Routledge Revivals

The Writings

Originally published in 1963, this work is a study of the Old Testament books known as 'The Writings' (Ketuvim). Introductory chapters supply the necessary background material and are followed by separate chapters on the books themselves, their origin, purpose, contents, date of composition, permanent influence and literary merit. The book is lucidly written and in a field in which scholars differ widely as to facts and interpretation, the author has succeeded in giving a wide range of views. The historical chapters describing the background to the literature are accurate and readable.

The Writings
The Third Division of the Old Testament Canon

T. Henshaw

First published in 1963 by George Allen & Unwin Ltd.

This edition first published in 2024 by Routledge
4 Park Square, Milton Park, Abingdon, Oxon, OX14 4RN
and by Routledge
605 Third Avenue, New York, NY 10158.

Routledge is an imprint of the Taylor & Francis Group, an informa business

© 1963 George Allen & Unwin Ltd.

The right of T. Henshaw to be identified as the author of this work has been asserted by him in accordance with sections 77 and 78 of the Copyright, Designs and Patents Act 1988.

All rights reserved. No part of this book may be reprinted or reproduced or utilised in any form or by any electronic, mechanical, or other means, now known or hereafter invented, including photocopying and recording, or in any information storage or retrieval system, without permission in writing from the publishers.

ISBN 13: 978-1-032-91339-1 (hbk)
ISBN 13: 978-1-003-56277-1 (ebk)
ISBN 13: 978-1-032-91353-7 (pbk)
Book DOI 10.4324/9781003562771

THE WRITINGS

The Third Division of the Old Testament Canon

BY

T. HENSHAW
M.A.

London
GEORGE ALLEN & UNWIN LTD
RUSKIN HOUSE MUSEUM STREET

FIRST PUBLISHED IN 1963

This book is copyright under the Berne Convention. Apart from any fair dealing for the purposes of private study, research criticism or review, as permitted under the Copyright Act 1956, no portion may be reproduced by any process without written permission. Enquiries should be addressed to the publisher.

© *George Allen & Unwin Ltd, 1963*

The Scripture quotations in this book are from the Revised Standard Version of the Bible, copyrighted 1945 and 1952.

PRINTED IN GREAT BRITAIN
in 11 point Fournier type
BY HAZELL WATSON AND VINEY LTD
AYLESBURY AND SLOUGH

PREFACE

The aim of the book is to present to the reader the main results of modern scholarship in the field of 'The Writings', to assess their permanent influence and to indicate their literary merits. I have endeavoured to treat the subject within a single volume of moderate size, but those who are familiar with the vast field which must be surveyed, will realize that to effect this selection and compression have been necessary, some matters having to be omitted and others treated more cursorily than one would have wished.

Controversy continues on many questions relating to 'The Writings', so that in dealing with these it is impossible to speak of the 'assured results which the future is not likely to reverse'. In a few of these cases I have endeavoured to express an independent judgment, but in the majority of them I have been content to express the main theories of the various theological schools, leaving the reader to draw his own conclusions.

An attempt has been made to summarize the individual books, though we realize that the poetical books, especially The Song of Songs, almost defy analysis. In the process of analysis their beauty is destroyed. In these summaries only a few notes on the text have been included. Those who desire fuller details should consult the larger commentaries.

Numerous quotations and references will be found scattered throughout the book. These should be considered an integral part of it. They have been deliberately added to illustrate a statement, to clinch an argument and to enable the reader to become familiar with the text. A statement is more likely to be remembered if it is illustrated by an apt quotation, while an argument loses much of its force if the words on which it is based are not read.

Readers who wish to pursue the study of 'The Writings' further will find a bibliography at the end of the book. Foreign works have been included in this for the benefit of those whose reading is not restricted to English.

I wish to acknowledge my indebtedness to many scholars whose names are well known in the field of Old Testament studies. It is impossible to express the debt which I owe to each one, but to the discerning mind their influence will be apparent throughout the book. My sincere thanks are due to the Reverend H. H. Rowley, M.A., D.D.,

F.B.A., Professor Emeritus of Hebrew Language and Literature in the University of Manchester, who read the manuscript, correcting it where necessary and making a number of valuable suggestions. The book has received the advantage of all the corrections and suggestions that he made. I must, however, make it clear that for any errors of thought or expression that it may contain, I alone am responsible. My grateful thanks are also due to my wife who helped me at every stage of the work, from the typing of the manuscript to the correction of the proofs.

T. HENSHAW

CONTENTS

PREFACE	*Page* 5
ABBREVIATIONS	9
I. The Canon of the Old Testament	11
II. Historical Background: Judah, 587–63 B.C.	20
III. Archaeology	37
IV. Apocalyptic Literature	45
V. Wisdom Literature	63
VI. The Forms and Characteristics of Hebrew Poetry	78
VII. Psalms	95
VIII. Psalms (continued)	111
IX. Proverbs	131
X. Job	147
XI. The Song of Songs	179
XII. Ruth	194
XIII. Lamentations	204
XIV. Ecclesiastes	218
XV. Esther	241
XVI. Daniel	255
XVII. 1 and 2 Chronicles	280
XVIII. Ezra-Nehemiah	301
APPENDICES	
A. *The Second Temple*	325
B. *Hebrew Music*	328

Contents

C. *The Samaritan Schism* — 334
D. *Particularism and Universalism* — 338
E. *Zoroaster and Zoroastrianism* — 344
F. *The Influence of Persia upon the Jews* — 349
G. *Hellenism: its Diffusion throughout the Near East and its Influence upon the Jews* — 354
H. *The Law* — 359
I. *The Dead Sea Scrolls* — 368
J. *Chronological Tables* — 375
K. *Bibliography* — 378

INDEX OF SUBJECTS — 389
INDEX OF AUTHORS — 395

ABBREVIATIONS

A.J.S.L.	*American Journal of Semitic Languages and Literatures.*
A.T.D.	*Das Alte Testament Deutsch.*
A.V.	Authorized Version.
B.A.S.O.R.	*Bulletin of the American Schools of Oriental Research.*
B.J.R.L.	*Bulletin of the John Rylands Library.*
B.W.A.N.T.	*Beiträge zur Wissenschaft vom Alten und Neuen Testament.*
B.W.A.T.	*Beiträge zur Wissenschaft vom Alten Testament.*
B.Z.A.W.	*Beihefte zur Zeitschrift für die alttestamentliche Wissenschaft.*
Camb. B.	Cambridge Bible.
C.U.P.	Cambridge University Press.
Cent. B.	*Century Bible.*
E.T.	*Expository Times.*
H.A.T.	*Handbuch zum Alten Testament*, ed. by Eissfeldt.
H.K.	*Handkommentar zum Alten Testament*, ed. by Nowack.
H.S.A.T.	*Die Heilige Schrift des Alten Testaments*, ed. Kautszch and Bertholet.
H.S.A.Tes.	*Die Heilige Schrift des Alten Testamentes* (Bonner Bibel).
H.T.R.	*Harvard Theological Review.*
H.U.C.A.	*Hebrew Union College Annual.*
I.C.C.	*International Critical Commentary.*
J.B.L.	*Journal of Biblical Literature.*
K.A.T.	*Kommentar zum Alten Testament*, ed. by Sellin.
K.H.C.	*Kurzer Hand—Commentar zum Alten Testament*, ed. by Marti.
O.U.P.	Oxford University Press.
R.H.P.R.	*Revue d'Histoire et de Philosophie religieuses.*
R.H.R.	*Revue de l'Histoire des Religions.*
R.S.V.	Revised Standard Version.
R.Th.Ph.	*Revue de Theologie et de Philosophie.*
R.V.	Revised Version.
T.C.A.	*Transactions of the Connecticut Academy of Arts.*
T.R.	*Theologische Rundschau.*
T.S.K.	*Theologische Studien und Kritiken.*
W.C.	*Westminster Commentaries.*
W.Z.K.M.	*Wiener Zeitschrift für die Kunde des Morgenlandes.*
Z.A.W.	*Zeitschrift für die alttestamentliche Wissenschaft.*

CHAPTER I

THE CANON OF THE OLD TESTAMENT

DEFINITION OF 'CANON'

THE word 'Canon' is derived from the Greek 'canna' = a 'reed'; it came to denote first a straight rod or bar and then a carpenter's or builder's rule or level. In the course of time it came to be used metaphorically for a 'rule' or 'standard', and in this sense we find it in Galatians vi. 16. 'Peace and mercy be upon all who walk by this rule, upon the Israel of God.' The title 'kanones' was given to the best models in Greek literature. Finally it was used of a collection of books normative of faith and practice. In this sense it is used of the books of the Bible by the Greek Fathers; it appears, for example, in the works of Athanasius (c. A.D. 296–373) with reference to the New Testament. By the Canon of the Old Testament, therefore, we mean a collection of books which conform to a certain standard and are regarded as authoritative for faith and practice.

THE CONCEPTION OF THE CANON AMONG THE JEWS

The first clear conception of the Canon meets us in the pages of the Jewish historian, Josephus. In his *Contra Apionem* (I. 38–42), written to establish the antiquity of the Jews and the trustworthiness of their history, he writes,

'We have not an innumerable multitude of books among us, disagreeing from and contradicting one another; but only twenty-two books, which contain the records of all the past times, and which are rightly believed in. And of these, five belong to Moses, which contain the laws and the tradition of the origin of mankind till his death for a period of nearly three thousand years. From the death of Moses until the reign of Artaxerxes, king of Persia, who reigned after Xerxes, the prophets who came after Moses wrote down the things that were done in their times in thirteen books. The remaining books contain hymns to God and precepts for the conduct of human life. But from Artaxerxes to our times all things have indeed been written down, but are not esteemed worthy of a like authority because the exact succession of the prophets was wanting. And how firmly we have given credit to these books of ours is evident by what we do; for during so many ages which have already passed, no one has been so bold as either to add anything to them, to take anything from them, or to make any change in them.[1] But it is become natural to all Jews, immediately and from their birth, to esteem these books to contain divine doctrines, and to stand by them, and willingly to die for them.'

From the above statement we see that the characteristic marks of canonical books are: (1) their number is strictly limited; (2) they were written by the prophets in the period from Moses to Artaxerxes; (3) they are divinely inspired and of unquestioned authority; (4) they are 'holy', that is, 'separate' from all other forms of literature; (5) their text is inviolable.

The Talmud adds nothing further to this description of the canonical books of the Old Testament except that it reckons the number as twenty-four instead of twenty-two. The Rabbis describe the books as 'defiling the hands', by which they mean, not that there was anything unclean about them, but that they were so sacred that ceremonial washing was necessary after handling them.

CONTENTS

The Hebrew Canon consists of twenty-four books, divided into three groups as follows:

(1) *The Law* (or Torah)

Genesis, Exodus, Leviticus, Numbers, Deuteronomy.

(2) *The Prophets*

(a) The Former Prophets: Joshua, Judges, Samuel (one book), Kings (one book).

(b) The Latter Prophets: Isaiah, Jeremiah, Ezekiel and The Twelve (Hosea, Joel, Amos, Obadiah, Jonah, Micah, Nahum, Habakkuk, Zephaniah, Haggai, Zechariah, Malachi). The Twelve so-called Minor Prophets count as one book, not because they are in any sense

---

[1] This statement is incorrect, for many additions were made to the Hebrew Scriptures after the death of Artaxerxes I (d. 424 B.C.).

inferior to the others, but because they are smaller than the three which precede them.

(3) *The Writings* (Hebrew, 'Kethubim') *or Hagiographa* (Greek, Sacred Writings)

Psalms, Proverbs, Job, Song of Songs, Ruth, Lamentations, Ecclesiastes, Esther, Daniel, Ezra-Nehemiah (one book), Chronicles (one book). Of these, Psalms, Proverbs and Job are known as the poetical books, but they do not include all the poetry in the Old Testament. The Song of Songs, Ruth, Lamentations, Ecclesiastes and Esther are called the five Megilloth or Rolls, and are appointed to be read publicly in the Synagogue at certain festivals—The Song of Songs at the Feast of the Passover, Ruth at the Feast of Weeks or Pentecost (marking the completion of the wheat harvest), Lamentations on the ninth day of Ab (the feast commemorating the destruction of Jerusalem in 587 B.C.), Ecclesiastes at the Feast of Tabernacles, and Esther at the Feast of Purim (commemorating the defeat of Haman's plot for the destruction of the Jews).

Thus we have five books of the Law, eight of the Prophets and eleven of the Writings, making twenty-four books altogether. The number twenty-four was probably chosen because it was regarded as a sacred number. In the English Bible these appear as thirty-nine books by subdivision. Josephus, however, reckoned twenty-two books in the Hebrew Canon but he probably arrived at the number by uniting Ruth with Judges and Lamentations with Jeremiah. The number twenty-two was preferred because it was the number of the letters in the Hebrew alphabet.

THEORIES OF ORIGIN

An early tradition found in 2 Esdras (xiv. 18–48) and repeated by many Christian writers down to the Reformation, attributes the formation of the Canon to Ezra, who was said to have been divinely inspired to write down from memory all the books of the Scriptures which had been destroyed by fire in the siege of Jerusalem in 587 B.C. At his dictation five scribes copied out ninety-four books, twenty-four of which were for public use and the other seventy for the wise among the people. 'For in them is the spring of understanding, the fountain of wisdom, and the river of knowledge' (2 Esdras xiv. 47). The twenty-four books for public use correspond to the twenty-two canonical books of Josephus. This tradition can have no foundation in fact, for Ezra's name is connected with the Pentateuch only (either in whole or in part) while several books in the Canon were not written till long after his death. In the sixteenth century a Jewish scholar, Elias Levita, expounded the theory according to which the 'Men of the Great Synagogue', a council under the presidency of Ezra, separated the inspired Scriptures from the spurious writings and fixed once for all the Canon with its threefold division. This theory passed into Protestant theology and persisted down to recent times, but it, too, is pure fiction, for there is no evidence that such an institution as the Great Synagogue ever existed.

THEORIES OF GROWTH

It is generally agreed that the formation of the Canon is the result of a long historical process extending over several centuries, but of the various stages in its growth little definite is known. It has been generally supposed that the three divisions of the Hebrew Canon represent three successive stages in the canonization. The first Canon to be formed was the Law, the second the Prophets, and the third the Writings. There is now a wide acceptance of Hölscher's view, according to which there was no canonization of separate collections of books. The Canon was fixed at the Council of Jamnia (c. A.D. 90). Before this date certain books had come to be venerated, but none of them had ever been officially recognized by any council as of divine authority. This view has much to commend it. The veneration of the Law was a very slow process, beginning about 621 B.C. and reaching its climax about the middle of the fourth century B.C. In the meantime, the prophetic books were being written from the eighth century B.C. onwards and some of them would be venerated before the Torah was a written book. Again, Jonah, a late book (c. 350–300 B.C.), is in the Prophets, yet some of the early Psalms (David's Psalms for example) would be regarded as sacred long before this, and the Psalms appear in the Writings. Lamentations was ascribed to Jeremiah, yet it is in the Writings. It is evident, therefore, that the canonical order could not have been simply the Law, the Prophets and the Writings.

FORMATION OF CANON

The Law

The first book to be recognized as authoritative Scripture was the Book of the Law, which was discovered in the Temple by the High

Priest, Hilkiah, about 621 B.C., and which may safely be identified with the central portion of our Deuteronomy (xii–xxvi). It was recognized as being divinely inspired by the prophetess, Huldah, the king and the people, and was solemnly accepted as the basis of a covenant with Yahweh. The next step in the history of the Canon was the arrival of Ezra in Jerusalem, probably in 397 B.C., with a law-book which he imposed upon the Jewish community. Unfortunately this law-book cannot be identified, but it was probably the Priestly Code. The impression made upon the people by the reading of it was of something new, for they wept when they heard it (Neh. vii. 9). It agrees with the Priestly Code (Lev. xxiii. 39) in requiring an eight-day celebration of the Feast of Tabernacles (Neh. viii. 18) instead of Deuteronomy's seven-day celebration (Deut. xvi. 13). Moreover it is more likely that Ezra would read a short code than the whole of the Pentateuch. If we knew the date of the Samaritan schism we should have a clue to the date when the Pentateuch reached its final form, for the Samaritans on their secession took it with them, and it has been found to agree substantially with the Hebrew Pentateuch. The first certain date we have of the Samaritans as a separate community is 128 B.C. when John Hyrcanus destroyed the Samaritan Temple on Mount Gerizim. Josephus tells us that it had been in existence for 200 years. If this is correct, we have a date which takes us back to the middle of the fourth century B.C. It is highly probable that the building of this separatist temple marks the definite breach between the Jews and the Samaritans. The Pentateuch, therefore, must have been completed and recognized as inspired and authoritative Scripture in the period c. 397–350 B.C., for the Samaritans are not likely to have taken it over after their breach with the Jews.

The Prophets

By the middle of the fourth century B.C. the Jews possessed the four historical books, Joshua, Judges, Samuel, Kings—called in the Hebrew Canon, the Former Prophets—substantially as they exist to-day, though many minor additions were probably made to them for the next hundred years or so. The memory of their close connexion with the Pentateuch, with which they originally formed a great historical work extending from Genesis to Kings, combined with the intense patriotism which they exhibit, would naturally cause them to be held in veneration. Though they were for the most part concerned with the history of the nation, they contained sufficient material concerning the prophets and prophecy to give rise to the idea that they had been written by the prophets and from their point of view.

As regards the Latter Prophets, Isaiah, Jeremiah, Ezekiel and the Twelve, they were being written from the eighth century B.C. onwards, and, as we have already indicated, some of them would surely be venerated before the Torah was a written book. The Fall of Jerusalem in 587 B.C. vindicated the truth of the prophetic utterances. The intense nationalism of the exilic and post-exilic prophets, which took the form of hostility towards foreign nations and promises of a glorious restoration, would also tend to increase the veneration for prophetic literature. The prophetic books were from time to time brought up to date by additions and corrections, and new ones appeared until finally the voice of prophecy ceased. With the cessation of prophecy the prophetic books, which had from pre-exilic times been increasingly venerated as being divinely inspired, were collected, though their inspiration was considered to be on a lower level than that of the Law. The precise date of this collection is unknown. Ben Sirach, in his famous eulogy of the great men of Israel in chapters xlv–xlix of his book Ecclesiasticus (c. 180 B.C.), shows clearly that he was familiar with the Law and the Prophets, and he actually refers to the Twelve Prophets as a definite collection. Some years later the author of Daniel (167–164 B.C.) refers to the 'books' and quotes from Jeremiah (ix. 2). It seems clear, therefore, that this group of writings, known as the Prophets was recognized as inspired Scripture by about the beginning of the second century B.C. There is, however, no evidence that they had been officially canonized.

The Writings

The earliest testimony to this group of writings is to be found in the Prologue to Ecclesiasticus, written by Ben Sirach's grandson about 132 B.C. In it he refers to 'the law and the prophets and the other books of our fathers' and 'the law itself, the prophecies, and the rest of the books'. These references suggest that the third division of the Canon was beginning to take shape but had not yet been given a name. By the beginning of the Christian era the writings in this group were generally recognized as being divinely inspired, though their inspiration was considered to be inferior to that of the Prophets. In some quarters, however, Esther, Ecclesiastes and the Song of Songs were disputed on theological grounds.

Before the beginning of the Christian era lessons from the Law and the Prophets were read in the synagogues on the Sabbath Day (cf. Lk. iv. 16-19; Acts xiii. 15, 27). In the New Testament the Jewish Scriptures as a whole are usually referred to as the 'law and the prophets' (Mt. v. 17) or as 'Moses in the law and also the prophets' (Jn. i. 45; cf. Acts xxviii. 23). It is generally thought that the triple division of the Jewish Scriptures is referred to in Luke xxiv. 44: 'These are my words which I spoke to you, while I was still with you, that everything written about me in the law of Moses and the prophets and the psalms must be fulfilled.' It is, however, by no means certain that all the books of the Writings are necessarily included under the heading 'psalms'. Quotations are taken from all the books of the Jewish Old Testament except Obadiah, Nahum, Ezra, Nehemiah, Esther, Song of Songs and Ecclesiastes, but no significance need be attached to their omission.

FIXATION OF CANON

The impetus which finally led to the formation of the Canon, probably came from the rivalry between Greek and Jewish culture after the conquests of Alexander the Great (356-323 B.C.) and from the rise of the Apocalyptic school of thought about the beginning of the second century B.C. Greek philosophical works and Jewish 'Apocalypses' circulated widely and became increasingly popular. The religious leaders of Judaism regarded such writings as erroneous and pernicious, so that it is natural that they should seek to combat their teaching by drawing up a list of books which all orthodox Jews should recognize as authoritative Scripture. It is generally supposed that the Hebrew Canon was finally fixed at the Council of Jamnia (c. A.D. 90), but for a long time afterwards the inspiration of Esther, the Song of Songs and Ecclesiastes was challenged. Even to-day it is difficult to see why these books should be in the Jewish Scriptures, while a book like The Wisdom of Solomon should be excluded. It is probable that Esther was admitted into the Canon because it was supposed to give a true historical account of the origin of the Feast of Purim, and that The Song of Songs and Ecclesiastes were admitted because they were ascribed to Solomon. But why The Wisdom of Solomon, also ascribed to Solomon and in many ways superior to Proverbs, should be excluded we do not know, unless it is that it was reckoned to be too Greek and philosophical in tone. *Baba Bathra*, a treatise in the Mishnah (c. A.D. 200) gives a complete list of the books of the Old Testament as we know them.

THE GREEK CANON

By the Greek Canon we mean all the books in the Greek version of the Hebrew Scriptures. During and after the Exile many Jews settled in Egypt, where they were compelled by force of circumstances to acquire the Greek language. Hence they began to forget classical Hebrew and even Aramaic, and it therefore became desirable, if not essential, that their Scriptures should be translated. According to tradition, the Law was translated into Greek by seventy-two distinguished Palestinian scholars working under the patronage of Ptolemy II Philadelphus (287-247 B.C.) at Alexandria during the first half of the third century B.C. The remaining books were translated by about the middle of the first century B.C. This translation is known as the Septuagint, sometimes shortened to LXX. This version includes not only the books of the Hebrew Canon, but also most of the books which we collectively call the Apocrypha. From the Jewish point of view the title Greek Canon is strictly speaking inaccurate, for there is no evidence that the books of the Apocrypha were ever canonized or that their claims to canonicity were ever discussed at the Council of Jamnia. It is in fact, highly probable that the name Septuagint was originally among the Egyptian Jews only attached to the translation of the Law. The Septuagint was taken over by the Christian Church, which during the first two centuries of our era recognized the whole of it as sacred Scripture.

By the fourth century A.D. controversy had arisen on the question of the canonicity of the Apocrypha. Jerome (c. A.D. 340-420) distinguished between 'canonical books' and 'ecclesiastical books', that is, books issued by the Church for the purpose of edification, but which it did not recognize as authoritative Scripture. All such books he declared to be 'apocryphal'. Augustine recognized no distinction between 'canonical' and 'ecclesiastical books', maintaining that all the books of the Septuagint were of equal value and canonical, and that apocryphal books simply implied those books whose origin was unknown or obscure. Augustine's views prevailed and the books of the Apocrypha were placed in the Vulgate, but their canonicity was disputed down to the Reformation. The Roman Catholic Church at the Council of Trent (1546) declared the books of the Apocrypha canonical, with the exception of 1 and 2 Esdras and The Prayer of Manasses, which were placed in an appendix at the end of the New Testament. In the Protestant Church the views of Jerome tended to prevail. Luther in his translation of the Bible (1534) relegated the books of the Apocrypha, omitting 1 and 2 Esdras to the end of the Old Testament with the title, 'Apocrypha; these are books which are not held equal to the sacred Scriptures and yet are useful and good for reading.' The Thirty-Nine Articles (1563) of the Church of England gives a list of the books of the Apocrypha, which, it declares, are read 'for example of life and instruction of manners', but are not used 'to establish any doctrine'. The Apocrypha was included in the Authorized Version of 1611, being placed between the two Testaments; but opposition to it gradually increased and it was omitted in the edition of 1629, though it was included in some of the later editions. The Westminster Confession (1647) declares that the books of the Apocrypha, 'not being of divine inspiration, are no part of the canon of the scripture, and therefore are of no authority in the church of God; nor to be in any otherwise approved, or made use of than other human writings'. In 1827, as the result of controversy, the British and Foreign Bible Society decided to exclude the Apocrypha from all its publications after that date (except for some pulpit Bibles).

CHAPTER II

HISTORICAL BACKGROUND: JUDAH, 587–63 B.C.

THE FALL OF JERUSALEM

IN 587 B.C. Jerusalem was sacked and the Temple destroyed by the Babylonians. The upper classes, which produced the political, religious and intellectual leaders of the people, were deported to Babylon, while the poorer classes were allowed to remain in the land as vine-dressers and ploughmen (2 Kgs. xxv. 11f.). Many Judaeans sought refuge in Edom, Moab and Ammon, whose people exulted over the downfall of their enemy, and whose rejoicing gave an added bitterness to their humiliation (Ob. v. 10–14; Ezek. xxv. 12–14; xxxv; Ps. cxxxvii. 7). In the course of time, however, these states, too, were conquered. A Babylonian officer, Nebuzaradan, was entrusted with the settling of affairs in Judah. After completing the destruction of the city, he appointed Gedaliah, a man of noble family, as governor (2 Kgs. xxv. 8, 23f.). Gedaliah established his headquarters at Mizpah and under him the land apparently began to recover. He inspired such confidence, that many of the inhabitants of Judah who had fled to the adjoining territories, were encouraged to return. Chief among his supporters was Johanan, the son of Kareah. Eventually, however, Gedaliah was treacherously murdered by a certain Ishmael of the royal house of Judah, whereupon Johanan and his companions, fearing the vengeance of Nebuchadrezzar because they had failed to maintain order, fled to Egypt, taking Jeremiah with them (2 Kgs. xxv. 22–26; Jer. xli–xliii. 7). A third deportation in 582 B.C., mentioned in Jeremiah lii. 30, may have been a belated reprisal for these disorders. Judah was probably incorporated in the province of Samaria, so that its governor was the subordinate of the governor of Samaria.

The destruction of Jerusalem and the subsequent exile are a landmark in the history of Israel. Judah as a political entity, and the Davidic

HISTORICAL BACKGROUND: JUDAH, 587–63 B.C.   21

monarchy, with all the promises and hopes attached to it, had come to an end. It is true that Jehoiachin was still regarded as king, but he was a prisoner in Babylon and died there without any of the hopes that had gathered round him having been realized (2 Kgs. xxv. 27–30).[1]

DIVISION OF JEWRY

The Hebrew people were now divided into three groups.

The Palestinian Group

Northern Palestine contained the remnant of the Ten Tribes, occupying Samaria, Galilee and Trans-Jordan. Here the people had intermarried with the colonists, settled in the country by the Assyrian kings, and had adopted a syncretistic form of religion—a combination of Yahwism and foreign cults. In southern Palestine were the Judaeans who had been allowed to remain in the land after the destruction of Jerusalem. Their land was in a sorry plight (Lam. v. 1–18). The population, which in the eighth century B.C. had numbered about 250,000, was now less than half that number. The people were surrounded by hostile enemies—Ammonites, Moabites, Edomites, Phoenicians and Philistines—and had no adequate means of defence against them, for archaeological discoveries show that all or virtually all the fortresses of Judah had been destroyed. They were poverty-stricken and wrested a precarious living from the land. Jerusalem soon became once more the political and religious capital. Though the Temple had been destroyed, it remained a holy spot to which pilgrims continued to journey to offer sacrifice among its ruins (Jer. xli. 5). It would seem that the worship of Yahweh was maintained at Jerusalem throughout the exilic period. Worship at the high places seems to have been revived and foreign cults practised. We read of Ishtar-worship (Jer. vii. 18), Tammuz worship (Ezek. viii. 9–18) and Sun-worship (Ezek viii. 16–18). There was also moral degradation (Jer. xxiii. 11–14; Ezek v. 5–10, xxii. 1–13; xxxiii. 22–35). Eventually, however, in spite of poverty, the intermittent attacks of enemies and the constant realization of their subjection, they settled down to a quiet life. So long as Babylon remained supreme, they must have seen that acquiescence was their only course of safety.

[1] On the death of Nebuchadrezzar in 562 B.C. Jehoiachin was released from prison by his successor Amel-Marduk (Evil-Merodach) and given a regular allowance until his death (2 Kgs. xxv. 27–30).

The Egyptian Group

The second group was to be found in Egypt. Probably many Jews sought a refuge there during the stormy last days of Judah. As we have already indicated, a party under the leadership of Johanan, had fled thither after the assassination of Gedaliah, taking Jeremiah with them. In the course of time the number of immigrants increased to such an extent that Egypt became a centre of world Jewry. It is interesting to note that in the fifth century B.C. there was a Jewish military colony at Elephantine (or Yeb), an island in the Nile 400 miles south of Cairo. Contrary to the Deuteronomic requirement of a single sanctuary, the members of this colony had their own Temple and worshipped in addition to Yahweh at least three subordinate deities, Anath-bethel, Asham-bethel and Haram-bethel. They celebrated the Jewish festivals and maintained their connexion with their fellow-countrymen in Palestine. According to their own witness, their fathers built the Temple in Elephantine, and the Persian king (Cambyses) found it already in existence when he conquered Egypt (525 B.C.). The fact that they practised a paganized cult of Yahweh lends support to the theory that they came originally from the environs of Bethel.

The Babylonian Group

The third group consisted of those Jews who had been deported to Babylon in 598, 587 and 582 B.C. Their lot does not appear to have been unduly severe. They were not enslaved but enjoyed a considerable measure of freedom. They were not dispersed among the local population but apparently placed in settlements of their own (Ezek. iii. 15; Ezra ii. 59; viii. 17) and allowed to build houses, engage in agriculture and live on the products of their labour (Jer. xxix. 5f.). Some of the exiles seem to have lived in cities (Jer. xxix. 7). Babylon was a centre of trade and some of them took the opportunity of trading and became wealthy (Ezra ii. 64–69). The Murashu tablets (see p. 41) show that in the fifth century B.C. the descendants of the Jewish exiles were allowed to engage in trade and accumulate wealth. They were allowed to meet together and enjoy some sort of community life (Ezek. viii. 1; xiv. 1; xxxiii. 30f.).

The destruction of Jerusalem and the captivity affected the exiles in different ways. There were those who felt that Yahweh was punishing them for their sins (Ezek. xxxiii. 10) or for the sins of their fathers

(xviii. 2), and questioned the divine justice (xviii. 25). In his wrath Yahweh had cast down from heaven to earth the splendour of Israel (Lam. ii. 1) and there was no hope of deliverance (Ezek xii. 22; xxxvii. 11). Many of the exiles identified themselves with the Babylonians, adopting their way of life and even their idolatrous worship (Ezek. xiv. 3–9; xx. 30–32; xxxvi. 25). They engaged in trade, and in the course of time grew rich, lived in ease and comfort and forgot their native land. There were some, however, and they were in the minority, who were ardent patriots and devoted followers of Yahweh, and were determined to preserve their national identity and their religion at all costs. Since they no longer existed as an independent nation and their Temple was destroyed, there was little to mark them off as Jews. Hence stress was now laid upon Sabbath-observance as the sign of the covenant between Yahweh and His people (Gen. ii. 2f.) and as the mark of differentiation between Jew and Gentile (Ezek. xx. 12–21; xxii. 8, 26; xxiii. 38). Circumcision, which hitherto had had no special significance and was apparently not practised among the Babylonians, likewise became a sign of the covenant (Gen. xvii. 11) and the mark of a Jew. Since Babylon was regarded as an unclean land stress was laid upon ritual cleanness (Ezek. iv. 12–15; xxii. 26). Deprived of their native land and of their Temple, they discovered that neither was essential to true religion, and that Yahweh could be worshipped in a private house in Babylon as well as in a magnificent temple in Jerusalem (cf. Ezek. viii. 1; xiv. 1; xxxiii. 30f.). Hence the tendency was for religion to become less formal and more spiritual. Religion too, became less exclusive. Closer contact and knowledge of other nations led them to see that Yahweh must have some relation to other nations as well as to their own. The result was that while they were still far short of a universal religion or of a clear monotheism, they grasped the conception of Yahweh as being the God of all the earth. Towards the close of the exile Deutero-Isaiah proclaimed the two great doctrines of monotheism (Is. xliv. 6; cf. xlv. 6, 14, 18, 21f.) and universalism (Is. xlii. 6f.; xlv. 23).

The Exile was a time of considerable literary activity. It was probably late in the exilic period that work began on the codification of the law. The Deuteronomic history, Joshua to 2 Kings, probably composed shortly before the fall of Judah, was re-edited, added to (2 Kgs. xxv. 27–30) and adapted to the situation of the exiles. The two prophetic books, Ezekiel and Deutero-Isaiah, are also generally assigned to the period.

Towards the end of the Babylonian Empire the exiles seem to have been subjected to persecution. There is a strong contrast between the tone of Jeremiah and Ezekiel on the one hand and Deutero-Isaiah on the other.

The death of Nebuchadrezzar in 562 B.C. marked the beginning of the break-up of the Babylonian power. Within six years four kings ascended the throne and there were two revolutions. The last king, Nabonidus (Nabunaid), was absorbed in the study of architecture and archaeology and left the administration of affairs very largely in the hands of his son, Bel-sharusur (Belshazzar). It was not long before he alienated the sympathies of many of his subjects by removing the images of the various local deities in the empire to Babylon, either to protect them, or more probably to secure their assistance against his enemies. He offended the priests of the Babylonian god, Marduk, by favouring the cult of the moon-god, Nannar, or Sin.[1] His innovations roused such hostility that he fled to Tema in southern Arabia, where he remained for about seven years (c. 553–546 B.C.).

The most dangerous rival of the Babylonian Empire had always been the state of Media whose king was now Astyages. In 553 B.C. Cyrus, the Persian vassal king of Anshan in southern Iran, revolted, and by 550 B.C. had captured the Median capital, Ecbatana, dethroned Astyages and united the Medes and the Persians under his sway. It was probably about this time that Deutero-Isaiah proclaimed that Yahweh had raised up Cyrus to be the instrument of His purpose (xliv. 28; xlv. 1; cf. xli. 2–4, 25; xlv. 1–7, 13; xlvi. 11; xlviii. 14f.). Nabonidus, alarmed by the sudden menace, entered into a defensive alliance with Croesus, king of Lydia, and Amasis, the Pharaoh of Egypt. Cyrus swept through Asia Minor, captured Sardis, the Lydian capital, and incorporated Lydia in his empire (546 B.C.). In 539 B.C. he launched an attack against Babylon. The forces of Nabonidus were defeated at Opis on the Tigris, and Gobryas, the governor of Gutium, who had deserted to Cyrus, occupied Babylon without striking a blow. Shortly afterwards Cyrus himself entered the city and was welcomed as a liberator. His territories now stretched from the western coast of Asia Minor to the Caspian Sea in the east, and from Armenia in the north to the deserts of Arabia in the south.

Cyrus was one of the most enlightened men of the ancient world.

---

[1] The fact that Nabonidus named his son, Belshazzar, after Bel-Marduk, and that at the end of his reign gods from other Temples were found collected in E-saglia, the Temple of Marduk, suggests that he had not abandoned the worship of Marduk.

HISTORICAL BACKGROUND: JUDAH, 587–63 B.C.

He saw the danger of having embittered alien peoples within his empire whose main aim was to overthrow the state and to return to their native land. His policy was to grant subject peoples a measure of self-government within the framework of the empire, at the same time keeping a firm control over them by means of a complex bureaucracy, the army and an efficient system of communication. One of his first acts was to allow many of the deported peoples within the empire to return to their homes, and to return to their sanctuaries the gods of Sumer and Akkad which Nabonidus had removed to Babylon. Among those allowed to return were the Jewish exiles in Babylon.

THE RETURN AND THE SECOND TEMPLE

The history of the return of the exiles is somewhat obscure. The sources from which our information is derived are Ezra, compiled by the Chronicler about 200 years after the restoration, and the prophetic books, Haggai and Zechariah i–viii, which are contemporary documents. According to Ezra, Cyrus issued an edict, permitting the exiles to return to their native land in order that they might rebuild the Temple (i. 2–4). The sacred vessels carried away by Nebuchadrezzar were restored, and about 50,000 people under the leadership of Shesbazzar, 'the prince of Judah', returned to Jerusalem (i. 7–ii. 65). In the seventh month of the year of their return they erected an altar, offered burnt offerings upon it, held the Feast of Booths (Tabernacles) and from that time kept the appointed feasts (iii. 1–5). In the second month of the second year of their return, under the leadership of Zerubbabel, the son of Shealtiel, and Jeshua (Joshua), the son of Jozadak, the foundations of the Temple were laid (iii. 8–11). But the work was interrupted by 'the people of the land' (that is, those who had not been in exile), and was not resumed until the second year of the reign of Darius I, king of Persia, that is, 520 B.C. (iv. 1–4, 24).

In Haggai and Zechariah i–viii there is no mention of a return of exiles on a large scale or of an earlier attempt to rebuild the Temple. It was not till eighteen years after the return, that is, in 520 B.C., that the proposal to build the Temple was first made (Hag. i. 1f.; Zech. i. 16). Haggai represents the Temple as being still in ruins (ii. 3), and urges its restoration on the ground that failure to build was the cause of all the calamities which had befallen the exiles (xxx. i. 5–11), and that it should be ready for the dawn of the Messianic Age when every nation would bring its treasure to the house of God (ii. 1–9). He makes no mention of any hostility between them and 'the people of the land', but actually represents the two as co-operating in the work (ii. 2; cf. Zech. viii. 6).

It is now possible to reconstruct the history of the return of the Jewish exiles from Babylon and of the rebuilding of the Temple. An edict was issued by Cyrus in 539 B.C. permitting the Jewish exiles to return. The substantial historicity of the edict has been confirmed by modern archaeological discoveries, its Jewish colouring being doubtless due to the Chronicler whose aim was to demonstrate that the return was in accordance with the will of Yahweh. The sacred vessels, carried away by Nebuchadrezzar, were restored, and a small company of the exiles, under the leadership of Shesh-bazzar returned to Jerusalem in 538 B.C., settled down with 'the people of the land' and joined in worship with them in the ruins of the Temple. Eighteen years of hardship, privation and insecurity followed. The territory at their disposal was quite small, stretching about twenty-five miles from north to south and about thirty miles from east to west and with a total population of about 20,000. A few people lived in pannelled houses (Hag. i. 4), but the majority must have lived under very primitive conditions. Drought and a series of bad harvests reduced them to a state of destitution. They were so preoccupied with the struggle for existence that they had neither the enthusiasm nor the energy for the task of rebuilding the Temple. 'This people say the time has not yet come to rebuild the house of the Lord' (Hag. i. 2).

Between 538 B.C. and the death of the Persian king, Cambyses, in 522 B.C. many more Jews had undoubtedly returned to Palestine, among whom were Zerubbabel, the son of Shealtiel, who became the civil leader, and Joshua, the son of Jehozadak, who became the High Priest (Hag. i. 1). The death of Cambyses (522 B.C.) was followed by widespread revolts and it looked as if the Persian empire would collapse. The prophets, Haggai and Zechariah, believing that the rule of the heathen was drawing to an end and that the Messianic Age was about to dawn, urged on the people to rebuild the Temple. Haggai fired them with the promise that Yahweh would shake all nations, fill the Temple with their treasures and make it more splendid than that of Solomon (ii. 6–9). He declared that Yahweh would make Zerubbabel 'as a signet ring', that is, invest him with His authority (ii. 20–23). Zechariah proclaimed that Yahweh was about to execute judgment upon the nations and to take up His abode in Zion (ii. 6–13). He spoke of a divine commission which came to him to make a crown and to place it on the head of Zerubbabel, who would rule as king with Joshua, the High Priest, by his side (vi. 9–14).

The foundations of the Temple were laid in 520 B.C. While the work was in progress, Tattenai, the governor of the province 'Beyond the River' (i.e. west of the Euphrates), and his officials, visited Jerusalem to question the Jews about their authority to erect the new building. They were referred to the permission originally given by Cyrus, and wrote to the Persian court for confirmation. Darius confirmed the edict of Cyrus, which was found in the archives of Ecbatana, and directed that the cost of rebuilding the Temple and of the maintenance of the cult was to be borne by the State, and that in return prayers were to be offered in the new sanctuary 'for the life of the king and his sons' (Ezra v. 3–vi. 10). The Temple was completed and dedicated with great rejoicing in the sixth year of the reign of Darius, that is, in 516 B.C. (Ezra vi. 14–16).

The hopes of Haggai and Zechariah were never realized, for the new king, Darius I (522–486 B.C.), quelled the revolt, reunited the empire, and gave it an organization which enabled it to endure undiminished for two hundred years. What happened to Zerubbabel is a mystery. Whether he was removed from office, or died a natural death, or was put to death we do not know, but nothing more is heard of him.

FROM THE DEDICATION OF THE TEMPLE TO NEHEMIAH

From the completion of the Temple in 516 B.C. to the coming of Nehemiah in 445 B.C. there is a gap of about seventy years in the historical records, but some information may be gathered from Trito-Isaiah and Malachi which are usually assigned to that period. It was evidently a time not only of disillusionment and despair, but also of moral and spiritual decline. In Trito-Isaiah we read of incompetent leaders (lvi. 9–12), oppression (lviii. 3–7), lawlessness (lix. 3), the corruption of the law-courts (lix. 4), gross idolatry and vice (lvii. 3–13; lxv. 1–7, 11f.; lxvi. 3f., 17), and formalism in religion (lviii. 1–4). From Malachi we learn that the priests were wearied with the routine of the Temple services and accepted inferior and blemished animals for sacrifice (i. 6–14), that people neglected to pay their tithes and offerings (iii. 7–10), that many were perplexed and began to doubt the justice of Yahweh and the wisdom of serving Him (i. 2; ii. 17; iii. 14f.), that men divorced their Jewish wives in order to marry foreign women (ii. 10–16) and that perjury, adultery and oppression prevailed (iii. 5). It was probably towards the end of this period that an attempt was made to rebuild the walls of Jerusalem, but the nobles of Samaria sent a letter to Artaxerxes I, charging the Jews with sedition, and the king ordered the work to cease until he had made a decree. The governor and his officials at once carried the king's order into effect (Ezra iv. 7–23).

NEHEMIAH AND EZRA[1]

Nehemiah

Nehemiah was a Jew who had risen to the position of cup-bearer to Artaxerxes I (465–424 B.C.) at Susa, the winter residence of the Persian kings. In 445 B.C. a delegation from Jerusalem, led by his brother, Hanani, informed him that the inhabitants of Judah were 'in great trouble and shame', and that the city was without a wall and gates (Neh. i. 1–3). Deeply distressed by the news, he appealed to the king to allow him to visit the city and rebuild the wall. Artaxerxes complied with his request, granting him leave of absence for a set period, letters of safe-conduct to show to the governor of the province, 'Beyond the River', a letter to the keeper of the king's forest, directing him to provide the necessary timber for the reconstruction of the city, and an armed escort (Neh. i. 4–ii. 9). Either at this time or later he was made governor of Judah (cf. Neh. v. 14; x. 1).

His arrival in Jerusalem roused the opposition of Sanballat, the governor of Samaria, and Tobiah the Ammonite, who was probably the governor of the neighbouring province of Ammon east of the Jordan (Neh. ii. 10). Three days after his arrival he inspected the walls by night on horseback and with only a few men with him (Neh. ii. 11–15). Then he divulged his plan to the leaders of the Jews and urged them to begin the work of restoration at once. They took up the plan with alacrity, saying, 'Let us rise up and build' (Neh. ii. 17f.). A labour force was recruited from the whole province, and the wall was divided into sections with a specific group of people responsible for each (Neh. iii. 1–32). Sanballat and his allies attempted to stop the work by ridicule (Neh. iv. 1–3), armed opposition (Neh. iv. 7–14) and intrigue (Neh. vi. 1–9) but it was in vain. So great was the zeal of the workers that the wall was built in fifty-two days (Neh. vi. 15), but according to Josephus (Antiquities, xi. v. 8), the work took two years and four months. Nehemiah entrusted the government of Jerusalem to his brother, Hanani, and Hananiah, the governor of the castle (Neh.

---
[1] For the date of Ezra's arrival at Jerusalem, see note on pp. 316f.

HISTORICAL BACKGROUND: JUDAH, 587–63 B.C.

vii. 1f.). As the city was only sparsely inhabited, he transferred thither a tenth part of the inhabitants of Judah who were chosen by lot (Neh. vii. 4; xi. 1f.). The wall was dedicated with great pomp and ceremony (Neh. xii. 27–43).

At some time during his administration of the province Nehemiah turned his attention to the alleviation of distress among the people. The poor had been compelled to mortgage their lands and even to sell their children into slavery in order to buy food and to pay the 'king's tax.' Nehemiah summoned the creditors before him, and induced them to take a solemn oath to restore the alienated property and to cease the practice of usury (Neh. v. 1–13).

Nehemiah was governor of Judah for twelve years, that is, from 445–433 B.C. (Neh. v. 14). At the end of the period he returned to Babylon, and after some time returned to Jerusalem (Neh. xiii. 6f.). During his absence a number of abuses had developed. Eliashib, the High Priest, had permitted Tobiah to occupy a room in the Temple because he was related in some unspecified way to him. The tithes had not been paid to the Levites, so that they had been compelled to work in the fields and neglect their Temple duties. People cultivated the land and brought their produce into Jerusalem on the Sabbath for sale. Tyrian merchants brought fish and other goods and sold them on the Sabbath. Jews had married foreign wives, one of the sons of Jehoiada, the son of Eliashib, the High Priest, even marrying the daughter of Sanballat. Many of the children of such marriages could not speak the language of their fathers. Nehemiah threw all the household furniture of Tobiah out of the room in the Temple, cleansed it from pollution and restored it to its proper function (Neh. xiii. 4–9). He summoned the Levites back from the fields to perform their proper duties, gave orders that the tithes should be paid and appointed honest treasurers to administer them (Neh. xiii. 10–13). He ordered the gates of the city to be shut on the Sabbath, and when merchants began to set up markets outside the city, threatened them with arrest and drove them away (Neh. xiii. 19–21). He made those who had contracted foreign marriages swear that they would not allow their children to contract such marriages in the future, and drove Jehoiada out of the country (Neh. xiii. 23–28).

Ezra

Ezra was a Jewish priest who lived in Babylon, probably in the reign of Artaxerxes II. He is described as a scribe, 'skilled in the law of Moses' (Ezra vii. 6) and as one who 'had set his heart to study the Law of the Lord, and to do it, and to teach his statutes and ordinances in Israel' (Ezra vii. 10). His official title was, 'the scribe of the law of the God of heaven' (Ezra vii. 12, 21), which suggests that he was regarded by the Persian authorities as their Jewish adviser. With the help, possibly, of influential Jewish courtiers, he enlisted the help of the king, who by imperial edict invested him with the authority to conduct home to Jerusalem such of his countrymen as desired to return (Ezra vii. 13), to instruct the people in the law and to enforce it (Ezra vii. 20f.). In addition he was granted the right to receive contributions from Babylonian Jews for the support of the Temple cult and to draw up to a fixed limit on the royal and provincial treasuries for its further requirements (Ezra vii. 15–20). His authority was not restricted to Judah but extended to all Jews living in the province, 'Beyond the River'. This probably does not mean that all the people of Jewish descent were to be forcibly subjected to the Law, but rather that all who desired to be considered Jews and to belong to the religious community in Jerusalem, had to submit to it. Having received his commission he collected a company of Jews, including priests, Levites, singers and Temple servants, and set out on the dangerous journey to Jerusalem without a military escort, preferring to trust in God alone (Ezra vii. 28–viii. 23).

On his arrival at Jerusalem, Ezra was distressed to hear that all Israel, especially the leading priests and Levites, had not separated themselves from the 'peoples of the lands' but had intermarried with them (Ezra ix. 1–3). He was appalled at the news, wept and confessed the sins of the congregation before Yahweh (Ezra ix. 4–x. 1). The people, deeply moved by the outburst of prayer, acknowledged their trespass against the Law, and the leading priests and Levites and all Israel took an oath to put away their foreign wives and their children (Ezra x. 2–5). A proclamation was issued ordering all the returned exiles to assemble at Jerusalem within three days. They answered the summons and Ezra appealed to them to put away their foreign wives. They agreed and a commission was appointed to investigate all such cases. Within three months a complete record was made of those who had been guilty of the offence, and all mixed marriages were dissolved (Ezra x. 7–44).

Ezra's main work was the proclamation of the Law. The people gathered in the square before the Water Gate. Standing on a wooden platform, he read from 'the book of the law of Moses' from early

HISTORICAL BACKGROUND: JUDAH, 587-63 B.C.

morning until mid-day, and certain Levites repeated it, giving the sense 'so that the people understood the reading' (Neh. viii. 1-8). The people were moved with contrition and broke out in demonstrations of grief (Neh. viii. 9). On the next day, after the leaders had been privately instructed in the Law, the Feast of Booths (or Tabernacles) was celebrated, with further readings from the Law on each day (Neh. viii. 13-18). Later (according to the Septuagint) Ezra publicly confessed the sins of the people and of their fathers before Yahweh, telling over the goodness and mercy of God and mourning over their own ingratitude (Neh. ix. 6-37).[1] Afterwards a covenant was drawn up and sealed binding the people to observe the Law (Neh. ix. 38-x. 39).[2] Ezra now disappears from history. According to Josephus ('Antiquities' xi. v. 5), he was buried in Jerusalem, but there is another tradition that he died in Babylon.

THE LATE PERSIAN PERIOD

Little is known of the province of Judah in the late Persian period. The hostility of the Jews and the Samaritans grew until it culminated in the building of a rival temple on Mount Gerizim, probably about the middle of the fourth century B.C. The Jews seem to have joined in a revolt against Artaxerxes III (464-440 B.C.) which resulted in the deportation of many of them to Babylonia and Hyrcania. Archaeology shows that they had a considerable measure of self-government, the High Priests having the right to levy their own taxes for the maintenance of the Temple and to strike their own silver coins. Greek influence increased steadily throughout the period. Coins were minted on the model of Attic drachmas and artifacts and pottery poured into Judah through the Phoenician ports. By the close of the period 'the material culture of Jewish Palestine was already saturated with Greek influence, which was soon to engulf the world and to usher in a new era, fraught with both evil and good.'[3]

THE GREEK PERIOD

Alexander's Conquests

In 334 B.C. Alexander, king of Macedonia, having destroyed Thebes, crossed the Hellespont into Asia Minor to liberate the Greek cities from the tyranny of Persia. He routed the Persians on the river Granicus

---

[1] See note on ix. 6-37 on p. 307.   [2] See note on ix. 38-x. 39 on p. 307.
[3] W. F. Albright, *The Biblical Period*, 1952, p. 55.

in Mysia (334 B.C.). The battle gave him the mastery of all Asia Minor. Then he determined to conquer the whole of the Persian empire. Passing through the Cilician Gates, a pass in the Taurus Mountains, he gained a great victory over Darius, the Persian king, at Issus in northern Syria (333 B.C.). He then marched against the cities of Phoenicia all of which submitted, except Tyre, which was reduced after a siege of seven months (332 B.C.). He next marched into Egypt which submitted without resistance (331 B.C.). The Egyptians welcomed him as a liberator and acclaimed him the legitimate Pharaoh. In the course of these operations Palestine came under his control. In the same year he marched through Palestine and Syria, crossed the Euphrates, defeated the forces of Darius on the plains of Gaugamela and entered Babylon, Susa and Persepolis. This victory really marks the end of the Persian empire and the beginning of the Hellenistic period in the Near East.

Alexander's Policy in Palestine

The conquests of Alexander seem to have made little difference to the general situation of the Jews in Palestine. According to Josephus, they were granted autonomy in religious matters.[1] Alexander favoured Jewish merchants and transferred many of them to his new city of Alexandria where they became a very important element in the population. The city became a stronghold of Greek philosophy and the combination of Jewish and Greek ideas had a profound influence upon early Christian thought.

The Struggle for Palestine

On the death of Alexander there was no logical successor to hold the empire together and his generals fell to quarrelling among themselves. After much fighting three kingdoms emerged. Egypt passed into the possession of Ptolemy I Soter (323–283 B.C.), who made the new city of Alexandria his capital. Seleucus I Nicator (312–280 B.C.) gained possession of the eastern part of Alexander's vast empire and established his capital at Antioch in Syria. The house of Antigonus had to be content with Greece and Macedonia. Only two of these kingdoms, namely the Ptolemaic and Seleucid kingdoms, are concerned with the history of the Jews. Ptolemy gained possession of Palestine but it was claimed by the Seleucids, and for a hundred years or so the

---

[1] Josephus, *Contra Apionem*, II. 4.

two houses struggled for its possession. Finally in 198 B.C. Antiochus III the Great (223–187 B.C.) defeated the Egyptian forces at Panion and gained control of it.

Internal Strife in the Jewish State

The conquest of Palestine by Antiochus III had a serious effect upon the history of the Jews. Even under the Ptolemies they had been exposed to Greek influence, but the Seleucids were far more enthusiastic missionaries of Hellenism than the Ptolemies had ever been. By this time there were among the Jews of Palestine two distinct parties, one advocating the adoption of Greek culture and the other, known as the Hasidim, the forerunners of the Pharisees, resisting it and clinging to their ancestral faith and way of life.

Antiochus III fell in battle in 187 B.C. and was succeeded by his son, Seleucus IV Philipator (187–175 B.C.), who ordered his chief minister, Heliodorus, to seize the Temple treasury but he failed in his purpose. Seleucus was murdered by Heliodorus and was succeeded by his brother, Antiochus IV Epiphanes.

The Maccabees

With the accession of Antiochus IV matters came to a head. The spark that fired the train was the deposition of the High Priest, Onias III, by Antiochus and the appointment to the office of a certain Jason. He in turn was superseded by a man named Menelaus who did not even belong to the high-priestly family. The orthodox Jews refused to accept him and challenged the right to nominate the High Priest which was claimed by Antiochus. In 169 B.C. Antiochus made an attempt to conquer Egypt but was compelled by the Romans to withdraw from the country. During his absence, Jason, who had fled to Ammonite territory, encouraged by a false report of his death, returned to Jerusalem and drove out Menelaus. On his return, Antiochus, interpreting the expulsion of Menelaus as rebellion, plundered the Temple and confirmed Menelaus in the High-priesthood. Supported by the Hellenizers among the Jews, he now determined to stamp out the Jewish religion which he apparently regarded as the cause of all the political unrest. The observance of the Sabbath and the rite of circumcision were forbidden, the Temple was turned into a temple of Zeus and swine's flesh was offered on the altar. An idol of Zeus—'the abomination that makes desolate'—was set up in the Temple, and Jews were commanded to build high places in the cities of Judah, to sacrifice to idols, to eat unclean food and to destroy all copies of the Scriptures. The penalty for refusing to obey these orders was death.

At first resistance to these repressive measures was passive but soon active aggression developed. An aged priest, Mattathias, belonging to the Hasmonaean house, raised a revolt at the little town of Modein in the hill country north-west of Jerusalem. When summoned to sacrifice to the heathen gods he refused and slew a Jew who was prepared to abandon his faith, together with the Syrian officer. With his five sons he fled to the hills and called upon all the faithful to follow him. On his death, Judas, named Maccabaeus (the 'hammerer'), took over the command. At first there was guerilla warfare in which Judas entered Jerusalem, and although the Syrians still held the citadel, he cleansed the Temple of pagan objects, rededicated it to the worship of Yahweh and re-established the daily sacrifices after three years' cessation (December 164 B.C.). The object of the revolt, namely religious freedom, had thus been attained, but Judas desired political freedom as well. Accordingly he continued the struggle, defeated the Syrian forces under Nicanor at Adasa but was himself defeated and slain at Elasa (160 B.C.).

After the death of Judas the leadership of the Jewish people was now assumed by Judas's brother, Jonathan (158–142 B.C.), who established himself at Michmash (158 B.C.). In 152 B.C. Jerusalem, with the exception of the citadel, was placed in his hands and he was allowed to assume the High-priesthood. He extended his territory, secured the abolition of the payment of tribute, but failed to eject the Syrian garrison from the citadel of Jerusalem. In 142 B.C. he was trapped and murdered by Tryphon, a Syrian general.

Jonathan's brother, Simon (142–134 B.C.), now succeeded to the leadership and to the High-priesthood. He recovered the citadel of Jerusalem and extended his territory by the conquest of Gazara (Gezer) and Joppa, in spite of an attempt made by the Syrians to overthrow him. He was murdered by his son-in-law, Ptolemy.

On the death of Simon, his son, John, commonly known as John Hyrcanus (134–104 B.C.), was appointed High Priest and civil ruler of the Jews. The Syrian king, Antiochus VII Sidetes, at once invaded Judaea to establish his authority, occupying Jerusalem and compelling Hyrcanus to pay a heavy tribute and to dismantle the wall of Jerusalem. Antiochus, however, used his victory with moderation, leaving him in full possession of the country and being content with a nominal sovereignty. Hyrcanus now embarked upon a career of conquest. He attacked the Nabataeans, east of the river Jordan, captured the towns of Medeba and Samaga and annexed the surrounding territory. In the north he captured Shechem and destroyed the Samaritan temple on Mount Gerizim. In the south he conquered Idumaea, the ancient Edom, and compelled the inhabitants to accept the Jewish faith. Finally he attacked the city of Samaria which was captured after a long siege. It was in this period that the two main sections of the Jewish people crystallized into the parties of the Pharisees and the Sadducees. During his early period Hyrcanus, though High Priest, was friendly with the Pharisees, but later he broke with them and joined the Sadducees.

John Hyrcanus was succeeded by his son, Aristobulus I (104–103 B.C.), who, according to Josephus, was the first Hasmonaean to assume the title of 'King.' In his short reign of one year he conquered a great part of Ituraea (probably Galilee) and compelled the inhabitants to accept the Jewish faith. He was a man of considerable ambition and energy and combined love of Greek culture with zeal for the traditions of the Jewish faith.

Aristobulus was succeeded by his brother, Alexander Jannaeus (103–76 B.C.), who continued the policy of his predecessors, so that he eventually ruled over almost the whole of the country from Dan to Beersheba. His ambition and his character roused opposition, especially among the Pharisees, who had by this time acquired great influence over the people generally. Civil war broke out and the Pharisees called in the help of their old foes, the Syrians. Alexander was forced to take refuge in the hills, but his sad plight produced a strong reaction in his favour among the Jewish people and they rallied to his support. The Syrians were expelled and Alexander returned in triumph. At the close of his life he advised his wife to conciliate the Pharisees.

On the death of Alexander, his widow, Alexandra, became queen (76–67 B.C.), making her eldest son, Hyrcanus, High Priest. She reversed the policy of hostility towards the Pharisees, taking them into her favour and complying to a large extent with their wishes and demands. Political power, however, made them arrogant and tyrannous. They persecuted the Sadducees who found a supporter in Aristobulus, the younger son of Alexandra.

On the queen's death Hyrcanus became king, but his brother, Aristobulus, refused to acquiesce in this state of affairs and civil war broke out between them. Hyrcanus was defeated and allowed to retire into private life while Aristobulus assumed the kingship and the High-priesthood. An Idumaean, named Antipater, however, stirred up

Hyrcanus to assert his rights, declaring that if he did not do so his life would be in danger. In the struggle which followed the two brothers appealed to Pompey, who was in Damascus, to arbitrate between them. Pompey delayed in giving his decision and Aristobulus prepared to act on his own, whereupon the former marched into Judaea, besieged Jerusalem, and after three months captured it with a terrible slaughter (63 B.C.). Hyrcanus was confirmed in the High-priesthood, the kingship abolished and Judaea incorporated in the province of Syria. With this settlement a new era in Jewish history began.

CHAPTER III

ARCHAEOLOGY

THE EXILE AND RETURN 587-538 B.C.

THE severe nature of the siege of Jerusalem (589-587 B.C.) is shown by the utter destruction which took place at the time. In 1935 eighteen inscribed potsherds were discovered in the debris of the guardroom by the city gate of Lachish (Tell-ed-Duweir). In 1938 three more were unearthed. Most of them were messages which passed between Hoska-yahu, the commander of an outpost, and Yaosh, the military governor of Lachish. The biblical narrative tells us that when the army of the king of Babylon was fighting against Jerusalem, Lachish and Azekah were the only fortified cities which had not been taken (Jer. xxxiv. 7). In one of the letters the writer says that they were watching for the fire-signals from Lachish, 'according to all the signs which my lord hath given, for we cannot see Azekah'. Lachish, Beth-shemesh and Debir were destroyed and the sites, as in many other places in Judah, were abandoned or only sparsely inhabited afterwards. No town in Judah has been found to have been continuously occupied throughout the exilic period. Only in the Negeb, the district north of Jerusalem and in the Babylonian province of Samaria, did towns escape destruction.

A clay seal was found in the ruins of Lachish, bearing on its back the impression of the fibres of the papyrus document to which it was attached and inscribed with the words, 'Gedaliah who is over the house'. The person mentioned has been identified with Gedaliah, 'the son of Ahikam, son of Shaphan' whom Nebuchadrezzar made governor of Judah after the destruction of Jerusalem (587 B.C.). His headquarters were at Mizpah (2 Kgs. xxv. 22-25).

The biblical narrative tells us that Jehoiachin, king of Judah, was taken into captivity in 598 B.C. (2 Kgs. xxiv. 15) and that Evil-Merodach, who succeeded Nebuchadrezzar on the throne, released him from prison and gave him a regular daily allowance as long as he lived

(2 Kgs. xxv. 27–30). During excavations carried out in Babylon from 1899–1917 a number of tablets were found in an administrative building near the Ishtar gate. Some of these tablets list deliveries of oil and barley from the government to captives and skilled workmen. Among them were 'Yaukin' (Jehoiachin) and his five sons. The evidence suggests that he was held as a hostage for the good behaviour of the Judaeans, and that he was regarded as the true king.

According to Daniel v. 1f., 22, 29f., Belshazzar was king at the time of the fall of Babylon, but contemporary records name Nabonidus, 'king of Babylon'. There is no evidence, but it is probable that during his absence in Tema (553–546 B.C.) he put the administration of the government in the hands of Belshazzar, who was his eldest son. In one inscription he prays for long life for Belshazzar, 'my first born, my dear offspring', and in another he tells us that in the seventh year of his reign he was in Tema, while his son, his officials and his army were in Akkad.

In the biblical record the name of the conqueror of Babylon is given as 'Darius the Mede' (Dan. v. 30; vi. 1, 28; ix. 1; xi. 1). The Nabonidus Chronicle and the Cyrus Cylinder prove conclusively that Babylonia was overthrown by Cyrus, the founder of the Persian empire. A stele from Harran, published by Gadd in 1958 describes the flight and exile of Nabonidus. His return in 546 B.C. was welcomed by 'the king of the Medes', who at this time must have been Cyrus. It has been suggested that 'Darius the Mede' was another name and title for Cyrus himself.

The Babylonian exile came to an end with the conquest of Babylon by Cyrus, king of Persia, in 539 B.C. In the first year of his reign in Babylon he issued a decree permitting the return of the Jewish community to Jerusalem and the rebuilding of the Temple. In the biblical record the decree is found in two forms. In Ezra vi. 3–5 it is in Aramaic and in the form of a 'dikrona', that is, a memoranda recording an oral decision of the king filed in the royal archives. It ordains that the Temple be rebuilt and the expenses defrayed from the royal treasury, and directs that the vessels seized by Nebuchadrezzar be restored to their rightful place. In Ezra i. 2–4 it is written in Hebrew and is in the form of a royal proclamation, in which Cyrus claims that the God of heaven has given him all the kingdoms of the earth, and has charged him 'to build him a house at Jerusalem which is in Judah'. It permits the Jewish exiles to return to their native land and invites the Jews remaining in Babylon to contribute towards the venture. This claim is strange when we remember that Cyrus was not a worshipper of Yahweh, and that the Jews were not the only people who had been deported to Babylonia. But archaeology provides us with a clue to the solution of the problem.

The Cyrus Cylinder gives an account of the events leading up to and culminating in the capture of Babylon, and of his general policy towards the people whom he had conquered.

'He (the god Marduk) scoured all the lands for a friend, seeking for the upright prince whom it would have to take his hand. He called Cyrus, king of Anshan. He nominated him to be ruler over all. ... He gave orders that he go against his city Babylon. He made him take the road to Babylon and he went at his side like a friend and comrade. His vast army, whose number like the waters of a river cannot be determined, with their armour held close, moved forward beside him. He got him into his city Babylon without fighting or battle. He averted hardship to Babylon. He put an end to the power of Nabonidus the king who did not show him reverence. The entire population of Babylon, the whole of Sumer and Akkad, princes and governors, bowed to him (Cyrus) and kissed his feet. ... From ... to the cities of Ashur and Susa, Agade, Eshnunna, the cities of Zamban, Meturnu, Der, as far as the region of the land of Gutium, the holy cities beyond the Tigris whose sanctuaries had been in ruins over a long period, the gods whose abode is in the midst of them, I returned to their places and housed them in lasting abodes. I gathered together all their inhabitants and restored (to them) their dwellings. The gods of Sumer and Akkad whom Nabonidus had, to the anger of the lord of the gods, brought into Babylon, I at the bidding of Marduk, the great lord, made to dwell in peace in their habitations, delightful abodes.'

It is obvious that Cyrus's concession to the Jews was not a mark of special favour but part of his policy of conciliation towards subject peoples. The Jewish colouring of the degree of Cyrus, found in Ezra i, 2-4 is due to the Chronicler who wished to show that Yahweh was using Cyrus as the instrument of His purpose for the return of the Jewish exiles to their native land.

THE PERSIAN PERIOD, 539-331 B.C.

The Jews in Egypt

In the early years of the present century a number of papyri in Aramaic were dug up at Elephantine (or Yeb), an island near the second cataract of the Nile: a further collection of papyri came to light in 1947. All these papyri came from a Jewish military colony in Elephantine which was entrusted with the important duty of guarding the frontier against attacks from Ethiopia. Many of them are dated and cover almost the whole of the fifth century B.C. They are mostly domestic, business and legal documents, but among them are copies of letters dispatched to the authorities in Palestine.

These documents shed considerable light on the social and religious life of the small religious community. From them it is clear that the fortress had been occupied by Jewish mercenary troops before the conquest of Egypt by Cambyses in 525 B.C. These mercenaries had their own temple with its priesthood and ritual. In one letter we find the words, 'Our fathers built this temple in the fortress of Elephantine in the days of the Kings of Egypt, and when Cambyses entered Egypt he found the temple already built, and though all the temples of the Egyptian gods were destroyed no one did any harm to that temple'. They were not monotheists in the strict sense of the term, since along with Yahweh they worshipped at least three subordinate deities, Anath-bethel, Asham-bethel and Haram-bethel. The syncretistic form of their religion suggests that they came originally from the environs of Bethel.[1] It is interesting to note that they either did not know of the Deuteronomic law which centralized all sacrificial worship in one place, which was taken to mean Jerusalem, or if they did know of it, they thought that it did not apply to them (Deut. xii. 1–14).

In the fifth year of Darius II, that is, in 419 B.C., a letter was sent to 'Yedoniah and his colleagues, the Jewish garrison' in Elephantine from Hananiah, who was apparently a Jew and an important official under the Persian governor, Arsames. The letter informed them that the king had issued an order commanding the Jewish garrison to observe the Passover. It is unlikely that the king took much interest in the details of Jewish ritual. No doubt he merely issued an order embodying the wishes of the Jewish leaders.

In 408 B.C., during the temporary absence of the Persian governor, Arsames, the priests of a local temple conspired with 'that scoundrel', Widrang, to raze the Jewish temple to the ground. The Jewish priest, Yedoniah, and his colleagues sent letters to Bagoas, governor of Judaea, 'and to the High Priest, Johanan (mentioned in Nehemiah xii. 22f.) and his colleagues the priests in Jerusalem and to Ostanes, the brother', requesting their support in rebuilding the temple. Their

[1] W. F. Albright, *Archaeology and the Religion of Israel*, 1953, pp. 171–175.

appeals met with no response, and as in 408 B.C., they wrote again to Bagoas informing him that they had reported the whole matter to Delaiah and Shelemiah, the sons of Sanballat, the governor of Samaria. In the biblical record Sanballat was a contemporary of Nehemiah, but we are not told that he was the governor of Samaria. Bagoas and Delaiah gave their consent verbally to an envoy, who apparently drew up a memorandum of the interview which has survived. It reads thus: 'Memorandum of what Bagoas and Delaiah said to me: Let it be a memorandum to you in Egypt to say to Arsames concerning the altar-house of the God of Heaven, which was built in the fortress of Elephantine long ago, before Cambyses, which that scoundrel Widrang destroyed in the fourteenth year of King Darius, that it be rebuilt in its place as it was before, and that meal-offering and incense be offered upon that altar as was formerly done.'[1] Whether the temple was ever rebuilt we do not know. Within a few years the Persian power collapsed and the Jewish garrison disappears from history.

The Jews in Babylon

At Nippur in south-east Babylon 730 tablets, written in the reigns of Artaxerxes I (465–424 B.C.) and Darius II (423–404 B.C.) and belonging to Murashu and Sons, a family of bankers, have been unearthed. The clients of the firm were mainly land-owners and farm-workers in central and southern Babylonia. Of these thirty-eight have Jewish names, showing clearly that in the fifth century B.C. there were numerous descendants of the Jewish exiles living in central and southern Babylonia and that they were allowed to engage in trade.

The Jews in Palestine

A few buildings of the Persian period have been excavated, but the only one of any importance is the Persian villa on the summit of the mound of Lachish dating from the end of the fifth or the beginning of the fourth century B.C. This suggests that Lachish must have been an important centre of Persian government. In Gezer tombs have been discovered belonging to the Persian period. They are probably the tombs of Persian officials and suggest that here was a minor centre of government.

Numerous jar-handle seals of the fifth and fourth centuries, bearing the words, 'Yehud', or 'Yerushalem', or 'Msh' (meaning unknown)

---

[1] A. Cowley, *Aramaic Papyri of the Fifth Century* B.C., 1923. E. G. Kraeling, *The Brooklyn Museum Aramaic Papyri*, 1953.

have been discovered. These jar-handle seals throw light on the administration of the province of Judaea under the Persians. The taxes were apparently paid in oil and wine which were collected in standard jars, made by certain licensed potters who were allowed to use official stamps.

The Persians seem to have learnt the art of minting coins from the Lydians or the Greeks. During the reign of Darius I (522–486 B.C.) gold coins, called darics, circulated throughout the empire. According to A. Reifenberg, the earliest Jewish-known coin was found in Hebron and is inscribed with the word 'beqa', which is the term used for the half-shekel.[1] The daric was a Persian coin but the 'beqa' was a Jewish coin, apparently minted in Judaea. Many silver Jewish coins, based on Greek models, with a human bearded head (with head-dress or helmet) on the one face and an owl (the emblem of the goddess Athena) on the other, and belonging to the fourth century B.C., have come to light. They show that the province of Judaea enjoyed a considerable measure of self-government under the Persian government. The discovery of these coins together with a large quantity of Greek vases and potsherds show that the Greek influence was strong in Palestine in the Persian period.

THE GREEK PERIOD, 331–63 B.C.

Archaeology has supplied us with little information concerning the life and religion of the Jews in the Greek period. The only important remains of this period are the painted tombs of Marisa (Sandahanna) discovered about 1902 and dating from the second half of the third century B.C. They were excavated from the rock for the heads of the Sidonian colony, established here about the middle of the third century B.C. The painted decorations on the walls show the Greek influence. Since Marisa lay in Idumaea, the inscriptions supply us with information concerning the life and religion of the Edomite settlements in southern Judaea. Among the papyri found in Egypt there is a group of documents from the archives of one Zeno, an Egyptian official of the time of Ptolemy II Philadelphus (285–246 B.C.). These include two letters from Tobiah, the governor of Ammon, who was doubtless a descendant of Nehemiah's enemy, 'Tobiah the servant, the Ammonite' (Neh. ii. 10, 19; cf. vi. 12; xiii. 4, 8). At Ataq-el-Emir in Transjordan are some rock-cut tombs one of which bears the name 'Tobiah' deeply cut on the rock in Aramaic characters of the third century B.C. This

---

[1] A. Reifenberg, *Ancient Jewish Coins*, 2nd. rev. ed., 1947.

ARCHAEOLOGY 43

Tobiah is probably to be identified with the Tobiah of the Zeno papyri. Excavations have brought to light Hellenistic fortifications at Samaria, Bethzur and Gezer. At Bethzur numerous coins have been discovered, bearing the names of Antiochus IV Epiphanes (175–163 B.C.) and Antiochus V Eupator (163–162 B.C.). Here too, have been found scores of stamped Rhodian jar handles, each bearing the name of the potter or the magistrate of the year. Similar jar handles have been found in large quantities in Samaria, which was a Hellenistic city. These coins and jar handles show that the Greek influence was strong in Palestine in this period.

THE DEAD SEA SCROLLS

The Dead Sea Scrolls, discovered in the period 1947–1956, are of the greatest importance for the textual criticism of the Old Testament.[1] Apart from the Nash papyrus (acquired in 1902), a small fragment containing the Ten Commandments (Deut. v. 6–21) and the Shema (Deut. vi. 4–9) and assigned by Albright to the second or early first century B.C., the oldest extant Hebrew text of the Old Testament, known as the Massoretic text, dates from about the middle of the ninth century of the Christian era. Early in the present century it was not thought possible that any ancient manuscript could have survived in the moist climate of Palestine. Now in the Dead Sea Scrolls we have many ancient Hebrew manuscripts of the Old Testament going back to the second or first century B.C., that is, nearly a thousand years nearer to the time when the Old Testament books were written.

The aim of modern biblical scholars is to establish as far as possible the original reading of the Scriptures. In pursuit of their aim they have had at their disposal in the past three main texts, namely, the Hebrew Massoretic text, the Greek translation of the Septuagint and the Samaritan text of the Pentateuch. Some of the Dead Sea manuscripts have close affinities with the Hebrew Massoretic text, some with the Septuagint text, and others with the Samaritan text. They show that the Hebrew Massoretic text, the Hebrew text underlying the Septuagint, and the Hebrew Samaritan text were varying types of text current among the people of Israel. Hence they can be used in conjunction with the three main texts in determining a more original text. 'If', says Rowley, 'in the passages that could be checked, they uniformly supported the Massoretic tradition, or uniformly supported the Greek tradition, this would be of the first significance. This, however, is not

[1] For an account of the Dead Sea Scrolls, see Appendix L, pp. 368–374

the case. Sometimes we find the one and sometimes the other supported, and sometimes a modern conjectural emendation finds the support here, while at other times we find readings hitherto unknown.'[1]

The manuscripts are important as enabling us to fix the dates of certain books with greater accuracy. For example, a fragment of Ecclesiastes comes from the middle of the second century B.C., suggesting that the date c. 200 B.C., assigned by some scholars to Ecclesiastes, is too late. The complete manuscript of Isaiah is dated in the second century B.C., suggesting that our Isaiah reached its present form long before that century.

[1] H. H. Rowley, *The Dead Sea Scrolls and their Significance*, 1954, p. 21.

CHAPTER IV

APOCALYPTIC LITERATURE

THE MEANING OF THE TERM

THE term 'apocalypse' is the Latin form of the Greek 'apocalypsis', meaning 'revelation' or 'disclosure', that is, something revealed or disclosed to a chosen few. The term was applied by the Jews to indicate a type of literature which was supposed to reveal the future, whether in this life or in the life to come. It was apocalyptic in form because it professed to be a revelation or disclosure, and eschatological (Greek 'eschatos' = 'last') in theme because it was concerned with the doctrine of the last things. This type of literature was not peculiar to the Jews. Homer made Odysseus visit the world of the dead beyond the stream of Ocean in which the heroes of history and legend led a shadowy existence; and his example was followed by Virgil in the sixth book of the *Aeneid*. The Egyptians were profoundly interested in the future, and in their literature (e.g. *The Wisdom of Amen-em-ope*) we find a doctrine of a final Judgment and of a Hereafter.

DATE AND PLACE OF COMPOSITION AND CAUSE OF DECLINE

The Jewish apocalyptic writings flourished during the period 200 B.C.–A.D. 100. It is generally supposed that they originated in Palestine, probably for the most part in Galilee, the home of the religious seer and mystic, and were very popular among the people. Towards the close of the second century A.D. their popularity began to decline. They continued to be written down to the thirteenth or fourteenth century A.D. when they were finally abandoned, partly because of their popularity among Christians, who found in them proofs of the Messiahship of Jesus and of the speedy advent of the kingdom of God, partly because they had played a part in inciting the people to embark on the disastrous revolt against the Romans which led to the destruction of Jerusalem in A.D. 70, and partly because the Rabbis became absorbed in the study of the Law, believing it to be the complete and final revelation of the will of God, so that no further revelations were possible.

The Jews apparently made no great efforts to preserve the apocalyptic writings with the result that they practically disappeared, so that it was once customary to speak of the interval between the Old Testament and the New Testament as 'the silent years'. In the last century, thanks largely to the labours of British and German scholars, many of them have been discovered. They have survived because they were taken over by the Christian Church and used by Christian communities. They seem to have been written originally in Hebrew or Aramaic and then translated into Greek, Latin, Syriac, Ethiopic or Slavonic, for use in the local churches of the Diaspora. For example, we have *The Testaments of the Twelve Patriarchs* and *The Testament of Abraham* in Greek, *The Life of Adam and Eve* in Latin and Greek, *The Apocalypse of Baruch* in Syriac, *The Book of Jubilees* in Ethiopic and Latin, 1 *Enoch* (or *The Ethiopic Book of Enoch*) in Ethiopic and 2 *Enoch* (or *The Slavonic Book of Enoch*) in Slavonic.[1] The discovery of these apocalyptic writings is one of the greatest achievements of modern biblical scholarship.

APOCALYPTIC WRITINGS

The following is a list of the apocalyptic books arranged approximately in chronological order.

WRITINGS OF THE LAST TWO CENTURIES B.C.

Canonical Books

The Book of Daniel (vii–xii). The book was written about 164 B.C. Chapters vii–xii consist of four visions in which Daniel is made to predict the course of history from the beginning of the Persian era to the time of Antiochus Epiphanes, the destruction of the heathen empires, the advent of the kingdom of God and the resurrection of the Jewish martyrs to everlasting life and of the apostates to everlasting contempt.

Non-canonical Books

The Ethiopic book of Enoch (or 1 Enoch). This is a composite work consisting of 105 chapters (chs. 106–108 are probably a late

---

[1] The Qumran Library has yielded fragments of *The Book of Jubilees*, 1 *Enoch* and *The Testament of Levi* in Aramaic, and of *The Testament of Naphtali* in Hebrew.

APOCALYPTIC LITERATURE

insertion) which can be divided into at least five independent sections. They belong to various dates ranging from about 163 B.C. to about 80 B.C.

The Book of Jubilees. The book is also known as the *Little Genesis* because it is inferior to canonical *Genesis*. It is called *Jubilees* because of the author's attempt to divide the period with which it deals, namely from the Creation to the Exodus (Gen.–Exod. i–xii), into periods of forty-nine years. It purports to be a vision which Moses received on Mount Sinai in which Yahweh is said to have unfolded to him all history from the Creation 'unto eternity' (Jub. i. 4, 26). It is generally agreed that it belongs to the second century B.C., probably to the period 134–104 B.C.

The Testaments of the Twelve Patriarchs. The book purports to be the last words of the twelve sons of Jacob, addressed to their children. In each Testament history, exhortation and prophecy are combined. It has commonly been believed that it is a Jewish work containing a number of Christian interpolations. According to Charles, it was probably written between 109–106 B.C.,[1] while De Jonge assigns it to the period A.D. 109–225.[2] Fragments of an Aramaic *Testament of Levi* have been found among the Dead Sea Scrolls. Philonenko believes that the work emanated from the Essenes, and that most of the supposed interpolations are original to it and are to be interpreted in relation to the Essenes as we meet them in the Qumran texts.[3]

The Sibylline Oracles. These oracles were originally contained in fifteen books of which twelve have survived. They contain both Jewish and Christian elements. The Jewish oracles are contained in Books iii–v which are of different dates, ranging from about 140 B.C. to A.D. 125. The remainder of the books are mostly of Christian origin and belong to the fifth century A.D. The aim of *The Sibylline Oracles* was the propagation of Judaism among the Gentiles.

The Psalms of Solomon. The book consists of eighteen Psalms belonging to about the middle of the first century B.C.

---
[1] R. H. Charles, *Religious Developments between the Old and the New Testaments*, 1914, pp. 227f.
[2] M. De Jonge, *The Testaments of the Twelve Patriarchs* 1953, p. 125.
[3] M. Philonenko, *Les interpolations chrétiennes des Testaments des douze Patriarches et les manuscrits de Qoumrân*, 1960.

The Zadokite Work. This work belongs to the period of the Dead Sea Scrolls.[1] In it reference is made to the coming of a Messiah of Aaron and Israel. The evidence of the Dead Sea Scrolls suggests that the singular word here replaced an original plural in the course of transmission in order to bring the language into line with current Jewish doctrine, and that the writer looked forward to the coming of two Messiahs—a priestly Messiah and a kingly Messiah. Reference is also made to a Teacher of Righteousness whose death would be followed by forty years of conflict between the sons of light and the sons of darkness after which the Messianic Age would dawn.

WRITINGS OF THE FIRST CENTURY A.D.

The Assumption of Moses. The work, written during the period 4 B.C.–A.D. 28 purports to be the final charge given to Joshua by Moses. The author gives a rapid sketch of Jewish history from the entry into Canaan to the time of writing, and an account of the advent of the kingdom of God and of the punishment of the heathen.

The Slavonic Book of Enoch. The book is so-called because it is known only in the Slavonic version. It is also called 2 Enoch or *The Book of the Secrets of Enoch*. Written probably in the first half of the first century A.D., it gives an account of Enoch's ascension through the seven heavens into the presence of God, of God's revelations to him, and of Enoch's admonitions to his sons.

The Life of Adam and Eve. The book was probably written in the first century A.D. before the destruction of Jerusalem in A.D. 70. It is cast in the form of a story of the experiences of Adam and Eve after their expulsion from Paradise. It contains a number of Christian interpolations.

4 Ezra. This consists of chapters iii–xiv of the book which stands in the Apocrypha as 2 Esdras. It consists of seven visions which Ezra is said to have seen in Babylon, but it was probably written towards the close of the first century A.D. The visions describe the signs of the end of the present world order, the advent of the Messianic Age, the general resurrection, and the condition of souls after death.

---

[1] For an account of the discovery of the *Zadokite Work* and of its connexion with the Qumran community, see Appendix I, p. 369.

APOCALYPTIC LITERATURE

The Syriac Apocalypse of Baruch (or 2 Baruch). It is called the Syriac Apocalypse because the final manuscript of the book is written in Syriac. Its theme is the destruction of Jerusalem in 587 B.C. The book is generally thought to be dependent on 4 Ezra, but the relation cannot be determined with any certainty. Some regard it as a unity and others as a composite work with elements falling in the period A.D. 53–90.[1]

The Testament of Abraham. The date of the work is uncertain. James maintains that it was written in the second century A.D. by a Christian writer, and that it embodies earlier material,[2] while others believe that it is a Jewish work with Christian interpolations, and that it belongs to the first century A.D. In the Apocalypse Abraham, before his death, was granted a vision of the world and of the judgment, and was afterwards borne away by Michael to Paradise.

The Apocalypse of Abraham. This belongs to the end of the first century or the beginning of the second century A.D. It is thought to be a Jewish work worked over by Christian hands. It consists of two parts (i–viii and ix–xxxii) the second of which alone is apocalyptic, containing a revelation to Abraham concerning the future of the Jewish race.

ORIGIN AND DEVELOPMENT OF APOCALYPTIC

The germ of Apocalyptic is to be found in the popular conception of the 'last times', frequently spoken of as the 'last day' and more specifically as the 'day of Yahweh'.[3] It was the day when Yahweh

---

[1] There is also *The Greek Apocalypse of Baruch*, often called *3 Baruch*. This gives a description of Baruch's journeys through the heavens and of his return. It probably belongs to the latter half of the second century A.D. and is, therefore, outside our period.

[2] M. R. James, *The Testament of Abraham*, 1892, pp. 23, 55.

[3] Gunkel (*Schöpfung und Chaos in Urzeit und Endzeit*, 1895) argues that the eschatological ideas associated with the Day of Yahweh were derived from the Babylonian creation myth. Primeval history is projected into the future, chaos returns and a new heaven and a new earth are created. Gressmann (*Der Ursprung der israelitisch-jüdischen Eschatologie*, 1905) holds that they were of great antiquity and were common to the ancient oriental world. For example, long before the appearance of prophecy in Israel there had existed in Egypt a literary genre of eschatology similar to that of the late Jewish apocalypses, comprising a description of awful calamities followed by an age of blessedness. Mowinckel (*Psalmenstudien* ii. 1922) maintained that they were derived from the day of Yahweh's enthronement in the New Year Festival. From the ritual associated with the Festival the Hebrews borrowed the ideas of the kingship of Yahweh, the catastrophes in nature, deliverance from enemies as a result of the new covenant, the eschatological

would intervene in human affairs, destroy His enemies, and bring in a new order in which Israel would be the dominant power. According to this conception, Yahweh would bestow His favours upon His chosen people irrespective of their manner of life. The canonical prophets introduced a moral and an eschatological content into it. They taught that Yahweh was not only the Lord of History but also a God of absolute righteousness whose judgments were not arbitrary but based upon the principles of right and wrong. Israel's special privileges as His chosen people involved them in special responsibilities. Much had been given to them and much would be required of them. For them, because of their wickedness, the 'day of Yahweh' would be a day, not of triumph but of catastrophe (Am. v. 18).

Prophet after prophet proclaimed the speedy advent of the judgment and of a kingdom of righteousness, peace and infinite bliss, in which God Himself or His representative, the Messiah, would reign as king. Time passed but the prophecies regarding the 'last things' were not fulfilled. The apocalyptists took them over, reinterpreting and developing them, each in his own way. A study of their works will show how they modified them.

Jeremiah predicted that the Jews would go into captivity in Babylon for seventy years (xxv. 11; xxix. 10), and that at the end of that period they would be restored to their native land (xxiv. 5f.) and the Messianic kingdom established (xxiii. 5f.). In Daniel x. 27 the seventy years are represented as seventy weeks of days, that is, 490 years, and in 1 Enoch lxxxix. 59 as the reigns of seventy shepherds or angels, commissioned by God to shepherd His people Israel. According to Daniel vii. 23–27, the fourth and last empire to be destroyed before the establishment of the everlasting kingdom would be the Greek, but according to 4 Ezra xi–xii. 35, it would be the Roman.

In the apocalyptic writings there is no fixed doctrine of the judgment. According to some accounts there would be only one judgment —a universal judgment which would usher in the eternal kingdom of God, whereas according to others, there would be two judgments, a preliminary one, introducing a Messianic kingdom of limited duration, and a final one, preceding the dawn of the eternal kingdom of God.

banquet (the sacrificial meal) and the Messiah, the divinely appointed leader. Hebrew eschatology was in fact a projection into the future of what had been dramatically presented in the cult. Morgenstern (*Amos Studies* 1941, 408ff.) believes that the origin of the concept of the Day of Yahweh was the annual observance of the New Year's Day at the autumnal equinox, which originated in the mythological idea of the primeval struggle at creation between light and darkness, good and evil, life and death.

Sometimes God Himself is represented as being the Judge (Dan. vii. 9f.; 1 En. i. 9; 4 Ezra vii. 33), and sometimes His Messiah (1 En. lxix. 27; 2 Bar. lxxii. 1ff.). There is no consistent view on the nature of the rewards of the righteous and of the punishment of the wicked. Sometimes the righteous were to be rewarded with unbounded prosperity and peace on the earth (1 En. x. 17; 2 Bar. xxix. 5–8; lxxiii. 1–7), and sometimes with eternal bliss in heaven (4 Ezra vii. 36, viii. 52; 2 Bar. li. 2). Sometimes the wicked were to be destroyed (Pss. of Sol. xv. 15), and sometimes they were to be condemned to endless torture in Gehenna (Ass. of Mos. x. 10; 4 Ezra xiii. 36–38; 2 Bar. xliv. 5).

Three fairly distinct, irreconcilable conceptions of the kingdom of God may be distinguished. The first conception is similar to that of the prophets. The everlasting kingdom of God would be established on the earth with the Jewish nation as the dominant power and with Jerusalem as the political and religious centre (1 En. xxv. 5; xc. 30; Sib. Or. Bk. iii. 772–776). It would be under the sovereignty of God Himself or His representative, the Messiah. With the establishment of the kingdom, the whole earth would be tilled in righteousness and should be full of blessing (1 En. x. 17; cf. 1 En. xi. 1f.). According to the second conception, the everlasting kingdom of God would be established, not on earth but in paradise or in heaven where God dwelt. There all goodness, joy and glory were prepared for the righteous; manifold good would be given to them in recompense for their labours, and their lot would be abundantly beyond the lot of the living (1 En. civ. 3f.). They would live eternally and know 'neither labour, nor sickness, nor humiliation, nor anxiety, nor need, nor violence, nor night, nor darkness, but great light' (2 En. lxv. 10). Time would no longer age them; they would be made like the angels, and would change into every form they desired, from beauty into loveliness, and from light into the splendour of glory (2 Bar. li. 10). To them would be given the joy of seeing their foes in torment in Gehenna (Ass. of Mos. x. 9). According to the third conception, the kingdom of God would be of limited duration and under the sovereignty, not of God but of His Messiah. That kingdom would not be identical with the everlasting kingdom of God but a partial and temporary manifestation of it. In 4 Ezra, we read that the Messianic kingdom would last for 400 years, and that at the end of that period the Messiah and all men would die, and that for seven years there would be complete silence on the earth (4 Ezra vii. 28–30). Then would come the resurrection and the final judgment, followed by the dawn of the eternal kingdom of God in which the righteous would enjoy the blessings of the 'paradise of delight' (4 Ezra vii. 31-36). A similar conception is found in 2 Baruch.

The Messiah is often associated with the advent of the kingdom of God, but he is not essential to the eschatological scheme. The figure of the Messiah is absent from Daniel, 1 Enoch (other than the Parables and Dream-Visions), The Assumption of Moses, 2 Enoch and 1 Baruch. Whenever he appears he plays a subordinate role.

There are two entirely different conceptions of the Messiah. On the one hand he is an ideal secular ruler of Davidic lineage (Test. of Jud. xxiv. 5f.; Pss. of Sol. xvii. 23-25), or a priest of the tribe of Levi (Test. of Reub. vi. 5-12; Test. of Levi xviii. 2ff.).[1] On the other hand he is a pre-existent heavenly being (1 En. xlvi. 1, 3; lxix. 26-29). The titles, character and functions of the Messiah are described in the Similitudes of Enoch (1 En. xxxvii-lxxi).

Apart from Isaiah xxiv-xxvii which is an apocalyptic element, there is no reference to the resurrection in the prophetic writings. In the apocalyptic writings, however, it is definitely taught, but the teaching is not uniform. The prevailing view of life after death in the post-exilic period was that at death the shade of man descended to Sheol, where he lived a dreary existence cut off from all communion with God and man. In Sheol there were no moral distinctions. According to Isaiah xxiv-xxvii, there would be a resurrection of the righteous Israelites: for the wicked there would be no resurrection (Is. xxv. 8; xxvi. 19). A similar view is found in 1 Enoch xxv. 4ff.; xxii. 13, The Psalms of Solomon, iii. 16, xv. 15, and 2 Baruch xxx. 1. In Daniel it is taught that there would be a resurrection of the Jewish martyrs and apostates (Dan. xii. 2). Presumably the rest of the righteous and the wicked would remain in Sheol. Some of the writings announced that all mankind were to rise from the dead (Test. of Benj. x. 6-8; 4 Ezra vii. 31ff.). In *The Assumption of Moses* there is no resurrection either of the righteous or of the wicked, but the righteous would be exalted to heaven and the wicked suffer endless torment in Gehenna (Ass. of Mos. x. 9f.).

Some of the writings declared that the body would rise again (Dan. xii. 2; 4 Ezra vii. 32). According to 2 Baruch i. 2, the dead would

---

[1] The evidence of *The Testaments of the Twelve Patriarchs* suggests that the author of the book believed in the emergence of two Messiahs, one kingly and the other priestly. It would appear that this belief was also shared by the members of the Qumran community (see pp. 372.)

be raised in exactly the same form in which they had been committed to the earth, in order that their identity might be established. After the judgment the aspect of the wicked would become worse than it was. The righteous would be transformed into the splendour of angels (2 Bar. li. 1–6).

Thus it will be seen that the apocalyptic writings contain a few common conceptions combined with a great variety of detail. We read, for example, of a single judgment and a double judgment, of a temporary kingdom on earth, an everlasting kingdom on earth and an everlasting kingdom in heaven; a kingdom under the direct rule of Yahweh, and a kingdom ruled over by the Messiah as His representative; a Messiah who is a Davidic prince of the tribe of Judah, and a Messiah who is a priest of the tribe of Levi; a Messiah who is a human figure and mortal, and a Messiah who is a pre-existent heavenly being; a world that would last for ever, and a world that would be destroyed by fire; a resurrection of all Jews who had died in the faith, a resurrection of faithful Jewish martyrs and apostates and a resurrection of all men.

PROPHECY AND APOCALYPTIC

The prophetic writings consist largely of brief oracles expressed for the most part in poetic form, and dealing either with the political, moral and social events of the day or predicting future events. Occasionally the prophetic utterances are longer, as for example, *The Song of the Vineyard* (Is. v. 1–7) and *The Taunt Song* (Is. xiv. 4b–21). The apocalyptic writings are more comprehensive, surveying the whole field of history from the Creation to the dawn of the kingdom of God.

In the pre-exilic period, prophecy was probably for the most part delivered orally and subsequently written down, while in the post-exilic period it was first written down and not necessarily spoken at all. The apocalyptist did not speak directly to the people, but addressed them indirectly through his book.

There is nothing mysterious in the prophetic writings. The prophets proclaimed their message openly and in language which could be readily understood by all. The apocalyptic writings claim to be revelations of divine secrets made known by God through dreams, visions, trances and auditions to certain elect individuals who purport to be the authors of the books. They are to be kept from general knowledge and handed down in secret to a chosen few. Daniel is told to seal up the vision 'for it pertains to many days hence' (viii. 26).

In 2 Enoch the writings are committed to the care of Michael until the last age (xxxiii. 10f.). In 4 Ezra the seer is told to write his visions in a book and put them in a secret place, 'and thou shalt teach them to the wise of thy people, whose hearts thou knowest are able to comprehend and keep these secrets' (xii. 37f.).

One of the functions of the prophet was prediction, most of which was concerned with the immediate future as it arose organically out of the present. In predicting the future he was unfolding to men the issues of the policies and sins of their day. Conscious of the wickedness of the people, he predicted that disaster would surely overtake them unless they repented of their evil ways. Hosea, for example, saw clearly that the nation was decadent and was hastening to its fall. 'For they sow the wind and they shall reap the whirlwind' (viii. 7). But for the righteous Remnant a Golden Age would dawn, in which every man would sit under his vine and his fig tree and none would make them afraid (Mic. iv. 4), and in which even the nature of the wild beasts would be transformed (Is. xi. 6–9; cf. lxv. 17–25). The apocalyptist, on the other hand, despaired of the present and placed his hopes in the future. He was aware that the prophets had foretold a glorious future for Israel, but their dreams had not been realized. To make matters worse the people were hopelessly corrupt and could never be transformed by the gradual transformation of their characters. The world seemed to be an arena of conflict in which not only the righteous and the wicked but also angels and demons, Yahweh and Satan fought for the mastery. To him it seemed that the forces of evil were triumphant. Though he despaired of the present, he was not, as some scholars suggest, a confirmed pessimist. He believed that Yahweh could deliver the people from the satanic forces which threatened to engulf them. Hence he proclaimed that the day was approaching when He would intervene catastrophically in the process of history, bring the present world order to an end and establish His kingdom.[1] 'Speaking generally, the prophet foretold the future that should arise out of the present, while the apocalyptist foretold the future that should break into the present'.[2]

The prophet spoke under direct inspiration, being absolutely convinced that he had been called by Yahweh to deliver His message

---

[1] The author of *The Book of Jubilees* held a different view. He looked for no catastrophic event but for the gradual coming of the kingdom by the progressive spiritual development of men and by a corresponding transformation of nature. Man's days would gradually grow longer until they attained a thousand years (xxiii. 27).

[2] H. H. Rowley, *The Relevance of Apocalyptic*, 1944, p. 34.

to the people. Frequently he prefaced his message with the words, 'Thus saith Yahweh' or 'The word of Yahweh came' or words of similar import. His call was irresistible. 'The lion has roared; who will not fear? The Lord God has spoken; who can but prophesy'? (Am. iii. 8). 'If I say, I will not mention him, or speak any more in his name, there is in my heart as it were a burning fire shut up in my bones, and I am weary with holding it in, and I cannot' (Jer. xx. 9). Like the prophet the apocalyptist claimed to be inspired by Yahweh, but he had not the prophet's overwhelming sense of mission or his sense of urgency and responsibility. He was primarily a teacher, his work being the fruit of study and reflection.

CHARACTERISTICS

Historical Setting

The apocalyptic writings have a definite 'Sitz-im-leben' or 'setting in life'. They arise out of a definite historical situation and reflect the conditions of the crises behind them. The pious Jews of the post-exilic period had become familiar with the teaching of the prophets. Ezekiel had stirred the imaginations of the Jewish captives in Babylon with his predictions of the return of the scattered tribes of Israel to their native land and their union under a single ruler of the Davidic line (Ezek. xxxvii. 19–25), and with his description of the new Jerusalem which would arise (Ezek. xl–xlviii). Deutero-Isaiah also encouraged the captives with his glowing picture of the Return and of the glory which awaited them (Is. lii. 1–12; liv. 11–17; lv. 5). But the predictions of the exilic prophets were never fulfilled. On their return in 538 B.C. they did not enter upon a time of peace, prosperity and security nor did they gain political independence. They returned to a diminished territory with its capital in ruins. Instead of being a free people they remained under the sovereignty of Persia until the conquest of the East by Alexander the Great (332–323 B.C.). During the Persian period the prophets Zechariah, Trito-Isaiah, Obadiah and Joel, raised their hopes with the expectation of a glorious future (Zech. ii. 10–13, vi. 9–15; Trito-Is. lxi. 5–9; Obad. 15a, 16–21; Joel iii. 9–17), but the predictions were not fulfilled. The conquests of Alexander the Great replaced Persia by Greece. From the death of Alexander in 323 B.C. to the destruction of Jerusalem in A.D. 70 they were, with the exception of a short period from 142–63 B.C., successively under the domination of foreign powers—Egypt, Syria and Rome. During their struggle against their oppressors they doubtless began to question the validity of the promises made to them by the prophets, and the righteousness of Yahweh who could allow His chosen people to suffer such oppression and humiliation. The main purpose of the apocalyptists was to sustain the courage of their compatriots in their struggles against oppression, and to strengthen their faith in the righteousness of Yahweh by holding out to them the expectation of divine intervention, a great deliverance from their enemies, and a glorious future. The apocalyptic literature has been aptly called 'the expression of a persecution complex'.

Nationalism and Universalism

In the apocalyptic writings we find a combination of nationalism and universalism. Most of the apocalyptists were ardent nationalists with a deep love of their country and an intense hatred of all heathen nations. They looked forward to the day when the righteous Jews would enjoy the bliss of the kingdom of God either on earth or in heaven, and when the Gentiles would be destroyed or condemned to suffer endless torment in Gehenna. According to 4 Ezra, God's concern was for the Jews only and the Gentiles as a whole were nothing to Him: in His sight they were like spittle or a drop on a bucket (vi. 55f.). The writer of *The Book of Jubilees* taught that there was no hope for the Gentiles. God had placed them under angelic guardians with the object of accomplishing their destruction (xv. 31). The time was coming when the righteous would rejoice with joy for ever and ever, and see all their judgments and all their curses on their enemies (xxiii. 30f.). In *The Assumption of Moses* Israel would be exalted to heaven and the people would look with joy on their foes in Gehenna (x. 9f.).

A few of the apocalyptists, however, held broader views concerning the attitude of God to the Gentiles. The writer of 1 Enoch i–xxxvi taught that the chosen race was 'the best part of mankind' (xx. 5) and that the joys of the coming kingdom of God would be for the 'elect' (i. 8; v. 7f.; xxv. 5); but he also declared, 'And all the children of men shall become righteous, and all nations shall offer adoration and shall praise Me, and all shall worship Me' (x. 21). In 1 Enoch lxxiii–xc we are told that the heathen nations would be destroyed by the Jews (xc. 20ff.), but the survivors would be converted and serve Israel (xc. 30). The object of *The Sibylline Oracles* was to propagate Judaism among the Gentiles. God was called 'the eternal Father of all men' (iii. 604). The day was coming when all the islands and cities would call upon God and go to the Temple in procession, abandoning their idolatry

(iii. 715–720). The writer of 1 Enoch xxxvii–lxxi looked forward to the day when the Son of Man would be the light of the Gentiles and the hope of all those who were troubled of heart, and when all who dwelt on the earth would fall down and worship before Him, and praise, bless and celebrate with song the Lord of Spirits (xlviii. 4 f.). In *The Testaments of the Twelve Patriarchs* we have the noblest teaching as regards the attitude of God to the Gentiles. Originally God gave light to all men, but the Gentiles 'went astray, and forsook Yahweh, and changed their order, and obeyed sticks and stones, spirits of deceit' (Test. of Naph. iii. 13). The writer looked for a Priest in whose days, 'the Gentiles shall be multiplied in knowledge upon the earth and enlightened through the grace of the Lord' (Test. of Levi xviii. 9). The Most High would save Israel and all the Gentiles (Test. of Ash. vii. 3). Yahweh would reveal His salvation to all the Gentiles (Test. of Beni. x. 5).

The Unity of History

According to Charles, apocalyptic and not prophecy was the first to grasp the great idea of the unity of history, a unity which followed naturally as a corollary of the unity of God preached by the prophets.[1] This statement is too sweeping and needs qualification. It may be true, as he suggests, that prophecy was mainly concerned with the present and the future so far as it rose organically out of the present, and only occasionally took account of the past, but it does not necessarily follow from this that the prophets did not grasp the conception of the unity of history. From their writings we infer that they did grasp it though they did not expound it, for they believed that the whole course of history was under the direction of God, and that He had a purpose for mankind, which would ultimately be fulfilled. The apocalyptists took over the conception of the unity of history and dealt with it more systematically. They surveyed the whole course of history, past, present and future, in an endeavour to prove that history was not a meaningless series of unconnected events but the unfolding of a divine purpose directed towards a goal—the establishment of the kingdom of God. In pursuit of their aim they divided all history into vast epochs which varied in number from book to book. In 1 Enoch xciii. 1–10; xci. 12–17, the number is ten; in 2 Enoch xxxiii. 1 and *The Testament of Abraham* 17, 19, seven; in 4 Ezra xiv. 11 and 2

[1] R. H. Charles, *Religious Development between the Old and the New Testaments*, 1914, p. 24.

Baruch xxvii. 1, liii. 6, twelve. They believed that the course of history was predetermined by God from the beginning to the end and that nothing could change it. 'What is determined shall be done' (Dan. xi. 36). He who had created the world would bring the present age to a close when the predetermined time was fulfilled (4 Ezra iii. 1–6). In their endeavours to discover a divine purpose running throughout history from the Creation to the final consummation the apocalyptists became the first men to essay a philosophy of history.

Pseudonymity

The apocalyptist ascribed his work to a venerated figure of the past such as Enoch, the Patriarchs, Moses and Isaiah. The reason for this pseudonymity is not known for certain. Some scholars think that the apocalyptist had no literary ambitions but thought only of the message which he hoped to deliver to the people. Some scholars maintain that he hid his identity because in an age of persecution it was too dangerous to attack rulers openly. Charles believes that the reason for pseudonymity is to be found in the prevailing belief that prophecy was dead and that the Law was the complete expression of the divine will. It was, therefore, impossible that there should be any fresh revelation: hence the only chance of gaining a hearing was to assume the role of a known prophet of olden times.[1] Rowley suggests that the convention arose from the way in which Daniel was written. The stories about Daniel were written first and the visions followed in his name in order to indicate identity of authorship with the stories. Succeeding writers slavishly copied this feature as though it were a part of the technique of apocalyptic. 'Pseudonymity was thus born of a living process, whose purpose was the precise opposite of deceit. It only became artificial when it was woodenly copied by imitators'.[2]

Symbolism

Throughout the apocalyptic literature frequent use is made of symbolism. The prophet made use of symbols to enforce or make intelligible his divinely inspired message. Isaiah, for example, saw six-winged seraphim one of whom had a live coal in his mouth (Is. vi. 2, 6), Jeremiah, the rod of an almond tree and a seething cauldron (Jer. i. 11, 13), and Amos, a plumb-line and a basket of summer fruit (Amos

---

[1] R. H. Charles, *Religious Development between the Old and New Testaments*, 1914, p. 42.
[2] H. H. Rowley, *The Relevance of Apocalyptic*, 1944, p. 152.

vii. 8; viii. 1f.). The apocalyptist also used symbols, but he allowed his imagination to run riot with the result that we have symbols of the most fantastic kind. In 1 Enoch lxxxiii–xc, for example, the patriarchs from Adam to Isaac are represented as white bulls, the fallen angels (the 'sons of God' in Gen. vi) as stars, the Gentiles as wild beasts, the Jews as blind sheep, and the Maccabaeans in revolt as horned and sighted sheep. In Daniel vii. 1–7, there appear a lion with eagle's wings, a bear with three ribs in its mouth between its teeth, a leopard with four wings of a bird on its back and with four heads, and a great beast with iron teeth and ten horns. The four heads represent the four great empires of the Babylonians, Medes, Persians and Greeks.

The meaning of the symbols was intelligible to those who possessed the key and to them only. In general it may be said that horns represent kings, stars fallen angels, wild beasts and birds of prey foreign nations, and domesticated animals Israel. In the course of time the symbols became stereotyped and reappeared again and again in the apocalyptic writings. The use of these symbols was doubtless dictated by prudential reasons, but they nevertheless reflected the mysterious character of the visions, so much loved by the apocalyptist who was conscious that the divine mysteries must contain in them something incomprehensible.

The Mythological Element

The apocalyptic writings contain a strong mythological element. This mythology probably originated in Sumeria and was acquired by the Hebrews as they passed through Mesopotamia on their way to Canaan. Four main myths may be distinguished, namely, the Creation Myth, the Saviour Myth, the Golden Age Myth and the Judgment Myth. Contact with the Babylonian culture during the Exile revived the memory of these ancient stories, and in the post-exilic period the apocalyptists made use of them, so purging them of their crude concepts and spiritualizing them that they are hardly recognizable in their new dress. In nothing is the Hebrew genius so clearly seen as in the power to transmute base metal into gold.

PERMANENT INFLUENCE

The influence of the apocalyptic writings was not wholly for good. The belief that they were the chosen people of Yahweh had engendered in the Israelites a spirit of pride and a feeling of superiority over all other nations. Forced into a state of subjection successively by Assyria, Babylon, Persia, Greece and Rome, they had become embittered and learned to hate their oppressors. The apocalyptic writings intensified their pride and fanned their hatred, teaching them to look forward to the day when an avenging God would destroy their oppressors, when Jerusalem would become the political and religious centre of a world-wide Jewish empire, when the surviving Gentiles would be converted and serve them (1 En. xxv. 5; xc. 20; Sib. Or. iii. 710ff.; Pss. of Sol. xvii. 31f.; Ass. of Mos. x. 2, 7; 2 Bar. lxxii. 1ff.), and when they would have the joy of seeing their foes suffering torment in Gehenna (Ass. of Mos. x. 10). By intensifying the spirit of nationalism and reviving the Messianic hope, they played no small part in inciting the Jewish populace to rebel against the Romans, an action which led to the destruction of Jerusalem and the downfall of the Jewish state (A.D. 70). The apocalyptic writings, however, are not merely an outlet for the repressed passions of an oppressed people. It is now generally recognized that in spite of their defects, they performed a great service not only to Judaism but also to Christianity.

The theological conception of a divine purpose running through history, which is enshrined in the apocalyptic writings, has been a source of inspiration, strength and comfort to both Jews and Gentiles throughout the centuries. In recent times this conception has been rejected by many people as unscientific. The pure mechanist, who denies the existence of God, will have none of it. To him the cosmos is but 'a fortuitous concourse of atoms' rolling impotently on, and man merely a by-product of the evolutionary process that works without mind and without heart. There are, he alleges, no compelling reasons for thinking that there is such a thing as a law of continuous progress, or that man is perfectible, or that universal happiness is attainable. To the devout Jew and Christian the cosmos is the creation of a purposeful God, who directs and controls it towards a definite goal. The evolutionary process is the method of the working of the divine mind, and the idea of the kingdom of God is not an impossible dream, but one which will, sooner or later, be realized. Without a divine purpose in history, the whole pageant of civilization is but 'a tale told by an idiot, full of sound and fury, signifying nothing'.

The apocalyptic writings have been aptly called, 'tracts for bad times'. Written in times of crises, they performed a great service by stimulating the hope and sustaining the courage of their readers when all the conditions tempted them to give way to despair.

To the apocalyptic writings we owe the doctrine of the resurrection and the future life, which, when purged of its crudities, made its way into the very centre of religion. The doctrine took various forms, 'but', says Rowley, 'through all these forms is the firm assurance of the writers that they who are loyal to the will of God shall not be excluded from the life of the kingdom of God. They shall live because the abiding God is the spring of their life, and they shall live in ineffable joy because they shall live with God.'[1] Through the centuries people have lived and died in the faith that 'this perishable nature must put on the imperishable, and that this mortal nature must put on immortality' (1 Cor. xv. 53).

The belief in the resurrection and the judgment marks the victory of individualism which had been developing from the days of Jeremiah and Ezekiel. The worth of the individual was recognized and he was set solitary before God. The struggle in the present world-order was not between Jews and Gentiles as nations, but between God and Satan and between good and evil men. At the final judgment every man would be held responsible for his own deeds, and, according to 4 Ezra vii. 102–115, the righteous would not be permitted to intercede for the ungodly. Father would not be permitted to intercede for son, or son for father, or brother for brother, or friend for friend, for every one 'must bear his own righteousness or unrighteousness'. Henceforth the individual and not the nation was to be the religious unit.

The apocalyptic writings help us to understand the mind and soul of those Jews who formed the nucleus of the early Christian Church. They were familiar with the concepts embodied in the apocalyptic writings and looked forward with eager expectation to the consummation of the present world, when, after a succession of horrors, moral, social, political and economic and the concentration of the forces of evil for a final resistance to the divine will, God would intervene and the Messiah come, and when the kingdom of God would be established on the earth. All these things, they believed, would occur in the near future. John the Baptist declared that the kingdom of God was at hand, and that there was one coming after him who would gather His wheat into the granary, but the chaff He would burn with unquenchable fire (Mt. iii. 12).

Christ Himself cannot be divorced from His environment. He lived during the years when the later Jewish apocalyptic writings were widely known. Whether He was acquainted with them may be doubted, but the ideas contained in them are plainly reflected in His teaching.

The apocalyptic writings exercised great influence on the writers

[1] H. H. Rowley, *The Relevance of Apocalyptic*, 1944, p. 174.

of the New Testament. There are apocalyptic elements in practically all the books of the New Testament (Mk. xiii. 3–47 and its parallels Mt. xxv. 31–46 and Lk. xxi. 5–36; Acts ii. 17–36; 1 Thess. iv. 13–17; 2 Thess. ii. 1–12; Jam. v. 3–9; 1 Pet. iv. 5, 7, 17; 2 Pet. iii. 3–13).

The early Christians not only took over the Jewish apocalyptic writings but also produced apocalypses of their own. Of these the most important is The Revelation, the only Christian apocalypse to be recognized as authoritative and to be admitted to the Canon.

The doctrine of the millennium, which is found in The Revelation, xx. 4–xxii. 5, and has persisted to the present day and given rise to many wild, fanatical movements, was the product of the Jewish apocalyptic writings. There is no authority for such a doctrine in the teaching of our Lord, but in the Jewish apocalyptic writings something approaching the concept can be found. In 1 Enoch xxxiii. 1f., the 'days' of creation are treated as symbols of later history, each creation 'day' representing a thousand years. After 6,000 years had elapsed there would come the judgment followed by a 'sabbath' period of a thousand years, corresponding to the Creator's 'day of rest'.

CHAPTER V

WISDOM LITERATURE

DEFINITION

HEBREW Wisdom literature is so-called because its authors, the wise men oft he nation, were primarily concerned with promoting the welfare and happiness of men by instructing them in the knowledge of right living, which they had acquired, partly by inheritance from previous generations, and partly by their own observation, experience and reflection.

WISDOM LITERATURE

The Wisdom literature of the Old Testament consists of three books, namely, Proverbs, Job and Ecclesiastes, together with some of the Psalms or portions of them (Pss. i, xix. 7–14, xxxiv. 11–22, xxxvii, xlix, l, lxxiii, xciv. 8–23, cxi, cxii, cxix, cxxviii, cxxxiii). There are two Wisdom books in the Apocrypha, namely, *Ecclesiasticus* or *The Wisdom of Ben Sirach* and *The Wisdom of Solomon*, together with sections of 1 Esdras (iii. 9–iv. 63), and Baruch, or 1 Baruch (iii. 9–iv. 4). Outside the Old Testament and the Apocrypha we have *The Letter of Aristeas*, 4 Maccabees, Pirke Aboth and Pseudo-Phokylides.

The following is a brief account of the non-canonical books. (For an account of the canonical books see relevant chapters.)

Ecclesiasticus. The book was written by Jesus the son of Sirach and translated into Greek about 132 B.C. by the author's grandson, who wrote a prologue in the Greek version. In most Greek MSS. it is called *Wisdom of Jesus, son of Sirach*, while in the Vulgate the title is *Ecclesiasticus*, so-called from its use as a Church Lectionary or Reading Book. The author's primary purpose was to show the superiority of Judaism over Hellenism.

The Wisdom of Solomon. The book purports to be the work of Solomon, but it was written in Greek in Alexandria about 80 B.C.

The author's purpose was to persuade worldly and apostate Jews to return to the fold, to strengthen the faith of pious Jews, and to prove the truth of Judaism and the folly of idolatry.

1 Esdras (iii–iv. 63). The book relates the Jewish history from Josiah's celebration of the Passover to the reading of the Law in the time of Ezra. It was probably written about A.D. 100. In the section, iii–iv. 63, three Jews of the bodyguard of Darius I, king of Persia, carry on an oratorical contest to determine what is the greatest power in the world. The first, says wine, the second, the king and the third, woman, and receives the prize when he adds that truth is the greatest. As his reward, Darius decrees the restoration of Jerusalem.

Baruch or 1 Baruch (iii. 9–iv. 4). The book was probably written soon after the destruction of Jerusalem in A.D. 70. The section iii. 9–iv. 4 is a poem in praise of Wisdom.

The Letter of Aristeas. The letter claims to have been written by Aristeas, an officer at the court of Ptolemy II (283–246 B.C.), to his brother, Philocrates. In it he gives an account of the origin of the Greek version of the Pentateuch, his object being the glorification of the Jews, their Law and their Wisdom. It was probably written in Alexandria about 100 B.C.

4 Maccabees. This is more or less a popular discourse on philosophical and religious matters. It was written in Greek about A.D. 30, its main purpose being to stimulate faithfulness to the Law, and to show that the Greek ideal of virtue could be realized only by Judaism.

Pirke Aboth. This is better known as the *Sayings of the Fathers*. It is a collection of sayings of Jewish sages who lived in the period c. 200 B.C.–A.D. 200.

Pseudo-Phokylides. This is a didactic work written by an Alexandrian Jew in the period 150 B.C.–A.D. 70. It combines elementary Wisdom-sayings with borrowings from the Pentateuch and the Greek philosophers.

THE WISE MEN

The wise men probably originated in a learned class of men from whose ranks state officials were drawn. Among the ministers of David we meet with Seraiah the scribe (2 Sam. viii. 17). According to 2 Kings xxii. 3–6, Shaphan, the scribe, held a high position at the court of king Josiah, while according to Jeremiah xxxvi. 11f., Elishama, the scribe, had charge of the State archives in the reign of Jehoiakim.

Comparatively few references are made to the wise men in the Old Testament. The first definite mention of them is found in Isaiah xxix. 14, where it is said that owing to the evil among the people the wisdom of their wise men would perish, indicating that they were known as a more or less distinct class as early as the latter part of the eighth century B.C. Later, towards the close of the seventh century B.C., they are referred to in Jeremiah xviii. 18 along with priests and prophets. 'Then they said, "Come let us make plots against Jeremiah, for the law shall not perish from the priest, nor counsel from the wise, nor the word from the prophet".' It is clear that in the days of Isaiah and Jeremiah the wise men were recognized teachers in Israel. The priests gave 'Torah' or 'Directions', the prophets declared the 'word' of God, and the wise men imparted advice on the practical problems of daily life. Another passage in Jeremiah suggests that they were identical with the scribes, for we read, 'How can you say, "We are wise, and the law of the Lord is with us?" But, behold, the false pen of the scribes has made it into a lie' (Jer. viii. 8). This identification is also found in Ecclesiasticus xxxix. 1–11, where the dual functions of the wisdom-scribe are set forth.

EDUCATIONAL AIMS AND METHOD

The wise men taught that wisdom was open to all and could be acquired by those who had the capacity to receive it. They were mainly concerned in training their hearers in right conduct in order that they might lead prosperous, contented and happy lives. They also aimed at imparting insight to the ignorant, and knowledge and discretion to the young and inexperienced, and at so inspiring and directing their intelligent disciples that they might increase in learning, appropriate their teaching, and know how to handle life (Prov. i. 1–6). They were prepared to impart their wisdom to all who sought it, especially the younger generation. They devoted much of their attention to the fools, who, they believed, constituted the majority of mankind. They were, however, also concerned with other kinds of people as well, such as husbands and wives (Prov. xii. 4; Ecclus. vii. 19, 26), parents and children (Prov. iv. 1–9; Ecclus. iii. 1–16), masters and servants (Prov. xxix. 19–21; Ecclus. vii. 20f.), rulers and subjects

(Prov. xxviii. 15f.; Wisd. of Sol. vi. 1–11), and rich and poor (Prov. xix. 4–7; Ecclus. iv. 1–10). In addition they had in mind the serious thinker who could grapple with such problems as those dealt with in Job and Ecclesiastes.

In the early period of Israel's history instruction was given by the wise men in the city gate or open spaces (Prov. i. 20f., viii. 2f.; Job xxix. 7–25). Later, according to Ben Sirach, it was given in the Beth-ha-Midrash or House of Learning, where the teacher sat with his pupils and proclaimed his wisdom (Ecclus. li. 23). He also speaks of the Yeshibah which was the name given to a larger place of instruction (Ecclus. li. 29). The instruction given was mainly oral, but it was committed to writing at an early date. It is probable that as teachers they were more effective than their great predecessors, the prophets.

RELATION BETWEEN THE WISE MEN AND THE PROPHETS

According to Lindblom, the prophets not only recognized the wise men as a definite class, but were also influenced by the Wisdom literature. They appreciated Wisdom in some measure, but condemned it when it was opposed to the divine word delivered through themselves. They took up certain features of the teaching of the Wisdom schools, especially the idea of God's wisdom manifested in Creation, and that of individual retribution. Their style was influenced by the Wisdom literature, as is shown by the use of parables, allegories, similes, metaphors, proverbial expressions, rhetorical questions, dialogues, reiteration of phrases and ideas, numbers and enumerations. Several late additions in the prophetic books originated in the Wisdom circles (Hos. xiv. 9; Is. ii. 22; Jer. x. 23–25).[1]

The wise men shared with the prophets the honour of being the chief media of revelation. Like the prophets they also were moved to speak by the Holy Spirit, but unlike them they did not have the same intense conviction that they were the representatives of Yahweh, commissioned by Him to proclaim His message to Israel. There was no 'Thus saith the Lord' in their teaching. The day of theophanies and divine interventions in human affairs was past. God confined Himself to visiting upon individuals the due reward of their conduct and let history take its own course. For His 'word' He had substituted His 'wisdom'.

The great contribution of the prophets was ethical monotheism.

[1] J. Lindblom, Article on 'Wisdom in the Old Testament Prophets' in *Wisdom in Israel and in the Ancient Near East*, ed. by M. Noth and D. Winton Thomas, 1955, p. 204.

In this the wise men followed them faithfully. To them Yahweh was the only God, supreme and absolute in power, wisdom and goodness. As a God of absolute righteousness He demanded right conduct from men before all things. 'To do righteousness and justice is more acceptable to the Lord than sacrifice' (Prov. xxi. 3). 'The sacrifice of the wicked is an abomination; how much more when he brings it with evil intent' (Prov. xxi. 27). If one turned away his ear from hearing the law, even his prayer was an abomination (Prov. xxviii. 9). Like the prophets they stressed the necessity of social justice. 'Do not rob the poor, because he is poor, or crush the afflicted at the gate' (Prov. xxii. 22). 'He who mocks the poor insults his Maker; he who is glad at calamity will not go unpunished' (Prov. xvii. 5). Cheating, lying, slandering, bearing false witness, and the shedding of innocent blood incurred the wrath of God. Like the prophets they taught dependence upon God. 'Commit your work to the Lord and your plans will be established' (Prov. xvi. 3). 'The name of the Lord is a strong tower; the righteous man runs into it and is safe' (Prov. xviii. 10).

In pre-exilic times there was probably a certain amount of estrangement between the prophets and priests on the one hand and the sages on the other. The prophets would naturally dislike the worldly wisdom and the apparent lack of spirituality of the wise men, while the priests would regard with disfavour their apparent indifference to the cult. Both prophets and priests would resent their popularity with people. The wise men on their part would no doubt consider that the priests and prophets were harsh and narrow minded. After the Exile a change took place. Prophecy gradually died out, and the priests, pre-occupied with the Temple ritual, looked more and more to the wise men to preserve the Hebrew culture and religion.

EARLY WISDOM

The origin of the Hebrew Wisdom literature is to be found in the proverb (Heb. mashal), that is, in the short, pointed saying, which embodied a truth based on long experience. Many sayings of this kind have been preserved in the Old Testament, such as the following:

(1) Is Saul also among the prophets? (1 Sam. x. 12).

(2) Out of the wicked comes forth wickedness (1 Sam. xxiv. 13).

(3) Let not him that girds on his armour boast himself as he that puts it off (1 Kgs. xx. 11).

(4) Let us eat and drink, for to-morrow we die (Is. xxii. 13).

(5) The fathers have eaten sour grapes, and the children's teeth are set on edge (Jer. xxxi. 29; Ezek. xviii. 2).

At a later stage came the riddle, the fable and the parable. Only one riddle is recorded in the Old Testament, namely that propounded by Samson at his wedding (Jud. xiv. 14). Only two fables are preserved, namely, the fable of Jotham (Jud. ix. 7–15) and that of king Jehoash (2 Kgs. xiv. 9), while the parable is represented by that of Nathan (2 Sam. xii. 1–4), that told by one of the 'sons of the prophets' to Ahab (1 Kgs. xx. 39f.), and that of the 'Song of the Vineyard' (Is. v. 1–7). For many centuries these wise sayings were current in an oral form. They were very popular for they challenged attention, provoked thought, and could easily be remembered because of their poetic rhythm and trenchant brevity. Eventually, Hebrew sages began to compile collections of these sayings, often, no doubt, adding proverbs of their own. In the course of time the short saying was extended until it became a king of miniature essay, as, for example, the path of wisdom and the way of the wicked (Prov. iv. 10–19), a warning against adultery (Prov. vi. 20–35), and the efficient housewife (Prov. xxxi. 10–31). In the final stage we get more elaborate works like Job, Ecclesiastes and Ecclesiasticus.

Tradition ascribes the introduction of the Hebrew Wisdom literature to Solomon. The ultimate origin of this tradition is the statement of 1 Kings iv. 32 that he uttered three thousand proverbs and a thousand and five songs. According to R. B. Y. Scott, the Hebrew Wisdom literature received its first great impetus from Hezekiah who wished to restore the vanished glories of Solomon's reign.[1]

HEBREW CONCEPTION OF WISDOM

Accurate definition of Wisdom is difficult, if not impossible, since the conception of it has changed during the centuries. In the Hebrew Wisdom generally it is never used in the sense of pure knowledge. The Hebrew word for it is 'Hokmah', which is derived from a root meaning 'firm', 'well-grounded', 'solid', and with this meaning it is used in the sense of skill in the administration of government (Gen. xli. 33, 39; Is. xxix. 14; Jer. xlix. 7), in spinning (Exod. xxxv. 25), in fashioning idols (Is. xl. 20), and in mourning (Jer. ix. 17). It is

---

[1] R. B. Y. Scott, Article on 'Solomon and the beginning of Wisdom in Israel', in *Wisdom in Israel and in the Ancient East*, ed. by M. Noth and D. Winton Thomas, 1955, pp. 278f.

WISDOM LITERATURE

also used in the sense of shrewdness (2 Sam. xx. 22; Jer. ix. 23), of craftiness (2 Sam. xiii. 3), and even of the intelligence of small creatures, such as ants, conies, locusts and lizards (Prov. xxx. 24-28). Thus, originally Wisdom stood for ability of any kind, whether of brain or of hand in the ordinary events of life.

Wisdom came to consist of two elements, the practical and the theoretical. The practical element, which was predominant, consisted of sound advice on questions of life and conduct, and the theoretical element of speculation on such matters as the nature of wisdom, the divine method of creation, the revelation of God in history and nature, and the principle of retribution in relation to the problem of suffering. The practical element is found chiefly in Proverbs, parts of Ecclesiastes, some of the Psalms and Ecclesiasticus, and the speculative element for the most part in Job, parts of Ecclesiastes, certain Psalms and The Wisdom of Solomon.

Wisdom rose to such heights of veneration that some writers personified it.[1] In Proverbs it is represented as a woman inviting people to receive her instruction (Prov. i. 20-33; viii. 1-6; ix. 1-6). Yahweh created her first of all His works (Prov. viii. 22f.). She was with Him at the Creation as a master-workman (or foster-child), and was daily His delight (Prov. viii. 27-31). In Job we are told that man cannot find the way to wisdom. God alone knows where she dwells (Job xxviii. 12-28). In Ecclesiasticus it is stated that Wisdom was created by God, that she covered the earth like a mist, and that alone she compassed the vault of heaven and walked in the depth of the abyss (Ecclus. xxiv. 3-5). In The Wisdom of Solomon Wisdom is called 'the fashioner of all things' (Wisd. of Sol. vii. 22), implying not that she created anything but that she carried out God's will in His created world. She was 'a reflection of eternal light, a spotless mirror of the working of God, and an image of His goodness' (Wisd. of Sol. vii. 26). It was Wisdom that brought men into contact with God. From generation to generation she passed into holy souls, making men friends of God and prophets (Wisd. of Sol. vii. 27).

[1] There are different opinions among scholars as to whether a distinct personality is attributed to wisdom. J. A. F. Gregg (*The Wisdom of Solomon*, 1909, p. xxxii.) regards wisdom merely as a poetical personification of the qualities of God. There is no thought of a real personal existence apart from Him. According to W. Fairweather (*The Background of the Gospels*, 1908, pp. 84ff.), Wisdom is a projection of the divine mind, something more than an attribute and something less than a hypostasis. According to W. O. E. Oesterley and T. H. Robinson (*An Introduction to the Books of the Old Testament*, 1934, p. 156), Wisdom is a personality existing alongside God, but in quite a definite sense distinct from Him.

THE RELIGIOUS CONTENT OF THE WISDOM LITERATURE

It is argued by some scholars that the Wisdom literature is too secular, that the maxims propounded are for the most part purely utilitarian, and devoid of any religious content. It is alleged that the appeal is to self-interest, the incentive to right conduct being the expectation of a reward—riches, honour, health, prosperity, length of days, etc.—and that the warnings against sin are grounded upon punishment—poverty, disgrace, ill-health, adversity, an early death etc.—rather than upon the sense of guilt and the fear of losing the favour of God.

There is some justification for the criticism, but it is not the whole truth. It cannot be denied that there are many passages, especially in Proverbs and Ecclesiasticus which appear to be devoid of any religious element. But it must be remembered that although the wise men did not possess the glowing religious enthusiasm of the prophets, they were, nevertheless, sincerely religious men and that their teaching had a religious basis. It is insisted again and again that wisdom is the gift of God. 'All wisdom comes from the Lord and is with him for ever' (Ecclus. i. 1; cf. Prov. ii. 6f.; viii. 22–31). It follows, therefore, that wisdom is essentially religious in its nature; there can in fact be no wisdom without religion. It is based upon a reverent attitude towards God and a deliberate turning away from all that is known to be wrong. 'Behold the fear of the Lord, that is wisdom; and to depart from evil is understanding' (Job xxviii. 28; cf. Prov. i. 7, ix. 10; Ecclus. i. 14; Ps. cxi. 10). In Ecclesiasticus wisdom is equated with the Law. 'All wisdom is the fear of the Lord; and in all wisdom there is the fulfilment of the law' (Ecclus. xix. 20; cf. xv. 1). 'His will was the final rule of righteousness. To embody that will in terms suitable for everyday life and conduct, and to lead their pupils and readers to obey it in detail, was the great aim of the wise men, and its extreme importance should be adequately recognized. A deeply religious spirit impregnates their utterances. They performed a very great function for God, and did it remarkably well. The whole range of life as well as the whole man—body, soul, mind—was claimed for Yahweh.'[1]

HEBREW WISDOM AND GREEK PHILOSOPHY

Wisdom was the nearest thing to philosophy that the Jews possessed. The wise men were not philosophers. The Hebrew mind is practical

[1] H. Ranston, *The Old Testament Wisdom Books and their Teaching*, 1930, p. 28.

and emotional and normally is not given to abstract thinking. Even when engaged in speculation it is not generally on the nature of ultimate reality, or the constitution of the universe or the end of life. The Hebrew language has few abstract terms, so that many philosophical ideas cannot be set forth with logical precision. There is nothing in the Wisdom literature to compare with the deep philosophical works of the Greek philosophers. It was contact with the Greeks and afterwards with the Arabs which stimulated the later Jews to true philosophical reasoning, their first writer of note being Philo of Alexandria (20 B.C.–A.D. 50).

As we have already indicated, Wisdom consisted of two elements the practical and the theoretical. Greek philosophy had a practical and a theoretical side. On the practical side it was concerned with questions of life and conduct and of the state; but such questions constituted only a small part of Greek philosophy. It was predominantly speculative, attempting by logical reasoning to solve the problems connected with the nature of ultimate reality, the constitution of the universe, and the end of life.

The Wisdom literature is the work of deeply religious men, who took for granted the existence of an omnipotent, omniscient and omnipresent God, who was absolute righteousness and demanded right conduct from mankind. From the first Yahweh proclaimed Himself as a living God, to be accepted by faith and transcending the utmost reach of speculative enquiry. His ways were beyond man's comprehension. The opening words of *Genesis*, 'In the beginning God created the heavens and the earth,' express not a philosophical hypothesis but an unquestioned conviction. Hebrew religion is a revealed religion, deriving its authority not from reason, but from its divine authorship.

Greek philosophy was partly the work of materialists and partly of theists. The early philosophers of the Greek cities in Asia were mostly materialists, and their philosophy was rather speculation on matters which we should now call natural science—the nature of the physical world—rather than on matters which we should now call philosophy. But in the course of time some schools of Greek philosophers became theistic. Pythagoras (570–500 B.C.), for example, founded a society in southern Italy, which was primarily a religious community. The way of life which he advocated was a combination of asceticism and scientific study,[1] and later Plato found an intellectual

[1] J. Burnet, Article on 'Philosophy' in *The Legacy of Greece*, ed. by R. W. Livingstone, 1921, pp. 57–95.

basis for a belief in immortality, which in any substantial sense was outside the Hebrew vision until Maccabaean times. The Greek philosophers, who held theistic views, came to their belief in God (or gods), not like the Jews through a special revelation, but through a process of reasoning. Wisdom accepted God and bowed before Him, while Greek philosophy regarded Him as a hypothesis to be proved. The axioms of the one were the conclusions of the other.

INTERNATIONAL CHARACTER OF THE WISDOM LITERATURE

The Wisdom literature is not the exclusive possession of the Hebrews but was cultivated by other nations in the Near East. In Egypt the wise men, who were called scribes, were state officials versed in the art of writing and in the laws of the state. They either collected 'the words of counsel of men of olden times' or delivered their own reflections on life for the instruction of those who aspired to exalted position. This 'wisdom' consisted of practical advice on how to act prudently in all the circumstances of life, and dealt with such matters as duties towards superiors, truthfulness and correct manners. These prudential maxims were delivered orally to their pupils and were copied out by them; and it is to this practice that we owe the preservation of a portion of the Egyptian Wisdom literature; Egypt probably had an extensive literature of this kind, but unfortunately much has been lost. Among the books which have survived are: *The Teaching of Ptah-hotep* (c. 1500 B.C.), *The Teaching of Ka-Gemni* (c. 1500 B.C.), *The Teaching of Amen-emhet* (c. 1300 B.C.), *The Teaching of Meri-ka-re* (c. 1450 B.C.), *The Teaching of Duauf* (1300 B.C.), *The Wisdom of Anii* (c. 1100 B.C.) and *The Teaching of Amen-em-ope* (c. 750 B.C.).

Similarly in Babylon and Assyria the wise men were state officials and were called scribes. Of the Babylonian and Assyrian literature, comparatively few examples have been discovered, the chief being *The Babylonian Job*, which is of great antiquity, and *The Proverbs of Ahikar*, discovered in an Aramaic version of the fifth century B.C. among the ruins of Elephantine in Egypt.

It is clear that Wisdom literature was cultivated in Syria, Arabia and Edom. Balaam, the son of Beor, who uttered the oracles found in Numbers xxiii, xxiv, was really a North-Syrian soothsayer from the Euphrates valley. In 2 Samuel xx. 18 we read, 'They were wont to say in old time, Let them but ask counsel at Abel'. 'To ask counsel' means 'to seek wisdom' which was often expressed in proverbial form.

Abel is identified with Abel-beth-Maacah, which is in Syria. In 1 Kings iv. 30f. it is said that Solomon 'surpassed the wisdom of all the people of the east', and that he was wiser 'than all other men, wiser than Ethan the Ezrahite, and Heman, Calcol, and Darda, the sons of Mahol'. The 'people of the east' were the Arabians and the Edomites, and doubtless the Babylonians, The Edomite city of Teman was famous for its wisdom (Jer. xlix. 7), while Obadiah v. 8 refers to 'the wise men out of Edom'.

Israel was not an isolated nation living without any contacts with the outside world. It is now universally agreed that the Hebrew sages were familiar with the Wisdom literature of the surrounding nations. They were not, however, mere slavish borrowers of other people's work: in their hands the materials which they adapted to their use became new creations. In their thought they reached heights which the Egyptians, Babylonian and Assyrian wise men never attained. Polytheism was characteristic of the Wisdom literature of these countries and their ethical standards were low. In the Hebrew Wisdom literature polytheism was rejected and monotheism was taken for granted; the ethical standard was high and morality was based upon religion. The survival of the religion of Yahweh was due to its own distinctive features, not to those which it had in common with other oriental religions.

THE TEACHING OF THE WISDOM LITERATURE

Individualism

With the advent of Greek culture the individual came into prominence. The canonical Wisdom books, Proverbs, Job and Ecclesiastes are concerned with the ordinary individual, irrespective of race or class rather than with the history and the institutions of the nation. Apart from the title, there is no reference to Israel in Proverbs, none in Job and only one in Ecclesiastes. Judah is mentioned but once and that in Proverbs xxv. 1, and Jerusalem only a few times in Ecclesiastes. Wisdom is for all who seek her and is not the exclusive possession of Israel. So free are the wise men from national prejudices, that of Proverbs it has been said with a certain amount of truth, that if for the name of Yahweh we were to substitute that of 'God,' the book would be just as suitable for any other people as for Israel. 'On account of their prevailing disregard of national points of view, and their tendency to characterize and estimate human nature under its most general aspects, they have been named not inappropriately, the Humanists of Israel.'[1]

In the uncanonical Wisdom books we find a different conception. By the beginning of the second century B.C. the Jews had become more conscious of their nationality and of their dignity as God's chosen people. In Ecclesiasticus Wisdom is represented as having sought a resting place among the nations of the worlds, but in vain. Israel alone is worthy of her, and among them, therefore God bids her abide (Ecclus. xxiv. 6–8). Obedience to the law is Israel's first duty (Ecclus. ix. 15; cf. x. 19; xxxiii. 1–3). Wisdom is identified with the law (Ecclus. i. 26; xix. 20; xxi. 11; xxxiv. 8).

The Messianic Hope

There is no reference in the canonical Wisdom books to the Messianic hope, which is prominent in the prophetic writings. It plays but a small part in the uncanonical Wisdom books. A few incidental references to it are found in Ecclesiasticus (xliv. 21; xlvii. 22; xlviii. 10, 24f.). It is also mentioned in *The Wisdom of Solomon* iii. 8, but without a Messiah.

The Sacrificial System

In the canonical Wisdom books the sacrifical system is accepted but no great enthusiasm is expressed for it. Stress, however, is laid upon the necessity of right conduct in the offerer. In Proverbs xv. 8 it is stated that the sacrifice of the wicked is an abomination to Yahweh, and in xxi. 3f. of the same book that justice and fairness are more pleasing to Him than sacrifice. Job, who was blameless and upright, feared God and turned away from evil, was accustomed to rise up early in the morning to offer burnt offerings on behalf of his sons (i. 5). In Ecclesiastes it is declared that in the house of God silence was more acceptable to the Most High than the sacrifice of fools (v. 1f.). In the uncanonical Wisdom books the sacrificial system is taken for granted, but in some books it receives more attention than in others. In Ecclesiasticus sacrifices are heartily welcomed, the author bearing eloquent testimony to his reverence for the Temple worship, and urging the duty of reverencing the priest and giving him his portion according to the law (vii. 29–31). At the same time he declared that

---

[1] S. R. Driver, *An Introduction to the Literature of the Old Testament*, 9th ed. 1913, p. 393.

God demanded righteousness of life from mankind. The Most High had no pleasure in the offerings of the ungodly and was not pacified by a multitude of sacrifices (xxxiv. 19).

Retribution

In both the canonical and uncanonical Wisdom books there are conflicting views on the problem of retribution. In Proverbs the doctrine of retribution is accepted without criticism (ii. 21f.; iii. 8, 10, 16; iv. 4, etc.). In *Job*, Eliphaz, Bildad and Zophar are represented as accepting it, while Job is first represented as holding it, but finally protesting against it since he was not conscious of having sinned. In Ecclesiastes the doctrine is rejected; good and bad fortune are the result of blind determinisn. There is no moral government of the world (ii. 14–16; vi. 7f.; vii. 15; viii. 14). The book, however, is not always consistent. Sometimes it teaches that wickedness will be punished on earth and the righteous rewarded by God (ii. 26; viii. 12f.). In the first part of The Wisdom of Solomon the reward of the righteous is immortality (i. 15; iii. 1–9; v. 15f.), but the portion of the wicked is death (i. 8; iv. 20; v. 17–23; viii. 13, 17). In the second part of the book (xi–xix), which some scholars believe to be the work of a different writer, the doctrine of retribution is strictly held. The righteous are assured of immortality, for to be acquainted with God is perfect righteousness, and to know His dominion is the root of immortality (xv. 3). The wicked are punished, the punishment being appropriate to the sin (xi. 15f.).

Sheol

In the background of all the Wisdom books is the belief in Sheol. In Proverbs the belief is taken for granted (i. 12; ii. 18f.; v. 5; vii. 27), but in one passage (xv. 11) there seems to be an advance on the common conception (see p. 143). Job normally accepts the current belief in Sheol (iii. 13–19; vii. 9f.), but as the poem progresses we see him moving towards a higher view (see pp. 173f.). The belief in Sheol is accepted in Ecclesiastes. The wise man dies just as the fool and there is no enduring remembrance of him (ii. 14–16). Belief in a future life is explicitly denied (iii. 19f.; ix. 3–6). Ecclesiasticus teaches that at death men go down to Sheol (xiv. 16; xvii. 28; xxi. 10; xli. 4). There is, however, the foreshadowing of a belief in something more than a mere shadowy existence beyond the grave. There are instances in which the dead are said to be at rest (xxii. 11; cf. xxx. 17; xxxviii. 23). In

The Wisdom of Solomon Sheol is reserved for the wicked, while the souls of the righteous are in the hand of God (iii. 1), and they shall live for ever (v. 15; cf. viii. 13, 17).

PERMANENT INFLUENCE

The Wisdom literature was a powerful influence in the life and thought of the Jewish people. After the Exile the priests ceased to be teachers, devoting their attention to the development of the ritual of the Temple. The prophets gradually disappeared until only the sages were left to teach the people. They accepted the teaching of the prophets and interpreted it in terms which the people could understand. They became the social, moral and spiritual guides of the nation, and it was largely due to their untiring efforts that the Jewish faith was preserved. 'They indeed saved the soul of Judaism and preserved it for the new crisis which came during the Maccabaean struggle. They also bore on the torch of Hebrew learning, which they in turn handed over to the scribes and rabbis, who from 165 B.C. on became the chief teachers of the race. To the rabbis they imparted that profound interest in the individual and that emphasis on social and moral values which partially delivered the work and writings of these later teachers from the blight of triviality and ceremonialism.'[1]

The influence of the Wisdom books can be traced in the New Testament. The Gospels make considerable use of them. There is no clear proof that our Lord quoted directly from them, but there can be no doubt that He was familiar with them and was influenced by them. Several of the beatitudes of the Sermon on the Mount remind us of those in Proverbs, though they are by no means identical. There is, for example, the happiness of the wise (iii. 13), the righteous (iii. 33; x. 6), the chaste (v. 18), the generous (xi. 26; xiv. 21; xxii. 9), and the law-abiding (xxix. 18). He stressed the principles already laid down by the sages (Mt. v. 42 and Prov. iii. 28; Mt. x. 42 and Prov. xix. 17). Some of the parables are apparently dependent on the Wisdom books. The parable of the two houses, the one founded on the sand and the other on the rock (Mt. vii. 24–27), was probably suggested by Proverbs x. 25, the Parable of the Great Supper (Mt. xxii. 1–13) by Proverbs ix. 1–6, and the parable of the Rich Fool (Lk. xii. 16–20) by Ecclesiasticus xi. 18f. The personification of Wisdom in the Proverbs, Ecclesiasticus and The Wisdom of Solomon ultimately led to the

---

[1] C. F. Kent, *The Growth and Content of the Old Testament*, 1926, p. 261.

development of the Logos doctrine as found in the prologue to the fourth Gospel.[1]

A careful study of the Epistles of Paul shows that the Apostle was indebted to the Wisdom books, especially to The Wisdom of Solomon for some of his ideas. In 1 Corinthians i. 24 Christ is called 'the power of God and the wisdom of God, while in Colossians ii. 3 it is stated that 'in him are hid all the treasures of wisdom and knowledge'. The teaching that the vices of pagans are the consequence of idolatry (Rom. i. 14–24), and that the prevalence of sin among men is due to Adam's transgression (Rom. v. 12) is found in The Wisdom of Solomon xiii–xiv and ii. 23f. respectively. The passage on the power of the potter over the clay (Rom. ix. 21) and that exhorting Christians to 'put on the whole armour of God' (Ep. vi. 11–17) are closely paralleled in the same book (Wisd. of Sol. xv. 7 and v. 17–20 respectively).

The unknown author of the Epistle to the Hebrews does not use the term 'Logos', but it is clear from his language that he thinks of Christ in this category. 'In many and various ways God spoke of old to our fathers by the prophets; but in these last days he has spoken to us by a Son, whom he appointed the heir of all things, through whom also he created the world' (i. 1f.).

Finally, the Epistle of James, written in the form of the Wisdom books, that is, exhortations on various points of conduct in a somewhat disjointed manner, has been called a 'body of Wisdom teachings'.[2]

[1] Philo, the Jewish philosopher of Alexandria (c. 20 B.C.–A.D. 50) in an endeavour to form a synthesis between the Jewish religion and Greek philosophy, identified the Jewish conception of the 'Word' or 'Wisdom', which signifies the sum of all the divine activities of the world, with the Stoic idea of the Logos ('word' or 'reason') the universal reason which is diffused through all things. He was also probably influenced by the expression, the 'Memra' or 'Word', used as an inoffensive substitute for 'the Lord' in the Aramaic paraphrases of the Old Testament, and known as 'Targums'. So we read, 'And the Word became flesh and dwelt among us, full of grace and truth; we have beheld his glory, glory as of the only Son from the Father' (Jn. i. 14). Canon Streeter (*The Four Gospels*, 1930, p. 468) calls the doctrine of the Logos 'the boldest restatement of Christianity in terms of contemporary thought ever attempted in the history of the Church'.

[2] T. Y. Mullins, *J.B.L.*, Dec. 1949, p. 338.

CHAPTER VI

THE FORMS AND CHARACTERISTICS OF HEBREW POETRY

THE FORMS

Introduction

A large part of the Old Testament is written in poetry. Some of its books are wholly poetic in form, namely, Psalms, Proverbs, Job, the Song of Songs and Lamentations. To these some would add Ecclesiastes. A large part of Isaiah, Jeremiah and the Minor Prophets, and a small part of Ezekiel are also written as such, while songs and fragments of songs survive embedded here and there in the historical books. The whole output of ancient Hebrew poetry is not included in the Old Testament. References are made to three collections of poems which are no longer extant. These are, the Book of the Wars of the Lord (Num. xxi. 14f.), probably a collection of songs celebrating great events in the history of the nation; the Book of Jashar (Josh. x. 12f.; 2 Sam. i. 18), probably a collection of songs, celebrating the achievements of national heroes; and a collection of lamentations, which is said to have contained Jeremiah's lament for Josiah (2 Chron. xxxv. 25).

The beginnings of a nation's poetry are to be found in its folk-poems. Some of the early Hebrew poems may be classed as spells, such as the blessings of Noah (Gen. ix. 25–27), Isaac (Gen. xxvii. 27–29), Jacob (Gen. xlix. 2–27), Moses (Deut. xxxiii. 1–29) and Balaam, the son of Beor (Num. xxiii. 7–10, 18–24; xxiv. 3–9, 15–19). The object of these spells was to ensure a blessing or a curse. Many proverbial sayings (Heb., Meshalim) were cast in poetic form, such as Samson's riddle and the answer (Jud. xiv. 14, 18a), and Samuel's condemnation of Saul (1 Sam. xv. 22f.).

The Israelites, like all the other eastern peoples, were fond of composing songs and singing them to the accompaniment of musical instruments. A great deliverance like that of the Israelites at the Red Sea, or a great victory like that of the Israelites over the Canaanites under the command of Sisera at the river Kishon, was celebrated with songs (Exod. xv. 1–18; Jud. v. 1–31). Taunt songs were sung exulting over the impending downfall of an enemy (2 Kgs. xix. 21–28; Is. xlvii. 1–15).

At the wedding festivities the dance of the bride was accompanied by songs, which a single voice chanted, while the choir took up the refrain. Some of the songs would exalt the bride and bridegroom while others would be love lyrics. A fragment of a wedding song has been preserved in Psalm xlv. Laments were sung at funerals, the finest examples being those of David over Saul and Jonathan (2 Sam. i. 19–27) and over Absalom (2 Sam. xviii. 33). Later, this type of poem became the literary model of Lamentations i, ii, iv, in which the poet (or poets) lamented over the destruction of Jerusalem in 587 B.C. as over a woman. It would appear that the ingathering of the vintage and the harvest was a time of mirth and song (Is. xvi. 10; Jer. xxv. 30, xlviii. 33). Songs were piped by shepherds at the watering places and among the sheep folds (Jud. v. 11, 16). Even the discovery or the digging of a well was an occasion for joyous song (Num. xxi. 17f.). That drinking songs were popular may be gathered from Isaiah's denunciation of them (Is. v. 11f.). Amos denounced those who sang idle songs to the sound of the harp and drank wine from bowls (Amos. vi. 4–6). Songs were sung in the homes of wealthy families from early times. When Laban realized that Jacob, his son-in-law, had fled, he pursued him to reproach him not so much for having fled as for having fled in secret, so preventing him from sending him away 'with mirth and songs, with tambourine and lyre' (Gen. xxxi. 27). Barzillai, the Gileadite, would not go to the court as David desired, because in his extreme old age, he could no longer take food or drink, or listen to the voices of singing men and women (2 Sam. xix. 35). The worship of Yahweh in His sanctuary was naturally accompanied by songs of praise, thanksgiving and supplication.

These early songs would be transmitted orally from generation to generation until they were finally fixed in writing. Thus, in the course of time, the nation would possess collections of oracles, proverbial sayings, triumphal odes, wedding songs (including love lyrics), laments, vintage and harvest songs, drinking songs and devotional hymns. Most of the poetry which has been preserved in the Old Testament is of a religious type, but there are poems of a purely secular character, such as the song of Lamech (Gen. iv. 23f.) and David's laments over Saul and Jonathan (2 Sam. i. 19–27) and over Abner (2 Sam. iii. 33f.). In these the name of Yahweh is not mentioned. These secular poems do not stand alone. The Song of Solomon for instance, is in no sense a religious work. It has been suggested that it is a collection of unconnected love lyrics such as were sung at Jewish wedding feasts. Some of these secular songs, however, are touched with religious emotion. The battle songs of Moses and Deborah might be called hymns of praise to Yahweh, who was regarded as the Leader of Israel's hosts and the Giver of victory.

Parallelism

The most important structural feature of Hebrew poetry is parallelism. Normally every line (technically called a 'verse') consists of at least two members, each of which is called a 'stichos' (pl. 'stichoi'). The two members of the line together form a 'distich' or 'couplet' in which the second member echoes, amplifies or completes the thought of the first. This device is known as 'parallelism', because the two members are parallel expressions of the same thought. For this reason parallelism has been called 'a rhyme of thought'. The principle of parallelism was first clearly recognized by Bishop Lowth in his famous lectures, *On the Sacred Poetry of the Hebrews* (1753). He defined it as 'a peculiar conformation of sentences, whereby the poets repeat one and the same idea in different words, or combine different ideas within the same form of words, like things being related to like, or opposites set in contrast to opposites'. Lowth distinguished three types of parallelism.

Synonymous Parallelism. The second member of the line repeats the thought of the first in a slightly different form.

> The spirit of God has made me,
> and the breath of the Almighty gives me life. (Job xxxiii. 4.)

> Give ear, O my people, to my teaching;
> incline your ears to the words of my mouth! (Ps. lxxviii. 1.)

This kind of parallelism produces an effect 'at once grateful to the ear and satisfying to the mind'.[1]

---

[1] S. R. Driver, *An Introduction to the Literature of the Old Testament*, 1913, pp. 362f.

Antithetic Parallelism. The second member of the line completes the thought of the first by the introduction of a contrast.

> A glad heart makes a cheerful countenance,
>   but by sorrow of heart the spirit is broken. (Prov. xv. 13.)

> The grass withers, the flower fades;
>   but the word of our God will stand for ever. (Is. xl. 8.)

This kind of parallelism is very common in the gnomic poetry in which antithetic truths are often contrasted.

Synthetic or Constructive Parallelism. The thought of the second member of the line supplements and completes that of the first.

> So teach us to number our days
>   that we may get a heart of wisdom. (Ps. xc. 12.)

> It is better to go to the house of mourning
>   than to go to the house of feasting. (Eccles vii. 2.)

Wherever a reason, or a consequence, or a comparison or a motive can be expressed, it can be readily done in this form.

Since Lowth's day three other types of parallelism have been distinguished.

Emblematic Parallelism. A truth is told in the first member of the line and is reproduced in the second by means of a comparison usually drawn from nature.

> You shall come to your grave in ripe old age,
>   as a shock of corn comes up to the threshing floor
>   in its season. (Job. v. 26.)

Sometimes the emblem comes first

> As an apple tree among the trees of the wood,
>   so is my beloved among young men. (Song of Sol. ii. 3.)

Climactic or Ascending Parallelism. The thought is built up to a climax by the repetition of a key-word or phrase.

> Who is the King of glory?
> The Lord strong and mighty,
> the Lord mighty in battle! (Ps. xxiv. 8).

> The voice of the Lord is powerful,
> the voice of the Lord is full of majesty. (Ps. xxix. 4.)

This kind of parallelism is rare since it is appropriate only to elevated poetry.

Introverted Parallelism. This involves at least two complete lines in which the four members are so arranged that the first is parallel to the fourth and the second to the third (a, b, b, a).

> My son, if your heart is wise,
> my heart too will be glad.
> My soul will rejoice
> when your lips speak what is right. (Prov. xxiii. 15f.)

By far the greater number of lines in Hebrew poetry consist of distichs or couplets of one or other of the types which have been illustrated. If, however, nothing but the couplet exemplifying the principle of parallelism were used, it would soon produce monotony. Hence, Hebrew poets did not hesitate to vary the form of the parallelism when the thought required it. So instead of the couplet we frequently find combinations of three and four lines, known as tristichs or tetrastichs respectively. The tristichs may be arranged in several different ways. For example, the three lines may be synonymous (Ps. c. 1); or the second line may be united with the first by constructive parallelism, and the third to the second by synonymous parallelism (Ps. iii. 7). Similarly, tetrastichs may exhibit various kinds of construction. For example, the first line may be parallel to the third and the second to the fourth (Ps. cxxvii. 1); or the first line may be parallel to the fourth and the second to the third (Ps. li. 1). Occasionally, we find combinations of five and six lines, known as pentastichs (Ps. xxxix. 12) and hexastichs (Song of Sol. iv. 8).

Although parallelism is the general rule in Hebrew poetry, it is sometimes absent. It does not occur in single lines or monostichs (Ps. xviii. 1; lxxxvii. 1). Single lines are generally used to express a thought with some emphasis at the beginning or occasionally at the end of a poem. There is no parallelism in the couplet found in 2 Samuel i. 23.

> Saul and Jonathan, beloved and lovely!
> In life and in death they were not divided.

In recent times G. B. Gray has made an independent and quite different analysis of parallelism. He distinguishes two kinds, namely, complete parallelism and incomplete parallelism. Complete parallelism occurs when every term in the first member of the line corresponds to a term in the second. Incomplete parallelism occurs when the terms in the first member of the line do not correspond to those in the second. Incomplete parallelism falls into classes, namely, incomplete parallelism with compensation, and incomplete parallelism without compensation. Incomplete parallelism with compensation occurs when the two members of the line contain the same number of terms, but one or more terms in the second member are not parallel to the term or terms in the first. Incomplete parallelism without compensation occurs when one member of the line (usually the second) contains a smaller number of terms than the other. For examples of all these forms of parallelism the reader should consult G. B. Gray's work on *The Forms of Hebrew Poetry*, 1915.

RHYTHM OR METRE

The second important structural feature in Hebrew poetry is the rhythm or metre. Hebrew poets in Old Testament times were not familiar with metre in our meaning of the term. In English poetry the metrical line (or verse) is divided into feet, each foot containing one stressed or accented syllable. If consisting of more than three feet, the line is usually further divided into two parts by a pause or caesura. (Latin 'caesura' = a cutting.) According to the most widely accepted view, metre in Hebrew poetry is reckoned in terms of the accented syllables. The line has a definite number of accented syllables and the unaccented syllables are not counted. The line is divided into two parts (sometimes three) by a strong pause, and there is also a definite pause at the end so that the sense does not run on from one line to the next.

The following are the chief rhythms or metres.

2:2 Each member of the line has two accented syllables.

> e.g. Offer right sacrifices
> and put your trust in the Lord. (Ps. iv. 5.)

This measure is rarely used. Its quick staccato movement is used to indicate a state of emotional tension due to fear or joy.

3:2 The first member of the line has three accented syllables and the second two.

> e.g. He has made my flesh and my skin waste away,
> and broken my bones. (Lam. iii. 4.)

This metre is called the 'Qinah' or 'Elegiac' metre because it was first identified in Lamentations. It is often employed in laments for the dead, but it is also used by Jeremiah in his warnings and appeals to the nation, and by Deutero-Isaiah and by many Psalmists to express praise and thanksgiving. The metre suggested with rare effectiveness the deep emotion which filled the heart of the poet.

2:3 The first member of the line has two accented syllables and the second three.

> e.g. Every valley shall be lifted up,
> and every mountain and hill be made low. (Is. xl. 4.)

3:3 Each member of the line has three accented syllables.

> e.g. He comes forth like a flower, and withers:
> he flees like a shadow, and continues not. (Job. xiv. 2.)

This metre, which is extremely common, is well adapted for the brief, forceful expression of an idea. It is used in the poetic portions of Job, in most of Psalms, and frequently in Proverbs and in the Prophets.

4:3 The first member of the line has four accents and the second three.

> e.g. I looked on the mountains, and lo, they were quaking
> and all the hills moved to and fro. (Jer. iv. 24.)

Occasionally, the line consists of three members, which may be in the 2:2:2 or 3:3:3 metre.

e.g. For he will deliver you
    from the snare of the fowler
        and from the deadly pestilence. (Ps. xci. 3.)

   Lift up your heads, O gates!
   and be lifted up, O ancient doors!
       that the king of glory may come in. (Ps. xxiv. 7.)

A study of Hebrew shows that the same metrical pattern is not invariably used throughout a particular poem. There is, in fact, hardly a poem in the Old Testament in which the metre indicated in the Massoretic text is absolutely regular. Some modern scholars assume that the irregularities are due to errors in the text and have suggested emendations. It is true that some of these emendations are confirmed by the Septuagint and other ancient versions, but for the majority of them there is no external evidence. It is obvious that the poets refused to follow the standard metrical pattern when it suited their purpose.[1]

Rhyme

Rhyme is not a fundamental but an occasional characteristic of Hebrew poetry. It was probably a favourite literary device of folk-poems. It is found in the ancient 'Song of the Sword' (Gen. iv. 23f.), Isaac's blessing of Jacob (Gen. xxvii. 29) and Jacob's blessing of Judah (Gen. xlix. 11), the poem on Sihon, king of the Amorites (Num. xxi. 28), Balaam's oracle against the Kenites (Num. xxiv. 21f.), the riddle propounded by Samson at his wedding feast (Jud. xiv. 14), and his reply to the Philistines when through his wife they discovered the answer to his riddle (Jud. xiv. 18). Numerous examples of it can also be found in Proverbs (i. 15f.; v. 7-14) and in the Song of Songs (vi .1-3; viii. 1-3).

Strophes or Stanzas

In Hebrew poetry there are no strophes or stanzas in the strict sense of the term. It is possible to divide any but the shortest poems into groups of lines, but it does not necessarily follow that a strophic structure is a fundamental characteristic of Hebrew poetry. A genuine strophic structure involves a correspondence in the number of lines and their metrical form between the various sections of a poem, but of this there is little or no convincing evidence in the old Testament. Attempts have been made by some scholars to reduce all Old Testa-

---

[1] T. H. Robinson, *The Poetry of the Old Testament*, 1947, pp. 37f.

ment poetry to a uniform strophic structure, but with little success. 'We need', says T. H. Robinson, 'stronger grounds than those frequently offered, before we can be reasonably satisfied that a particular poem has been subjected to the very large amount of modification, which a strict stanza theory often requires'.[1]

If a strophe is taken to mean a group of lines connected by a certain unity of thought, it may be claimed that Hebrew poetry has a strophic structure. Accepting this definition of a strophe, we can often detect the strophic arrangement of a poem. A refrain repeated at regular intervals is decisive evidence of the strophic form (Is. ix. 8–x. 4). Some of the acrostic poems are strophic in form (Ps. cxix). The term 'Selah' is often said to indicate a strophic structure, but since the meaning of the term is obscure, we cannot say for certain that it was used for that purpose.

Acrostics

Normally, an acrostic poem is one in which the initial letters of the successive lines or groups of lines follow the order of the letters of the Hebrew alphabet. The acrostic form is found in Psalms ix–x (originally one), xxv, xxxiv, xxxvii, cxi, cxii, cxlv, Lamentations i–iv and Proverbs xxxi. 10–31. Nahum i. 2–ii. 2 is an incomplete acrostic. Variations occur in the acrostic pattern. Some acrostic poems are composed of single lines, each half of the line having the appropriate letter (Ps. cxi, cxii). Psalms ix–x and Lamentations iv are arranged in pairs of lines, the first line of each pair beginning with the appropriate letter. Lamentations i, ii are arranged in groups of three lines, the first line of each group beginning with the proper letter. Lamentations iii is arranged in groups of three lines, each of which carries the acrostic letter.[2] Psalm cxix is the most elaborate of all the acrostic poems. It is divided into twenty-two groups, each beginning with one of the letters of the Hebrew alphabet in regular order. Each group contains eight lines each of which begins with the same letter which introduces the group.

LITERARY CHARACTERISTICS

Nature

In Hebrew poetry great prominence is given to nature. This is not surprising since the Hebrews were a pastoral and agricultural people,

---

[1] T. H. Robinson, *The Poetry of the Old Testament*, 1947, pp. 42–43.

[2] Lamentations i presents the usual order of letters in the Hebrew alphabet, 'ayin' preceding 'pe', whereas in Lamentations ii–iv 'pe' precedes 'ayin'.

Forms and Characteristics of Hebrew Poetry 87

whose occupations brought them in close contact with nature. There are innumerable references to the sights and sounds of the country— to the sun which came forth 'like a bridegroom leaving his chamber' (Ps. xix. 5), the stars which sang together when the foundations of the earth were laid (Job xxxviii. 7), the mountains that stood round about Jerusalem (Ps. cxxv. 2), the rivers that ran into the sea, yet never filled it (Eccles. i. 7), the valleys that decked themselves with grain (Ps. lxv. 13), the green pastures where the sheep lay down in safety (Ps. xxiii. 2), the horse that could not stand still at the sound of the trumpet and smelt the battle from afar (Job. xxxix. 24f.), the hippopotamus (behemoth) that ate grass like an ox and lay under the lotus plants in the covert of the reeds and in the marsh (Job xl. 15–24), the crocodile (leviathan) that made the sea boil like a pot and left behind him a shining wake (Job. xli. 31f.), the lion that emerged from the thicket to destroy (Jer. iv. 7), the hart that longed for the flowing streams (Ps. xlii. 1), the stork, turtledove, swallow and crane that kept the time of their coming (Jer. viii. 7), and the young ravens in their nest clamouring for food (Ps. cxlvii. 9).

The Hebrew poets saw in nature the manifestation of the infinite power, wisdom and majesty of God. The heavens proclaimed His glory and the firmament spoke of His handiwork (Ps. xix. 1). It was His hand that made the dry land and that shut in the sea when it burst from the womb of chaos, swathed it in mist, swaddled it in clouds of darkness and fixed its boundaries (Job xxxviii. 8–10). His voice was heard in the thunder that shattered the cedars of Lebanon, shook the wilderness and stripped the forests bare (Ps. xxix. 5–9). He gave snow like wool, scattered the hoar-frost like ashes, and made the wind blow and waters flow (Ps. cxlvii. 16–19). He poured the streams into the valleys where all the beasts of the field drank and the wild asses quenched their thirst, where the birds had their habitation and sang among the branches of the trees (Ps. civ. 10–12). He watered the earth, softening it with showers and blessing its growth, so that the meadows clothed themselves with flocks and the valleys decked themselves with corn, shouting and singing for joy (Ps. lxv. 9–13).

It is sometimes said that although the Hebrew poets were keen observers of nature, they did not love it for its own sake. Unfortunately, most of their nature-poetry has not survived, so that we cannot speak with certainty. There are, however, indications that they were not entirely blind to the beauty and charm of nature. References are found to the wings of the ostrich that waved proudly (Job. xxxix. 13), to the silver and green-gold plumage of the dove (Ps. lxviii. 13), to its soft eyes (Song of Sol. i. 15) and the murmuring sound of its voice (Is. lix. 11). In the Song of Solomon the maiden is in the eyes of her lover 'a cluster of henna blossoms in the vineyards of Engedi' (i. 14) and 'a rose of Sharon, a lily of the valleys' (ii. 1). The young man is as comely and graceful as a gazelle or a young stag (ii. 9). The lovers go early to the vineyard to see whether the vines have budded, whether the grape blossoms have opened and whether the pomegranates are in bloom (vii. 12). The description of the coming of spring shows a real appreciation of the beauty and charm of nature.

> For lo, the winter is past,
>   the rain is over and gone,
> The flowers appear on the earth,
>   the time of singing has come,
> And the voice of the turtledove
>   is heard in our land.
> The fig tree puts forth its figs,
>   and the vines are in blossom,
>   they give forth fragrance. (ii. 10-13.)

Imagination

Imagination is a fundamental characteristic of all great poetry. Without it poetry is commonplace, dull and uninteresting, and hardly worthy of the name. Imagination shines through Hebrew poetry, sometimes raising it to the level of the sublime. The Hebrew poets were acute observers who saw not only the outward aspects of things —their shapes, forms and colours—but also their inner nature and spiritual significance. Without imagination they would have been aware of objects and nothing more. But they perceived the strength and durability of the mountain, the power and turbulence of the sea, the instability of the river, the cruelty of the wild beasts, the industry of the ant, the swiftness of the eagle and the gentleness of the dove. Moreover to them objects were images or symbols of things which were beyond literal description. The sky was a symbol of God's steadfast love (Pss. xxxvi. 5; ciii. 11), the mountains of His eternity (Ps. xc. 2) and His righteousness (Ps. xxxvi. 6), the sea of His justice (Ps. xxxvi. 6), the dew of His goodness (Hos. xiv. 5), and the bird sheltering its young under its wings of His protection (Ps. xci. 4). Similarly the fading flower was a symbol of the brevity of human life

(Is. xl. 6), the shuttle of the swift passage of time (Job. vii. 6), the snapping of the silver cord by which the golden bowl was suspended, the pitcher smashed at the fountain, and the water-wheel broken at the cistern of death, the tree planted by streams of water of a man who delighted in the Law of Yahweh (Ps. i. 1–3), and the watered garden of the prosperous, contented and happy lives of the returned exiles (Jer. xxxi. 12).

In the poetical portions of the Old Testament there are many passages of inimitable beauty, which could only have been written by men richly endowed with imagination. Such, for example, are Job xxviii, on the divine wisdom, Job xxxviii–xli, Yahweh's answer to Job out of the whirlwind, Psalm cxxxix, on the omnipresence and omniscience of Yahweh, Ecclesiastes xii. 1–7, on the infirmities of old age, Isaiah xxxv, xl, lv, on the return of the exiles from Babylon, Isaiah ii. 2–4, on the dawn of the kingdom of peace and righteousness, and Isaiah liv. 11–13; lx, on the glory of the New Jerusalem.

Intensity of Feeling and Sincerity.

Hebrew poetry is distinguished by intensity of feeling. It is highly subjective, for its authors were more concerned with themselves than with other people. The Hebrews generally were an emotional people, who, when roused, were not afraid to express their feelings and to reveal their inmost thoughts. When stirred by their religious convictions and experiences, they poured forth in song their feelings of contrition, supplication, despair, hope, doubt, faith, devotion, passionate love of God and hatred of their enemies. They made no attempt to conceal their feelings or to give a false impression of themselves. It is said that sincerity is the basis of all art, the one thing needful. The Hebrew poets were sincere in all that they wrote. In their works there is no wordiness, no useless ornamentation and no artificiality. They wrote, not because they had to say something, but because they had something to say. Their sincerity is seen especially in their expression of violence and hatred. Nahum exulted over the destruction of Nineveh, 'the bloody city, all full of lies' (Nah. iii. 1). Isaiah violently denounced the 'daughters of Zion' with their fine clothes, their earrings and nose rings, their bracelets and signet rings, their perfume and handbags (Is. iii. 18–23). Jeremiah prayed for vengeance upon his enemies (Jer. xviii. 21). The author of Psalm cxxxvii, remembering the destruction of Jerusalem by the Babylonians in 587 B.C. and the conduct of the Edomites on that occasion, could not restrain his wrath.

> Remember, O Lord, against the Edomites
>   the day of Jerusalem,
> how they said, 'Rase it! rase it!
>   Down to its foundations!'
> O daughter of Babylon, you devastator!
>   Happy shall he be who requites you
>   with what you have done to us!
> Happy shall he be who takes your little ones
>   and dashes them against the rock! (Ps. cxxxvii. 7–9.)

Simplicity

One of the distinctive features of Hebrew poetry is its simplicity. The original Hebrew language possessed certain characteristics which made for simplicity. Its vocabulary was small with few abstract nouns. To make up for the lack of these, writers often resorted to symbols ('bowels' = compassion, 'wind' = spirit, 'horn' = power, 'house' = family or dynasty). It had few adjectives; writers had their favourite epithets like 'goodly' and 'pleasant' which they used again and again.

> The lines have fallen for me in pleasant places;
>   yea I have a goodly heritage. (Ps. xvi. 6.)

> Hyenas will cry in its towers,
>   and jackals in the pleasant palaces. (Is. xiii. 22.)

The complex sentence, that is, one containing a principal clause and one or more subordinate clauses, was rarely used, preference being given to the simple sentence, that is, one containing only one finite verb; or the compound sentence, that is, one containing two or more independent clauses, connected by co-ordinate conjunctions like and, but, or, therefore.

> I loathe my life;
>   I will give free utterance to my complaint;
>   I will speak in the bitterness of my soul. (Job x. 1.)

> I will restore the fortunes of my people Israel
>   and they shall rebuild the ruined cities
>   and inhabit them;

> They shall plant vineyards and drink their wine,
> and they shall make gardens and eat
> their fruit. (Amos ix. 14.)

There is no elaboration in Hebrew poetry, much being left to the imagination. Instead of a detailed account of the defeat and death of Saul and Jonathan we have the simple statement:

> Thy glory, O Israel, is slain upon thy high places!
> How are the mighty fallen! (2 Sam. i. 19.)

There is no unnecessary description in the Psalmist's call to worship.

> O come, let us worship and bow down,
> let us kneel before the Lord our Maker! (Ps. xcv. 6.)

Vigour of Expression

Hebrew poetry is marked by vigour of expression. This is especially the case of the earlier poetry. The Hebrew language contained many hard consonants and heavy guttural sounds, which suggested a greater power for emphasis than for beauty in its literary use. Moreover it was primarily a language of the senses and the emotions. Nearly all Hebrew roots expressed a physical action or denoted a material object. Words, therefore, were pictures which startled the senses and roused the emotions. This somewhat defective language was suited for curses, war-cries and prayers for vengeance rather than for prophecies and psalms. In the course of time, however, Hebrew writers succeeded in making it a fitting medium for the expression of nearly every form of literature.[1] In poetry, while its basic structure remained the same, the lines became longer, the constructions more flexible and the rhythm more melodious. In the process something of the old vigour was lost. This is seen if we compare a passage from the Song of Deborah with a passage from a psalm written several centuries later.

> She put her hand to the tent peg
>   and her right hand to the workmen's mallet;
> she struck Sisera a blow,
>   she crushed his head,
>   she shattered and pierced his temple.

---

[1] G. A. Smith, Article on 'The Hebrew Genius as exhibited in the Old Testament' in *The Legacy of Israel*, ed. by E. R. Bevan and C. Singer.

> He sank, he fell,
>   he lay at her feet;
>   at her feet he sank, he fell;
>   where he sank, there he fell dead. (Jud. v. 26f.)

> Whither shall I go from thy Spirit?
>   Or whither shall I flee from thy presence?
> If I ascend to heaven, thou art there.
> If I make my bed in Sheol, thou art there!
> If I take the wings of the morning
>   and dwell in the uttermost parts of the sea,
> even there thy hand shall lead me,
>   and thy right hand shall hold me. (Ps. cxxxix. 7–9.)

Vivid Imagery

One of the outstanding features of Hebrew poetry is its vivid imagery, which was taken largely from nature, both animate and inanimate, or from the home or occupations in towns and villages, or from national history. The assailants of Nineveh dashed through the streets and across the broad spaces, their war-chariots flashing like torches and darting like lightning (Nah. ii. 4). The 'daughter of Zion' was left 'like a booth in a vineyard, like a lodge in a cucumber field' (Is. i. 8). In the ancient Blessing of Jacob (Gen. xlix) Judah is a lion's whelp (v. 9), Issachar a strong ass (v. 14), Dan a serpent in the way (v. 17), and Benjamin a ravenous wolf (v. 27). The writer of Psalm cii felt himself 'like a vulture of the wilderness, like an owl of the waste places' (v. 10). Leviathan made the deep boil like a pot (Job. xli. 31). Ephraim was a cake not turned (Hos. vii. 8). Yahweh would feed His flock like a shepherd (Is. xl. 11). The once precious sons of Zion had become 'as earthen pots, the work of a potter's hands' (Lam. iv. 2). When Israel went forth from Egypt,

> The sea looked and fled,
>   Jordan turned back.
> The mountains skipped like rams,
>   the hills like lambs. (Ps. cxiv. 2f.)

Figures of Speech

Another striking feature of Hebrew poetry is the frequent use of apt figures of speech like similes (Job. xiv. 2; Ps. cxxvi. 1; Song of Sol. iv. 1–5), metaphors (Job. viii. 9; Ps. lxi. 2f.; Is. xxviii. 5f.) and

Forms and Characteristics of Hebrew Poetry 93

personification (Job xxviii. 14, 22; Ps. xcviii. 7-9; Is. xliv. 23); and of various literary devices like repetition (Jer. v. 15; Is. xl. 1; Ob. vv. 12-14), the rhetorical question (Hos. vi. 4; Jer. ii. 31f.; Is. xl. 27f.), the imperative (Amos. iv. 4; Hos. xiv. 1; Jer. v. 1), the exclamation (2 Sam. i. 27; Nah. iii. 2; Is. lii. 7), and contrast (Amos. ix. 2; Is. v. 20; Lam. v. 12-15).

Spirituality

Familiarity with nature, imagination, intensity of feeling and sincerity, simplicity, vigour of expression, vivid imagery and apt figures of speech, are not peculiar to Hebrew poetry, but it has one quality, namely, an exalted spirituality, which is not found in the poetry of any other nation. Hebrew thought was theocentric, that is, everything began and ended with God. He was the Creator of the world, the Source of all life and the Controller of history. Everything that happened took place in accordance with His will. He was in everything, from the crash of an empire to the healing of the brokenhearted. He was omnipotent, omnipresent and omniscient, and therefore nothing could prevent the ultimate fulfilment of His purpose. He was the only God beside whom there was no other. He was not a universal spirit nor a mere abstraction, but a personal living God to whom men could speak and pray. He made man in His own image (Gen. i. 27), and called him to a life of holiness (Lev. xix. 2). In Hebrew thought the conception of God as Creator was secondary in importance to the conception of Him as Saviour. He called Abraham from Ur of the Chaldees, that he might be a co-partner with Him in the promotion of righteousness on the earth, delivered the Israelites from bondage in Egypt, gave them the land of Canaan for an inheritance, called in first the Assyrians and then the Babylonians to destroy their kingdoms and to carry them away into captivity, and raised the Persian conqueror to restore them to their native land. In His own good time He would usher in His Kingdom of peace and righteousness, when the earth would be filled with the knowledge of Yahweh as the waters covered the sea (Is. xi. 9).

The thought of God was never absent for long from the minds of the Hebrews for the earth was full of His glory.

> I will call to mind the deeds of the Lord;
>   yea, I will remember thy wonders of old.
> I will meditate on all thy work
>   and muse on thy mighty deeds.

> Thy way, O God, is holy.
> What god is great like our God?
> Thou art the God who workest wonders,
> who hast manifested thy might among the peoples.
>
> (Ps. lxxvii. 11–14.)

They longed to enter into fellowship with Him as a hart longed for flowing streams (Ps. xlii. 1). On their journey through life they saw the spiritual in the material, the unseen in the seen, the eternal in the temporal. This exalted spirituality or quality of vision gave Hebrew poetry, with the exception of a few short poems and *The Song of Solomon*, a unique position in the history of the world's literature.

CHAPTER VII

PSALMS

GENERAL TITLE AND PLACE IN CANON

THE English title of the book comes from the Greek 'biblos psalmon' (Book of Psalms) or 'Psalmoi' (Psalms). In classical Greek 'psalmos' signifies the 'twanging of strings' and especially the musical sound produced thereby; but in the Septuagint it has the meaning of a song or hymn accompanied by a stringed instrument, from the translation of the Hebrew word, 'mizmor,' which is found fifty-seven times in the titles of individual Psalms. In the Codex Alexandrinus we find the title Psalterion (Psalter), which originally meant a 'stringed instrument' and then a collection of sacred songs. The Hebrew title of the book is Tehillim, the plural of Tehillah, meaning 'hymn of praise', but it is inappropriate since many of the Psalms cannot be called 'hymns of praise'.

The position of the book within the third division of the Hebrew Canon is not fixed but it usually stands first in order. In the modern printed Hebrew Bibles, which follow the great majority of the German manuscripts, it also comes first and is followed by Proverbs and Job. It was given the first place among the Writings because it was regarded as the most important of them. That this was the case may be judged by the words of our Lord. 'These are my words which I spoke to you, while I was still with you, that everything written about me in the law of Moses and the prophets and the psalms must be fulfilled' (Lk. xxiv. 44).

TITLES OF INDIVIDUAL PSALMS

In the Hebrew text all the Psalms, except thirty-four which are called 'orphans', bear titles. These titles, though they are not original, must go back to comparatively ancient times, for in the third century B.C. the translators of the Septuagint could not understand them. It is probable that by that time they had become obsolete and unintelligible. They may be grouped as follows.

(1) Titles denoting traditional authors.
   (a) Moses (xc).
   (b) David (iii–ix; xi–xxxii; xxxiv–xli; li–lxv; lxviii–lxx; lxxxvi; ci; ciii; cviii–cx; cxxii; cxxiv; cxxxi; cxxxiii; cxxxvi–cxlv; 73 in all).
   (c) Solomon (lxxii; cxxvii).
   (d) Asaph (l; lxxiii–lxxxiii; 12 in all).
   (e) The Sons of Korah (xlii; xliv–xlix; lxxxiv; lxxxv; lxxxvii; lxxxviii; 11 in all).
   (f) Heman the Ezrahite (lxxxviii, with the Sons of Korah).
   (g) Ethan the Ezrahite (lxxxix).

The Septuagint ascribes twelve more Psalms to David than does the Hebrew text, while others are attributed to the Sons of Jonadab and the first captives, Jeremiah, Haggai and Zechariah.

(2) Titles containing references to events in David's life.
   Psalms iii; vii; xviii; xxxiv; li; lii; liv; lvi; lvii; lix; lx; lxiii; cxlii; 13 in all.

(3) Titles giving the literary types.
   (a) Mizmor. Fifty-seven Psalms have in their titles the term 'Mizmor', translated 'Psalm'. It appears originally to have meant 'to make melody', but came to be applied specially to instrumental music as distinguished from vocal music.
   (b) Shir. The term 'Shir', translated 'Song', occurs thirty times in the titles, generally preceded or followed by 'Mizmor' (xxx; xlviii; lxv–lxviii, etc.). It is applied to secular as well as sacred songs (Gen. xxxi. 27; Jud. v. 12; Kgs. iv. 32, etc.).
   (c) Maskil. This term is found as the title of thirteen Psalms, chiefly in Books II and III (xxxii; xlii; xliv; xlv; lii–lv; lxxiv; lxxxiv; lxxxviii; lxxxix; cxlii). Its meaning is obscure. It has been thought to mean 'instruction' or 'meditation' or 'a skilful Psalm'.
   (d) Miktam. Six Psalms have the title 'Miktam' (xvi; lvi–lx), the meaning of which is unknown. It may come from a word meaning 'gold', implying that the Psalm is of unusual excellence. According to Mowinckel, it is a song the object of which is to atone for sin, or uncleanness, or sickness the result of sin.
   (e) Shiggaion. This term occurs in the title of Psalm vii. Its meaning is obscure. It is thought to mean 'a wild passionate song with rapid changes of rhythm'.

(f) Tehillah. This term is the title of Psalm cxlv, and means 'praise' that is, 'Psalm of praise'. It came to be used in the plural (tehillim) as the Hebrew title of the Psalter.

(g) Tephillah. Five Psalms bear the title 'Tephillah', meaning 'prayer' (xvii; lxxxvi; xc; cii; cxlii). In the subscription to Psalm lxxii the preceding collection of Davidic Psalms is called 'The prayers of David'.

(4) Titles containing musical directions.

(a) Lammenaṣṣeah. This term, translated 'To the choirmaster',[1] occurs in the titles of fifty-five Psalms, fifty-two of which are in Books I–III and three in Book V (iv–vi; viii; ix; xi–xiv, etc.). Its meaning is uncertain. The word probably refers to the conductor of the Temple choir, while the preposition prefixed to it indicates that the Psalm belonged to a collection of Temple hymns bearing the name of the choirmaster for use in the Temple services.

(b) Selah. This term (Heb. 'salal' = 'to lift up') occurs seventy-one times in the Psalter in thirty-nine Psalms. Its precise meaning has not been determined. It has been suggested that it may have been a cry of the worshippers at a specified point in the Psalm or at its close, or a musical direction indicating a pause in the music, or telling the orchestra to play louder.

(c) Higgaion. Higgaion occurs once with Selah in Psalm ix. 16 as a musical direction. It has been understood to mean 'resounding music', but more probably refers to solemn, meditative music.

(d) Al Neginoth. The title occurs six times in the Psalter (iv; vi; liv; lv; lxvii; lxxvi) and means 'with stringed instruments'.

(e) El Nehiloth. The title is found in Psalm v and means 'with the wind instruments' or 'for flutes'.

(f) Al Alamoth. The term is found in the title of Psalm xlvi and is translated 'according to Alamoth'. It is thought to mean 'for maidens' voices' or 'in the manner of maidens' and refers to soprano or falsetto voices.

(g) Al Sheminith. Two Psalms (vi; xii) have in their titles the term 'Al Sheminith', which is rendered 'according to the Sheminith' or 'according to the eighth', probably indicating that the melody was to be sung an octave lower. Moffatt translates it 'for bass voices'.

(h) Al Gittith. Three Psalms (viii; lxxxi; lxxxiv) have in their titles

---

[1] The A.V. has 'To the chief Musician', the R.V. 'For the Chief Musician', and Moffatt, 'From the Choirmaster's collection'.

'Al Gittith' which is rendered, 'According to the Gittith'. This term has been supposed to mean that the Psalms were to be sung to the accompaniment of the Gittite instrument, which took its name from the city of Gath. This, however, is questionable, as there is no mention of an instrument of this kind in the Old Testament. Some scholars suggest that 'Gittith' comes from a Hebrew word 'Gath' which means 'a wine press', indicating that the melody of the Psalms was to be sung to a vintage tune. Moffatt renders the term, 'set to a vintage melody'.

(i) Le or Al Jeduthun. Psalm xxxix has in its title 'Le Jeduthun', which is rendered 'to Jeduthun' and appears to be the name of the chief musician. Psalms lxii and lxxvii have in their titles 'Al Jeduthun', which is rendered 'according to Jeduthun', and probably means that the Psalms were set to a melody composed by or called after the chief musician.

(5) Titles of popular melodies.

(a) Al tashheth. Psalms lvii, lviii, lix and lxxv have the title, 'according to Do Not Destroy'. The term may be the beginning of a vintage song cited in Isaiah lxv. 8.

(b) Al-ayyeleth hash-shahar. Psalm xxii has the title Al-ayyeleth hash-shahar, that is, 'according to The Hind of the Dawn'. It is thought that the reference is to the sacrifice of a ewe in connexion with which the Psalm was sung by the offerer or by the priests in his name. The sacrifice was made at dawn.

(c) Al Shoshannim. Psalms xlv and lxix bear the title Al Shoshannim, which means 'according to lilies'. The same melody is probably referred to under the title 'Al Shushan Eduth' in Psalm lx and 'Al Shoshannim Eduth' in Psalm lxxx. It is thought that the title refers to the use of flowers in the sacrifice.

(d) Al Jonath-elem-rehokim. Psalm lvi has the title 'Jonath-elem-rehokim', which is rendered 'according to the Dove on Far-off Terebinths'. It has been suggested the Psalm was designated to be sung over the dove which symbolically carried away the guilt of the purified to the far-off gods. It was a sacrifice designed to placate the evil spirits that caused the sickness or misfortune of the sufferer.

(e) Al Muth-labben. Psalm ix has the title 'Al Muth-labben', that is, 'according to Muth-labben'. It may possibly mean 'Die for the son' or 'Death makes white'.

(f) Al Mahalath, Al Mahalath Leannoth. The former title occurs in

Pss. liii and lxxxviii and the latter title in Ps. lxxxviii. The meaning of these two titles is unknown, but they are probably names of melodies.

(6) Titles referring to the liturgical use of the Psalms.

(a) Psalm xcii was to be sung on the Sabbath.[1]

(b) Psalms xxxviii and lxx bear the title 'Lehazkir', meaning 'to bring to remembrance'; but some scholars hold that the word should be 'Azkarah', meaning 'to make memorial' or 'for making memorial', which is the technical word in Leviticus ii. 2, 9 for the meal-offering. Hence it is probable that the two Psalms were sung at the meal offering.

(c) Psalm xc bears the title 'Lethodah', meaning 'for thanks'. It is thought that the Psalm was sung when the thank-offering was presented in the Temple.

(d) Psalm xxx has the title, 'A Song at the Dedication of the House'. It was probably used either at the dedication of the Second Temple (Ezra vi. 16), or in later times at the Festival commemorating the rededication of the Temple by Judas Maccabaeus in 164 B.C. (1 Macc. iv. 59; 2 Macc. x. 6-8).

(e) Psalm lx has in its title 'to teach' or 'for teaching'. It was probably to be committed to memory and recited on public occasions.

(f) Psalms cxx–cxxxiv are called 'Songs of Ascents'. They were probably sung by pilgrims going up to Jerusalem from the country at the time of the great festivals (Ps. xlii. 4; Is. xxx. 29).

DIVISIONS

In the Hebrew version the Psalter contains 150 Psalms.[2] The same number is also found in the Septuagint (not counting the spurious Psalm 151, which is stated in the title to be 'outside the number' and is ascribed to David), but the numeration is somewhat different. Psalms ix and x are combined so that the psalm numbers are one short of those in the Hebrew version so far as Ps. cxiv, which is joined to

---

[1] An early Jewish tradition tells us that in the worship of the Second Temple a special Psalm was sung on each day of the week at the time of the offering of the morning sacrifice. The only reference to this custom in the Hebrew text is found in the title of Psalm xcii; but in the Septuagint, Psalm xxiv is assigned to the first day of the week, Psalm xlviii to the second day, Psalm xciv to the fourth day and Psalm xciii to the sixth day. In the Mishnah, Psalm lxxxii is assigned to the third day, and Psalm lxxxi to the fifth day.

[2] The latest Dead Sea Scroll to be unrolled is a Psalter older than any other Hebrew version, dating from at least the first century of the Christian era and probably earlier, and including a new 151st Psalm.

Ps. cxv, the two counting as Ps. cxiii. Psalm cxvi is divided into two, Pss. cxiv and cxv. The order is restored at Ps. cxlvii, which is also divided, being reckoned as Pss. cxlvi and cxlvii.

In some cases in the Hebrew version one Psalm has been divided into two. Psalms ix and x once formed one Psalm, as it appears from the acrostic arrangement of the verses and by the absence of the title in Ps. x: they form one Psalm in the Septuagint. Psalms xlii and xliii are obviously one, as is shown by the poetic structure and the refrain. There is reason for thinking that some Psalms, which now appear as one, really consist of two elements which have been incorrectly joined together. This is certainly the case with Pss. xix and cxliv where vv. 1–6 and 7–14 in the former and vv. 1–11 and 12–15 in the latter are separate.

The book is divided into five parts, probably in imitation of the Pentateuch. The Authorized Version does not reveal this, but in the Revised Version and the Revised Standard Version the divisions are indicated. The five books in the Hebrew Version are arranged as follows. Book I, Pss. i–xli; Book II, Pss. xlii–lxxii; Book III, Pss. lxxiii–lxxxix; Book IV, Pss. xc–cvi; and Book V, Pss. cvii–cl. Each book closes with a doxology. These doxologies end with an Amen, a double Amen, or Hallelujah ('Praise ye the Lord'), while in the case of the fifth division the whole of Ps. cl is a great burst of praise.

THE GROWTH OF THE BOOK

The Psalter was not created by a number of writers living in the same period who undertook the task of composing sacred songs suitable for public worship and private devotions. It is rather the result of a slow growth extending over several centuries. Different men living in widely separate periods wrote their Psalms as the spirit moved them, and long after their death their compositions were gathered together to form collections. It was from these independent collections that the Psalter was eventually compiled, and thus it has been called 'a collection of collections'.

That the Psalter is composed of several originally independent collections is shown from the following considerations.

(1) Certain psalms are repeated in slightly different forms. Thus Ps. xiv = Ps. liii; Ps. xl. 13–17 = Ps. lxx; Ps. lvii. 7–11 and Ps. lx. 5–12 = Ps. cviii. The presence of these doublets can be explained satisfactorily only by the fact that they were found in more than one collection.

(2) There is a striking difference between Pss. i–xli and Pss. xlii–lxxxiii in the use of the Hebrew term for deity. In Pss. i–xli 'Yahweh' occurs 272 times and 'Elohim' 15 times, whereas in Pss. xlii–lxxxiii 'Yahweh' occurs 42 times and 'Elohim' 200 times. The preponderance of 'Elohim' over 'Yahweh' in Pss. xlii–lxxxiii cannot be attributed to a preference of their authors for the former name. It is obvious that these Psalms must have passed through the hands of an editor, who changed 'Yahweh' of the original authors to 'Elohim'. The reason for this change probably is that the editor lived at a time when the name 'Yahweh' was no longer pronounced because it was considered too sacred to be used.

Thus far we have evidence for two main collections, namely, Pss. i–xli and Pss. xlii–lxxxiii, the former being commonly called the Yahwistic Psalter and the latter the Elohistic Psalter from their respective use of the terms 'Yahweh' and 'Elohim' for the deity.

In the first collection thirty-seven Psalms are attributed to David. Psalms i and ii are clearly introductory to the Psalter and have no title. Psalm x lacks a title since it is the second part of Ps. ix. Psalm xxxiii lacks a title in the Hebrew Version, but in the Septuagint it is attributed to David. Thus Pss. i–xli may be called the first Davidic collection.

In the second collection (xlii–lxxxiii) the following minor collections can be distinguished.

(1) Psalms li–lxxii. The words at the end of Ps. lxxii, 'The Prayers of David, the son of Jesse, are ended,' clearly mark the close of a second Davidic collection. Of the Psalms contained in it, three, namely, lxvi, lxvii and lxxi lack the title 'Of David' in the Hebrew version but they have it in the Septuagint, while Ps. lxxii is attributed to Solomon.

(2) Psalms xlii–xlix. These are assigned to the Sons of Korah.

(3) Psalms l, lxxiii–lxxxiii. These are assigned to the Sons of Asaph.

An appendix, consisting of six Psalms (lxxxiv–lxxxix), has been added to the Elohistic Psalter, without the editorial change from 'Yahweh' to 'Elohim'. Of these Psalms four are ascribed to the Sons of Korah (lxxxiv, lxxxv, lxxxvii, lxxxviii), one is ascribed to David (lxxxvi) and one to Ethan the Ezrahite (lxxxix).

Psalms xc–cl form a third main collection, which has been called 'the anonymous collection' since most of the Psalms in it lack a title. Seventeen are ascribed to David, one is ascribed to Moses (xc) and one to Solomon (cxxvii), but the majority have no name. In this collection several minor collections may be distinguished of which the most important are the 'Songs of Ascents' or 'Psalms of Degrees' (cxx–

cxxxiv) and the 'Hallel Psalms' (civ–cvi; cxi–cxiii; cxv–cxviii; cxxxv; cxlvi–cl). The former were probably chanted by the pilgrims on their way to Zion and are sometimes, therefore, called the 'Pilgrim Psalms'. The latter were apparently sung by the Temple choir, and at the close the people shouted 'Hallelujah' ('Praise ye the Lord').[1]

The growth of the Psalter may be summarized thus:

(1) Formation of the first Davidic collection (i–xli).
(2) Formation of the second Davidic collection (li–lxxii).
(3) Formation of the collection of the Sons of Korah (xlii–xlix).
(4) Formation of the collection of the Sons of Asaph (l, lxxiii–lxxxiii).
(5) Formation of the Elohistic Psalter by the combination of collections 2, 3 and 4.
(6) The Enlargement of the Elohistic Psalter by the addition of Pss. lxxxiv–lxxxix.
(7) Formation of the collection xc–cl.
(8) Formation of the Psalter in its present form.

It is generally believed that the Psalter originally consisted of three books, namely, Book I comprising Pss. i–xli, Book II, comprising Pss. xlii–lxxxix, and Book III, comprising Pss. xc–cl, and that it was subsequently redivided into five books in imitation of the Pentateuch.

CLASSIFICATION

An accurate classification of the Psalms is difficult owing to the paucity of the data and the variety of their contents. Various classifications have been proposed but none of them can be considered entirely satisfactory. Many scholars have accepted that of Gunkel, who, by discovering for each Psalm its 'setting in life', that is, the sort of occasion for which it was used, distinguished five main 'types' or 'classes'.[2] These are as follows:

(1) Hymns of Praise.

(a) Pss. viii, xix, xxix, xxxiii, lxv, lxviii, xcvi, xcviii, c, ciii, civ, cv, cxi, cxiii, cxiv, cxv, cxvii, cxxxv, cxxxvi, cxlv, cxlvi, cxlvii, cxlviii,

---

[1] In the synagogue liturgy the term 'Hallel' was applied to Pss. cxiii–cxviii. It was known as the 'Egyptian Hallel' and was sung at the great Jewish festivals—the Feast of the Passover, the Feast of Tabernacles, the Feast of Pentecost and the Feast of Dedication of the Temple.

[2] H. Gunkel, *Die Psalmen*, 1926; and H. Gunkel and J. Begrich, *Einleitung in die Psalmen*, 1933.

cxlix, cl. These are entirely devoted to the celebration of the praise and goodness of Yahweh.

(b) Pss. xlvi, xlviii, lxxvi, lxxxiv, lxxxvii, cxxii. These are called 'Songs of Zion' because they extol Zion, the dwelling place of Yahweh.[1]

(c) Pss. xlvii, xciii, xcvi. 10ff., xcvii–xcix. These are called 'Enthronement Songs' because they were apparently composed to celebrate the enthronement of Yahweh as the universal king.

(2) Laments of the Community.

Pss. xliv, lxxiv, lxxix, lxxx, lxxxiii. They were sung by the congregation on the occasion of some national calamity, or when the community was threatened by some dire peril, such as that of famine or foreign invasion. For the most part they consist of the recital of the disasters, which have befallen or might befall the nation, and prayers for deliverance.

(3) Royal Psalms.

Pss. ii, xviii, xx, xxi, xlv, lxii, ci, cx, cxxxii, cxliv. 1–11. These were sung on festive occasions in honour of the king and the royal house.[2]

(4) Individual Laments.

Pss. iii, v, vi, vii, xiii, xvii, xxii, xxv, xxvi, xxvii. 7–14, xxviii, xxxi, xxxv, xxxviii, xxxix, xlii–xliii, li, liv, lv, lvi, lvii, lix, lxi, lxiii, lxiv, lxix, lxx, lxxi, lxxxvi, lxxxviii, cii, cix, cxx, cxxx, cxl, cxli, cxlii, cxliii. These constitute the largest single class in the Psalter. They appear to have been originally at least the immediate concern of individual worshippers rather than the congregation as a whole. The authors deal with their own personal troubles, such as the attacks of enemies (iii; xiii), or sickness (vi; xxii), or anguish of thought arising from their enforced absence from Zion (xlii; xliii), or the fear of death (lxix; lxxxviii).

(5) Individual Psalms of Thanksgiving.

Pss. xviii, xxx, xxxii, xxxiv, xli, lxvi, xcii, cxvi, cxviii, cxxxviii. These were sung by individual worshippers during the offering of sacrifice. They express gratitude for deliverance from trouble or re-

---

[1] Gunkel sometimes assigns a Psalm to more than one class. Pss. lxxxiv and cxxii are also classed as 'Pilgrim Psalms'.

[2] The Royal Psalms, which celebrate a human king, must not be confused with the Enthronement Psalms which celebrate the enthronement of Yahweh as universal king.

covery from sickness. Both the sacrifice and the song bear the same Hebrew name, 'todah'.

Gunkel distinguishes several other minor types, namely, Pilgrim Psalms (e.g. lxxxiv), Communal Psalms of Thanksgiving (e.g. cxxiv), Psalms in praise of the Law (cxix), and Wisdom Psalms (e.g. lxxiii). Some Psalms cannot be classified since they represent a mixture of different types. To these Gunkel gives the name of 'Mixed Poems'.

Mowinckel believes that about forty-three Psalms are Enthronement Psalms composed to form part of the ritual connected with an annual New Year's Festival similar to that in honour of the god, Marduk, in Babylon. He alleges that in pre-exilic times the Ark was carried in procession through the streets of Jerusalem to the Temple where Yahweh was enthroned as king.[1] Mowinckel's views have not won universal acceptance. There is no direct evidence of such a festival in Israel in Old Testament times. Snaith shows that the New Year's Festival is not earlier than the second century A.D., and is therefore not valid as evidence for such a festival in the pre-exilic period.[2]

AUTHORSHIP

The question of the authorship of the Psalms is of interest chiefly in reference to David. In the Hebrew Version of the Psalter seventy-three of the Psalms bear his name. It is very doubtful if the Hebrew preposition in the phrase 'of David' was ever used before the Exile to denote authorship. In the Authorized Version of the Bible the same preposition is rendered by 'to' in the phrase 'To the Chief Musician' (the Revised Version has, 'For the Chief Musician' and the Revised Standard Version, 'To the choirmaster'), but neither 'to' nor 'for' denotes authorship. Similarly we have the phrases 'of Asaph' (used collectively for the 'sons of Asaph') and 'of the sons of Korah', which probably indicate, not that the Psalms bearing these titles were written

---

[1] A. R. Johnson (*Sacral Kingship in Ancient Israel*, 1955) accepts the theory of a New Year's Festival, but holds that its principal features were (1) a celebration presumably in song of Yahweh's great deeds of the past (His triumph over the primeval chaos and His creation of the world), and (2) a ritual drama in which the Davidic king was enthroned as Yahweh's viceregent on earth, and worshippers were given assurance of final victory over death, a summons to renew their faith in Yahweh and a challenge to be faithful to His demands so that the vision of a universal realm of righteousness might be realized. The exclamation 'YHWH malak', used in the ceremony, did not announce the annual enthronement of Yahweh (i.e. 'Yahweh has become king') but affirmed His eternal kingship (i.e. 'Yahweh is king'). The king, while playing the central role in the ritual drama and occupying the central place in the anointing of Yahweh, was, nevertheless, not divine and in relation to his subjects only first among equals.

[2] N. H. Snaith, *The Jewish New Year Festival: Its origin and Development*, 1947.

by members of the two guilds of singers, but that in some sense they belonged to them. In the same way the phrase 'of David' probably means 'belonging to David'. Such a phrase, therefore, does not imply or prove Davidic authorship. There is no doubt, however, that it came to be regarded as such: until recent times it was believed that David was the author of all the Psalms which bore his name. This view can no longer be sustained as the evidence against it is too convincing. It is now generally recognized that while there is no reason for doubting the presence of a Davidic element in the Psalms ascribed to him, the majority of them cannot be his work. The chief grounds on which this view is based are as follows:

(1) The Psalms vary in literary quality, ranging from the commonplace to the sublime, and suggesting that they are not the work of one man.

(2) Some of the Psalms are strongly tinged with Aramaisms (ciii; cxvi; cxxii; cxxxix; cxliv) which suggest the post-exilic period when Hebrew was gradually superseded by Aramaic.

(3) Many of the Psalms are out of harmony with the historical situation as it existed in David's time. Some of them imply the existence of the Temple (v. 7; xxvii. 4; xxviii. 2); but the first Temple was not built until the reign of Solomon, and the second not until some years after the Return from captivity in Babylon. Others again imply that the Psalmist is living in evil times when the wicked are flourishing and oppressing the righteous (ix; x; xii; xiv, etc.). Such conditions are not consistent with those which are said to have existed in David's lifetime.

(4) Some of the Psalms presuppose the circumstances of a later age. Psalms li. 18f. and lxix. 35 presuppose the approaching restoration of Jerusalem and Judah, while others reflect the teaching of the prophets.

(5) From what is known of David's character it is hard to believe that he could have reached the high spiritual level and the maturity of theological reflection revealed in many of the Psalms ascribed to him. The author of Ps. xvii declares his innocence and desires to live in fellowship with Yahweh for ever. To the author of Ps. ciii Yahweh is eternal and His mercy never fails. The theological conceptions expressed in Ps. cxxxix are among the noblest in the Old Testament. 'Every indication', says Driver, 'converges to the same conclusion, viz. that the Davidic Psalms spring, in fact, from many different periods of Israelitish history, from the time of David himself downwards;

and that in the varied moods which they reflect—despondency, trouble, searchings of heart, penitence, hope, confidence, thankfulness, exultation; or the various situations which they shadow forth—distress, sickness, oppression or persecution, deliverance—they set before us the experiences of many men, and of many ages of the national life.'[1]

DATE

It is generally recognized that the oldest of the three collections in the Psalter is Book I, which is probably not earlier than the Return from captivity. Then followed the Eloistic Psalter (Books II and III) and later still its appendix (lxxxiv–lxxxix). Books IV and V are probably the last of all. The Psalter in its present form was probably completed before 100 B.C. This is borne out by the following considerations:

(1) The Hebrew Scriptures containing the Psalms were translated into Greek by about 100 B.C. and there is substantial agreement between the two versions.

(2) Psalm lxxix. 2f. is quoted as Scripture in 1 Maccabees vii. 17 (c. 90 B.C.).

(3) A collection of eighteen Psalms, called the 'Songs of Solomon', appeared about 50 B.C. The fact that none of these Psalms was included in the Psalter suggests that it was closed and not open to further additions.

The precise dates of the individual Psalms cannot be fixed since the internal evidence is indecisive. The language is often general and the thought would be as applicable to one century as to another. All attempts to date them have resulted in such a conflict of opinion that it seems almost futile to continue with the task. We can do no more than summarize the various views which have been advanced on the subject.

During the latter half of the nineteenth and the beginning of the twentieth centuries it was customary to assign practically all the Psalms to the post-exilic period, and to see in the king portrayed in them one of the Maccabaean princes or a friendly foreign ruler. Cheyne regarded the whole of the Psalter as the creation of the Jewish Church and as therefore post-exilic.[2] Briggs assigns the majority of them to the Persian period, and especially to the time of Ezra and Nehemiah,[3] while

---

[1] S. R. Driver, *An Introduction to the Literature of the Old Testament*, 9th ed., 1913, p. 377.

[2] T. K. Cheyne, *Origins of the Psalter*, 1891.

[3] C. A. and E. G. Briggs, *A Critical and Exegetical Commentary on the Book of Psalms*, 1906 and 1907.

Duhm ascribes nearly all to the Maccabaean period.[1] Of recent years there has been a tendency to find a larger pre-exilic element in the Psalter. Engnell declares that there is only one Psalm (cxxxvii) in the whole Psalter of which he is convinced that it is post-exilic.[2] Bentzen is prepared to assign a considerable number to the pre-exilic period. 'As a rule', he says, 'we must keep in mind that the psalms may date from all periods in the history of Israel and Judaism, and that the classical period of this poetry is the ancient times, when the poems were expressions of the relations of men and God.'[3] Albright 'would date the contents of the Psalter in their present form between the eleventh and the fourth centuries B.C., and would admit a date many centuries higher for the Canaanite substratum of many Psalms.'[4]

The chief reasons for this reaction against the older theory that practically all the Psalms are post-exilic is as follows:

(1) Psalmody was known in Israel from its earliest days. The Song of Deborah (Jud. v. 2–31), written about 1150 B.C., is a Psalm.

(2) The Egyptians, Babylonians and Canaanites made use of Psalms in the worship of their gods long before the days of David and Solomon, from which it may be inferred that the Israelites, who were familiar with the cultures of these peoples and were influenced by them, would probably use similar compositions in the services of the first Temple.

FOREIGN INFLUENCE

The Hebrew Psalms are not an isolated phenomenon in the literature of the world. Archaeological investigation has shown that the Egyptians, Babylonians and Canaanites had similar compositions long before the building of the Temple and the growth of Hebrew psalmody. The question of the indebtedness of the Hebrew Psalmists to this foreign literature is a subject of controversy, some scholars finding clear evidence of Hebrew borrowings, either direct or indirect, and others finding little or none.

Gressmann maintains that the Psalter shows clear parallels in both language and thought to similar compositions from Egypt and Babylon, and that this points to dependence, direct and indirect, upon the older psalmody of the ancient Near East. He alleges, for example, that Psalm civ is clearly dependent upon an Egyptian prototype with which

[1] B. Duhm, *Die Psalmen*, 1899.
[2] I. Engnell, *Studies in Divine Kingship in the Ancient near East*, 1943, p. 176, n. 2.
[3] A. Bentzen, *Introduction to the Old Testament*, Vol. II, 1948, p. 168.
[4] W. F. Albright, *Journal of Biblical Literature*, Vol. LXI, Part 2, p. 122.

the Hebrews became acquainted through the Phoenicians (i.e. Canaanites). This accounts for the mention of the 'cedars of Lebanon' (v. 16), and the transformation of the description of the Nile with its ships and crocodiles into that of the Mediterranean in which there are no crocodiles (vv. 25, 26). 'Just as the Temple of Jerusalem was modelled on an Egyptian-Phoenician sanctuary, so behind Ps. civ we sense an Egyptian-Phoenician original, not specifically the Psalm of Ikhnaton (as is often urged), but more generally an Egyptian Psalm in Phoenician guise.'[1] Babylonian influence can be traced in Psalms xix and lxxii.

Blackman also cites parallels in language and thought from these two fields, but believes that there was mutual indebtedness between the Semitic world and Egypt in the second millennium B.C. The Semitic world gave to Egypt its idea of divine providence and its realization of the fact of sin and the need of forgiveness, and in return Egypt gave to the Semitic world 'a genuine appreciation for the beauties of Nature, a love for all living things, even for hippopotami and crocodiles, cheerfulness, a sense of fun, great sociability and remarkable kindness of heart.'[2] Driver admits that there are striking parallels in form, language and thought between the Hebrew Psalms and their Babylonian counterparts, but finds little or no evidence of direct dependence. The resemblances, he alleges, can be explained partly by an independent parallel development, and partly by a common origin in prehistoric times before the expansion of the Semites had driven them out of their primitive home to form separate nations. At the same time he admits the possibility of indirect influence from Babylon through the ancestors of the Hebrews or through the Canaanites.[3]

It is also claimed that the Psalter shows direct dependence upon the earlier cultic literature of the Canaanites. Patton has shown that there is a surprising number of parallels in language and thought between the Psalms and the Ugaritic texts.[4] According to Albright, 'the literary texts of Ugarit do demonstrate that many of the Psalms are saturated with Canaanite stylistic and verbal reminiscences, and even with direct quotations from passages found in Ugaritic sources already known to us.' Furthermore, he considers that the parallels

---

[1] H. Gressmann, 'The Development of Hebrew Psalmody' in *The Psalmists*, ed. by D. C. Simpson, 1926, p. 20.

[2] A. M. Blackman, 'The Psalms in the Light of Egyptian Research', in *The Psalmists*, ed. by D. C. Simpson, 1926, p. 197.

[3] G. R. Driver, 'The Psalms in the Light of Babylonian Research' in *The Psalmists*, ed. by D. C. Simpson, 1926, pp. 109–175.

[4] J. H. Patton, *Canaanite Parallels in the Book of Psalms*, 1944.

with xviii, xxix, xlv and lxviii are so close that they may approximately be provisionally attributed to the tenth century. As for Pss. lxxxviii and lxxxix they simply 'swarm with Canaanitisms'.[1]

On the evidence it seems impossible to deny that the Psalter is, to some extent at least, dependent upon Egyptian, Babylonian and Canaanite literature. It must not be forgotten, however, that none of the peoples of the Near East could approach the Hebrews in religious experience and depth of spiritual insight, which made their sacred literature unique. In their theological and ethical conceptions they were immeasurably superior to them.

THE PSALMS AND TEMPLE WORSHIP

The Psalter has been called the 'Hymnbook of the Second Temple' but the title is misleading. It suggests not only that all the Psalms belong to the post-exilic period, but also that they were composed expressly for use in public worship. We have already shown that many of the Psalms must be assigned to the pre-exilic period, some of them going back to the time of David and even earlier.

As regards the purpose for which they were written, there is a wide diversity of opinion. Duhm maintains that the Psalter was not designed primarily as a hymnbook for public worship, but as a manual of meditation and devotional reading to keep people in the right path and to encourage them to study the Law and to keep its precepts.[2]

According to Mowinckel, all the Psalms, with the possible exception of Psalms i and cxix, originated in the cult and were associated with the worship of the community. He believes that many of the Psalms were written to be used to break magic spells, but to break them not by magic but by an appeal to Yahweh. Persons, assuming that some enemy has put a spell upon them, would seek the help of a priest who would recite or cause them to recite the proper Psalm to break the spell. The 'workers of iniquity' mentioned in the Psalms were the sorcerers who cast their spells upon people. He also believes, as we have already indicated, that about forty-three Psalms were employed in the ritual connected with the Annual New Year's Festival, the purpose of which was to secure the welfare of the community during the ensuing year. Furthermore, he maintains that the Individual Laments were not the spontaneous outpourings of pious individuals but were wholly cultic in origin, the authors being the professional poets in the

---

[1] W. F. Albright, *Archaeology and the Religion of Israel*, 3rd. ed., 1953, pp. 128f.
[2] B. Duhm, 'Die Psalmen,' *K.H.C.*, 1889, pp. xxivff.

Temple personnel, who could enter sympathetically and imaginatively into the experience of the worshipper and compose Psalms suitable for use on behalf of the believer in connexion with some form of purificatory rite.[1] It is, however, difficult to believe that such Psalms as li, ciii and cxxxix could have been written by professional poets of the Temple personnel. They create the impression of being the outpourings of devout individuals.

Gunkel recognizes that the Psalms had their origin in the cult, but he believes that psalm-writing was later taken over by devout individuals outside it. Using the psalm-forms derived from the cult, they wrote their Psalms to describe their spiritual experiences, or to express their thoughts and emotions on some particular occasion. Many of these Psalms were eventually taken over into the service of the sanctuary and employed in public worship. Gunkel's theory has not been universally accepted but it is nearer the truth than that of Mowinckel.

In our opinion the Psalter contains Psalms of both cultic and non-cultic origin. Since both vocal and instrumental music was employed in the Temple services, and since there are numerous references in the Psalms to musical instruments, to Temple singing and to Temple activities, it is reasonable to suppose that some of the Psalms are of cultic origin. On the other hand, there are some Psalms which, as we have already indicated, are the spontaneous outpourings of devout individuals, and which originally could not have had any connexion with the cult. Such Psalms would eventually be accepted by the priesthood and used, either with or without alterations, for liturgical purposes.

---

[1] S. Mowinckel, *Psalmenstudien IV. Die technischen Termini in den Psalmenüberschriften*, 1923; *Psalmenstudien III. Kultprophetie und prophetische Psalmen*, 1923; *Psalmenstudien VI. Die Psalmdichter*, 1924.

CHAPTER VIII

PSALMS (Continued)

TEACHING

Cosmology

THE conception of the constitution of the world as revealed in the Psalms is that which had prevailed among the Hebrew people from early times. It was supposed that the world was flat and supported on pillars (Job ix. 6; Pss. lxxv. 3; civ. 5). Over it stretched the firmament, a great solid dome resting apparently on mountain pillars (2 Sam. xxii. 8; Job xxvi. 11), and in it were set the sun, moon and stars (Gen. i. 16f.; Pss. viii. 3; xix. 4–6). Above the firmament was water (Ps. cxlviii. 4), and above that three heavens one above another, the highest of which—the heaven of heavens—was the dwelling place of God[1] (Deut. x. 14; Pss. lvii. 5; cxxiii. 1). In the recesses of the earth lay Sheol, the abode of the dead (Deut. xxxii. 22; Pss. ix. 17; xxx. 3; cxv. 17). Beneath the earth was water—the 'great deep', where lived Leviathan and the Dragon (Is. xxvii. 1; li. 9f.; Pss. lxxiv. 13f.; civ. 26). Floods surged up from the 'great deep' and rain came through openings in the firmament (Gen. vii. 11; viii. 2; Pss. lxix. 15; lxxii. 6).

This primitive conception of the constitution of the world survived for many centuries, but the growth of knowledge, the development of science and the deeper and richer understanding of the ways of God ultimately led to its abandonment.

GOD

Anthropomorphism

The Psalms belong to different periods of Hebrew history and are the work of many writers. Since an advanced theology does not spring up fully developed but is the result of a slow evolutionary process

---

[1] In the apocalyptic literature of the post-exilic period there is no consistent theory regarding the constitution of the world. Some writers speak of three heavens and others of seven. The third heaven is usually identified with Paradise, the abode of the righteous after death and of God.

often extending over many centuries, it is not surprising that we should find in Psalms crude and exalted conceptions of the deity. Anthropomorphic expressions occur again and again in the book. The people who walk in the light of Yahweh's countenance are blessed (lxxxix. 15): His eyes behold and His eyelids test the children of men (xi. 4). He hears the cry of the righteous for help (xxxiv. 17). His right hand and holy arm have gained Him the victory (xcviii. 1). The heavens are the work of His fingers (viii. 3). He makes the clouds his chariots and rides on the wings of the wind (civ. 3). He awakens as from sleep like a strong man wild with wine (lxxviii. 65). The anthropomorphic expressions used by the early Psalmists would be understood in a literal sense, while those used by the later Psalmists would probably be understood metaphorically since they would employ such expressions long after anthropomorphism had died out.[1]

Monotheism

Monotheism is implied in a few Psalms (e.g. cxv. 4–7; cxxxv. 15–17) but nowhere do we find the belief in the doctrine fully expressed. The language frequently employed is that of monolatry, that is, the belief in one God, while at the same time acknowledging the existence of others. The later Psalmists were probably monotheists who referred to other gods only to ridicule them and to exalt Yahweh.

The Creator and Sustainer

Yahweh is the 'living God' as opposed to the 'empty idols' of other nations, which are made of silver and gold by the hands of men, and cannot speak, or see, or hear, or smell, or feel or walk (cxv. 4–7). He is an omnipotent being who works wonders (lvii. 14) and neither slumbers nor sleeps (cxxi. 4). He has created the world and all life upon it (viii. 3; xxxiii. 6–9; xcv. 3–6; civ. 1–9, 24; cxix. 90f.). The world and all that is in it belong to Him—every beast of the forest, the cattle on the hills, the birds of the air and all that moves in the field (l. 10f.). He is not only the Creator but also the Sustainer of all life. The eyes of all look to Him and He gives them their food in due season (cxlv. 15; cf. cxlvii. 9). He causes grass to grow for the cattle and plants for man to cultivate. He supplies him with wine and bread to gladden and strengthen his heart, and with oil to make his face shine. He plants the cedars of Lebanon in which the birds build their nests,

---

[1] Anthropomorphism (Greek anthrōpos = 'man' and morphē = 'form' or 'shape') is the attribution of human form or personality to the deity.

PSALMS (CONTINUED)

and the fir trees which are the home of the stork. He raises the high mountains on which the wild goats roam, and establishes the rocks which are a refuge for the badgers. The young lions with angry roar seek their food from Him (civ. 14-22).

The physical world is the revelation of Yahweh's infinite power and wisdom. The heavens tell His glory and the firmament proclaims His handiwork (xix. 1). The clouds are His chariots, the winds His messengers and fire and flame His ministers (civ. 3f.). His voice (i.e. the thunder) is heard pealing across the waters, shattering the cedars, shaking the wilderness and stripping the forests bare (xxix. 3-9). Those who go down to the sea in ships see His works and His wonders in the deep (cvii. 23f.).

Some of the Psalmists express their delight in the workmanship of Yahweh. All His works are done 'in faithfulness' (xxxiii. 4) and are characterized by firmness and permanence. The world is established and shall never be moved (xcvi. 10). By His strength He has established the mountains and girded them with might (lxv. 6). He has made all things to last 'for ever and ever', and fixed their boundaries which cannot be passed (cxlviii. 6).

Universal Ruler

Yahweh is not only the Creator of the world and the Sustainer of all life, but also the universal ruler of mankind—'a great king over all the earth' (xlvii. 2). He made nations subject to Israel, choosing her heritage, the goodly land of Canaan, her pride and delight (xlvii. 4). He rejected the 'tent of Jacob' and chose the tribe of Judah, building His sanctuary on Mount Zion which He loved. He took David from the sheepfold to tend His people Jacob and to shepherd Israel (lxxviii. 67-72). Because of the sins of His people He drove them into exile, making them the taunt of their neighbours and a laughing-stock among the nations (xliv. 11-14). He reigns over the nations (xlvii. 8) and His eyes behold the children of men (xi. 4; xiv. 2; xxxiii. 13). His enemies shall perish and all evil-doers shall be scattered (xcii. 9). The day is coming when all men shall praise and worship Him (xxii. 27-29; lxxxvi. 9; cii. 15; cxxxviii. 4f.). His kingdom is an everlasting kingdom and His dominion shall endure throughout all generations (cxlv. 13).

His Omnipresence

Yahweh is said to dwell in heaven (xiv. 2; lxxx. 14; cii. 19) and in the Temple at Jerusalem (xi. 4; xxvii. 4; lxv. 4; cxxxii. 13f.); but in

Psalm cxxxix we find a more exalted conception, namely, that His presence is everywhere. A man may ascend to heaven, or make his bed in Sheol, or flee to the uttermost parts of the sea, or hide in the darkness, but he cannot escape from His presence (vv. 7–12).

His Omniscience

Yahweh is also omniscient. He knows the secrets of the heart (xliv. 21); a man's guilty secrets are laid bare before Him (xc. 8). He is acquainted with all his ways, reads his thoughts from afar, and knows every word before it is uttered (cxxxix. 1–6).

His Eternity

Yahweh is characterized not only by His omnipotence, omnipresence and omniscience, but also by His eternity. Though the Psalmists use language which implies that His life is of endless duration, it is not certain that they always think of it as such. It would appear that in some Psalms His life is thought of as being immeasurably longer than that of man, but nevertheless limited. There are, however, other Psalms which seem to imply that it is of infinite duration (xc. 1f.; cii. 25–27).

His Righteousness

Stress is laid throughout the Psalms on the righteousness of Yahweh. Righteousness and justice are the foundation of His throne (xcvii. 2). His righteousness is like the mountains of God and His judgments are like the great deep (xxxvi. 6). The gates of the Temple are gates of righteousness because they lead to His sanctuary (cxviii. 19). His ordinances are true and righteous altogether (xix. 9; cf. cxix. 7, 106). He has executed justice and righteousness in Jacob (xcix. 4). All nations will receive justice at His hands (xcvi. 13).

His Mercy (or Hesed)

Yahweh is not a stern, inflexible judge meting out strict justice. His justice is tempered with mercy. The Hebrew word which is often translated 'mercy', or 'kindness', or 'loving-kindness' or 'steadfast love' is hesed, but it has a richer content than these words suggest. It also includes the qualities of loyalty and grace, and is of the very essence of Yahweh's heart. The earth is full of His steadfast love (xxxiii. 5). He is merciful and gracious, 'slow to anger and abounding in steadfast love and faithfulness' (lxxxvi. 15). He crowns man with steadfast love and mercy (ciii. 4). The author of Psalm lxxiii declares his intention of blessing Him as long as he lives and of calling upon His name, because His steadfast love is better than life (vv. 3f.). The whole of Psalm cxxxvi is devoted to the praise of His mercy which endures for ever. His mercy embraces the whole of life. He upholds the righteous sleeping and waking and protects them from all their enemies (iii. 1–5). He covers them with favour as with a shield (v. 12). He is ever ready to forgive the penitent sinner, pardoning his iniquities and healing all his diseases (ciii. 3). The Psalms not only dwell with joy on the thought of His 'hesed', but also describe it in image and symbol. He is a shield protecting men from their enemies (iii. 3; v. 12; cxv. 10), a rock and a fortress, where they can find refuge (lxxi. 3), and their strength, song and salvation (cxviii. 14). He is a mother-bird in the shadow of whose wings they can find safety (xci. 4) and sing for joy (lxiii. 7); the shepherd who makes men to lie down in green pastures and leads them beside the still waters and through glens of gloom, comforting them with His rod and staff (xxiii. 1–4); a host who spreads for them a table in the presence of their enemies, anoints their heads with oil and follows them with His goodness and mercy all their days (xxiii. 5f.); the father of the fatherless and the protector of widows (lxviii. 5). There is no contradiction between the justice and the mercy of Yahweh. They are supplementary qualities and fundamental to His character.

MAN

His Weakness and Mortality

Man is a being created by Yahweh and as such he is characterized by weakness and mortality. Compared with Yahweh he is but dust. He flourishes like a flower, which at the breath of the wind is gone to be seen no more in its place (ciii. 14–16). His days are as a shadow that passes away (cxliv. 4).

His Exalted Position

Nevertheless, though he is a weak creature and doomed to die, he occupies a position of dignity and honour in the scale of creation. Yahweh has made him little less than divine and crowned him with glory and honour, giving him dominion over all that His hands have made (viii. 4–8). He is not left to struggle alone. Yahweh supplies him with food (civ. 14f.), protects him with unsleeping care (cxxii. 3f.), guides him by His counsel (lxxiii. 24), heals his diseases (ciii. 3) and binds up the wounds of the broken-hearted (cxlvii. 3). He raises the poor from the dust and lifts the needy from the ash-heap 'to make them sit with princes' (cxiii. 7f.). To crown all His mercies He has given men the Law, which is more to be desired than 'much fine gold' and in the keeping of which there is great reward (xix. 10f.).

WORSHIP

The view commonly held among the Hebrews was that Yahweh dwelt in heaven and in a special sense in Jerusalem, 'the city of the great King' (xlviii. 2). Access to His presence was by worship in His holy Temple (v. 7; xi. 4; cxxxviii. 2). Throughout the Psalms stress is laid upon the importance of Temple worship. Again and again men are exhorted to worship in His Temple.

(1) O come, let us worship and bow down,
    let us kneel before the Lord, our Maker! (xcv. 6.)

(2) Extol the Lord our God,
    and worship at his holy mountain;
    for the Lord our God is holy! (xcix. 9.)

(3) Enter his gates with thanksgiving,
    and his courts with praise!
    Give thanks to him, bless his name! (c.4.)

In many Psalms the traditional view that sacrifice is the chief element in worship is accepted (iv. 5; xxvii. 6; li. 19; liv. 6). But there are a few Psalms in which a more spiritual view is expressed. According to Psalm xl, Yahweh does not require sacrifice but obedience to His will (6-8). A similar view is expressed in Psalm li. 16f. The sacrifice acceptable to Yahweh is that of a soul with its evil crushed and a heart broken with penitence (vv. 16f.). The author of Psalm l declares that Yahweh will accept no bull from a man's house, nor he-goats from his folds, for every beast of the forest is His and the cattle on a thousand hills. He knows all the birds of the air and all that moves in the fields belong to Him. He does not eat flesh or drink blood. Thanksgiving, the payment of vows and prayers are better than sacrifice (vv. 9-15). Psalm xv describes the man whose worship is acceptable to Yahweh. He is one who leads a blameless life, doing what is right and speaking truth from his heart. He indulges in no slander, does no evil to his friend, heaps no insult upon his neighbour, despises rogues, honours those who reverence Yahweh, keeps his oath though he may lose by it, takes no interest on a loan and accepts no bribe against the innocent (vv. 1–5). In Psalm xxiv the requirements for entrance to the sanctuary are similar.

> Who shall ascend the hill of the Lord?
> And who shall stand in his holy place?
> He who has clean hands and a pure heart,
>   who does not lift up his soul to what is false,
>   and does not swear deceitfully. (vv. 3f.)

Thus we see that the noblest minds among the Psalmists think of Yahweh as deserving not sacrifice but the devotion of a pure heart. In other words they stress the spirituality of true worship.

SIN AND FORGIVENESS

The Psalmists without exception accept the theory of the eighth century prophets, Amos, Hosea, Micah and Isaiah, that sin is fundamentally rebellion against Yahweh (v. 10; lxxviii. 8; cvii. 10f.). The author of Psalm li, overwhelmed by the consciousness of his sin, declares, 'Against thee, thee only, have I sinned, and done that which is evil in thy sight' (v. 4). Though the Psalmists do not teach the doctrine of original sin, that is, the doctrine of inherited guilt, they recognize the inherent sinfulness of men. It seemed to them that sin was handed down from one generation to another by the physical process of procreation. 'Behold I was brought forth in iniquity, and in sin did my mother conceive me' (li. 5). 'The wicked go astray from the womb, they err from their birth, speaking lies' (lviii. 3). Sins are of various kinds. There are the thoughtless sins of youth (xxv. 7), sins committed inadvertently and unconsciously (xix. 12), presumptuous sins, that is, conscious sins of rebellion and pride (xix. 13) and secret sins (xc. 8). The effect of sin is to sever a man from Yahweh and to destroy the joy and peace which come from fellowship with Him. The author of Psalm li prays that Yahweh will not cast him away from His presence but will restore to him the joy of His salvation (vv. 11f.). If Yahweh marked every sin there would be no hope for anyone (cxxx. 3), but He is good and forgiving, abounding in steadfast love to all who call upon Him (lxxxvi. 5). If a man truly repents and confesses his sins, he will be forgiven and the old happy fellowship will be renewed. The floods may roar but they will never reach the righteous, for they will find in Yahweh a shelter, preserving them in peril and surrounding them with deliverance (xxxii. 1–7).

RETRIBUTION

All the Psalmists stoutly maintain the doctrine of retribution, according to which Yahweh rewards the righteous and punishes the wicked. The doctrine is proclaimed in Psalm i and runs through the whole of the Psalter (i; xi; xxxiv; lxxv; xci; xcii; cxxviii; cxlv; cxlvi; cxlvii). But the facts of human experience are in conflict with the doctrine, for it is obvious to any person of ordinary intelligence that sometimes the wicked prosper and the righteous suffer.

Many of the Psalmists accept the doctrine without questioning it. They must have had sufficient intelligence to realize that it was contrary to the facts of life; but if doubt ever assailed their minds they kept silent. Some of the Psalmists accept the doctrine, though they know from personal experience that undeserved suffering is a grim reality. In their pain and sorrow they cry out that God has forsaken them.

> My God, my God, why hast thou forsaken me?
> Why are thou so far from helping me,
> from the words of my groaning? (xxii. 1; cf.
> xiii. 1f.; xlii. 9f.)

They are bewildered in face of undeserved suffering but make no effort to explain it. They cling to their faith, convinced that the steadfast love of Yahweh will not fail them, and that one day they will again praise Him as their God and Saviour (xlii. 5, 11; xliii. 5; cf. xiii. 5f.). Among the Psalmists are a few who are deeply conscious of the presence of undeserved suffering in life and attempt to reconcile it with the orthodox doctrine of moral retribution. They admit that the wicked sometimes prosper and the innocent suffer, but affirm that the prosperity of the wicked and the suffering of the innocent are only temporary. The day will surely come when justice will be done. Yahweh, who is a righteous God, will see to it that victory is with the righteous. The author of Psalm xxxvii counsels those who fret over the wicked and are envious of their success, to be 'still before the Lord, and wait patiently for him' (v. 7), 'for they will soon fade like the grass and wither like the green herb' (v. 2). The author of Psalm xlix declares that the justice of Yahweh will be vindicated, not in this life but in the Hereafter. The wicked, who boast of their wealth, cannot take it with them at death. They will die leaving it to others, and descend to Sheol where their form shall waste away and they will never see the light to all eternity. But the righteous, of whom the author reckons himself one, shall be delivered from the grasp of Sheol and received by God (vv. 5-20). The author of Psalm lxxiii, having seen the prosperity of the wicked, had almost lost his faith in Yahweh (vv. 1-15). But when he considers the latter end of the wicked, he realizes that they are destroyed in a moment, swept away by terrors, 'like a dream when one awakes' (v. 20). He himself enjoys unbroken communion with Yahweh who holds his right hand, guides him with His counsel, and will finally receive him to glory (vv. 23f.).

THE LAW

There are comparatively few references to the Law in the Psalter. This is rather surprising, seeing that many of the Psalms belong to the post-exilic period when the conviction grew that the law was the complete revelation of the divine will, and that the religion of Yahweh could only be preserved by strict fulfilment of legal precepts. Probably the Law to the Psalmists included all the ways by which Yahweh revealed His will; but it was the 'Written Law' that was specially in their minds. The author of Psalm ciii. 7 says, 'He made known his ways to Moses, his acts to the people of Israel'.

The nature of the Law is described in Psalm xix. 7-9 and interpreted by six terms, namely, law, testimony, precepts, commandment, fear and ordinances. The Law, conceived as the 'teaching' or the 'instruction' of Yahweh, is 'perfect, reviving the soul'. The Law, reviewed as the 'testimony', which bears witness to the divine will, is 'sure, making wise the simple'. The Law, understood as 'precepts', is 'right, rejoicing the heart'. The Law, considered as 'a set of commandments' is 'pure, enlightening the eyes'. The Law, looked upon as 'an object of reverence' is 'clean, enduring for ever'. The Law, interpreted as a body of 'ordinances' is 'true and righteous altogether'.

The supreme importance of the Law in the life of the nation is recognized. The author of Psalm lxxviii, assuming the role of a teacher, exhorts the people to make known to their children Yahweh's glorious deeds and wonders in Israel's history and to impart to them a knowledge of His law, in order that the coming generations might not forget His works but keep His commandments. Such instruction will keep them from being stubborn and rebellious as their fathers were—'a generation whose heart was not steadfast, whose spirit was not faithful to God' (vv. 1-8).

It is evident that the observance of the Law was not regarded as a grievous burden. The good man finds his chief delight in its fulfilment, poring over it day and night (i. 2). The author of Psalm xix declares that the ordinances of Yahweh are more to be desired than gold and that it is sweeter than honey (v. 10). In observing them a man is warned from evil and receives a great reward. He prays that he may be saved from sins against it, among which he mentions 'hidden faults' and 'presumptuous sins'. He presents the meditation of his heart to Yahweh, with the prayer that it may be as acceptable to Him as a material sacrifice upon His altar (vv. 11–14). Psalm cxix extols the Law and reveals the author's passionate devotion to it. He loves the Law (v. 97), finds his chief delight in observing it (vv. 16, 35, 47, 77, 92, 174), meditates on it (vv. 15, 23, 48, 78, 148), and finds it a lamp to his feet and a light to his path (v. 105). Every one of Yahweh's righteous ordinances endures for ever (v. 160).

IMMORTALITY

The doctrine of immortality appears to have been developed slowly in religious thought. In early times certain primitive conceptions were current concerning the state of man after death and the abode of the dead. They were not, however, peculiar to the religion of Israel but were the common background of Semitic belief. Traces can be found in the Psalms of a cult of the dead. In Psalm cvi. 28, 38, the author reminds the people that their forefathers had worshipped the Moabite god, Baal-peor, offered sacrifices to the dead, and sacrificed their sons and daughters to demons who were perhaps the departed in the underworld. Later the common belief, which is found in the Psalms, is the belief in Sheol, which is practically identical with that of the Babylonians on the same subject. Sheol, the abode of the dead, is located beneath the earth (xxii. 29; xlix. 17) and is sometimes referred to as the 'Pit'. It is thought of as a place of silence (cxv. 17) and of darkness and forgetfulness (lxxxviii. 12). There the dead, now ghostly replicas of men, live a dreary existence deprived of everything that made life desirable (xlix. 7–12), and cut off from fellowship with God (lxxxviii. 5). Since death offers no prospect of joy and happiness and death awaits all, the Hebrews desire 'length of days'.

(1) What man can live and never see death?
Who can deliver his soul from the power of Sheol?
(lxxxix. 48.)

> (2) When he calls to me, I will answer him;
> I will be with him in trouble.
> I will rescue him and honour him,
> With long life will I satisfy him,
> and show him my salvation. (xci. 15f.)

In a few Psalms more advanced conceptions can be found, but whether they contain the fully developed doctrine of immortality is doubtful. In this respect four Psalms call for consideration. In Psalm xvi. 10f. we have the words:

> For thou dost not give me up to Sheol,
> or let thy godly one see the Pit.
> Thou dost show me the path of life;
> in thy presence there is fulness of joy,
> in thy right hand are pleasures for evermore.

Here the Psalmist is expressing the conviction that with Yahweh as his guide he can tread the path of life in safety and that he has the unbounded joy of being close to Him for ever. He does not definitely formulate the doctrine of immortality, but it is the logical conclusion of his conviction that he can enjoy fellowship with Yahweh for ever. Psalm xvii. 15 declares:

> As for me, I shall behold thy face in righteousness;
> when I awake, I shall be satisfied with
> beholding thy form.

In this case everything depends upon the meaning of the words, 'when I awake'. They may refer to the awaking from sleep with a renewed sense of Yahweh's presence, or from death conceived as sleep. It is, therefore, doubtful if the doctrine of a future life can be found in the passage.

In Psalm xlix. 15, the author contrasts his own misfortunes with the prosperity of the wicked. Death shall shepherd the souls of the wicked down to Sheol.

> But God will ransom my soul from the power of Sheol,
> for he will receive me.

Here the words may mean that the righteous will be translated to heaven like Enoch (Gen. v. 24) and Elijah (2 Kgs. ii. 11), or that death will be abolished. No mention is made of the immortality of the wicked. Gunkel considers that the verse is a late addition, but Duhm sees in it a passage similar to that of Isaiah xxvi. 19 and Daniel xii. 2. The most significant passage is Psalm lxxiii. 23-25.

> Nevertheless I am continually with thee;
> thou dost hold my right hand.
> Thou dost guide me with thy counsel,
> and afterwards thou wilt receive me to glory.
> Whom have I in heaven but thee?
> And there is nothing upon earth that I desire besides thee.

In these words the Psalmist expresses his conviction that he enjoys constant fellowship with Yahweh—a fellowship which death cannot sever. Such a conviction inevitably leads to the belief in immortality.

Though the Psalms contain no definitely formulated belief in a future life, they illustrate the height to which faith was capable of rising under the sense of communion with Yahweh, and so they provide the fruitful soil out of which the doctrine of immortality was bound sooner or later to be developed. 'This conviction of a personal relation to God, independent of time and change, and not any particular theory as to the character of life after death, is the lasting contribution of the Old Testament to the doctrine of the future life.'[1]

THE ESCHATOLOGY OF THE PSALMS

The Enthronement Psalms

There are wide differences of opinion among scholars on the question of the Eschatology of the Psalms. As we have already indicated (see p. 103), there is, in Gunkel's classification of the Psalms, a group entitled the 'Enthronement Psalms' (xlvii, xciii, xcvi-xcix) because, he alleges, they were composed to celebrate the enthronement of Yahweh as the universal ruler of the world. These Psalms contain more than one of the characteristic features of Eschatology. The coming of Yahweh to rule over mankind is accompanied by the manifestation of His power in nature. He is girt about with storm-clouds. His lightnings lighten the world; the earth sees and trembles and the mountains melt like wax before His presence (xcvii. 1-5).

---

[1] C. F. Burney, *Israel's Hope of Immortality*, 1909, p. 104.

The manifestation of His power is also seen in the world of men—in the destruction of the enemies of Israel and in her exaltation to the dominant position among the nations. He is terrible. He has made all nations subject to Israel and returned to His sanctuary amid the shouts of acclamation and the sound of trumpets (xlvii. 1–5). He has won a marvellous victory, which has made it plain to all the world that He has remembered His steadfast love and faithfulness to the house of Israel. Again He has taken His seat upon the throne, robed in majesty, and now the world is firmly established and immovable. Again and again the floods have lifted up their angry voices, but He is mightier than the thunder of many waters and mightier than the waves of the sea (xciii. 1–4). In these Psalms we are told that Yahweh is a lover of justice (xcix. 4), and that 'He will judge the world with righteousness and the peoples with equity' (xcviii. 9), but there is no reference to a final judgment or to a Messiah.

If, as Gunkel maintains, the 'Enthronement Psalms' were composed to celebrate the enthronement of Yahweh as the ruler of all mankind, they must be interpreted in eschatological terms, even though some of the elements of Eschatology are absent from them.

Mowinckel rejects both the historical and the eschatological interpretation of the Enthronement Psalms.[1] In his view they were composed to form part of the ritual connected with an annual New Year Festival (see p. 104) and must be interpreted from this point of view. Though they are not eschatological, they are, however, the origin of Eschatology, for the day of Yahweh's enthronement in the festival was projected by the prophets into the future, and became the 'day of Yahweh' when He would come with power to assert His kingship over all mankind.

Other Psalms

Eschatological ideas can be found in other Psalms besides those classified as 'Enthronement Psalms' by Gunkel. In Psalm xxix Yahweh's power is manifested in the storm. His voice breaks the cedars of Lebanon, makes Lebanon skip like a calf and Sirion like a young wild ox, flashes forth flames of fire, shakes the wilderness, whirls the oaks, and strips the forests bare (vv. 5–9). He sits enthroned as king for ever (v. 10). In Psalm lxxvi He has established His abode in Zion and

---

[1] S. Mowinckel, *Psalmenstudien*, II. *Das Thronbesteigungsfest Jahwäs und der Ursprung der Eschatologie*, 1922.

from there He has destroyed His enemies (vv. 4–6).[1] The authors of Psalms i and vii express their belief in a final judgment (i. 5; vii. 7f.).

The Royal Psalms

As regards the belief in the coming of the Messiah to rule the earth as the viceregent of Yahweh, there are certain Psalms known as Royal Psalms because of the references in them to a human king. It has been customary to call these Psalms 'Messianic' because the king is always regarded as the 'Anointed' of Yahweh. Some modern scholars maintain that the Messianic interpretation cannot be sustained for the following reasons:

(1) The king mentioned in these Psalms is a reigning Hebrew king, not an ideal king of the 'last days'. Gunkel, for example, declares that these Psalms deal with a king who must be regarded as a native Israelite king of the pre-exilic period.

(2) It is known that the 'Anointed' was a common royal title in Israel (1 Sam. ii. 35; xii. 5; xvi. 6; xxiv. 7; 2 Sam. i. 14; 2 Chron. vi. 42).

(3) These Psalms were composed for use in religious ceremonies in which the king played a prominent part, such as those associated with his accession and coronation (ii), a royal marriage (xlv), his engagement in war (cxliv) and his return in triumph (xviii).

(4) The people expected great things from every new king, and when their expectations were not fulfilled they transferred them to an ideal ruler of the future. Hence though these Psalms are not Messianic in the usual meaning of the term, they are the soil from which the Messianic hope has grown.[2]

The view that none of the Royal Psalms is Messianic has not won universal acceptance. T. H. Robinson thinks that it is quite possible that Psalms ii, xviii and cxxxii, are Messianic,[3] while Rowley says of Psalm lxxii that it 'almost certainly has the Davidic Messiah in mind though he is not described as such'.[4]

PERMANENT INFLUENCE

The Psalms are important for the insight they give us concerning the spiritual life of the Hebrew community, more especially the pious

---

[1] Mowinckel includes Psalms xxix and lxxvi in the 'Enthronement Psalms'. According to his theory, therefore, they have no eschatological significance.

[2] H. Ringgren, *The Messiah in the Old Testament*, 1956, p. 21.

[3] T. H. Robinson, Chapter on 'The Eschatology of the Psalmists' in *The Psalmists*, ed. by D. C. Simpson, 1926, pp. 100–102.

[4] H. H. Rowley, *The Rediscovery of the Old Testament*, 1945, p. 195.

members of it, during several centuries of its history. After reading through them, we feel that we know the people of those far-off days intimately both in their strength and in their weakness. It is clear that they were overwhelmed with the sense of God. He was the Creator of the world and the Sustainer of all life upon it, the Controller of nature and the Lord of history. He was good to all, and His compassion was over all that He had made (cxlv. 9). To know Him and to possess Him was all that mattered.

> Whom have I in heaven but thee?
>   And there is nothing upon earth that I desire
>   beside thee.
> My flesh and my heart may fail,
>   but God is the strength of my heart
>   and my portion for ever. (lxxiii. 25f.)

They longed to enter into communion with Him. Their souls longed for Him, the living God, 'as a hart longs for flowing streams' (xlii. 1), and waited for Him 'more than watchmen for the morning' (cxxx. 6). Those who kept His testimonies and sought Him with all their hearts were blessed (cxix. 2). They loved His sanctuary, the place where His glory dwelt (xxvi. 8). A day in His court was better than a thousand elsewhere. They preferred to be doorkeepers in His house rather than dwell in the tents of wickedness (lxxxiv. 10). They were never tired of acknowledging His goodness (xxvii. 13; lxv. 11; lxxiii. 1) and expressing their trust in Him (xx. 7; xxxi. 6; xxxiv. 22; cxviii. 8; cxxv. 1). At the thought of His goodness and mercy the author of Psalm xcii declared,

> It is good to give thanks to the Lord,
>   to sing praises to thy name, O Most High;
> To declare thy steadfast love in the morning,
>   and thy faithfulness by night,
> To the music of the lute and the harp,
>   to the melody of the lyre. (xcii. 1f.)

They were conscious of their own powerlessness, and of the transitoriness of human life compared with His incomparable power and His eternity. Man was but dust (ciii. 14); his days were but a few handbreadths and as nothing in His sight (xxxix. 5). He had no more permanence than a dream, or the grass of the field which flourished in the morning and faded and withered in the evening (xc. 5f.). Moreover he had no hope of survival after death (not as we know it). Since life was so short and there was no hope of a blessed immortality, he clung to this life, desiring that Yahweh would bestow upon him prosperity and length of days (xxi. 4; cxv. 12-15; cxviii. 25).

The Psalms, especially the so-called Penitential Psalms (vi; xxxii; xxxviii; li; cii; cxxx; cxliii), show that the people were deeply conscious of their sins and of their need of forgiveness. In anguish of spirit they threw themselves upon the mercy of Yahweh in the assurance that He would forgive them, for with Him there was plenteous redemption (cxxx. 7; cf. ciii. 10-14).

The 'Imprecatory Psalms' (lviii; lix; lxix; lxxxiii; cix; cxxxvii) show that the people could hate as well as love, appeal to God for vengeance as well as for mercy, curse as well as pray. The author of Psalm cix cursed his enemy in the anguish of his spirit.

> May his days be few;
> > may another seize his goods!
>
> May his children be fatherless,
> > and his wife a widow!
>
> May his children wander about and beg;
> > may they be driven out of the ruins they
> > > inhabit. (vv. 8-10.)

The author of Psalm cxxxvii declared that he who dealt with Babylon as she had dealt with Judah would be blessed.

> O daughter of Babylon, you devastator!
> Happy shall he be who requites you
> > with what you have done to us!
>
> Happy shall he be who takes your little ones
> > and dashes them against the rock! (vv. 8f.)

The Psalms reveal the people as ardent patriots. Yahweh had destroyed their enemies, given them Canaan for their inheritance (cv. 11) and chosen Zion for His habitation (cxxxiii. 13). To them Canaan was a holy land, and Jerusalem was a holy city with a Temple in its midst where dwelt a holy God. Jerusalem was the city of the great King and the joy of all the earth (xlviii. 2). Yahweh would bless it abundantly, satisfying the poor with bread, clothing its priests with salvation, causing its saints to shout for joy and raising to honour a scion of the house of David to continue his line for ever (cxxxii. 15-17). Nothing would ever destroy their love for Jerusalem or erase the memory of it from their hearts. Even in exile their thoughts turned to their beloved city even though it was in ruins.

> If I forget you, O Jerusalem,
>   let my right hand wither!
> Let my tongue cleave to the roof of my mouth,
>   if I do not remember you,
>   if I do not set Jerusalem
>   above my highest joy! (cxxxvii. 5f.)

The Psalms have had a profound influence upon the lives of both Jews and Christians.

As regards the Jews we learn from the 'Mishnah', a collection of Jewish oral laws composed about A.D. 200, that the Psalms were used in the services of the Temple. The Levites used to sing one Psalm daily in the Temple (xxiv; xlviii; lxxxii; xciv; lxxxi; xciii; xcii). A levitical choir sang Psalm xxx when the first fruits were brought into the sanctuary and the Hallel (cxiii-cxviii) at the celebration of the Passover. The latter was also recited at the Feast of Tabernacles and at the Feast of Dedication. Little is said about the use of the Psalms in the liturgy of the synagogue. It is generally assumed, however, that part of the liturgy was taken over from the services of the Temple and that it included the employment of Psalms. The recitation or singing of the Psalms has continued in the synagogue down to the present day.

It was doubtless the employment of the Psalter by the Jews in the Temple and the synagogue that led to its introduction into the Christian Church. 'More than any other book in the Old Testament', says Davison, 'it has been baptized into Christ'.[1] That it was very popular in the early Church may be judged by the numerous quotations from it which appear in the New Testament. The singing or recitation of Psalms soon became common (Acts xvi. 25; 1 Cor. xiv. 26; Eph. v. 19; Col. iii. 16; Jas. v. 13). When Christian hymns were first introduced they were modelled on the Psalms. The Psalter was the first book which the early Church put into the hands of the young converts, and no man could be admitted to the highest order of the clergy unless he knew it by heart. During the Middle Ages the Psalter was

---

[1] W. T. Davison, *The Praises of Israel*, 1902, p. 2.

systematically recited in the monasteries. The great reformers of the sixteenth century found in it guidance, encouragement, comfort and inspiration. To-day the Psalms (with the exception of the Imprecatory Psalms) are sung or recited by Christians of all denominations in all parts of the world. Even when the Psalms themselves are not used, their thoughts and words have been appropriated so that some of the best-known hymns such as 'All people that on earth do dwell', 'The Lord's my shepherd I'll not want' and 'I to the hills will lift mine eyes' are but paraphrases of the Songs of the ancient Jewish Church.

The reason for the popularity of the Psalter in all branches of the Christian Church is not difficult to find. Man in his essential nature does not change: he can pass through no religious experience which has not found expression in the Psalms. 'The Psalms, then, are a mirror in which each man sees the motions of his own soul. They express in exquisite words the kinship which every thoughtful human heart craves to find with a supreme, unchanging, loving God, who will be to him a protector, guardian and friend. They utter the ordinary experiences, the familiar thoughts of men; but they give to these a width of range, an intensity, a depth and an elevation, which transcend the capacity of the most gifted. They translate into speech the spiritual passion of the loftiest genius; they also utter, with the beauty born of truth and simplicity, and with exact agreement between the feeling and the expression, the inarticulate and humble longings of the unlettered peasant. So it is that, in every country, the language of the Psalms has become part of the daily life of nations, passing into their proverbs, mingling with their conversation, and used at every critical stage of existence.'[1]

LITERARY MERIT

The Psalter is an anthology of Hebrew Poetry, comprising works which are the product of several centuries of literary development. Since they are the work of many writers belonging to different periods, they naturally vary in literary quality. Some are dull and commonplace in thought and expression, repetitious and lacking in emotional appeal, but most of them are highly imaginative, original in thought and expression and deeply moving in their appeal. Among the latter are a few, like xxiii, xc and cxxxix, which attain the level of the sublime.

The Psalms generally possess certain characteristics in common. They are not cold, artificial productions elaborated with great labour

---

[1] R. E. Prothero, *The Psalms in Daily Life*, 4th ed. 1920, p. 2.

Psalms (continued)

in the privacy of the study, but the spontaneous outpourings of hearts charged with deep emotions. With simplicity and sincerity the authors express their thoughts of God, their hopes and aspirations, their joys and sorrows, their doubts and fears, their confessions and thanksgivings.

Many of the Psalms reveal an intimate knowledge of nature and the power of graphic description on the part of the authors. To them the earth belonged to Yahweh, and so they saw it irradiated with something of His ineffable glory. Their eyes were open to the wonders of earth, sky and sea—the sun coming forth like a bridegroom, leaving his chamber, and running its course with joy like a strong man (xix. 5); the moon and the stars which were made to rule over the night (cxxxvi. 9); the sea, great and wide, teeming with innumerable things, both small and great (civ. 25); the storm, when the clouds poured out water, when the crash of Yahweh's thunder was in the whirlwind, when the lightning lit up the world, and the earth trembled and shook (lxxvii. 17f.); the mountains where the wild goats lived, and the rocks where the badgers found a refuge (civ. 18); the cattle grazing on the hills (l. 10); the desert where the vulture and the owl had their homes (cii. 6); the meadows clothed with flocks and the valleys decked with grain (lxv. 13); the grass that flourished in the morning and faded and withered in the evening (xc. 6); the trees planted by streams of water and yielding their fruit in their season (i. 3); the cedars of Lebanon where the birds made their nests, and the fir trees which were the home of the stork (civ. 17); the lions lurking in ambush (xvii. 12); the horse and the mule, which had no understanding and had to be curbed with bit and bridle (xxxii. 9); the wild asses quenching their thirst at the spring (civ. 10f.); the lonely bird on the housetop (cii. 7), and the swallow which had made its nest over the altar in the Temple (lxxxiv. 3).

The chief glory of the Psalms is the wealth of imagery, which is drawn from the landscape, or the home, or the daily occupations of the people in town or village, or the birds and animals. Apt similes and metaphors abound. Yahweh is round about His people 'as the mountains are round about Jerusalem' (cxxv. 2). He will make His enemies 'as a blazing oven' (xxi. 9). A thousand years in His sight 'are but as yesterday when it is past, or as a watch in the night' (xc. 4). He is represented as a 'shepherd', (xxiii. 1; lxxx. 1), a 'rock' (xix. 14; xxviii. 1), a 'sun and shield' (lxxxiv. 11), and 'a refuge and fortress' (xci. 2). His word is a 'lamp' to a man's feet and a 'light' to his path (cxix. 105). Judah is His 'sceptre' and Moab His 'washbasin' (cviii. 8f.). Personification is frequently employed. The floods are bidden to 'clap their hands and to sing for joy' (xcviii. 8). The earth is called upon to tremble at the presence of Yahweh (cxiv. 7) and Jerusalem to praise Him because He had strengthened the bars of her gates and blessed her sons (cxlvii. 12f.). Often a sentence is cast in the form of an exclamation,

(1) Oh, how I love thy law! (cxix. 97.)

(2) Behold, how good and pleasant it is
when brothers dwell in unity! (cxxxiii. 1.)

(3) How precious to me are thy thoughts, O God!
How vast is the sum of them. (cxxxix. 17.)

Use is made of several literary devices, such as the rhetorical question (xlii. 5; lxxxviii. 10; cxxxvii. 4), the imperative (lxxxi. 1; xcvii. 12; cxxxi. 3), repetition (xxix. 4f.; xcvi. 7f.; cxv. 12f.) and contrast (xxx. 5; civ. 27-30; cxxxix. 7-12).

CHAPTER IX

PROVERBS

TITLE AND PLACE IN CANON

The Hebrew title of the book is 'Mishle Shelomoh' (The Proverbs of Solomon), or simply 'Mishle' (Proverbs), which are abbreviations of the opening sentence, 'The Proverbs of Solomon, son of David, king of Israel'. In the Septuagint the title is 'Paroimiai Salomontos' or only 'Paroimiai', and in the Vulgate 'Liber Proverbiorum' or 'Proverbia', whence comes our English title. In the Hebrew Canon it is the second book in the 'Writings' and comes immediately after Psalms.

CONTENTS

The book is a compilation of several originally independent collections of which eight may be distinguished.

Outline

Chs. i–ix.	In praise of wisdom and virtue, and a warning against folly and vice.[1]
Chs. x. 1–xxii. 16.	The Proverbs of Solomon, consisting of 375 maxims in couplet form.
Chs. xxii. 17–xxiv. 22	The words of the wise.[2]
Chs. xxiv. 23–34.	Sayings of the wise.
Chs. xxv–xxix.	The 'Proverbs of Solomon which the men of Hezekiah, king of Judah, copied'.[3]
Ch. xxx.	'The words of Agur, son of Jakeh of Massa.'

[1] Ch. i. 1–6 is generally regarded as an introduction to the whole book, added by the atest compiler.

[2] Ch. xxii. 17 has the words, 'Incline your ear, and hear the words of the wise'. The Septuagint shows that this collection was originally headed, 'The words of the wise'.

[3] There are reasons for thinking that two separate collections, namely, xxv–xxvii and xxviii, xxix have been united, since in the last two chapters greater stress is laid upon the observance of the Law, while the religious element is much more prominent.

Ch. xxxi. 1–9.   'The words of Lemuel, king of Massa, which his mother taught him.'
Ch. xxxi. 10–31.   An acrostic poem in praise of the ideal wife.

Summary: Chs. i–ix

Ch. i. The purpose of the book is to teach wisdom (vv. 1–6). The sage tells a young man that reverence for Yahweh is the first thing in knowledge, and warns him against throwing in his lot with those who live by theft and murder (vv. 7–19). Wisdom (personified) warns the simple that because they have ignored her counsel, calamity will overtake them. The simple are destroyed by their own self-will, but those who listen to her will dwell securely and will be wholly free from harm (vv. 20–33).

Ch. ii. If the young man searches for wisdom as for hidden treasures, he will find out what the knowledge of God really means, for it is God alone who gives wisdom, but only to the upright whom He protects (vv. 1–8). He will understand righteousness and injustice and keep to every honest course, for wisdom will come into his heart, and sound judgment will save him from evil men and the loose woman whose house leads to death (vv. 9–19). The upright will inherit the land but the wicked will be rooted out (vv. 20–22).

Ch. iii. The sage exhorts the young man to listen to his teaching, to trust in Yahweh and to honour Him with his wealth and the first fruits of his produce, for then he will enjoy great prosperity, health, long life and happiness (vv. 1–10). The young man should not despise the discipline of Yahweh, for He reproves him whom He loves (vv. 11f.). Happy is the man who finds wisdom for no treasure can compare with her. She gives long life, honour, tranquil ease and peace (vv. 13–18). By wisdom, Yahweh created the world (vv. 19f.). The young man should hold to sound wisdom and discretion, for they will give him security (vv. 21–26). He should not refuse help to a neighbour if he has the power to give it, or quarrel with a man who has done no harm, or envy a man of violence. Yahweh's curse is on the house of the wicked, but He blesses the abode of the righteous. Wise men come to honour but fools get disgrace (vv. 27–35).

Verses 27–35 are totally different in style from the rest of the collection and are probably a later insertion.

Ch. iv. The young man is exhorted to get wisdom and discretion, for they will promote him and bring him to honour (vv. 1–9). He should not follow the road of evil men, who cannot eat unless they have done some wrong, eat ill-gotten food, and drink wine won by cruelty. Their way lies through the deep darkness, but the course of good men shines brighter and brighter to the full light of day (vv. 10–19). The young man should guard his inner-self, banish wayward words and adhere to the path of righteousness (vv. 20–27).

Ch. v. The young man is warned against following the loose woman whose lips drip honey but whose feet go down to death (vv. 1–6). He should keep clear of her lest he lose his honour, his position and his health, and live to be filled with remorse, regretting the day when he despised all warning and was nearly sentenced to death by the community (vv. 7–14). He should find the sources of his pleasure at home with his wife and should let her affection fill him at all times with delight. There is no reason why he should be infatuated with a loose woman and embrace an adventuress (vv. 15–20). The iniquities of the wicked ensnare him and he dies for lack of discipline (vv. 21–23).

Ch. vi. The young man is warned against going bond for a person (vv. 1–5), sloth (vv. 6–11) and the scandal monger (vv. 12–15). God hates haughty eyes, a lying tongue, hands that shed innocent blood, a mind with crafty plans, feet that make haste to run to evil, a false witness who breathes out lies and a sower of discord among brothers (vv. 16–19). The young man is warned against the adulteress and the loose woman's smooth tongue. The harlot may be hired for a loaf of bread but the adulteress preys upon a man's very life (vv. 20–26). A man cannot commit adultery with impunity. The thief is despised if he steals to satisfy his hunger, but he escapes further punishment by the payment of a fine. But the adulterer destroys himself, for he can never wipe out the disgrace or buy off a jealous husband, who will show no mercy in his revenge and accept no compensation (vv. 27–35).

The section, vi. 1–19, breaks the connexion between v. 1–23 and vi. 20–35 and is probably a later insertion.

Ch. vii. The sage advises the young man to observe his commandments and teachings that he may be preserved from the loose woman (vv. 1–5). The former describes how, dressed like a harlot, she meets a brainless youth in the street and by her blandishments lures him to her home. He follows like an ox going to the slaughter, not knowing that it will cost him his life (vv. 6–23). She has slain many a victim; her house is the way to Sheol, leading down to the chambers of death (vv. 24–27).

Ch. viii. Wisdom (personified) appeals to all men to learn sense and listen to her. Though all men are invited to listen to her, only those who love truth and righteousness can appreciate her message (vv. 1–9). All that men may desire cannot compare with her (vv. 10f.). Wisdom possesses prudence, knowledge, discretion, counsel, skill, insight and strength. It is by her that kings reign and rulers deal out justice (vv. 12–16). Those who seek her not only find her, but also gain prosperity and honour (vv. 17–21). Yahweh formed Wisdom as the first of all His works. She was beside Him at the creation of the world, rejoicing constantly before Him and delighting in mankind (vv. 22–31). He who finds her finds life and wins the favour of Yahweh, while he who ignores her injures himself (vv. 32–36).

Ch. ix. Wisdom has built her mansion and invited the simple and him devoid of sense to a feast (vv. 1–6). Instruction is wasted on the scoffer and the wicked man but bears fruit and increase in the wise. Reverence for Yahweh is the beginning of wisdom; this adds years to life. If a man is wise, he is wise for himself: if he scoffs, he alone will suffer for it (vv. 7–12). A foolish woman is wanton and knows no sense of shame. She invites the simple and him devoid of sense to her mansion, but they do not know that the dead are there, that her guests are in Sheol (vv. 13–15).

Verses 7–12 are disconnected maxims, apparently inserted by a later scribe, either to separate the two pictures of Wisdom and Folly, or because this was a convenient place for the preservation of this small collection.

Chs. x. 1–xxii. 16

Consists of 375 proverbs written in couplet form (except xix.7c which is clearly part of a lost couplet).

In chs. x–xv. the parallelism is mainly antithetic, and in xvi–xxii. 16 mainly synonymous or synthetic. Several proverbs are repeated in full or in part, either in identical form or with slight variations (e.g. x. 1 = xv. 20; x. 2 = xi. 4; xiv. 12 = xvi. 25).

Chs. xxii. 17–xxiv. 22

Consists of proverbs on various subjects arranged mainly in quatrains instead of couplets. Sometimes proverbs on the same subject, are developed into a larger unit. Ch. xxiii. 29–35, for example, is a short poem of five quatrains on 'the drunkard'. In it the young man is warned against the disastrous effects of intemperance, and is advised not to look on wine 'when it sparkles in the cup and goes down smoothly'.

The parallelism is synonymous or synthetic. Within the collection several proverbs are repeated in part, either in identical form or with slight variations (e.g. xxii. 23 = xxiii. 11; xxii. 28 = xxiii. 10; xxiii. 17 = xxiv. 1).

Ch. xxiv. 23–34

In these few verses there are three extended proverbs, the chief being that on 'idleness'. In it the sage describes how, passing by the field of the sluggard, he noticed that it was overgrown with thorns and nettles and that the wall was broken down. From its neglected condition he learned the lesson that sloth would reduce a man to poverty.

The parallelism is mainly synonymous or synthetic.

Chs. xxv–xxix

This collection, consisting of 137 proverbs, bears a close resemblance to the second collection. Couplets are numerous though not to the same extent as in the second collection. There are, however, extended proverbs of varying length, the chief being a poem of ten lines on the value of industry to the farmer (xxvii. 23–27). The farmer should look well to the condition of his flocks and herds, for riches do not last for ever. After the hay and after-growth have been harvested, the lambs will provide him with clothing and the goats with the price of a field and with ample milk for his household.

In xxv–xxvii, the commonest form of the couplet is the synthetic, while in xxviii–xxix. the antithetic couplet prevails. Throughout the collection are found proverbs wholly or partly identical with sayings in the second collection (e.g. xxv. 24 is verbally identical with xxi. 9 and xxvii. 13 with xx. 16, while similarities are to be found in xxvii. 21 and xvii. 3, and xxvi. 13 and xxii. 13).

Ch. xxx

A confession of scepticism (vv. 1–4) followed by an orthodox confession of faith (vv. 5f.), a prayer for sincerity and a moderate competency (vv. 7–9), a warning against the slander of a servant (v. 10), a description of four types of wicked men—the despisers of parents, the self-righteous, the proud and the extortioners (vv. 11–14), four insatiable things—Sheol, the barren womb, the earth ever thirsty for water, and fire that is never satisfied (vv. 15f.); the fate of the disobedient son (v. 17); four mysterious things—an eagle in the sky, a serpent on a rock, a ship on the high seas, and a man with a maid (vv. 18–20); four intolerable things—a slave who rises to be king, a fool who makes a fortune, an unloved woman who at last gets married, and a maid who supplants her mistress (vv. 21–23); four wise creatures—the ants, badgers, locusts and lizards (vv. 24–28); four stately things, the lion, strutting cock, he-goat, and a king striding before his people (vv. 29–31); a warning against haste in speech or action which produces strife (vv. 32f.).

Verse 17 is probably a gloss on v. 11 and v. 20 a gloss on v. 19f.

Ch. xxxi. 1–9

The king is warned against sensuality and intoxication, and exhorted to champion the cause of the poor.

Ch. xxxi. 10–31

The ideal wife is worth far more than jewels. She is an industrious housewife, working early and late to provide food and clothing for her family and servants, a keen business woman, buying land prudently and supplying linen garments and girdles to traders, and a friend of the poor and the forlorn. She talks shrewd sense and offers kindly advice. Her husband is a man of note and sits among the elders in council. Both he and his children sing her praises. Charms may fade and beauty wither, but she, as a woman of intelligence, is worthy to receive the admiration of the people.

In v. 30 the Revised Version has 'a woman that feareth the Lord', and the Revised Standard Version, 'a woman who fears the Lord', but the religious note has probably been introduced by a pious interpolator. The Septuagint has, 'a woman of intelligence'.

AUTHORSHIP

An early tradition ascribed the book to Solomon. This ascription was probably due to the fact that Solomon was famous for his wisdom. In 1 Kings iv. 29 we are told that God 'gave Solomon wisdom and understanding beyond measure', and in 1 Kings iv. 34 that 'men came from all peoples to hear the wisdom of Solomon, and from all the kings of the earth, who had heard of his wisdom', and in 1 Kings iv. 32

that Solomon was the author of 3,000 proverbs and 1,005 songs. The early Jewish tradition of Solomonic authorship was accepted by the Christian Church and survived until modern times, but is no longer tenable and has been abandoned for the following reasons.

(1) The book itself makes no claim to be entirely the work of Solomon. If we accept ch. i. 1–6 as an introduction to the whole book, added by the latest compiler, only two of the eight collections are attributed to Solomon, namely, chs. x–xxii. 16 and chs. xxv–xxix. It cannot be definitely proved that these two collections are from his hand. Some scholars believe that the title of the second collection (x–xxii. 16) was probably Proverbs. A scribe who copied out the book, found that it contained 375 proverbs. In Hebrew each letter has a numerical value; and since the letters of the name 'Solomon' add up to 375, the scribe assigned the collection to him. The fifth collection (xxv–xxix) assigns the proverbs to Solomon but states that they were copied by 'the men of Hezekiah, king of Judah.' The verb translated 'copied' is used in this sense only in late Hebrew. 'This superscription ... only bears testimony to the disposition, in later times, to ascribe all wise sayings to Solomon, and a special suggestion of Solomonic authorship may have been found in the mention of kings with which the collection opens.'[1] The sixth collection is attributed to Agur, the seventh to Lemuel and the eighth is anonymous.

(2) Many of the proverbs are unsuited to the character of Solomon, who was famous for his wealth and extravagance and had a large harem. It is difficult to believe that such a man would depreciate wealth (xi. 28; xv. 16), or praise monogamy (xii. 4; xviii. 22; xix. 14f.), or condemn his own government (xxix. 4).

(3) Ethical monotheism, which is taken for granted throughout the book, was not definitely taught until the time of Deutero-Isaiah.

(4) The social life depicted is that of a city rather than that of a semi-pastoral order of society. The sages deal chiefly with such subjects as kingly attributes (xvi. 10–15), conduct at court (xxv. 2–7), business affairs (vi. 1–5; xvii. 18; xx. 10, 14), fraud, violence, crime and vice (xxi. 6–8), immorality (v. 1–20; vii. 1–27), drunkenness and gluttony (xxiii. 20–35) and the oppression of the poor (xiv. 31; xxii. 22f.).

The book contains many late elements, but there is doubtless a certain amount of early material embodied in it, going back to the

---

[1] C. H. Toy, *A Critical and Exegetical Commentary on the Book of Proverbs*, 1914, p. 437.

days of Solomon and even earlier. Though it cannot be proved, it may well be that some of this earlier material originated with him.

DATE

The first collection (i–ix) is probably the latest of the book. It is not a collection of proverbs, but a series of loosely connected discourses on such subjects as crimes of violence (i. 10–19), the pleasures of wisdom (ii. 1–22), a warning against adultery (vi. 20–35), the wiles of a loose woman (vii. 6–23). The expansion of the proverb into a miniature essay is a mark of a late date. The personification of wisdom due to an increasing sense of God's transcendance (i. 20–33; iii. 13–20; iv. 5–9; viii. 1–ix. 6), the close affinity of the collection with *Ecclesiasticus*, and the presence of a certain number of late Hebrew words and expressions and of Aramaisms suggest the Greek period. It is usually assigned to the fourth or third century B.C. The presence, however, of many words and grammatical constructions of Ugaritic and Phoenician origin in the collection make it certain that a certain amount of material dating back to early times is embodied in it.

The consensus of opinion is that the second collection (x–xxii. 16) is the oldest in the book and that it belongs to the pre-exilic period. This view rests on the following considerations. Normally each verse is an independent and self-contained couplet, which is the earliest form of the proverb. There is evidence for the existence of a class of the 'wise' in pre-exilic days (Is. xxix. 14; Jer. xviii. 18), and it is reasonable to assume that some of these saying would be preserved. There are frequent references to a king or kings, which are thought by some scholars to indicate the Israelite kings, suggesting that the monarchy was still in existence when the collection was made. Other scholars, however, maintain that the references to kings do not necessarily demand a pre-exilic origin.[1] The date of the collection cannot be determined precisely. Gressmann and Oesterley assign it to about 750 B.C., while Pfeiffer, who holds that it is improbable that any collections of maxims were made before 600 B.C., assigns it to the fourth century B.C.

Chapters xxii. 17–xxiii. 14 of the third collection (xxii. 17–xxiv. 22)

---

[1] G. B. Gray (*A Critical Introduction to the Old Testament*, 1913, pp. 145ff.) shows that the king is mentioned in other wisdom books besides *Proverbs*, namely *Ecclesiastes* (iv. 13–16; v. 9; viii. 2–4; x. 16, 17, 20) and *Ecclesiasticus* (vii. 4f; viii. 2; x. 3), and suggests that none of the references necessarily demands a pre-exilic date. R. H. Pfeiffer (*Introduction to the Old Testament*, 1948, p. 659) holds that it is a fallacy to regard proverbs about the king as *ipso facto* pre-exilic. A. Bentzen (*Introduction to the Old Testament*, vol. II, p. 173), asserts that in *Proverbs* we cannot use the references to kings as criterion of pre-exilic date since Wisdom literature has always spoken of kings.

PROVERBS 139

is an adaptation of the Egyptian Wisdom book, *The Teaching of Amen-em-ope*, which probably belongs to the eighth or seventh century B.C. There are close verbal parallels, the most striking of which is the phrase in xxii. 20, formerly translated 'excellent things'. The Egyptian text reads, 'Consider these thirty chapters'. It is now generally recognized that the Hebrew should read 'thirty (sayings)'. The date of this collection can hardly be earlier than the seventh century B.C., and may be much later, since the Egyptian Wisdom book may not have been utilized till long after its composition.[1]

The fourth collection (xxiv. 23–34) is closely connected with the third and may be assigned to about the same period.

Most scholars now accept the tradition that the fifth collection (xxv–xxix) was compiled by 'the men of Hezekiah, king of Judah' (c. 715–687 B.C.). In general character it closely resembles the second collection. Like the latter it employs the isolated couplet though they are not so common. An attempt is made to group the sayings according to subject. Thus, xxv. 1–7 deals with conduct at court, xxvi. 3–12 with the senseless fool, xxvi. 13–16 with the sluggard and xxvi. 23–26 with the false flatterer. The presence of these continuous pieces indicate a later stage of literary development. The collection also contains numerous references to kings, but as we have already shown, they do not necessarily demand a pre-exilic date.

The dates of the sixth, seventh and eighth collections (xxx, xxxi. 1–9; xxxi. 10–31) respectively, cannot be determined. The confession of scepticism (xxx. 2–4), the numerical form (xxx. 15–31) and the alphabetic acrostic poem (xxxi. 10–31) seem to indicate the post-exilic period.

Assuming that the book as a whole did not grow by successive stages, and that the first of the eight collections comprising it (i.e. i–ix) is the latest and dates from the fourth or third century B.C., it cannot be earlier than 400 B.C. It cannot be later than about 200 B.C. since it is known to Ben Sirach, who in Ecclesiasticus xlvii. 17 refers to Proverbs i. 6. We shall not be far wrong if we assign it to about 250 B.C.

THE PUPILS OF THE SAGES

The sages directed their teaching mainly to the 'fools' of society. In Hebrew several words are used for 'fool' and it is difficult to give the precise meaning of each. In Proverbs we find the following:

---

[1] Many scholars hold that xxiii. 13f. is borrowed from *The Proverbs of Ahikar* (c. 550–500 B.C.). If their view is correct, then the collection must be post-exilic. But there is no proof that xxiii. 13f. is dependent on *The Proverbs of Ahikar*.

Pethī. The simple or ignorant man who cannot avoid danger (xxvii. 12), and believes everything that is told him (xiv. 15). He falls a victim to evil (xxii. 3) and naturally inclines towards folly (xiv. 8). He may be taught both good and evil and both wisdom and folly appeal to him (viii. 5; ix. 4, 6, 16). He may be taught prudence by sound teaching (i. 4) or by seeing the corporal punishment of the scorner (xix. 25).

Kesīl. The dull, stupid coarse man, who has a glib tongue which is his ruin (xviii. 7). He hates knowledge (i. 22), has no pleasure in understanding (xviii. 2) and no desire to acquire wisdom (xvii. 16). It is not fitting for him to live in luxury (xix. 10) or to receive honour (xxvi. 1, 8). The lash is his lot (xix. 29) though it will have little effect upon him (xvii. 10).

Ewīl. He is very similar to the Kesīl. He despises wisdom (i. 7) which is too high for him (xxiv. 7). He is easily angered (xii. 16) and it is useless to argue with him (xxix. 9). He cannot be cured of his folly (xxix. 9) and dies for lack of sense (x. 21).

Chāser Lēb. The man without sense (vii. 7f.).

Lētz. The scoffer or scorner who will never discover wisdom (xiv. 6) for he delights in scoffing (i. 22). He insults his rebukers (ix. 7), is arrogant (xxi. 24) and the cause of discord (xxi. 10). He is an abomination to men (xxiv. 9) and scorned by Yahweh (iii. 34).

Nābāl. The churlish and ignoble man, lacking all sense of decency and honour. From him one would never expect to hear fine speech (xvii. 7). In 1 Samuel xxv. 25 he is described as a man who is a churl by name and a churl by nature, and in Psalm xiv. 1 as a man who says that there is no God.

TEACHING

God

Monotheism is taken for granted throughout the book. Yahweh is omnipotent. No wisdom, no understanding, no counsel can avail against Him (xxi. 30). His presence is everywhere. His eyes are in every place, keeping watch over the evil and the good (xv. 3); even Sheol and Abaddon are within His field of vision (xv. 11). He is the Creator of the world (iii. 19f.; viii. 22–31) and of man (xiv. 31; xx. 12; xxii. 2) who is under His complete control. Even kings are under His authority. 'The king's heart is a stream of water in the hand of the Lord; he turns it wherever he will' (xxi. 1). He not only controls the thoughts (xvi. 1) and deeds (xvi. 9; xx. 24) of men, but also tests their hearts. 'The crucible is for silver, and the furnace is for gold, and the Lord tries hearts' (xvii. 3). He knows them better than they know themselves. 'All the ways of a man are pure in his own eyes, but the Lord weighs the spirit' (xvi. 2). The ways of God are mysterious and His nature beyond man's comprehension (xxv. 2; xxx. 1–4).

Man and Sin

Man, who is the creation of God, is prone to evil. Often he chooses a path which seems to be right but ends in ruin (xiv. 12). The corruption of the human heart is universal: no man can say that he is free from sin (xx. 9). The word 'conscience' is not mentioned but its presence in man is recognized. It is described under the metaphor of 'the lamp of the Lord' which flashes through his inmost soul. 'The spirit of man is the lamp of the Lord, searching all his innermost parts' (xx. 27). The chief sins which men commit and which are abominations and hateful to God, are pride, lying, mischief-making, sowing discord, impure thinking, the use of false weights and measures, murder and adultery. God is merciful to those who confess and forsake their transgressions. 'He who conceals his transgressions will not prosper, but he who confesses and forsakes them will obtain mercy' (xxviii. 13). But there are limits to His forbearance. Those who reject the counsel of Wisdom and spurn her warnings will find no mercy in the day of their calamity. They will call upon her, but will only hear her mocking laughter, 'because they hated knowledge and did not choose the fear of the Lord' (i. 29). From Yahweh men get justice (xxix. 26).

Retribution

From man Yahweh demands righteousness of life. 'Trust in the Lord with all your heart, and do not rely on your own insight' (iii. 5; cf. xvi. 3; xxii. 19; xxix. 25). Man's lips must speak 'what is right' and his heart must 'continue in the fear of the Lord all the day' (xxiii. 16f.). On the one hand Yahweh loves those who pursue righteousness (xv. 9), delights in their prayers (xv. 8), shields them from harm (ii. 8; xxx. 5), bestows upon them prosperity, riches, honour and life (iii. 9f.;

xxi. 21; xxii. 4) and blesses their habitations (iii. 33). His love for them is seen even in His chastisement (iii. 11f.). On the other hand, the wicked with their evil thoughts, lying lips, and wicked ways are loathsome to Him. His curse lies upon their houses (iii. 33) and their days are shortened (x. 27). The punishment of the wicked and the reward of righteousness are well brought out in the following passage.

> What the wicked dreads will come upon him,
>   but the desire of the righteous will be granted.
> When the tempest passes, the wicked is no more,
>   but the righteous is established for ever.
>
> The fear of the Lord prolongs life,
>   but the years of the wicked will be short.
> The hope of the righteous ends in gladness,
>   but the expectation of the wicked comes to nought.
> The Lord is a stronghold to him whose way is upright,
>   but destruction to evil-doers.
> The righteous will never be moved,
>   but the wicked will not dwell in the land. (x. 24f., 27–30.)

Ethics

The ethical stand set forth in the book is universally recognized to be high. There are proverbs advocating honesty and truthfulness in public and private life (ii. 21; viii. 6–9; xi. 1–3; xxi. 3, 28), respect for life and property (i. 10–15; xxi. 6f.), diligence in business (xxii. 29), kindness to man (iii. 3) and animals (xii. 10), the care of the poor and needy (xiv. 31; xix. 17; xxxi. 9), and the forgiveness of enemies (xxiv. 17f.; xxv. 21f.). Other proverbs extol love and condemn hatred (x. 12; xv. 17) and the taking of revenge (xx. 22; xxiv. 29). Again, other proverbs contain warnings against immorality (v. 1–14; vi. 20–35; xxiii. 26–28), drunkenness and gluttony (xx. 1; xxiii. 20f.; 29–35; xxxi. 4f.), and idleness (vi. 6–11; x. 4f.; xii. 24; xiii. 4; xv. 19; xxi. 25). Woman is given a higher position than in any other book of the Old Testament. A wife is prized (xviii. 22; xix. 14), marriage is a covenant (ii. 16f.) and monogamy is directly taught (v. 18f.). With her husband she takes part in the education of their children (i. 8f.). In the family she occupies as important a position as the husband and has the power to make or mar family life (xii. 4; xxvii. 15f.; xxxi. 10–31).

Wisdom

All wisdom comes from God who alone possesses it fully. 'For the Lord gives wisdom; from his mouth come knowledge and understanding' (ii. 6). His wisdom is manifested in the creation of the world (iii. 19f.; viii. 22–31) and of man (xiv. 33; xvii. 5; xxii. 2). Wisdom is conceived as the companion and helper of God in the creation of the world (viii. 22–31).

The mysterious and unfathomable wisdom of God is beyond man's reach but he can acquire a portion of it, sufficient to enable him to lead the good life. It is a gift of God, bestowed not upon all men indiscriminately, but only upon those who earnestly seek it. Wisdom is represented as a woman who calls aloud in the public places, warning the simple of the consequences of refusing to follow her counsel and assuring them of the benefits to be derived from it (i. 20–33; viii. 1–21). She has built her mansion and sent her maids to call the simple to the banquet which she has prepared for them.

> Come, eat of my bread
> and drink of the wine I have mixed.
> Leave simpleness and live,
> and walk in the way of insight. (ix. 5f.)

The wisdom of God is also manifested in history, but this aspect of it is brought out especially in the uncanonical Wisdom books, such as Ecclesiasticus and The Wisdom of Solomon.

Immortality

There is no doctrine of immortality in the book. Sheol is taken for granted (i. 12; ii. 18f.; v. 5; vii. 27). At death the shades of all men, both good and bad, go down to Sheol, a place of darkness beneath the earth, where they live a dreary, shadowy existence, cut off from all relations with the living and from communion with Yahweh. But a growing experience of communion with Yahweh would naturally lead a few choice spirits to more advanced views regarding life beyond the grave. In xv. 11 Sheol and Abaddon are said to lie open before Yahweh, that is, He is in some way concerned with the underworld and its inhabitants. In the same passage reference is made not just to death alone, but to the stern punishment that awaits the man who has forsaken the way of Yahweh. In other words, Sheol seems to be taking on a moral aspect.

PERMANENT INFLUENCE

Proverbs is probably one of the least known of all the books of the Old Testament, but it has, nevertheless, exercised considerable influence in the history of both Jews and Gentiles. It supplies a certain amount of information regarding the activities of a class of teachers known as 'wise men'. We gather that they were deeply religious men, with an exalted moral standard, who sincerely desired to promote the welfare and happiness of mankind. It reflects the teaching of the canonical prophets, showing that they had not laboured in vain. By stressing the necessity of observing the Law (vi. 23; xix. 16; xxviii. 4, 7, 9) it helped to make Judaism the religion of a sacred book (the Pentateuch). Throughout the book monotheism is taken for granted, showing that by the time it was written heathenism had been finally vanquished. Its ethical standard is a noble one. Its teaching on loving one's enemies is hardly transcended in the New Testament, and is an advance on that of a spiritually minded man like Jeremiah, who never reached the stage where he could find it possible to forgive his enemies (Jer. xi. 20; xv. 15; xvii. 18; xviii. 23; xx. 12) or that of Ben Sirach who warned his readers never to trust an enemy (Ecclus. xii. 10). Its teaching that education must be based upon religious foundations (i. 7; ix. 10; xv. 33), that the strength of a nation depends upon the character of the people composing it (xiv. 34; xxv. 5f.) and that religion and morality are indissolubly united (ii. 1–20) is as relevant to-day as when it was first enunciated.

The book had considerable influence on the writers of the New Testament, and even on our Lord Himself who wrote nothing (see p. 76).

As literature the book has had some slight influence on the English language. It contains many idiomatic expressions, some of which have been introduced into our language and are in common use to-day, though most of the people who use them are unaware of their origin. Among them may be mentioned, 'a crown of glory' (xvi. 31), 'a soft answer' (xv. 1), 'a word in season' (xv. 23), 'coals of fire' (xxv. 22), and 'throw in your lot' (i. 14). Many English proverbs are also based upon it. For example, 'It's a poor heart that never rejoices' is based on 'A glad heart makes a cheerful countenance' (xv. 13), 'Knowledge is power' on 'A wise man is mightier than a strong man, and a man of knowledge than he who has strength' (xxiv. 5), and 'Like master like man' on 'If a ruler listens to falsehood, all his officials will be wicked' (xxix. 12).

LITERARY MERIT

The book is poetic in form like Psalms and Job but it cannot compare with them as literature. It lacks inspiration, imagination and intensity of feeling, which are characteristics of great poetry. Almost all the verses are composed of couplets which are either independent and self-contained or grouped together to form sections, each dealing with a particular theme. The style of the isolated couplets is condensed, abrupt, forcible and sometimes obscure, while that of the sections is smoother and more flowing. The short epigrammatic sentences, the constant use of parallelism, and the numerous repetitions tend after a time to become monotonous. Occasionally the sections form charming short poems, such as those on, 'In Praise of Wisdom' (iii. 13-20), 'The Sluggard' (vi. 6-11), 'Against Drunkenness' (xxiii. 29-35) and 'Four Small Things' (xxx. 24-28).

The frequent use of apt similes and metaphors adds vividness and beauty to many of the couplets.

Simile

> But the path of the righteous is like the light of dawn,
>   which shines brighter and brighter until full day. (iv. 18.)

Metaphor

> Wisdom is a fountain of life to him who has it,
>   but folly is the chastisement of fools. (xvi. 22.)

Added force is sometimes given to sayings by the use of various literary devices, such as the following:

The Imperative

> Buy truth, and do not sell it;
>   buy wisdom, instruction, and understanding. (xxiii. 23.)

The Rhetorical Question

> A man's steps are ordered by the Lord;
>   how then can man understand his way? (xx. 24.)

Repetition

> A little sleep, a little slumber,
>   a little folding of the hands to rest,
> and poverty will come upon you like a robber
>   and want like an armed man. (xxiv. 34.)

Contrast

> He who guards his mouth preserves his life;
> he who opens wide his lips comes to ruin. (xiii. 3.)

Occasionally a touch of humour is present.

> Like a gold ring in a swine's snout
> is a beautiful woman without discretion. (xi. 22.)

> Do not withhold discipline from a child;
> if you beat him with a rod, he will not die. (xxiii. 13.)

CHAPTER X

JOB

TITLE AND PLACE IN CANON

JOB takes its name from the man whose history it records. In the Hebrew Canon it comes third in the 'Writings', immediately after Psalms and Proverbs, while in the Septuagint it is reckoned among the historical books and placed after Chronicles and before Psalms. In the English versions, following the arrangement which ultimately prevailed in the Vulgate, it stands between Esther and Psalms. In the Syriac version—the Peshitta—it comes immediately after Deuteronomy, probably owing to the tradition of its Mosaic authorship.

CONTENTS

Outline

Chs. i, ii. The Prologue, recording how Satan is allowed by God to test the sincerity of Job's religion by overwhelming him with calamity, and how three friends come to comfort him.

Ch. iii. Job bewails his birth and longs for death.

Chs. iv–xxvii. Three series of debates between Job and his friends on the cause of the former's sufferings.
   (a) First series. Eliphaz, iv. v, Job, vi, vii; Bildad, viii, Job, ix, x; Zophar, xi, Job, xii–xiv.
   (b) Second series. Eliphaz, xv, Job, xvi, xvii; Bildad, xviii, Job, xix; Zophar, xx, Job, xxi.
   (c) Third series. Eliphaz, xxii, Job, xxiii, xxiv; Bildad, xxv. 1–6, xxvi. 5–14, Job, xxvi. 1–4, xxvii. 1–6, 11f.; Zophar, xxvii. 7–10, 13–23.

Ch. xxviii. The search for wisdom.

Chs. xxix–xxxi. Job reviews his former prosperity and happy days and contrasts them with his present misery, clears himself of certain flagrant sins and calls on God to state the charges against him.

Chs. xxxii–xxxvii. Elihu sets forth the doctrine that suffering is a discipline, and proclaims that God is great in power, yet not unjust.

Chs. xxxviii–xli (omitting xl. 3–5). God calls on Job to consider the divine power revealed in nature and his own insignificance.

Chs. xl. 3–5, xlii. 1–6. Job's submission.

Ch. xlii. 7–17. The epilogue, recording the divine censure of the three friends and Job's restoration to prosperity.[1]

Summary: *Chs. i, ii.*

Job is a perfectly righteous man with a large family and great possessions (i. 1–5). In a heavenly council the Satan insinuates that his piety depends upon the blessings bestowed upon him, and is allowed by God to put him to the test. Job is deprived of his family and possessions and smitten with a painful disease, but he resists the temptation to renounce God and die. Three friends come to comfort him (i. 6–ii. 13).

Ch. iii

Job curses the day of his birth and the night of his conception (vv. 1–10). Why did he not die at his birth and enjoy the quiet and rest of Sheol (vv. 11–19)? What he dreads comes upon him and he knows neither quiet nor rest (vv. 20–26).

Chs. iv–xxvii

Chs. iv, v. Eliphaz is surprised that Job should collapse at the touch of trouble. His religion and his blameless life should give him confidence. He should remember that it is only the wicked who are destroyed by God (iv. 1–11). Eliphaz has learnt in a vision of the night that no man can be accounted righteous before God. After a brief life man dies unnoticed without having attained wisdom (iv. 12–21). It would be futile for Job to appeal to the angels against God for it would mean his death. The foolish come to an evil end through im-

[1] For the rearrangement of the text, see notes on the relevant chapters.

patience. Trouble does not come without a cause (v. 1–7). Job would do far better to commit his cause to God who controls nature and mankind (v. 8–16). He should accept the chastening of the Almighty, who will deliver him from trouble and bestow upon him prosperity, long life and a peaceful death (v. 17–27).

Chs. vi, vii. Job replies that his lament is justified by the intensity of the pain which God has inflicted upon him. He loathes his afflictions and longs for death, for he cannot endure his sufferings (vi. 1–13). In his despair he had looked to his friends for kindness but had been bitterly disappointed. He had not asked them for a gift or protection. Their arguments are worthless; they should understand that they are censuring the wild words of a desperate man. He appeals to them to give him a fair hearing because his cause is just (vi. 14–30). He complains about man's hard service on the earth, and appeals to God to remember the brevity of his life and that he will go down to Sheol, never to return (vii. 1–10). He asks why God should pay so much attention to an insignificant creature like man, testing him continually and never taking his eyes off him. If he has sinned it cannot hurt Him. Why, therefore, does He not forgive him before death overtakes him? (vii. 11–21.)

Ch. viii. Bildad declares that God is not unjust. If Job is righteous and will appeal to God, He will restore him to greater prosperity than before (vv. 1–7). If he questions the men of bygone ages, they will teach him that God does not reject a blameless man or uphold the wicked (vv. 8–22).

Chs. ix, x. Job maintains that man is unequal to the task of stating his case before God, since He is all-wise and all-powerful and none can question His actions (ix. 1–12). If he were to cite Him to appear He would force him, though blameless, to condemn himself. Injustice reigns throughout the earth and God is responsible for it (ix. 13–24). Job complains that his life is hastening to its close without his seeing good, and that God is determined to condemn him. God and he cannot meet on equal terms and there is no umpire to enforce his decision upon them. If God would not afflict and terrify him he would speak without fear (ix. 25–35). Job asks God what He has against him, His own handiwork and innocent. He has bestowed upon him life and love yet all the while purposing to destroy him. He assails him no matter whether he is guilty or innocent. Why then was he born? Let God give him a brief respite before he passes into the darkness of Sheol (x. 1–22).

Ch. xi. Zophar replies that if God were to meet his challenge, He would show him that He was punishing him less than he deserved (vv. 1–6). It is foolish of him to think that he can discover the deep things of God or reach the Almighty's range of wisdom. He sees guilt and trains a worthless creature to be wise (vv. 7–12). If Job repents, a life of blessedness will be his portion, but as for the wicked there is no escape except in death (vv. 13–20).

Chs. xii–xiv. Job mocks the wisdom of his friends. It is natural for those in pleasant circumstances to despise the unfortunate. Robbers prosper and those who provoke God are secure (xii. 1–6). The animals and the earth know that God rules over nature and mankind. We should not accept all the teaching we hear, even though given by the aged, but discriminate (xii. 7–12). Wisdom and might belong to God and none can undo His work. He overthrows the mighty and turns the wisest into fools (xii. 13–25). Job would reason with God. His friends bring unfair arguments for God and lie on His behalf. All their maxims and arguments are worthless (xiii. 1–12). At the risk of his life he will plead his cause before God, confident of his innocence. He desires two things, namely, that God will release him from pain and that He will not terrify him (xiii. 13–22). He demands to know the charges brought against him, and why God pursues one so insignificant and frail and rakes up the sins of his youth (xiii. 23–28). Man's life is brief and full of trouble. God should cease tormenting him that he may make the most of the time left to him (xiv. 1–6). Man dies and will never awake (xiv. 7–12). If only God would hide him in Sheol until His wrath were spent and then remember him! If only man might die and live again, he would gladly wait until God should once more desire His servant, release him, watch over him and forget his sin (xiv. 13–17). But man dies and henceforth knows nothing about his dear ones on earth, but is conscious only of his own pain (xiv. 18–22).

Ch. xv. Eliphaz reproves Job for undermining religion (vv. 1–6). He is not primeval man who listened in the council of God: he is no more informed than his aged friends. He is carried away by passion and turns angrily on God. No man is pure before God (vv. 7–16). The wise men have taught that the wicked man suffers torment all his life and comes to an untimely end (vv. 17–35).

Chs. xvi, xvii. Job wishes to hear no more 'windy words' from his miserable comforters (xvi. 1–6). God has made a savage onslaught against him in spite of his innocence (xvi. 7–17). Job has, however, a witness in heaven (i.e. God) to whom he appeals to uphold his right,

JOB 151

and to grant him a pledge that he will vindicate his honour, for soon he must die. God has made him a byword among the people and reduced him to the last extremity. Upright men are so appalled at his calamities that they rouse themselves against the godless; but the righteous man does not falter but grows ever stronger (xvi. 18–xvii. 9). Job's heart is broken and all that he can hope for is a home in Sheol (xvii. 10–16).

Verses 8f. of xvii are rejected by many scholars as interrupting the flow of Job's lament, and as contradicting his assertion that men regard him with abhorrence.

Ch. xviii. Bildad refuses to be considered as foolish as a beast, and asks Job if he imagines that the world will be deranged for his sake (vv. 1–4). The wicked shall be destroyed and his house made accursed; his memory shall perish and his posterity shall be cut off, while men shall be appalled at his fate (vv. 5–21).

Ch. xix. Job rebukes his friends for tormenting him (vv. 1–5). It is God who has unjustly afflicted him, blocking and darkening his path, stripping him of honour, robbing him of hope, and treating him as an enemy (vv. 6–12). His friends, his family and even his servants have forsaken him; children despise him, friends abhor him and his body is decaying (vv. 13–20). He appeals to his friends to have pity on him (vv. 21f.). He wishes that his words might be engraved in the rock for ever. But he knows that his Vindicator lives and that after his death he shall, without his flesh, see God on his side—no longer estranged (vv. 23–27). The slanders of his friends will inevitably bring punishment upon them (vv. 28f.).

Ch. xx. In reply Zophar declares that the joy of the wicked is brief (vv. 1–5). His children will be reduced to poverty; he will be forced to disgorge his ill-gotten wealth and will vanish like a dream (vv. 6–11). He will be destroyed by the poison of his own wickedness; his prosperity will not endure, and a fire that no man lit will consume him and his possessions. This is the wicked man's portion from God (vv. 12–29).

Ch. xxi. Job requests the attention of his friends (vv. 1–6). Some wicked men prosper all their lives and die in peace, yet they deliberately denounced God. Only a few of them are overwhelmed by calamity (vv. 7–18). God should punish the wicked, not their children of whose sufferings they would have no knowledge after death. It is foolish to attempt to teach wisdom to God (vv. 19–22). He does not differentiate between men. All men, both rich and poor, die (vv. 23–26). Travellers tell how the wicked man is spared calamity rests peacefully in the tomb and has many imitators. It is futile for his friends to offer him their idle consolations since all they urge is false (vv. 27–34).

Ch. xxii. Eliphaz replies that since God has no interest or pleasure in his righteousness he cannot punish him for his piety. It is obvious that Job must be a great sinner (vv. 1–5). Because of his innumerable sins panic has seized him and he is overwhelmed by calamities (vv. 6–11). He thinks that God cannot see the deeds of men on earth, and that he can, therefore, tread the path which evil men took long ago. They renounced God but perished to the joy of the righteous (vv. 12–20). If Job submits humbly to God he will be restored to communion with Him, his life will be prosperous and even the guilty will be saved through his innocence (vv. 21–30).

Chs. xxiii, xxiv. Job still rebels though he tries to repress his complaints. He would like to lay his case before God but cannot find Him (xxiii. 1–9). God knows his ways, and when He has tested him he will come forth as gold, for he has never disobeyed His commands. God does what He likes and terrifies him (xxiii. 10–17). Job asks why God has not set times of judgment (xxiv. 1). Evil men seize the property of others and drive their wretched victims into hiding. Though the wounded and dying groan, God takes no heed (xxiv. 2–12). There are those who shun the light—the murderer, the thief and the adulterer (xxiv. 13–17). The wicked are swept away and their greatness is no longer remembered (xxiv. 18–21). God preserves the lives of the mighty and watches over them; they are exalted a little while and then are cut off like the ears of corn (xxiv. 22–25).

Verses 18–21 of xxiv do not express the views of Job, since they assert the punishment of the wicked. The Revised Standard Version attributes the words to Job's friends by prefixing the words 'You say'. The verses are possibly misplaced and belong to Bildad's speech in xxv or are a later interpolation.

Ch. xxv. 1–6, xxvi. 5–14. Bildad replies that God wields a dread authority. He keeps the peace in His high heaven. His armies are innumerable and nothing is hid from Him. Man cannot be pure in His sight (xxv. 1–6). Before Him the primeval giants tremble and Sheol lies open to His gaze. He is the Creator and Upholder of the world. His voice made the pillars of heaven tremble. He quelled the sea by His power, smote the Dragon by His wisdom, cleared the sky by His breath and pierced the fleeing serpent with His hand. All this is the mere fringe of His force, the faintest whisper we can hear of Him. No one knows the full thunder of His power (xxvi. 5-14).

It has been suggested that xxv. 4-6 is a gloss since it repeats with slight variation the words of Eliphaz (xv. 14-16, cf. iv. 17-21). Ch. xxvi. 5-14 is generally thought to be the conclusion of Bildad's speech.

Chs. xxvi. 1-4, xxvii. 1-6, 11f. Job speaks sarcastically of the help and instruction which Bildad has given. He must have been inspired (xxvi. 1-4). Job swears by God that he speaks the truth. He will not admit that his friends are right in their accusations against him, but will maintain his innocence unflinchingly (xxvii. 1-6). He will teach them how God's power works. They have seen it for themselves and should not be so foolish as to deny it (xxvii. 11f.).

Ch. xxvii. 1 is probably a later insertion.

Ch. xxvii. 7-10, 13-23. Zophar wishes that his enemy may fare like the wicked (vv. 7-10). The children of a wicked man are destroyed, his wealth is taken from him, and he is swept to destruction by God (vv. 13-23).

Zophar does not speak in the third debate. Most scholars ascribe these verses to him on the ground that Job would not assert the miserable fate of the wicked. Verses 21-23 are omitted in the Septuagint.

Ch. xxviii

Wisdom is unattainable by man. Precious metals are found in the earth by man, who sinks a shaft into the darkness below and reaps the harvest of wealth just as a farmer reaps the harvest of grain. He cuts channels in the rocks and brings to light the hidden treasure (vv. 1-6, 9-11). No bird of prey knows the path to wisdom and no wild beast has trodden it. Man does not know the path to it, nor can it be found in the land of the living. The deep does not possess it; it cannot be purchased for it is priceless (vv. 12, 7f., 13-19). Abaddon and Death have heard but a rumour of it. It is God alone who knows its home. At the Creation He studied (or created) it, and declared that for man to fear Him was wisdom and to shun evil was knowledge (vv. 20-28).

Many scholars regard v. 28 as a later addition, since the poet has denied wisdom to all but God. If the verse is retained it must mean that the fear of God is the only wisdom that man can attain.

Chs. xxix–xxxi

Job reviews his former happy days when God's favour rested upon him. He was blessed with a happy and prosperous family, respected by young and old and influential in the assembly. His smile encouraged them and his decision was their law (xxix. 1–10, 21–25). He was praised for his benefactions to the needy and for his championship of justice. He naturally looked forward to a long, untroubled life (xxix. 11–20). He is derided by his juniors who are nothing more than wretched outcasts (xxx. 1–8). They loathe and persecute him because God has forsaken him (xxx. 9–15). Now he is tormented by a horrible disease. God assails him and means to destroy him. Instead of receiving sympathy such as he extended to others, evil has overtaken him and his music has turned to wailing (xxx. 16–31). He clears himself of sensual desires, falsehood, deceit, covetousness and adultery (xxxi. 1–12). He has treated his servants fairly, helped the poor, the fatherless and the beggar. He has not oppressed the orphan, relying on his influence with the judges (xxxi. 13–23). He has not placed his confidence in wealth or worshipped the sun and moon, or hated his enemy, or been inhospitable, or concealed his sins for fear of public opinion (xxxi. 24–34). He wishes that God would give him His indictment, for then he would come into His presence and declare his innocence (xxxi. 35–37). He has never violently dispossessed others of their land (xxxi. 38–40).

Many scholars regard xxx. 1–8 as a misplaced section of the description of the outcasts in xxiv. 5ff. Duhm treats v. 1 as an insertion, designed to connect vv. 2–8 with their present context. Peake allows it to stand; this is perhaps better as v. 9 seems to require some introduction. The passage xxxi. 38–40 is undoubtedly out of place. It is generally agreed that originally it stood in a different part of the chapter. Moffatt places it immediately after v. 22.

Chs. xxxii–xxxvii

Elihu intervenes because Job has made himself out to be more righteous than God, and because the three friends have failed to refute him (xxxii. 1–5). He had not intervened previously because he was young and the three friends were old. But wisdom comes by the direct inspiration of the Almighty; it is not always the old who are wise and understand what is right. Elihu is full of ideas and feels that he can sit silent no longer. He will not favour or flatter any man (xxxii. 6–22).

He invites Job to reply for he is a man and not God (xxxiii. 1–7). Job has affirmed that he is innocent, and that God persecutes him and will not answer him (xxxiii. 8–13). God answers man in two ways, namely, through dreams and through severe illness. If an angel intercedes for him, he is restored to perfect health, renews his communion with God and proclaims before men his own sins and God's grace. God does this again and again to bring him from death into the sunshine of life (xxxiii. 14–30). Job should continue to listen to Elihu unless he has anything to say in self-defence (xxxiii. 31–33). His assertion that God has dealt unjustly with him is blasphemous (xxxiv. 1–9). God cannot do wrong for He rewards every man according to his works. He is no viceroy lording it on the earth but the supreme ruler; if He were to withdraw His spirit the human race would perish (xxxiv. 10–15). One cannot condemn a just and mighty God, in whose sight kings and nobles are wicked men and who is no respecter of persons. He has no need of fixed seasons in order to bring men to justice, for He smites the mighty without trial for abandoning His ways (xxxiv. 16–28). If He did nothing, no one had the right to complain. Job's trials should continue for he adds rebellion to his sin (xxxiv. 29–37). Elihu argues that neither man's sin nor his righteousness can injure or profit God (xxxv. 1–8). Men cry out for help because of the oppression of the wicked, but they do not enquire of God, who can turn their sorrow into joy and make them wiser than beast or bird. They appeal to God in vain for He does not hear an idle cry. Job argues that because He does not strike in anger He is not serious about sin, and so he utters foolish and empty words (xxxv. 9–16). Elihu asserts that he will defend the righteousness of God for he speaks with perfect knowledge (xxxvi. 1–4). God is mighty but despises none. He does not preserve the wicked but exalts the righteous. If he afflicts men it is for their instruction; if they repent they prosper, but if not they perish (xxxvi. 5–14). God saves the afflicted by affliction and opens their ears to His teaching. Job's wide freedom and prosperity have brought him the full doom of the wicked. He has chosen sin rather than affliction (xxxvi. 15–21). God is exalted in power and no one can command or criticize Him. Job should extol His work in creation. He produces rain, distributes the clouds, sends thunder and lightning, judges and blesses the nation and hurls the lightning to its mark. The thunder speaks of His anger blazing against iniquity (xxxvi. 22–23). Elihu trembles at the flash of the lightning and the roar of the thunder. God sends snow and rain; storms blow from the south and cold winds from the north, and ice is formed by His breath. He fills the clouds with moisture and scatters the lightning, either smiting with a curse or bestowing a blessing (xxxvii. 1–13). Job cannot comprehend the wonderful works of God—the flash of the lightning, the poising of the clouds, the heat and stillness that accompany the sirocco, and the mirror-like sky. Men with their darkened minds cannot argue with Him. They cannot even gaze on the dazzling sun. The majesty of God is terrible and men should fear Him (xxxvii. 14–24).

Duhm omits xxxvi. 10 and places vv. 15–17 between vv. 9 and 11. Ch. xxxvi. 31 breaks the connection between vv. 30 and 32 and may be a later insertion. It would be more in place after v. 28.

Chs. xxxviii–xli (omitting xl. 3–5)

Yahweh, answering Job out of a storm, challenges him to the contest which he has so often demanded (xxxviii. 1–13). By a series of questions He makes Job realize that he knows nothing about the inanimate creation—the founding of the earth, the taming of the sea, and the fixing of its boundaries (xxxviii. 4–11), the coming of the dawn (xxxviii. 12–15), the depths of the abyss, the realm of death and the breadth of the earth (xxxviii. 16–18), the abodes of light and darkness (xxxviii. 19–21), the storerooms of snow and hail (xxxviii. 22f.), the mysteries of wind, lightning, thunder, rain and ice (xxxviii. 24–30), the movements of the constellations and the laws which govern the heavenly bodies (xxxviii. 31–33), the control of rainfall and lightning (xxxviii. 34f.), the numbering of the clouds and the pouring down of the rain (xxxviii. 36–38). By a similar series of questions Yahweh makes Job realize that he knows nothing about the animate creation—the hungry lions lying in wait for their prey and the young ravens clamouring for food (xxxviii. 39–41), the mountain goats and the hinds calving at their appointed times (xxxix. 1–4), the untamable wild ass and wild ox (xxxix. 5–12), the thoughtless ostrich (xxxix. 13–18), the fiery war-horse that smells the battle from afar (xxxix. 19–25), the migratory hawk and the high-soaring sharp-eyed eagle (xxxix. 26–30). Yahweh invites Job to answer His questions (xl. 1, 2). Will he condemn God to justify himself? Is he as powerful as God? If he can prove himself the equal of God in majesty and power, then Yahweh will admit that Job can save himself (xl. 6–14). Yahweh calls Job's attention to two animals, behemoth and leviathan. Behemoth has enormous strength and is at home both on land and in the water. No one has assailed him and been safe (xl. 15-24, xli. 9-12). Leviathan is unconquerable and will not serve anyone (xli. 1-8). No one can penetrate his double coat of mail or open his jaws with their terrible teeth. He is covered with scales, inseparably fitted together; fire and smoke pour from his mouth and nostrils; he makes the sea boil and leaves behind him a shining wake. He has no rivals and is the king of all the beasts (xli. 13-34).

Ch. xli. 9-12 forms a suitable conclusion to the description of behemoth and is placed by Duhm and Peake after xl. 24.

Chs. xl. 3-5, xlii. 1-6. Job acknowledges his insignificance and will speak no more (xl. 3-5). He admits that he has spoken of things he did not understand. Having now seen God he repents in dust and ashes (xlii. 1-6).

As the text stands there are two speeches of Yahweh, namely, (a) xxxviii. 1-xl. 2 and (b) xl. 6-xli. 34, and two confessions of Job, namely, (a) xl. 3-5 and (b) xlii. 1-6. There is almost universal agreement that xl. 3-5 is misplaced and should be taken immediately before xlii. 1-6 (omitting xlii. 1), since Yahweh in His second speech ignores Job's confession and continues to rebuke him, and then Job confesses once only. Hence the second divine speech, xl. 6-xli. 34, should be regarded as the conclusion of the first, xxxviii. 1-xl. 2 (omitting xl. 1).

Ch. xlii. 7-17

Having spoken to Job, Yahweh censures the three friends for not speaking the truth about Him and commands them to offer up a burnt offering. Job shall intercede for them and they shall not be punished as they deserve (vv. 7-9). Job is restored to prosperity and his possessions are doubled. He has seven sons and three daughters, lives to see his descendants to the fourth generation and dies an old man after a full life (vv. 10-17).

LITERARY FORM

Many attempts have been made to fit the book into a particular literary category but without success. It has often been classed with the Wisdom Writings, but according to Gray and Driver it differs from them in three respects, namely, (1) in its combination of prose and poetry, (2) in its use of dialogue and (3) in its sustained treatment of a single theme. Milton called it an epic poem, but it does not satisfy the definition of an epic as a poem describing the deeds of one or more heroes in an elevated style. The style is certainly lofty and inspiring, but the action is not physical but spiritual. Since the action takes place in the soul, some call it a spiritual epic, but Literature knows nothing of such a category. Because of the use of dialogue in the poem the term drama has been applied to it. But there is no action and no cut and thrust in debate; any attempt to present it on the stage would be foredoomed to failure. It is not a lyric poem for it is much too long to be classed as such, nor is it a didactic poem for there is no direct attempt at edification. It may be readily conceded that the poem contains epic, dramatic, lyrical and didactic elements, but it cannot be assigned to any particular literary category. The poem is unique—the only one of its kind.

PURPOSE

The author's main purpose in writing the book was to reconcile the suffering of the righteous with the existence of a just God. The problem of suffering was first concerned with the nation before it touched the individual. The prophets of the eighth century B.C. proclaimed that calamity would inevitably fall upon the people if they disobeyed the commandments of Yahweh. Amos warned them that because they were His people He would visit upon them all their iniquities (iii. 2). He was raising up the Assyrians against them (v. 27, vi. 14): the 'day of the Lord', which they constantly expected, would be 'darkness and not light, and gloom with no brightness in it' (v. 20). Hosea declared that they had sowed the wind and would reap the whirlwind (viii. 7). Micah predicted that Yahweh would execute judgment upon them because of the sins of Samaria and Jerusalem (i. 2–9). Isaiah proclaimed that Yahweh would 'raise a signal for a nation afar off', that is, Assyria (v. 26), to punish Israel for her iniquities, for 'he looked for justice, but behold bloodshed; for righteousness, but behold a cry!' (v. 7). The theory of retribution first found full expression in the Deuteronomic Code (c. 621 B.C.), which declared that the people had made a covenant with Yahweh by the terms of which they would be blessed or cursed according as they obeyed or disobeyed the divine will (xxviii). The theory was applied by the writers of the Deuteronomic school as an interpretative principle in editing the historical records of Israel. Until towards the close of the seventh century B.C. the suffering of the individual raised no problem since his personality was merged in the life of the nation. 'The individual's share in the common suffering of the nation, brought upon it by its corporate wickedness, did not raise any problem. For the Hebrew recognized the solidarity of society to a much greater extent than is characteristic of ourselves. He was carried in the tide of the nation's life, and his fortunes were involved in the fortunes of society.'[1]

With the growth of individualism in the late pre-exilic period the thinkers of Israel began to turn their attention to the problem of the suffering of the individual. Jeremiah was puzzled at the prosperity of the wicked.

> Righteous art thou, O Lord, when
> I complain to thee;
> yet I would plead my case before thee.
> Why does the way of the wicked prosper?
> Why do all who are treacherous thrive? (xii. 1.)

He could find no justification for his own suffering since he had done no wrong. 'Why is my pain unceasing, my wound incurable, refusing to be healed?' (xv. 18.) He usually held the doctrine of corporate responsibility, but looked forward to the time when no man should suffer for the sins of others (xxxi. 29f.). Habakkuk could not reconcile the suffering of the innocent with the existence of a righteous God.

> Thou art of purer eyes than to behold evil
> and canst not look on wrong,
> why dost thou look on faithless men,
> and art silent when the wicked swallow up
> the man more righteous than he? (i. 13.)

He came to the conclusion that the righteous man would live by his steadfastness, that is, his moral steadfastness, in the assurance that Yahweh would ultimately triumph over evil.

The destruction of Jerusalem (587 B.C.) and the Exile probably hastened the process of the recognition of the individual. In captivity the exiles complained that Yahweh was unjust in punishing them for the sins of the fathers, but Ezekiel declared that they should no more have occasion to quote the proverb, 'The fathers have eaten sour grapes, and the children's teeth are set on edge' (xviii. 2), for no man was punished for the sins of others. 'Behold, all souls are mine; the soul of

---

[1] H. H. Rowley, *The Rediscovery of the Old Testament*, 1945, p. 128.

the father as well as the soul of the son is mine: the soul that sins shall die.' (xviii. 4.)

By the close of the Exile the problem of undeserved suffering must have become acute. The orthodox doctrine that God rewarded the righteous and punished the wicked could no longer be accepted without question, for observation and experience showed that there was a vast amount of undeserved suffering in human life which could not be reconciled with the existence of a righteous God. The problem was all the more acute because there was no belief in a real after-life. It was believed that at death the man's shade descended to Sheol, where it lived a shadowy existence cut off from communion with God and mankind. Since there was no hope of compensation in this life the justice of God must be vindicated on earth. It is not surprising that the orthodox view was challenged by the courageous thinkers of Israel, and that they attempted to find a solution of the problem. Deutero-Isaiah taught that suffering could be vicarious and redemptive (liii). The author of Malachi, answering those who were constantly complaining about the prosperity of the wicked, declared that the day was coming when the wicked would be destroyed, but that on those who feared Yahweh the sun of righteousness would arise with healing in its wings (iv. 1f.). The author of Psalm xlix affirmed that both the righteous and the wicked died but that the righteous alone had the prospect of immortality. The author of Psalm lxxiii, who had cleansed his heart and washed his hands in innocence, almost lost his faith when he saw the prosperity of the wicked, but in the sanctuary the truth flashed upon him that the wicked perished while the righteous found joy in unbroken communion with God.

It is in Job that we find the most thorough attempt to reconcile the suffering of the righteous with the existence of a just God. The three friends of Job were representatives of the orthodox doctrine that calamity was a punishment for sin, Eliphaz appealing to revelation, Bildad to tradition and Zophar to common sense. Eliphaz suggested the further view that suffering might be not only a punishment for sin, but also a discipline sent by God. Elihu, a young man who intervened in the debate, added little to it. Like the three friends he believed that all suffering was due to sin, but also stressed the view that sin might be disciplinary to purge the heart of pride, which was Job's sin. Job, however, rejected the orthodox view as inadequate. There was no necessary connexion between sin and suffering. He himself was conscious of no sin yet he was suffering. There were numerous examples of the wicked prospering and escaping trouble all their lives. The only logical inference must be that God, at least so far as human intelligence could ascertain, was omnipotent but unjust. The Almighty did not answer Job's charge of His injustice in the moral government of the world and especially in His treatment of him. Instead He directed Job's thoughts to His infinite power and wisdom as manifested in the wonders of creation. The only conclusion to be drawn from the divine speeches was that since the wonders of the physical world were beyond man's comprehension, he could not expect to understand the mystery of suffering. The presence of evil in the world was not explained but Job was no longer a rebel. Face to face with God and overwhelmed by the thought of His infinite power and wisdom, he acknowledged his ignorance and calmly submitted to the divine will. His doubts were dispelled and his tortured spirit found rest, not because he had found a satisfactory answer to the problem of suffering, but because he had had a vision of God and henceforth was content to walk by faith.

UNITY

It is now almost universally recognized that the book is not a literary unit.

Prologue and Epilogue

Many scholars think that the prologue and the epilogue come from a different hand from the dialogue, chiefly for the following reasons.

(1) The prologue and the epilogue are written in prose and the dialogue in poetry.

(2) There is a marked difference in the use of the divine names. The name 'Yahweh' is frequently used in the prologue and the epilogue, while it is studiously avoided in the dialogue where we find 'El' thirty-three times, 'Eloah' thirty-three times and 'Shaddai' twenty-four times.[1]

(3) In the prologue it is stated that all Job's children had been killed (i. 18f.), while in the dialogue they are represented as still living (xix. 17).

(4) In the epilogue God declares that Job had spoken rightly (xlii. 7), but in the dialogue He accuses him of making dark the divine plan of the world (xxxviii. 2).

---

[1] The name 'Yahweh' is found in the redactional superscriptions of the divine speeches and in Job's answers, and once in the dialogue (xii. 9), but it is generally considered to be an oversight of the author or an error of a copyist.

(5) In the epilogue Job is rewarded for his righteousness, whereas in the dialogue he is represented as rejecting the orthodox view of retribution.

The cumulative effect of the arguments is strong but not convincing. According to Bentzen, for example, 'the postulated differences between the narrative and the dialogue are not strong enough to account for a separation'.[1] The prose narrative contains statements in poetry (e.g. i. 21; ii. 9f.), while even its prose at times has a stately rhythm. In the dialogue the narrative introductions to the various speeches are in prose (cf. iii. 1; iv. 1; xxxii. 1-6; xxxviii. 1; xl. 1, 3, 6). A linguistic comparison of the prose narrative and the dialogue reveals numerous similarities between the vocabulary and grammar of the two sections. It is quite natural that Job's three foreign friends should use more general Semitic terms for God, and that Job in addressing them should use these more general terms. In Job xix. 17 the phrase, 'the children of my womb' (or 'body') could refer to the womb of his mother because he emerged from it. The Revised Version has 'the children of my mother's womb', and the Revised Standard Version 'the sons of my own mother'. It is true that Job is condemned in the dialogue and commended in the epilogue, but the condemnation and commendation are not on the same issue. He is condemned for making dark the divine plan of the world and commended for having stood the test of the Satan and for having vindicated God's trust in him. 'It would have been intolerable to leave him still in the hands of the Satan. No longer would this have been the test of Job, but mere malice and vindictiveness. A human court which left a defendant to languish in gaol after a verdict of acquittal would be denounced as unjust. Job was acquitted, and therefore he must be delivered from his misfortunes since they are the form his trial takes.'[2]

In Ezekiel xiv. 14, 20 reference is made to three righteous men, Job, Noah and Daniel, who, had they been alive, could not have saved Jerusalem from destruction. Many scholars believe that in the pre-exilic period there existed a book containing a popular story giving an account of a righteous man named Job, and that the author of our book took over the introduction and conclusion of this 'Volksbuch' and used them as the framework of his poem, working them over and inserting certain passages to make the framework and the poem more

---

[1] A. Bentzen, *Introduction to the Old Testament*, Vol. ii, 1948, p. 175.
[2] H. H. Rowley, Lecture on 'The Book of Job and its Meaning' in the *B.J.R.L.*, Vol. 41, No. 1, September 1958.

suitable to each other (ii. 11–13; xlii, 7–10a), or to harmonize his own bitter, defiant Job with the patient, submissive Job of the legend (i. 22; ii. 10). Some scholars agree that there is little reason to doubt that such a story was in existence, but maintain that the author of our book took from it nothing more than its fundamental elements—the scene in which the story is laid, the righteousness of Job, his endurance under affliction and the names of the characters. The weight of the evidence is insufficient to prove the truth of the theory that the author of our book borrowed the whole or part of the prologue and the epilogue from a folk-tale and adapted them as a framework for his poem.

A few scholars hold that the prologue and epilogue are later additions and that the dialogue preceded them. It is, however, hard to believe that the dialogue ever circulated independently. Without the prologue there is no setting for the dialogue. From the prologue we learn how the Satan, the prosecuting angel, was allowed by God to test His servant Job, first by depriving him of his family and his possessions, and then by smiting him with a painful disease, how in his misery he refused to curse God and die, and how three friends came to visit him. Without the epilogue the book would be left unfinished, for we should not know whether Job withstood the test and vindicated God's trust in him. W. B. Stevenson suggests that in later times the dialogue was felt to be incomplete and perhaps not wholly intelligible without the prose additions, and that those familiar with the folk-tale may reasonably have thought that part of it at least was worthy of preservation. A preference for a happy ending and a wish to encourage virtue in distress, may also have helped to accomplish the union of the prose narratives and the dialogue.[1] The theory that the prologue and the epilogue of our book are later additions cannot be substantiated and is mere conjecture.

N. H. Tur-Sinai suggests that the prologue and the epilogue are later than the dialogue, but that they may have replaced a lost older framework.[2] There is no evidence to prove that the dialogue had a different beginning and ending. No trace of a different setting has survived.

Elihu Speeches

It is almost certain that the Elihu speeches (xxxii–xxxvii) are no part of the original work. The main arguments advanced against their genuineness are as follows.

---

[1] W. B. Stevenson, *The Poem of Job*, 1947, p. 86.
[2] N. H. Tur-Sinai, *The Book of Job*, 1957, p. 31.

(1) Elihu is not mentioned either in the prologue or the epilogue. The fact that no reference is made to him in the prologue is of little consequence, but we should expect his name to be mentioned in the epilogue when judgment is passed on Job and his friends.

(2) His speeches interrupt the argument; they follow immediately after xxxi in which Job appeals to God to answer him, and the divine reply is found in xxxviii–xli.

(3) His speeches elicit no reply from Job and no notice is taken of him in the divine speeches.

(4) In the epilogue God commends Job and condemns Eliphaz, Bildad and Zophar, but completely ignores Elihu.

(5) He adds nothing new to the discussion. The three friends also believed that Job's sufferings were due to sin, and Eliphaz had taught the doctrine of the disciplinary character of suffering.

(6) The style of the speeches is inferior to that of the rest of the dialogue. 'It is', says S. R. Driver, 'prolix, laboured and often tautologous. The power and brilliancy which are so conspicuous in the poem generally are sensibly missing.'[1]

(7) The language is more strongly marked by Aramaisms and uses words which rarely or ever occur elsewhere in the dialogue.

A few scholars, notably Budde and Cornill, defend the authenticity of the Elihu speeches on the ground that they contain the author's solution to the problem, which is that suffering is divinely sent to purge the heart of pride. But pride is mentioned only twice by Elihu (xxxiii. 17; xxxvi. 9), while in the prologue there is no hint of any such weakness in Job. He is portrayed as a perfectly upright man who was afflicted not to purge his heart of pride, but to vindicate God's trust in him. Hence Elihu's solution is irrelevant to the book.

Poem on Wisdom

Most scholars agree that chapter xxviii on Wisdom is an independent poem which had no connexion with the original work. It is apparently spoken by Job, but it is not appropriate to the speech he is making nor is it a reply to the arguments of the previous speaker. If part of the previous chapter is Zophar's missing speech, then chapter xxviii follows without any introduction, but it is not appropriate to Zophar. If Job has reached the position where he recognizes the inscrutable wisdom of Yahweh, the divine speeches (xxviii–xli) expressing the same idea are irrelevant.

[1] S. R. Driver, *Introduction to the Literature of the Old Testament*, 9th ed., 1913, p. 429.

First Divine Speech

A few scholars reject the first divine speech (xxviii–xl. 2) on the grounds that (1) it contributes nothing material to the discussion of innocent suffering which is the theme of the dialogue, and (2) it is inconsistent with the epilogue; in the former Job is rebuked and in the latter he is declared to be in the right. The arguments advanced for its rejection are unconvincing. It is hard to believe that a literary genius would leave the dialogue in suspense with Job's protest of innocence. As regards the inconsistency between the speech and the epilogue, the difference of judgment is not on the same issue. In the epilogue Yahweh declares that Job has been right in maintaining his innocence in face of the charge made against him by the Satan, while in the speech he is rebuked for criticizing Yahweh whose ways are beyond man's comprehension. The language and style of the speech closely resemble those of the dialogue. It is hard to believe that a late writer could, as a literary artist, equal and at times surpass the author of the dialogue.

Second Divine Speech

The general consensus of opinion is that the descriptions of behemoth (xl. 15–24, xli. 9–12) and leviathan (xli. 1–8, 13–34), which appear in the second divine speech (xl. 6–xli. 34), are late insertions for the following reasons. (1) They are irrelevant, adding nothing material to the discussion of innocent suffering; (2) other creatures are briefly described in Yahweh's first speech, but the descriptions of behemoth and leviathan are much longer and contain a disproportionate amount of material. Fourteen lines are given to the former and no less than thirty to the latter. The descriptions of the two creatures attain a high literary standard, but they are not on the same level as that reached in the first divine speech. If the speech is omitted Job's words in xl. 4f. and xlii. 2–6 become a single speech of submission.

CONFUSIONS

In the judgment of scholars there is a certain amount of confusion in the dialogue arising from omissions, misplacements and later additions (apart from those already mentioned), and various attempts have been made to reduce the confusion to order by rearranging certain passages, excising others, and ascribing others to different speakers. It is generally agreed, for example, that xxvii. 7–10 and xxvii. 13–23 should be assigned to Zophar, not as in the text to Job, since the latter in these verses abandons his own view and adopts that of his friends.[1]

FOREIGN INFLUENCES

It is claimed that the book shows dependence upon foreign literature. Some scholars believe that the author was familiar with the philosophical dialogues of Plato and imitated their form. But Driver and Gray argue that the differences between the long and set poetical dialogues of the Hebrew book and the quick responses of the closely knit analytical prose arguments of the Greek dialogues are too great to indicate dependence.[2] A resemblance has been traced between the book and the *Prometheus Bound* of Aeschylus, but there is no evidence of any connexion between the two.

An Edomitic origin is claimed for the book. According to Pfeiffer, 'the folk tale, which furnished the plot, the geographical, social and natural background, the philosophy and the language of the book are characteristically Edomitic'.[3] Lindblom thinks that the original work was Edomitic.[4] While it is true that there is a strong Edomitic influence in the author's background, there is no definite proof that he himself was an Edomite. It is quite possible that he was a Jew born in the south of Judaea, near the border of Edom, where he would become familiar with the geography and culture of that country.

In the Babylonian Wisdom literature there is preserved in a series of cuneiform tablets a poem known as the *Babylonian Job*, because in some of its ideas and expressions it is said to resemble our book. The tablets on which the poem is inscribed belong to the seventh century B.C., but the poem was composed much earlier. The poem records the story of a good man, Tabi-utul-Bel, who was sorely afflicted, mocked by his friends, and ultimately restored to health and strength by his god Marduk. The differences, however, are more striking than the resemblances. Our book is specifically Hebrew with its pure monotheism in contrast with the polytheism of the Babylonian poem. In the latter the sufferer, unlike Job, admits his sin, and the purpose of the story is not to show that sin is inevitably punished, but to discover how the sufferer had offended his god. The names of the persons, the geography, and the rank of the sufferer are different. The Babylonian

---

[1] A. S. Peake, 'Job,' in *The Century Bible*, 1904, p. 33.
[2] S. R. Driver and G. B. Gray, *Job*, 1921, p. xxiv.
[3] R. H. Pfeiffer, *Introduction to the Old Testament*, Rev. ed. 1948, p. 682.
[4] J. Lindblom, *La Composition du livre de Job*, 1945, pp. 3ff.

poem is a monologue not a dialogue or a combination of prose and poetry. The differences are too great to admit of any dependence.¹

Resemblances have been found between our book and an Egyptian Wisdom book of the second millennium B.C., called *The Dialogue of a Misanthrope with his own Soul*. It describes the sufferings and doubts of the author, a poor man who longs for death as a man longs to see his home again after many years spent in captivity. Here again the differences between the two stories are so great as to rule out any idea of dependence. It is possible, however, that the sages of the three countries, Palestine, Babylon and Egypt, were familiar with the story of a suffering Job, which had been handed down in the Near East with local variations from early times.

It is claimed that there are parallels between our book and the ancient classics of India. The latter tell of a pious king who gave up his kingdom to a sage and fell into dire poverty, but was eventually restored to his throne by the intervention of the gods. There is, however, no proof of any connexion between our book and this ancient story.

THE DATE

The date of the book cannot be determined with precision. It was once supposed that the book was one of the earliest books in the Old Testament, probably because the Babylonian Talmud (Baba Bathra, 14b, 15a) stated that 'Moses wrote his own book, and the passages about Balaam and Job'. This view, however, is no longer tenable and has been abandoned.

External Evidence

The external evidence is of little value in determining the date of the book. It was in existence about 180 B.C., for a passage from the

¹ Since the discovery of the *Babylonian Job*, other texts dealing with the problem of human suffering have been brought to light. The text of a Sumerian poem, inscribed on tablets discovered at Nippur during excavations there, have recently been translated. The tablets belong to about 1700 B.C., but the poem was composed much earlier, perhaps as early as 2000 B.C. In the poem a wealthy, wise and righteous man was suddenly overwhelmed with sickness and suffering. He did not doubt the justice of his god or defy him. Instead he came humbly before him and prayed for mercy. As a result his god answered his prayer, delivered him from his misfortunes and turned his sufferings into joy (see article on 'Man and his God', by S. N. Kramer in *Wisdom in Israel and in the Ancient East*, ed. by M. Noth and D. Winton Thomas, 1955, pp. 170–182).

The text of a poem, also recording the story of a righteous sufferer, has recently been discovered in a seventh-century temple near Harran. The poem has been dated towards the close of the second millennium B.C. (See W. G. Lambert and O. R. Gurney, *Anatolian Studies*, 4, 1954, pp. 65–99; and W. von Soden, *Bibliothica Orientals*, 10, 1953, pp. 8–12.)

Greek historian Aristeas implies familiarity with a Greek version of it, and with Elihu as a person in the story. Ben Sirach in Ecclesiasticus xlix. 10 (c. 180 B.C.) alludes to Job as a person mentioned in Ezekiel (c. 180 B.C.), but this is no proof that he knew of our book.

Internal Evidence

The internal evidence is stronger and suggests that the book belongs to the post-exilic period.

(1) Although Job is represented as living in the patriarchal age (i, ii), it must not be inferred that the book was written at that time. The conditions depicted are the creation of the author's imagination or taken from Genesis. He set the story in the patriarchal age and depicted the conditions which he judged to be characteristic of that age. The references to various classes of society (xxiv, xxx. 1–8), an established system of judicial procedure (xxxi. 9–11, 26–28), judgment at the gate (xxix. 7, xxxi. 21), the law (pledges, xxii. 6, xxiv. 9; vows, xxii. 27; landmarks, xxiv. 2) indicate a much later period.

(2) The writer seems to be familiar with national catastrophes, such as the destruction of Samaria by the Assyrians in 722 B.C. and that of Jerusalem by the Babylonians in 587 B.C. (iii. 18ff.; vii. 1; ix. 24; xii. 6f., 17–25; xxiv. 12).

(3) There is a close resemblance between Job iii. 3–10 and Jeremiah xx. 14–18, and it is highly probable that the priority is on the side of the prophet. It is extremely difficult to believe that Jeremiah, who was not, like the writer of Job, composing an elaborate imaginative work, would borrow his ideas from Job. Again Job vii. 17 is a parody of Psalm viii. 4, but it cannot be used as evidence since the date of the Psalm cannot be fixed.

(4) The central problem of the book could not have been discussed before the emergence of the teaching of Jeremiah and Ezekiel on the value of the individual. The national problem was raised before the personal one.

(5) It presupposes a lofty monotheism, indicating a later stage than that found in Deutero-Isaiah.

(6) Its angelology is post-exilic (see pp. 273f.).

(7) The inwardness of its ethics indicates a time later than Jeremiah's prophecy of the New Covenant.

(8) In the book 'the Satan' is a title borne by a particular spirit whose duty it was to discover the sins of men and to oppose their

claims to righteousness before God. He is practically identical with 'the Satan' in Zechariah iii. 2 (520–518 B.C.), where he is condemned by Yahweh for his zeal in pointing out the sins of the Jewish people, so that it is probable that the two books do not stand far apart from each other in point of time. In 1 Chronicles xxi. 1 'Satan' (without the article) is a proper name, and he is represented as tempting David to sin. It is, therefore, almost certain that Job is earlier than Chronicles (c. 300 B.C.–250 B.C.).

(9) The numerous Aramaic words, the vocabulary and the syntax suggest a relatively late period.

(10) The literary craftsmanship of the book suggests that it belongs to a period in which an advanced stage of literary culture had been reached.

The book in its present form was probably written about 400 B.C. This is the date favoured by Budde, Peake and Driver. Some scholars, notably Pfeiffer, place it in the time of Jeremiah, and others, including Eissfeldt, Steuernagel and Volz in the fourth century B.C. Cornill dates it 'in the latest period of Hebrew literature'. Pedersen and Bentzen refrain from giving any date.

HISTORICITY

The idea that the book is strictly historical, which persisted down to recent times, has been practically abandoned. It is now almost universally recognized as being largely a creation of the imagination. Job was a familiar figure in Hebrew tradition (Ezek. xiv. 14, 20), and it is possible that he was a real historical figure round whom in the course of time legends had gathered. That the book is in the main unhistorical is shown by the reference to the heavenly council (i. 6; ii. 1), by the symbolic numbers three (i. 2, 3, 4, 17; ii. 11; xlii. 13) and seven (i. 2, 3; xlii. 8, 13) used to describe Job's children and his flocks, by the escape of one messenger only from each of the catastrophes which befell Job's possessions, servants and family (i. 13–19), and by the doubling of Job's possessions after his restoration to prosperity (xlii. 10, 12). The divine speeches (xxxviii–xli, omitting xl. 3–5), of course, cannot be historical. The strongest argument against the historicity of the book is the fact that the speeches of Job and his friends cannot be verbatim reports of actual speeches, for they are the work of a great literary genius and could not have been delivered on the spur of the moment.

THE AUTHOR

Nothing is known of the author beyond what we learn from the perusal of his book which is largely autobiographical. His nationality is unknown since the 'land of Uz' (i. 1) to which he belonged cannot be identified. Some think that he was a Jew living in the south of Judaea near the border of Edom, and others that he was an Edomite, living in Edom or perhaps in Palestine.[1] The desert and caravan life seem to have been familiar to him. All the creatures in his book, except the hippopotamus (xl. 15) and the crocodile (xli. 1), belong to the desert. We are told how the brooks in the desert were swollen in the winter with water and dried up by the heat of summer, and how sometimes members of a caravan sought for water in vain and perished in the desert. It is probable that he had visited Egypt where he had seen the hippopotamus and the crocodile, the papyrus growing in the mud of the Nile and the reed flourishing in its waters (viii. 11). From his home in the interior of the country he had travelled to the coast and gazed across the sea, which impressed him by its vastness and reminded him of the omnipotence of the Almighty (ix. 8; xxvi. 12; xxxviii. 8). The restraints of civilized life seem to have been irksome to him. He was envious of the wild ass and the wild ox that were free to roam far from the haunts of man (xxxix. 5–12), and the hippopotamus and crocodile that no man could capture (xl. 24; xli. 1–14, 25–29).

All scholars agree that he must have been one of the most learned men of his day. He had some knowledge of mythology (vii. 12; ix. 13; xxvi. 12f.), astronomy (ix. 9; xxxviii. 31f.), the wisdom lore and the sacred writings of Israel. He was an original thinker with a philosophical turn of mind, and a superb literary artist.

A man of wide human sympathies, he hated oppression and was ever ready to help those in distress (xxix. 12–17; xxxi. 5–40). He

---

[1] There is much discussion on the question of the author's nationality. Those who hold that he was a Jew do so for the following reasons. (1) He shows familiarity with the Law (xxii. 6; xxiv. 9) and with a number of Old Testament writings (Jer. xx. 14–18). (2) He must have been a worshipper of Yahweh since the name of Israel's God occurs frequently in the prologue and epilogue. (3) The essential ideas of the book are Jewish. Those who maintain that he was an Edomite do so on the following grounds. (1) The references to the Law represent practices in force among all civilized nations. (2) The author was evidently a learned man, familiar with the Wisdom literature of other nations, and therefore with Israelite writings. (3) The name 'Yahweh' is never used in the dialogue (except in xii. 9, which is probably an oversight of the author or an error of a copyist) where various terms are used for God, one of which, 'Eloah,' is that of a deity from Teman in Edom. (4) The ideas of the book are not particularly Jewish. (5) The geographical background is Edomite. (6) The Hebrew of Job is strongly influenced by Arabic and Aramaic.

pitied the naked, starving outcasts, huddled under the rocks for shelter against the drenching rains and compelled to steal to keep themselves and their children alive (xxiv. 5-12). He was deeply conscious of the frailty and insignificance of man (iv. 19; xxv. 6; xl. 4), of the drudgery of his life on earth (vii. 1), and of the brief span of his days (vii. 6; xiv. 1f.). Unlike his fellow-countrymen he had escaped from the bonds of a narrow nationalism. Except for the mention of the river Jordan in xl. 23, there is no specific reference in the book to Israel. When he spoke of man he had in mind mankind in general.

He was a man capable of intense emotions and varying moods. Now he is struck dumb with pain and grief (ii. 13), and now he is in a rage, cursing the day of his birth and longing for death (iii. 1-26). Now he rails against God and challenges Him to a contest in court (xxiii. 1-7; xxxi. 35-37), and now he humbly submits to the divine will and repents 'in dust and ashes' (xlii. 6).

Finally he was a deeply religious man with a moral standard far in advance of that of his contemporaries (xxxi). Longing for fellowship with God, he became estranged from Him, because, after pondering on the problem of human suffering, he arrived at the conclusion that though God was omnipotent He was unjust. In the end, however, he realized that the ways of God were beyond man's comprehension, and that the only course open to him was to submit to the divine will. Thus, 'in humble submission to God's inscrutable wisdom, and in a profounder sense of fellowship with Him, he had escaped into a region of unclouded trust'.[1]

THE TEACHING

Monotheism

Monotheism is not stated explicitly but is taken for granted throughout the book, while idolatry is left almost out of account. God is the all-wise, omnipotent Creator, and the Controller of all things (ix. 4-10; xii. 13; xxxviii. 4-7). He is so infinitely superior to man that the latter is utterly insignificant before Him. 'For he is not man, as I am, that I might answer him, that we should come to trial together' (ix. 32; cf. x. 4-6). He is not a God who is 'merciful and gracious, slow to anger, and abounding in steadfast love and faithfulness' (Exod. xxxiv. 6). Although He listens to Job and speaks to him out of the whirlwind, He is an inscrutable cosmic force rather than a person.

[1] A. S. Peake, *Job*, 1904, p. 46.

Angelology

God is surrounded by certain spiritual beings called 'sons of God' (i. 6; ii. 1). They present themselves before Him at stated times and form His council (xv. 8). They are represented as being older than creation, for with the morning stars they formed the choir which sang at the laying of the earth's foundation stone (xxxviii. 4-7). Though they are called 'holy ones' (v. 1), they are not morally perfect but subject to folly and sin. 'Even in his servants he puts no trust, and his angels he charges with error' (iv. 18, cf. xv. 15). There is no distinction between good and bad angels. Since they are spiritual beings they are more akin to God than to men who are material, dwelling in houses of clay rooted in the earth (iv. 19). They act as intermediaries and intercessors for men (v. 1).

The Satan

In Job the Satan (Heb., 'adversary') is the title of one of the 'sons of God', whose function it is to test the integrity of good men by bringing calamity upon them. He has freedom to wander 'to and fro in the earth' (i. 7), but, nevertheless, acts with the express permission of God and keeps within the limits God has fixed for him (i. 12; ii. 6). He is not a malevolent being, but has evidently become cynical as to the reality of human goodness and irritated by the blameless character of Job. In the New Testament he is called 'the devil' (Greek, 'diabolos') and 'the tempter' as well as 'satan' (Mt. iv. 10). He has an evil army—'the angels of Satan'—who strive to hinder the divine purposes (Mt. xxv. 41; Rev. xii. 7-9). The Revelation even speaks of 'Satan's throne' (ii. 13).

Man

Man is the creation of God (xxxi. 15) who fashioned him like clay, clothed him with skin and flesh and knit him together with bones and sinews (x. 9-12). He dwells in a house of clay whose foundations are in the dust (iv. 19). He is a creature of little significance being no more than a maggot, a worm (xxv. 6). His days on earth are brief and full of trouble (xiv. 1); they are swifter than a weaver's shuttle and flee away without hope (vii. 6) and without good (ix. 25). After a brief life of drudgery (vii. 1) he perishes and his shade descends to the darkness of Sheol, there to dwell for ever cut off from communion with God and man (iii. 11-19; vii. 8-10; x. 20-22; xiv. 10-12; xviii. 13-16;

xviii. 18–21), while his body lies in the dust and is covered with worms (xxi. 26).

Retribution

Job's three friends together with Elihu hold the orthodox doctrine of retribution, namely, that God punishes the wicked and rewards the righteous. Eliphaz and Elihu also advance the doctrine that punishment may be sent by God upon a man to purge him of sin and to wean him from evil which leads to destruction (v. 17; xv. 11; xxii. 15–30; xxxvi. 8–23). Job had held the doctrine of retribution, but in his afflictions he rejects it because he is conscious of his integrity and therefore feels that he is being punished unjustly (vi. 10; ix. 20f.; xvi. 7–17; xxiii. 11f.; xxvii. 2–6; xxix. 12–17; xxxi. 1–34).

Ethics

The ethical ideals are the noblest in the Old Testament, transcending those of the Decalogue and even the teaching of the Prophets, and almost attaining the level of those of the Sermon on the Mount. Job condemns adultery (xxix. 14–16), falsehood (xxxi. 5), injustice to slaves (xxxi. 13–15), the harsh treatment and oppression of the widow and orphan, the poor and the helpless (xxii. 6; xxiv. 2f.; xxxi. 16–23). The secret sins of the heart are also condemned—sensual desires (xxxi. 1), covetousness (xxxi. 7), and joy in one's wealth (xxxi. 24f.), gloating over the destruction of an enemy (xxxi. 29f.), idolatrous thoughts (xxxi. 26) and hypocrisy (xxxi. 33f.). His conduct is marked not merely by abstention from wrong, but also by active benevolence. He feels that since God has cared for him from his youth he must also care for the weak. He has always fed the starving, clothed the naked and offered hospitality to the stranger and the traveller (xxxi. 16–23, 34).

Immortality

Job normally accepts the popular belief in Sheol, but as the poem progresses we see him moving towards the doctrine of immortality. In vii. 8, 21 he expresses the belief that when he is dead and beyond recall, God will long to renew the old communion with his devoted servant and search diligently for him. In xiv. 13–22, he expresses the wish that God might hide him in Sheol until His wrath be past, and then remember him. He would gladly wait until God should call him, watch over him and forget his sin. But it is only a dream, instantly dismissed. Such a future life is not to be hoped for, especially for such a frail creature as man. God destroys his hope and he passes, descending to Sheol where he neither knows nor cares for the concerns of his family, but is conscious only of his own pain. In xix. 25 he expresses the conviction that after his death he shall see God, no longer estranged and hostile but as a friend.[1] This is not a doctrine of immortality in the fullest sense: there is no suggestion of a life of endless duration after death. It is but a passing conviction that death will not separate him from God. It is, however, a great advance on the popular doctrine of Sheol. 'Till men see that death is no longer an impassable barrier, there can be no advance towards a belief in full immortality. But when once it is seen that death is not the end, it is inevitable that the new life, as men conceive it, should extend indefinitely. So Job opened a door through which later generations could pass, and reach a picture of eternal life which is a true counterpart of the eternal God. For personal contact with an eternal God must of necessity be itself eternal.'[2]

PERMANENT INFLUENCE

The book is valuable for the light it sheds on Judaism in the post-exilic period. On their return from exile the Jews, purified by their sufferings and surrounded by heathen influences, clung more tenaciously than ever to their ancestral faith, finding their chief joy in their obedience to the Law and in the worship of the Temple. It would be wrong, however, to suppose that the nation was intellectually stagnant, and that there was complete unanimity in matters of religion. With the growth of individualism in religion, the people became more critical so that there was not the same ready acceptance of popular beliefs. As we have already shown, the question of suffering had become real and intense by the close of the exile. Job is symptomatic of

[1] There are wide differences of opinion on the meaning of xix. 25–27. A. S. Peake (*Job*, 1904, p. 192) thinks that the hope of immortality is not expressed here, but only of a momentary vision of God, assuring him of his vindication. N. H. Snaith (*The Distinctive Ideas of the Old Testament*, 1944, p. 90n.) says, 'The famous passage in Job xix. 25–27 can be made to refer to life after death only by a most liberal latitude in translation, a strong attachment to the Latin version, and reminiscences of Handel's "Messiah." The Hebrew text is difficult, but it is unlikely that the vindicator is God, and Job almost certainly means that he will be vindicated before he is dead.' H. H. Rowley (*B.J.R.L.*, Vol. 32, 1949–1950, p. 205) believes that the author is reaching out after something more satisfying than the dreary doctrine of Sheol, but that he has not securely grasped it. 'There is no clear faith in a worthwhile after-life, but at best the belief that God will one day vindicate him and that he will be conscious of that vindication.'

[2] T. H. Robinson, *Job and his Friends*, 1954, p. 103.

the intellectual unrest, which also found expression in Ecclesiastes, written in the same age. These two books (and possibly others which have not survived) must have awakened a ready response in many hearts and created a deep impression, otherwise they would not have come to be venerated as Scripture and admitted to the Hebrew Canon. At first sight it seems strange that they should be canonized, but it should be remembered that it was never the policy of the creators and upholders of Judaism to crush out all freedom of thought. They tolerated the heretic and allowed him to disseminate his views, provided he did not strike at what they conceived to be the foundations of the faith. Any attempt, for example, to destroy the validity of the Law or to propagate an alien faith would have met with persecution. The Jewish Church rested not on uniformity of belief but on obedience to the Law.

The book has had little influence on the development of religious ideas. Although it must have been read with deep interest by many Jewish thinkers, it failed to discredit the doctrine of retribution. In New Testament times the doctrine was the working faith not only of the rank and file, but also of the leaders of the people (cf. Jn. ix. 2). The book seems to have had little influence on the writers of the New Testament. There is only one explicit quotation from it. 1 Corinthians iii. 19 (prefixed by the formula 'it is written'), 'He catches the wise in their craftiness' is from Job. v. 13. Romans xi. 35, 'Or who has given a gift to him that he might be repaid?' refers to Job xli. 11. Philippians i. 19a, 'it will turn out for my deliverance', is identical with Job xiii. 6a in the Septuagint. In James v. 11 there is a reference to the 'steadfastness of Job'.

The book offers no intellectual solution of the problem of human suffering which has puzzled the minds of men throughout the centuries. The doctrine of retribution, popular in Job's day, has long since lost all interest for us, for it is obviously false to the facts of life. But if it does not solve the problem of human suffering, it does teach that disinterested religion is a reality, that there is such a thing as undeserved suffering and that it can lead to a deeper knowledge of God, and that the universe is under the control of an all-wise and omnipotent Creator whose ways are beyond man's comprehension.

> 'Lo, these (i.e. the marvels of the universe) are but the outskirts
>   of his ways;
> and how small a whisper do we hear of him!
> But the thunder of his power who can understand?' (xxv. 14.)

LITERARY MERIT

As a work of art the book is by universal consent the greatest literary masterpiece in the Old Testament. The only other portion of the Old Testament which can compare with it is Isaiah xl–lv, dealing with the suffering of the Jewish exiles in Babylon. It is also reckoned as one of the greatest masterpieces in the literature of the world, ranking with the Homeric sagas, *The Iliad* and *The Odyssey*, the dramas of Euripides and Aeschylus, Virgil's *Aeneid*, Dante's *Divine Comedy*, Shakespeare's *Hamlet*, Milton's *Paradise Lost* and Goethe's *Faust*. In Carlyle's opinion there is nothing written in the Bible or out of it of equal merit.

The book is marked by intense and highly personal emotion and reflects a variety of moods. The poet has undoubtedly identified himself with the suffering Job. He had suffered acutely and was so conscious of the miseries of the world that he could not discuss the problem of human suffering calmly and dispassionately. As he contemplated the suffering of mankind in general and of himself in particular, he was stirred to the depths of his soul and wrote out of a full heart. In the whole work there is not the slightest trace of insincerity or artificiality. He wrote not as a philosopher or a dialectician, but as one who was tortured in body, mind and soul.

The book shows that the poet was richly endowed with imagination which never failed him. It is apparent in every chapter, more especially in those chapters containing the divine speeches. Among the many passages which glow with his imagination are those describing Sheol (iii. 13–19), the revelations given to Eliphaz in visions of the night (iv. 12–16), the false friends (vi. 15–21), the laying of the foundations of the earth (xxxviii. 4–11) and the war-horse (xxxix. 19–25). His vivid imagination personifies natural phenomena. Job prayed that the night of his birth might never behold 'the eyelids of the morning', (iii. 9), appealed to the earth not to cover up his blood (xvi. 18), and called Sheol his father and the worm his mother (xvii. 14). Fields and furrows would cry out against him if he injured them (xxxi. 38). At the creation the morning stars sang together (xxxviii. 7). Sometimes he puts into the mouths of the three friends imaginative utterances which we cannot imagine falling from their lips.

The poet reveals a wider knowledge and a keener appreciation of nature than any other poet in the Old Testament. In a series of pictures he brings before the mind's eye, the sea (xi. 9; xxvi. 12; xxxviii. 8, 16), the constellations (ix. 11; xxxviii. 31f.), the treasures of the snow and the hail (xxxviii. 22), the clouds (xxvi. 8f.; xxxviii. 9, 34, 37), grass and flowers (viii. 11f.; xiv. 2; xv. 33), leaves, stubble and chaff (xiii. 25; xxi. 18), the lions in their dens (xxxviii. 39f.), the horse (xxxix. 19-25), the wild ass and the wild ox (xxxix. 5-12), the wild goat and the hind (xxxix. 1-4), the hawk (xxxix. 26) and the eagle (xxxix. 27).

The poet is a master of similes and metaphors, being quick to note resemblances between two things. Man 'comes forth like a flower and withers' (xiv. 2); he comes to the grave as 'a shock of grain comes up to the threshing floor in its season' (v. 26); 'as waters fail from a lake and a river wastes away and dries up, so man lies down and rises not again' (xiv. 11); 'those who plough iniquity and sow trouble reap the same' (iv. 8); man's life on earth is a warfare (vii. 1; xiv. 14); Job's roots spread out to the waters, with the dew all night on his branches (xxix. 19). He makes frequent use of the imperative mood (iii. 1-9; xiii. 6, 13), the rhetorical question (v. 1; xv. 11; xxxi. 4), and the expletives, 'behold!' (iv. 3; v. 17; xxiii. 8), 'lo!' (v. 27; xiii. 1; xxv. 14) and 'Oh!' (xiii. 5; xxix. 2; xxxi. 35). He also uses the literary device of contrast with striking effect. Job reviews his former prosperity and happy days, and contrasts them with his present misery (xxix-xxxi). The deep things of God are higher than heaven and deeper than Sheol (xi. 8). The wicked man 'is thrust from light into darkness and driven out of the world' (xviii. 18). In the divine speeches the wisdom and omnipotence of the Almighty are contrasted with the ignorance and impotence of man (xxxviii-xli, omitting xl. 3-5).

There are in the book numerous instances of irony. Job tells his three friends that no doubt they are the people and wisdom will die with them (xii. 2). He speaks ironically of the helpfulness and instructiveness of Bildad's speech; he must have been inspired (xxvi. 2-4). God tells Job that he doubtless knows the way to the home of light and where darkness dwells, for the number of his days is great (xxxviii. 19-21).

The pathos of the book is deeply moving. Job pleads with his three friends to have pity on him. 'Have pity on me, have pity on me, O you my friends, for the hand of God has touched me!' (xix. 21). He pleads with God that he may be left in Sheol till His wrath be spent and then remember him (xiv. 13). He declares that when he is dead, God will seek him diligently in order to renew the old communion, but it will be too late, for he will have gone beyond recall (vii. 21).

The characters of the story are differentiated from one another, but they are not highly individualized. The three friends are devout kindly men, who are anxious to do all they can to help Job. Eliphaz is the mystic who has visions and receives revelations. Bildad is the scholarly sage whose mind is stored with the wisdom of the ancients to which he loves to appeal. Zophar appeals neither to revelation nor to the wisdom of the past but to reason. Job is a devout man, who fears God and shuns evil. Because of his intense pain he loses his faith in God, charging Him with injustice, but in the end, in the contemplation of the wisdom and might of God, he admits his mistake and submits humbly to the divine will (xl. 4f.; xlii. 2–6).

CHAPTER XI

THE SONG OF SONGS

TITLE AND PLACE IN CANON

THE book in Hebrew is called 'Shirath Shirim', Song of Songs. This expression, like 'vanity of vanities' and 'holy of holies', is used to indicate the superlative and means 'the finest song of all'. This title has been adopted in the Greek and Latin versions. Canticles, another title for the book, is a translation of the Vulgate, 'Canticum Canticorum'.

In the Hebrew Canon it stands in the 'Writings', between Job and Ruth, and is the first of the five Megilloth or Rolls. In the English versions it comes immediately after Ecclesiastes.

CANONICITY

In the first century A.D. many Jewish scholars refused to accept the book as sacred Scripture because of its obviously secular character. Its theme is love between man and woman and the religious element is entirely lacking. The name of Yahweh is mentioned only once—in the passage in which jealousy is described as 'a very flame of the Lord' (viii. 6). It was treated by some people as a common ditty and passages from it were sung at banquets.[1] It was finally admitted to the Canon at the Council of Jamnia (c. A.D. 90); but in the first half of the second century A.D. there were still Jewish scholars who hesitated to accept it as canonical. The famous Jewish Rabbi, Akiba, lent the weight of his great influence in support of its canonicity, declaring that, 'All the Hagiographa are holy, but the Song of Songs is the most holy, and the whole world is not of such importance as the day on which it was given to Israel'. Its inclusion in the Canon was due to

---

[1] Tosephta, *Sanhedrin*, xii. 10, and Babylonian Talmud: *Sanhedrin*, 101a.

the association with the name of Solomon and to its allegorical interpretation.[1]

CONTENTS

Outline

Ch. i. 1.	The title.
Ch. i. 2–8.	The maiden praises her lover.
Ch. i. 9–ii. 7.	The lovers sing each other's praises.
Ch. ii. 8–17.	The young man sings of love and springtime.
Ch. iii. 1–5.	The maiden's dream.
Ch. iii. 6–11.	A description of a wedding procession.
Ch. iv. 1–v. 1.	The maiden's charms.
Ch. v. 2–vi. 3.	The maiden searches for her lost lover and describes his comeliness.
Ch. vi. 4–12.	The young man praises the maiden's beauty.
Ch. vi. 13–vii. 9.	The young man praises the maiden's beauty as she dances.
Ch. vii. 10–viii. 7.	The maiden's longings and her description of the irresistible power of love.
Ch. viii. 8–10.	The solicitude of the brothers.
Ch. viii. 11–12.	The two vineyards.
Ch. viii. 13–14.	The young man desires to listen to the maiden's voice.

Paraphrase: Ch. i. 1

The whole book is described as the most beautiful of Solomon's Songs.

Ch. i. 2–8

The maiden longs for his kisses. His caresses are dearer than wine; the fragrance of his perfumes is rare and the sound of his name is wafted like scent; every maiden is in love with him. She desires him to bring her to his chamber where they will thrill with delight. His caresses will be dearer to her than wine; it is no wonder that maidens adore him (vv. 2–4).

---

[1] Recently, the theory that the allegorical interpretation was a factor in securing the inclusion in the Canon has been challenged. It is now suggested that the Song was held in high esteem owing to its popularity. The allegorical interpretation placed upon it simply increased its popularity and its worth in the eyes of the people and was in no way responsible for its admission to the Canon. (See article on 'The Wisdom Literature' in *The Old Testament and Modern Study*, 1951, p. 233).

She tells the maidens of Jerusalem that she is dark but comely—dark as the black tents inhabited by the people of Kedar and as beautiful as the curtains of Solomon. They must not scorn her for being dark for the sun has tanned her. Her brothers in anger made her look after their vineyards, but she did not look after the vineyard of her own charms (vv. 5f.).

Addressing her lover, she wishes to know where he rests his flock at noon, for there is no reason why she should go roaming from flock to flock of his companions. He advises her to follow the sheep-tracks and pasture her kids by the shepherds' tents (vv. 7f.).

Ch. i. 9–ii. 7

The young man compares her to a noble filly in Pharaoh's chariot; her cheeks are fair with braided plaits and her neck is fair with strings of jewels; they will make for her circlets of gold studded with silver (i. 9–11).

The maiden returns the compliment; when her king lies on the divan, her charms breathe out their fragrance. He is like a bunch of myrrh that lies between her breasts, and like a cluster of henna-flowers from the vineyards of Engedi (i. 12–14).

The young man continues his praise of her. She is fair with dove-like eyes. She replies that their bed of love is the green sward, and that the beams of their house are cedar boughs and the rafters firs (i. 15–17).

The maiden compares herself to humble wild flowers—the rose of the plain (Sharon) and the lily of the valley. To this her lover replies that in comparison with other women she is like a lily among thorns. She replies that he stands out from other men like the apple tree among the trees of the wood. She loves to lie under his shadow, tasting his sweet fruits. He has brought her into his 'house of wine', hung over with love. She desires to be sustained with raisins and revived with apples, for she swoons with love. She wishes that his left hand may be under her head and that his right hand may embrace her. She charges the maidens of Jerusalem never to disturb the enjoyment of lovers until they are satisfied (ii. 1–7).

Ch. ii. 8–17

The maiden hears the voice of her beloved and sees him hastening over the mountains and gazing through the lattice-window. He calls to her and beseeches her to go with him, for the winter has past and the summer come. The flowers appear on the earth and it is time for pruning. The turtle-dove's note is heard, the figs are ripening red and the vines are all blossoms and fragrance. He urges her to leave her hiding-place and to let him see her form and hear her voice. She calls upon him to save her from those who seek to destroy her happiness, declares that they are for ever united in their love, and asks him to leave her until the evening breeze rises and there are no shadows, and to play like a gazelle or a stag upon the mountains of spices.

Ch. iii. 1–5

Night after night the maiden dreamt that she sought her beloved through street and square, but all in vain. She asked the watchmen if they had seen him; no sooner had she left them that she found him and brought him to her mother's house (v. 5 is a repetition of ii. 7).

Ch. iii. 6–11

The palanquin of Solomon (i.e. of the bridegroom) is seen approaching like pillars of smoke perfumed with myrrh and frankincense, with all the fragrant spices of the trader. Sixty mighty men of Israel (i.e. sixty companions of the bridegroom), armed with swords and trained to war, protect the king from perils by night. The palanquin is made of wood from Lebanon; the pillars supporting the roof are covered with silver and the back of it is made of gold; the seat is of purple and the inside is inlaid with ivory. The king is crowned by his mother on the day of his marriage—on the day of his rapture.

Ch. iv. 1–v. 1

The bride is fair to look upon. Her eyes are dove-like beneath her veil. The tresses of her hair are like flocks of goats that trail down the slopes of Mount Gilead, her teeth like a flock of shorn ewes fresh from the dipping, paired together in rows, not one missing, and her lips like a scarlet thread. Her mouth is delicious; her cheeks are like slices of pomegranate behind her veil; her neck is like David's tower decorated with trophies; and her breasts are like a pair of fawns. In the cool of the evening when the shadows depart, the bridegroom will repair to the open country where everything is sweet and fragrant like myrrh and frankincense. She is all fair and spotless (iv. 1–7).

The bridegroom invites his beloved to leave Lebanon. She has ravished his heart with a glance from her eye and a turn of her neck. Her love is sweeter than wine and no spice is so sweet as the fragrance of her ointments. Her words are as sweet to him as the honey that drops from the honeycomb, and the scent of her robes is as the scent of Lebanon (iv. 8-11).

His bride is like an enclosed garden or a sealed spring. Her charms are like a paradise full of delicious fruit and all the best spices. She is like a garden fountain, a well of fresh water and streams from Lebanon. The bride invites the wind to blow upon her garden (i.e. herself) and carry its fragrance to her beloved, so that he may come into his garden to eat his choice fruits. He accepts the invitation, comes into the garden to gather his balsam and myrrh, to eat his honey and to drink his wine and milk. The joys of love cause him to invite all lovers to taste the sweets of love and to drink of its joys (iv. 12-v. 1).

Ch. v. 2-vi. 3

The bride narrates a dream she has had. Her beloved knocked at the door one night and asked her to open, for his head was bedrenched with dew and with the moisture that dropped from the night-clouds; but she told him that she had doffed her robe and bathed her feet. He put his hand through a hole in the door; her heart yearned for him and her soul fainted when she heard him. She rose to open the door, her hands all moist with myrrh and her fingers wet with liquid myrrh. She opened the door but he had gone. She searched for him in vain. The watchmen met her on their rounds, struck and wounded her and took her mantle from her. Meeting the maidens of Jerusalem she asked them to tell her beloved, if they found him, that she was lovesick They asked her what was her beloved more than another that she charged them so (v. 2-9).

She describes her beloved. He is white and ruddy, the pick of ten-thousand. His head is like the finest gold; his curls are black as the raven, his eyes like doves upon the water, bathed in milk, limped and swimming, his cheeks like beds of balsam and banks of sweet perfume, his lips like lilies breathing liquid myrrh, and his hands like golden tapers, tipped with topaz; his body is like ivory, overlaid with sapphires; his limbs are like marble columns resting on sockets of gold. His whole aspect is like Lebanon, as lordly as a cedar; his mouth is sweetness itself; he is altogether lovely (v. 10-16).

The maidens of Jerusalem ask her where her beloved has gone in order that they also may search for him. She replies that he has gone to his garden to feed and to gather lilies. They are for ever united in their love (vi. 1-3).

Ch. vi. 4–12

The young man describes the beauty of his beloved. She is as beautiful as the city of Tirzah, as fair as Jerusalem, and as awe-inspiring as an army with banners. He cannot look into her eyes without being overcome by them. The tresses of her hair are like goats that stream down the slopes of Mountain Gilead; her teeth are like a flock of shorn ewes, fresh from the dipping, all paired together in rows and not one missing; her cheeks are like slices of pomegranate behind her veil (vi. 4–7).

Solomon had sixty queens, eighty concubines, and maidens without number. He would rather have his one beloved, who is an only daughter, than all the ladies of the court. Women see her and honour her; queens and concubines praise her. She glows like the dawn; she is as fair as the moon, as clear as the sun, and as awe-inspiring as an army with banners (vi. 8f.).

The maiden, interrupting her beloved, says that she went to the walnut-bower to see the green plants of the valley, and to see if the vines were budding and if the pomegranates were in flower (v. 12 is unintelligible and probably corrupt) (vi. 10–12).

Ch. vi. 13–vii. 9

The young man implores the maid of Shulem to turn that they may see her. She asks him what he can see in her, and he replies that he desires to see her in the dance of Mahanaim. As she dances he praises her charms. Her swaying thighs are the links of chain, moulded by a master-hand; her navel is like a round goblet filled with wine mixed with spices, her belly like a bundle of wheat encircled by lilies, her bosom like two fawns and her neck like an ivory tower. Her eyes are like the pools of Heshbon; her nose is like the tower of Lebanon that faces Damascus and her head like the summit of Carmel. Her hair is as glossy as purple and her king is held captive in its tresses. She is fair and pleasant for love's delight. She stands as straight as the palm with breasts like clusters of grapes. He will climb the palm, taking hold of the boughs. He hopes that her breasts may be like clusters of grapes, her breath sweet as an apple, and her kisses like the best wine that slips smoothly down, gliding over the lips and the teeth.

Ch. vii. 10–viii. 7

The maiden declares that she belongs to her beloved and that he is longing for her. She longs to walk with him in the fields in the spring, to sleep among the henna flowers, to go at dawn to the vineyards to see if the vines are budding, if the blossoms are open, and if the pomegranates are in flower. There she will give him her love, the mandrakes yielding their fragrance. She has stored up for him all manner of choice fruits, old and new (vii. 10–13).

If he were her brother she would kiss him whenever she met him and no one would despise her. She would bring him to her mother's house and give him to drink spiced wine and draughts of pomegranate wine (v. 3 is a repetition of ii. 6 and v. 4 almost identical with ii. 7 and iii. 5) (viii. 1–4).

The maiden is seen coming from the country leaning on her beloved. She woke him under the apple-tree where his mother gave birth to him. She asks him to wear her as a seal close to his heart and like a ring upon his hand. Love is as irresistible as death and jealousy as cruel as the grave. Its flashes burn like flame—true lightning flashes; the floods cannot quench love and no rivers can drown it. If a man were to offer all he has for love he would be utterly scorned (viii. 5–7).

Ch. viii. 8–10

When the maiden was young and undeveloped, her brothers decided that if, when lovers came, she continued to be virtuous, like a battlement withstanding an invader, they would reward her with an ornament of silver. If she yielded to lovers like a door, they would enclose her with boards of cedar. She was virtuous and was in her lover's eyes as one who brings peace (vv. 8–10).

Ch. viii. 11–12

Solomon once had a vineyard which he leased out to keepers for a thousand silver pieces for its fruits; but the maiden keeps her vineyard (i.e. she remains loyal to her lover). Solomon is welcome to his silver and the keepers to their fruit.

Ch. viii. 13–14

The young man and his companions wish to hear the maiden's voice. She urges him to hasten and play like a gazelle or a stag upon the mountains of spices (v. 14 is a repetition of ii. 17).

INTERPRETATION

Allegorical Interpretation

In the course of the centuries the Song has been interpreted in many different ways, but none of the explanations which have been advanced has gained universal acceptance.

Jewish scholars interpreted it as an allegory, signifying the love of Yahweh for His people from the Exodus to the dawn of the Messianic Age. The allegorical method of interpretation was taken over by the Christian Church, and the Song was held to be a symbolic representation of the love of Christ for His Church or for the individual soul. Some of the early Christian Fathers saw references in it to the Virgin Mary (cf. iv. 7). During the Middle Ages it was a favourite occupation of Commentators to find fresh interpretations of the Song, which were so absurd as to need no refutation. The allegorical method of interpretation can be seen in the chapter headings of the Song in the Authorized Version of the Bible, and has been retained in some quarters down to the present day. By this method of interpretation the Song could be made to mean anything according to the fancy of the commentator. With the rise of the modern school of criticism in the eighteenth century it fell into disfavour.

Dramatic Interpretation

Instead of regarding the Song as an allegory some critics have seen in it a drama with human love as the theme. The early dramatic interpretations contained two principal characters, namely, Solomon and a Shulamite maiden. In this form of the drama, Solomon, on a royal progress through Northern Israel, meets a beautiful maiden, woos her in the disguise of a shepherd, removes her from her home to his harem at Jerusalem and eventually wins her love. In the later dramatic representations there are three principal characters, namely, Solomon, a Shulamite maiden and a shepherd boy, and the story is more romantic. Solomon, on a royal tour through Northern Israel, surprises a beautiful maiden and brings her to Jerusalem, where efforts are made by the king and the ladies of the court to induce her to give up her shepherd and to enter the royal harem. The maiden, however, resists all the king's advances and is finally allowed to return to her home where she is united with her lover.

The theory that the Song is a drama has now been largely abandoned.

When the various dramatic interpretations, which have been advanced, are compared with the Song, as we know it, it is clear that they are largely imaginative reconstructions. In the Song there is no clear plot and the names of the characters are not given: there is no division into acts and scenes and there are no stage directions. However, in the Old Testament, passages can be found containing dramatic elements, but in the ancient Hebrew literature there is, strictly speaking, no drama. It is, therefore, difficult to see how the Song could be a drama except on the assumption that it was the only one of its kind to be written in Israel and that it has survived the centuries.

Wedding Song Interpretation

Another view is that the book is a collection of wedding songs. They refer to wedded love only and deal with marriage, its ceremonies, the beauty of bride and bridegroom, and their love for each other. According to Origen (c. A.D. 185–253), the occasion of the Song was the marriage of Solomon and Pharaoh's daughter (cf. 1 Kgs. iii. 1). This view was revived by Bossuet (1693) and Lowth (1753) who held that the Song was written for use during the seven days of the wedding festivities of Solomon and his Egyptian princess. In 1860 Renan called attention to the similarity between the Song and modern Syrian wedding poetry,[1] and in 1873 Wetzstein, the German consul at Damascus, published a study of modern marriage customs in Syria. After the wedding there is a seven days' feast, called the 'King's Week', during which the bride and bridegroom are enthroned on rustic seats, placed on the threshing-board, and saluted as king and queen. Songs, called 'wasfs', describing their physical beauty, are sung in their honour, and also songs of war, while the bride, brandishing a naked sword, dances before the guests. Wetzstein suggested that the marriage festivities of ancient Israel proceeded along similar lines.[2] In 1894 Budde presented the theory with such cogency that it gained wide support, but it is now losing its popularity.[3] The songs are songs of peace, but many of those of the Syrians are war songs. They are too few in number to last for seven days. Apart from the description of the wedding procession and the crowning of the bridegroom as king by his mother (iii. 6–11) and that of the beauty of the bride as she dances (vi. 13–vii.

---

[1] E. Renan, *Le Cantique des Cantiques*, 1860, p. 86.
[2] J. G. Wetzstein, 'Die syrische Dreschtafel' in *Zeitschrift für Ethnologie*, v, 1873, pp. 270–302.
[3] K. Budde, 'The Song of Solomon', in *The New World*, III. 1894, 56–77.

9), there is nothing in the Song that can be definitely connected with wedding festivities. The Syrians are a mixed race and their customs have no bearing on Jewish poetry. It is not certain that the customs described by Wetzstein exist in Palestine.

Secular Love Song Interpretation

The book has been interpreted as a single secular love song. In the first century A.D. passages from it were sung in taverns. Rabbi Akiba (d. c. A.D. 135) pronounced a curse on all those who treated it as a common ditty. At the close of the fourth century A.D., Theodore of Mopsuestia attributed it to Solomon and connected it with his marriage to an Egyptian princess. More than a century after his death he was condemned as a heretic in the fifth General Council which met at Constantinople in A.D. 553, for not subscribing to the allegorical interpretation. In the sixteenth century Castellio, one of the early Protestant reformers, declared that it should be excluded from the Canon since it dealt merely with earthly love—a view which led to his departure from Geneva in A.D. 1545. In 1567 Luis de Leon was brought before the Inquisition for holding a similar view. In 1723 Whiston declared that the Song was immoral and unworthy of a place in the Canon.[1] In 1879 Reuss regarded it as profane poetry which should be excluded from the Canon.[2] The view that it is a single secular love song has persisted down to the present day. Beek, for example, thinks that it would be wrong to look upon the book as a series of separate love songs, for it is held together by a central thread—the harsh treatment of a girl by her brothers, her appointment as the keeper of their vineyards and the consequent neglect of her own. 'This central thread holds together all the lovely songs of love and joy that have made this book so rightly famous.'[3]

Some scholars reject the view that the book constitutes a single whole on the ground that it contains no central theme, and that the various sections follow one another without logical sequence, giving the impression of a patchwork of incongruous fragments. They see the book as a collection of independent secular love songs which for the most part have no connexion with wedding festivities. From

---

[1] W. Whiston, *A supplement to Mr Whiston's late Essay, 'Towards restoring the true text of the Old Testament, proving that the Canticles is not a sacred book of the Old Testament'*, 1723, pp. 5f.

[2] E. Reuss, *Le Cantique des Cantiques*, 1879, p. 3.

[3] M. A. Beek, *A Journey through the Old Testament*, Eng. Trans. 1959, pp. 230f.

twenty-five to thirty separate songs have been counted. As early as 1778 Herder suggested that the book was not a single composition but a collection of independent love songs linked together 'like a bunch of pearls upon a string'.[1] Since then this view has been advocated in various forms and is one of the prevailing views to-day. 'The view I adopt', says Rowley, 'finds in it nothing but what it appears to be, lovers' songs, expressing their delight in one another and the warm emotions of their hearts'.[2]

Liturgical Interpretation

It has been suggested by Meek that the Song was originally a liturgy of the Tammuz-Adonis cult.[3] Tammuz is the Babylonian counterpart of the Syrian Adonis. In the myth the death and resurrection of the god symbolized the death of vegetation in autumn and its revival in spring. The cult flourished in Babylon and Syria and was practised in Palestine in Old Testament times. In Ezekiel viii. 14 there is a picture of women at the entrance of the north gate of the Temple weeping for Tammuz, while in Isaiah xvii. 10f. reference is made to the gardens of Adonis. In the cult the death of the god Tammuz, his descent into the underworld, followed by the goddess Ishtar in search of him, and their subsequent return to the upper world were represented in a ritual drama. After the return there were the wooing of the two persons, who represented the god and goddess, and their union in marriage. The ritual dance figured in the ceremonies, and they were accompanied by much licentiousness in which the Temple prostitutes played their part. According to Meek, the liturgy was reinterpreted in order to bring it into harmony with the higher Yahweh cult of the Hebrews.

The evidence for this theory is not convincing. It is most unlikely that the leaders of Judaism would have included in the Canon a liturgy with such pagan associations. Some scholars, while rejecting the liturgical interpretation of the Song, admit that the Adonis-Tammuz cult had some influence upon it. 'At the same time', says Rowley, 'it may be freely allowed that many of the allusions in the Song may

[1] J. G. von Herder, *Lieder der Liebe*, 1778, pp. 89–106.
[2] H. H. Rowley, 'The Interpretation of the Song of Songs' in *The Servant of the Lord*, 1953, p. 233.
[3] T. J. Meek, 'Canticles and the Tammuz Cult', in *A.J.S.L.*, xxxix, 1922–23, pp. 1–14; 'The Song of Songs and the Fertility Cult,' in *The Song of Songs: a Symposium*, ed. by W. H. Schoff, 1924, pp. 48–79; 'Babylonian Parallels in the Song of Songs,' in *J.B.L.*, xliii, 1924, pp. 245–252.

genuinely refer to elements of the Adonis-Tammuz cult, whether found in the practice of the poet's contemporaries, or inherited in speech from an earlier age, and we owe a real debt to Meek and his associates for the light they have shed on some things in the Song, even though they have failed to carry conviction in their main thesis[1].

We have now outlined the main interpretations placed upon the book. For our part we favour the view that the book is a collection of love songs, having little connexion with wedding festivities and containing reminiscences of the Tammuz-Adonis ritual.

AUTHORSHIP AND DATE

The authorship and date of the book cannot be determined with precision. Apart from a few short pieces (e.g. iii. 6–11; vi. 13–vii. 5), it exhibits a uniformity of style and numerous repetitions (ii. 6f. and viii. 3f.; ii. 17a and iv. 6a; ii. 17b and viii. 14) which suggest unity of authorship. Tradition ascribes the book to Solomon (i. 1). This ascription was doubtless due to the repeated mention of Solomon's name in it (i. 5; iii. 7, 9; viii. 11f.), and to the fact that in 1 Kings iv. 32 he is said to have written 1,005 songs. The tradition of Solomonic authorship can no longer be accepted since the linguistic evidence indicates clearly that the book belongs to a much later period than that of the monarchy. Aramaic words and constructions are frequent and the language resembles most that of the latest books of the Old Testament. The Persian word, 'pardes' = 'garden' (iv. 13) and the word 'appirion' = 'palanquin' (iii. 9), which is the Hebrew form of the Greek word, 'phoreion', suggest a late date. The book was perhaps written in the period 300–250 B.C.

From the manner in which Tirzah is linked with Jerusalem in vi. 4, it has been suggested that part of the book at least was written during the time that Tirzah was the capital of the Northern Kingdom (1 Kgs. xiv. 17–xvi. 23f.), that is, from the beginning of the reign of Baasha to the sixth year of the reign of Omri (c. 900–870 B.C.). The argument, however, is not decisive. The city of Tirzah is mentioned later (2 Kgs. xv. 14f.) and it was known down to the fifteenth century A.D. It is quite possible that a post-exilic writer might use the name Tirzah instead of Samaria because of the evil repute in which the latter was held.

---

[1] H. H. Rowley, 'The Interpretation of the Song of Songs' in *The Servant of the Lord*, 1952, pp. 230f.

It should be stated that not all scholars by any means are agreed that the book is the work of a single author. Many hold that it is a collection of love songs written by different authors in the course of several centuries, and worked over in the third century B.C. by a poet who was a conscious literary artist.

PERMANENT INFLUENCE

The book has had no influence in the realm of religious ideas. It is a collection of secular songs extolling the natural and even the physical love of a man and a maid. Though it is in no sense a religious work, there is no need to regret its inclusion in the Canon. Love is the greatest emotion in the human heart and the most powerful force in society and civilization. The ecstasy of union in perfect love, which true lovers know, is the gift of God. Any book, therefore, that glorifies pure love is worthy of a place in the Canon.

LITERARY MERITS

As a work of art the book ranks high in the literature of the world. Its chief characteristics are an appreciation of the beauty of nature for its own sake, vivid imagery, and intensity of feeling.

The poet is a lover of the country. We see the flocks of goats streaming down the slopes of Mount Gilead (iv. 1; vi. 5), or feeding among the lilies (ii. 16; vi. 3), or resting at noon (i. 7); the gazelles bounding over the hills (ii. 9); the doves hiding in the clefts of the rock (ii. 14) or resting beside the water brooks (v. 12); the little foxes spoiling the vines (ii. 15), the streams and cedars of Lebanon (iv. 15; v. 15); the fig-tree ripening her green figs and the vines blossoming and giving forth their fragrance (ii. 13); the rose blooming in the plain of Sharon and the lily in the valley (ii. 1); the garden filled with the choicest fruits and with all manner of valuable herbs (iv. 12-14). The poet's observations are not confined to one particular locality. He has evidently wandered far and wide in his native country—to Kedar (i. 5), Engedi (i. 14), Sharon (ii. 1), Lebanon (iii. 9; iv. 8, 11, 15, etc.), the mountains of Gilead (iv. 1; vi. 5), Amana, Senir and Hermon (iv. 8), Tirzah (vi. 4), Mahanaim (vi. 13), Heshbon (vii. 4), Carmel (vii. 5) and Baalhamon (viii. 11).

Some of the passages in which the love of nature is revealed possess a beauty and a haunting charm which place them among the finest examples of Hebrew poetry.

(a) I am a rose of Sharon,
    a lily of the valleys.
As a lily among brambles,
    so is my love among maidens.
As an apple tree among the trees of the wood
    so is my beloved among young men.
With great delight I sat in his shadow,
    and his fruit was sweet to my taste.
He brought me to the banqueting house,
    and his banner over me was love. (ii. 1–4.)

(b) For lo, the winter is past,
    the rain is over and gone.
The flowers appear on the earth,
    the time of singing has come,
and the voice of the turtledove
    is heard in our land. (ii. 11f.)

(c) Come, my beloved,
    let us go forth into the fields,
    and lodge in the villages;
let us go out early to the vineyards,
    and see whether the vines have budded,
whether the grape blossoms have opened
    and the pomegranates are in bloom.
There I will give you my love. (vii. 11f.)

Numerous images are scattered throughout the book, some of which are very striking, simile being added to simile and metaphor to metaphor in an attempt to depict the charms of the lovers (e.g. ii. 1–4; iv. 1–5, 11–15; v. 10–16; vi. 4–9; vii. 1–9).

Not all the similes and metaphors are appropriate. Some of them are mere fanciful exaggerations, such as when the maiden is likened to 'a mare of Pharaoh's chariots' (i. 9), her two breasts to 'two fawns, twins of a gazelle' (iv. 5, vii. 3), her neck to 'an ivory tower' and her nose to 'a tower of Lebanon overlooking Damascus' (vii. 4). Some of the images describing the physical charms and the wooing of the lovers are distasteful to western minds, but it should be remembered that they are common features in oriental love songs.

The Song is infused with passionate feelings. The lovers reveal their inmost soul without shame and without reserve. No love poem has ever surpassed the strength and passion of the following passage.

'Set me as a seal upon your heart,
    as a seal upon your arm;
for love is strong as death,
    jealousy is cruel as the grave.
Its flashes are flashes of fire,
    a most vehement flame.
Many waters cannot quench love,
    neither can floods drown it.
If a man offered for love
    all the wealth of his house,
    it would be utterly scorned.' (viii. 6f.)

CHAPTER XII

RUTH

TITLE AND PLACE IN CANON

RUTH derives its title from the chief character, Ruth, whose charming personality pervades its pages. In the Hebrew Scriptures it is the second of the five Megilloth or Rolls. In the Septuagint, the Vulgate and the modern English versions of the Bible the book is placed immediately after Judges, its transference from its position in the Hebrew Scriptures being due to the fact that the scene of the story is laid in the time of the Judges. 'In the days when the judges ruled there was a famine in the land' (i. 1).

DATE

There is no unanimity among scholars as to the date of the book. According to Jewish tradition, 'Samuel wrote his book and Judges and Ruth', but this view is now regarded as no longer tenable. In the last century it was customary to assign it to an early date—as early as the time of David, but in recent times the majority of scholars have assigned it to the post-exilic period, mainly for the following reasons.

(1) In the Septuagint, the Vulgate and the modern English versions, the book is placed immediately after Judges, but in the Hebrew Scriptures it is placed among the 'Writings', that is, in the third division of the Hebrew Canon, in which generally only late books appear. Had it belonged to the pre-exilic period, it is reasonable to suppose that it would have been placed after Judges in the second division.

(2) The writer sets the story in the days of the Judges, but he does not claim to be contemporaneous with the incidents which he describes. In fact the opening words (i. 1) suggest that the incidents described took place in the remote past.

(3) By the time the book was written David had become a famous historical figure, and it was evidently considered an honour to be

reckoned among his ancestors. Ruth's son is described as 'the father of Jesse, the father of David' (iv. 17).

(4) The opening verse (i. 1) suggests that the writer was familiar with the Deuteronomic edition of Judges (c. 550 B.C.).

(5) The old custom of removing a shoe to confirm a transaction, familiar in the seventh century B.C. (Deut. xxv. 9f.), has become obsolete and needs explanation (iv. 7).

(6) The style appears to indicate a comparatively late date. Some of the words, expressions and grammatical forms are characteristic of later Hebrew literature. It is true, as Driver maintains, that the style 'is palpably different, not merely from that of Esther and Chronicles, but even from Nehemiah's memoirs or Jonah, and stands on a level with the best parts of Samuel;'[1] but it does not necessarily follow that the book belongs to the pre-exilic period. The writer sets his story in the distant past and may be deliberately imitating the style of Samuel and Kings, which belong to the classical period of Hebrew literature.[2]

If the main purpose of the book was to protest against the rigorous policy of Nehemiah and Ezra it may be dated about the beginning of the fourth century B.C.

PURPOSE

Several theories have been advanced regarding the purpose of the book, but none of them has received universal acceptance. A careful study of the book shows that it is chiefly concerned with the question of inter-marriage. Nehemiah banned foreign marriages, while Ezra went further and insisted upon the Jews putting away their foreign wives; and particular objection was taken to marrying Ammonite or Moabite wives (Neh. xiii. 1–8, 23–27). The hostility of the Jews to the Moabites was of long duration. In Genesis xix. 30–38 the origin of the Moabites is ascribed to the disgraceful conduct of Lot, probably in order to disparage them as a race. A law ordained that they (and the Ammonites) should not enter the congregation till the tenth genera-

---

[1] S. R. Driver, *Introduction to the Literature of the Old Testament*, 9th ed., 1913, p. 454.
[2] A few modern scholars still assign the book to an earlier period. Steinmueller (*Companion to Scripture Studies*, II., 1942, p. 82) and Lattey (*The Book of Ruth*, 1936, pp. xxxiii–xl) assign it to the period of the early monarchy, and Jepsen ('Das Buch Ruth,' *T.S.K.*, N.F. III, 1937–8, pp. 416–422) to the exilic period. Bentzen (*Introduction to the Old Testament*, vol. II, 1948, p. 185) fixes the date any time from the period of the later monarchy to post-exilic days.

tion (Deut. xxiii. 3; cf. Neh. xiii. 1). The temper which dictated the law is shown in the words, 'You shall not seek their peace or their prosperity all your days for ever' (Deut. xxiii. 6). Many scholars regard the book as a political tract written to protest against the prohibition of mixed marriages enforced by Nehemiah and Ezra, by reminding the Jews that their most illustrious king, David, had Moabite blood in his veins. Ruth is repeatedly called the Moabitess (i. 22; ii. 2, 6, 21; iv. 5, 10) and is portrayed as a loyal, loving, virtuous woman, with sufficient faith to accept Israel's God as her own (i. 16f.). In the field she is allowed to eat with the Jews (ii. 14) and is accounted worthy to become the ancestress of David (iv. 17). Rowley holds that it is just as easy to read the book as a defence of the policy of Nehemiah and Ezra, for Ruth was no longer an alien but a proselyte at the time of her marriage to Boaz, and the Jews, in spite of their exclusiveness, were not averse to the receiving of proselytes.[1] According to Slotki, the purpose of the book was, *inter alia* (a), to protest against intermarriage, unless it occurs in exceptional circumstances, and (b) to check indiscriminate proselytization.[2]

Another theory is that the purpose of the book is to commend levirate marriage.[3] This theory is rejected by some scholars because the marriage of Boaz and Ruth was not levirate, since neither Boaz nor the nearer kinsman was a brother of the deceased. But it would appear from the story of Tamar in Genesis xxxviii that the duty of raising children to bear the name of the dead kinsman was not restricted to a brother-in-law. Tamar, who could not marry her brother-in-law, Shelah, because of his youth, tricked her father-in-law, Judah, and became the mother of her twin sons. It may well be, however, that Ruth preserves an older custom than that embodied in Deuteronomy. Other scholars hold that there was no levirate marriage, since it is clearly stated that Boaz acquired Ruth along with Naomi's property

---

[1] H. H. Rowley, *Israel's Mission to the World*, 1939, pp. 46ff., *The Growth of the Old Testament*, 1950, p. 151. Article on 'The Marriage of Ruth' in *The Servant of the Lord*, 1952, pp. 164f.

[2] J. J. Slotki, *The Five Megilloth*, ed by A. Cohen, 1946, p. 39.

[3] The law of levirate marriage provided that if a man died leaving no son, his brother, if he lived on the same estate, should marry the widow, and that the first-born should succeed to the name and to the inheritance of the deceased, 'that the name of his brother may not be blotted out of Israel'. If the brother refused, the widow had the right to complain to the elders of the city. If in their presence he still refused, the widow was to express her contempt for him by removing his shoe and spitting in his face (Deut. xxv. 5-10). In this law nothing is said about any other person accepting the responsibility of marrying the widow.

(iv. 5; v. 10).¹ But against this view it may be urged that Ruth was not part of the property and could not be sold with it. Boaz simply meant that the nearer kinsman in buying the property was also required to marry Ruth as well. The nearer kinsman was willing to buy the property in accordance with the law governing the redemption of property, but he was not prepared to marry Ruth as well in accordance with the law of levirate marriage, since it would diminish his own children's inheritance, as the property would revert to Ruth's first-born child as the heir of Mahlon. Boaz, however, as the next-but-one-of-kin, accepted the double responsibility, buying the property and at the same time marrying Ruth in order that the name of the deceased might be carried on along with his inheritance.²

Two other theories regarding the purpose of the book may be mentioned. Staples gives the book a cultic interpretation. He denies that the book has anything to do with David and eliminates every reference to him. He holds that the town of Bethlehem was named after the god Lehem (Lahmu), who was once worshipped there until he was supplanted by the god Adonis. The names of the characters in the book are interpreted in connexion with these two fertility cults. Elimelech represents the dying god and Naomi the mother-goddess, while Ruth is her devotee.³ This theory may be rejected at once as little more than conjecture.

Some scholars, notably Gunkel, Gressmann and E. Robertson, support the view that the book is a novel, the work not of an ardent reformer, but of a conscious literary artist, intent on telling a story merely to please his readers. Against this theory it may be urged that when the Jews of the post-exilic period wrote in support of heathen peoples, they must have had a distinct purpose for doing so other than that of mere entertainment.

CONTENTS

Outline

Ch. i. Circumstances leading to Ruth's marriage. Left a widow she accompanies her mother-in-law, Naomi, to Bethlehem.

---

[1] In Leviticus xxv. 25 it was enacted that if a man by reason of poverty was forced to sell his property, his nearest kinsman (the go'el) should redeem it, if possible. If the fortune of the original owner improved, he had the right to redeem the property; but it was laid down that in any case it was to revert to him in the year of Jubilee.

[2] For a full discussion of the problem of the marriage of Ruth and Boaz see the article on 'The Marriage of Ruth' by H. H. Rowley in *The Servant of the Lord*, 1952, pp. 163–186.

[3] W. E. Staples, *A.J.S.L.*, LIV. 1936–7, pp. 145–157.

Ch. ii. Ruth gleans in the field of Boaz who treats her kindly.
Ch. iii. Ruth, urged on by Naomi, seeks marriage with Boaz.
Ch. iv. Boaz marries Ruth, and has a son who becomes the ancestor of the royal house of David.

Summary: *Ch. i*

In the days of the Judges, Elimelech, a native of Bethlehem, under stress of famine, emigrates to Moab with his wife, Naomi, and her two sons, Mahlon and Chilion. There Elimelech dies and his two sons marry Moabite women; but after a lapse of about ten years the two sons die also. Naomi resolves to return to her native land and takes farewell of her two daughters-in-law. Ruth, however, in spite of Naomi's earnest entreaty, refuses to leave her, and so together they proceed to Bethlehem where their arrival causes much excitement.

Ch. ii

Owing to their poverty Ruth goes gleaning, as it happens, in a field belonging to Boaz, a wealthy kinsman of the family of Elimelech, who shows her great kindness, inviting her to share the food and drink of the reapers and bidding his young men pull out some of the stalks from the sheaves for her to glean. 'So she kept close to the maidens of Boaz, gleaning until the end of the barley and wheat harvests; and she lived with her mother-in-law' (v. 23).

Ch. iii

Naomi discloses to her daughter-in-law a plan for inducing Boaz to do his duty by her as next of kin (i.e. as go'el). Knowing that Boaz is spending a night at the threshing floor, she advises Ruth to go and lie down at his feet. Ruth proceeds to the threshing-floor, reminds him that he is a near kinsman and asks to be taken under his robe (symbolical of a promise to make her his wife). He points out that there is a nearer kinsman than he who has a better right to marry her, but if the latter refuses to fulfil his obligation, he will undertake the responsibility himself. In the morning he sends her home, 'before one could recognize another', with a gift of barley.

Ch. iv

The same morning Boaz goes to the city gate, and there hails the nearer kinsman of whom he had spoken the previous night. In the presence of ten elders of the city he tells him that Naomi intends to sell the property which had belonged to Elimelech, and asks him if he will do his duty as go'el by buying it. The nearer kinsman at first agrees to buy the property, but on learning that he must at the same time marry Ruth in order to preserve the name of the dead along with his inheritance, he refuses to accept the twofold obligation and offers the right of redemption to Boaz, who thereupon buys the property and marries Ruth. A child is born who is destined to become the grandfather of David.

UNITY

There is almost universal agreement that apart from the genealogy (iv. 18–22) the book is a unity. The genealogy is thought to be a later insertion, mainly because it presents a point of view different from that of the preceding narrative. Whereas in the preceding narrative Ruth's son is recognized by a legal fiction as Mahlon's, in the genealogy he is regarded as the child of Boaz. This argument for the rejection of the genealogy is unconvincing. Rowley points out that 'if Boaz had taken Ruth to be his legal wife and had not merely played the part of kinsman, then the same child would be his heir as well as Mahlon's.... There is thus no conflict on this view between the appendix and the preceding verses.'[1] A more likely reason for the rejection of the genealogy is that it is merely an amplification of verse 17, added in order to supply the missing links between Boaz and Perez (iv. 12). It seems to be based on the genealogy in 1 Chronicles ii. 4–15, or it may be that both passages are derived from a common source.[2]

HISTORICITY

A few scholars still hold that the book is a record of events which actually occurred in the period of the Judges. There is, however, almost universal agreement that it is not sober truth but fiction. The reasons given in support of this view are as follows:

(1) The conditions of life depicted are different from those which prevailed in the period of the Judges.

[1] H. H. Rowley, article on 'The Marriage of Ruth' in *The Servant of the Lord*, 1952, pp. 185f.
[2] E. Robertson (article on 'The Plot of Ruth' in *B.J.R.L.*, vol. 32, 2, 1950, pp. 207–228) suggests that the author based his story on (1) a tradition that Israel's most illustrious king, David, had Moabite blood in his veins; (2) the story of Tamar and Judah (Gen. xxxviii. 1–26); (3) Hosea ix. 1 in which Israel is charged with having loved 'a harlot's hire upon all threshing floors'.

(2) It is impossible to believe that such a happy contented community could have existed in that dark and stormy period.

(3) The names of Elimelech ('my God is king'), Mahlon ('sickness'), Chilion ('wasting'), Naomi ('my pleasant one'), Orpah (meaning uncertain—perhaps 'stiff-necked'), Ruth (meaning uncertain—perhaps 'the friend' or 'the companion') and Boaz ('in him is strength') are so appropriate to the story that they must have been chosen by the author to suit the creations of his imagination.

(4) The incidents of the plot from the sad opening to the happy ending could not have occurred in the same order in actual life. They have evidently been arranged in a particular order by a conscious literary artist in order to produce a dramatic effect.

PERMANENT INFLUENCE

Historically the book is of little value. Since it probably belongs to the post-exilic period, it can supply little reliable information concerning the social conditions existing in the country in the days of the Judges. The only item of value may be the tradition of David's Moabite ancestry. In the sphere of religion the book is of value as anticipating the teaching of the New Testament that God is no respecter of persons. 'For there is no distinction between Jew and Greek; the same Lord is Lord of all and bestows his riches upon all who call upon him' (Rom. x. 12).

LITERARY MERIT

Scene

It is in the realm of literature that the book has won lasting fame. The story is set in the period of the Judges, but it does not mirror the life of that period with its lawlessness, bloodshed and cruelty. The author seems to have deliberately omitted the dark side of life in order to place his characters amid idyllic surroundings. The picture presented to us is that of a rural community, consisting of rich and poor, engaged in agriculture and dwelling together in peace and contentment. We see the reapers cutting the standing barley and gathering together for their mid-day meal; Ruth gleaning the ears, beating out the corn and carrying it home to her mother-in-law; Boaz winnowing the barley at the threshing-floor and sleeping at night in the open air; the elders meeting at the city gate in the morning; the people invoking the blessing of Yahweh upon the union of Boaz and Ruth, and Naomi clasping Ruth's first-born child to her bosom in the knowledge that now the name of her dead son will not be forgotten in Israel.

Plot

The plot is well-conceived and skilfully developed through a variety of open-air scenes. The interest of the reader is roused and maintained throughout the narrative—from the time when famine compels Elimelech and his family to leave Bethlehem to the time when Naomi holds Ruth's child in her arms.

Characterization

The chief characters, Naomi, Ruth and Boaz, though lightly sketched, are not dim shadowy figures but real living people. No attempt is made to analyse their characters. Their words and deeds are recorded and the reader is left to form his own conclusions about them.

Naomi stands out as a God-fearing woman, patriotic, tolerant towards strangers, capable of deep affection and shrewd. As soon as she hears that Yahweh has given his people bread, she resolves to return to her native land though she has lived in Moab about ten years (i. 1-6). At a time when the Jews hate the foreigner she accepts Orpah and Ruth, two women of Moab, into her family. She is deeply attached to them, and prays that Yahweh will recompense them for all the kindness they have shown her, and that He will grant each of them a new home in the house of a husband (i. 8f.). Her sufferings have caused her to meditate upon the mystery of pain and sorrow, and made her doubt the truth of the prevailing Jewish doctrine that Yahweh rewards the good and punishes the wicked. She leaves Bethlehem with a husband and a family and returns widowed and childless, lonely and poor. In her bitterness she says to her old neighbours, 'Do not call me Naomi, call me Mara, for the Almighty has dealt very bitterly with me' (i. 20).

She is clearly a stronger character than Ruth. It is she who tells Ruth where to glean (ii. 22) and contrives to bring her and her wealthy kinsman together (iii. 1-4). Some scholars maintain that in order to gain her ends she places Ruth in grave moral danger by advising her to visit Boaz by night at the threshing floor. But she knows that Boaz is a man of honour and that Ruth will come to no harm. In the last picture we have of her she is clasping Ruth's child to her bosom (iv. 16).

Ruth is the most lovable woman in the whole of Jewish literature. The secret of her charm lies not in her beauty—for we are not told that she is fair to look upon—but in her love and loyalty, her industry, gentleness and kindness. So great is her love for Naomi that she is prepared to renounce not only her own people and her own country, but also her religion and the melancholy privilege of being buried in her native land. The words in which she expresses her determination to follow Naomi wherever she may go, are among the most beautiful in all literature (i. 16f.). To provide food for herself and her mother-in-law she goes gleaning in the field of Boaz where she attracts the attention of the overseer by her industry, for she works 'without resting even for a moment' (ii. 7). To-day her conduct in visiting Boaz by night at the threshing-floor would be considered reprehensible in a woman, but she must not be judged by modern standards but in accordance with the customs of the time. Boaz himself declares that all the people of his city know that she is a virtuous woman (iii. 11). The people, too, believe that she is worthy to become like Rachel and Leah who together built up the house of Israel (iv. 11).

Boaz is described as 'a man of wealth' (ii. 1). He has an overseer in charge of his reapers and he himself makes a visit of inspection (ii. 4f.). He is evidently a man in advancing years, for he addresses Ruth as 'my daughter' (ii. 8) and is pleased that she prefers him to the young men of the district, rich or poor (iii. 10). He seems to wield considerable influence among the people, for at the city gate he speaks to the elders with the voice of authority (iv. 1f.). Though he is wealthy, he assists the reapers in gathering in the harvest in the daytime and winnows the barley at the threshing-floor in the evening. His relations with his servants are of the friendliest nature, greeting them with the words, 'The Lord be with you', and receiving the reply, 'The Lord bless you' (ii. 4). Such greetings were and still are conventional in the East, but we feel that they have been deliberately introduced to reveal the kindly disposition of Boaz and the cordial relations existing between himself and his servants. It is obvious that he is attracted to Ruth at the first sight of her (ii. 5, 8f., 11f., 14–16). Unlike the vast majority of his countrymen he is not prejudiced against foreigners. It matters not to him that Ruth is a Moabitess. He is the soul of honour. We feel that even when Ruth is alone with him in the darkness of the night, no harm will come to her (iii. 1–14). He is fair to the nearer kinsman, reminding the latter of his prior right to redeem Naomi's property and to marry Ruth, before undertaking the twofold responsibility himself (iv. 1–10). He stands out as one of the most attractive figures in the Old Testament.

Style

The story is written entirely in prose, which is characterized by simplicity, directness and restraint. It is written in simple language with few obscurities, and partly in direct speech which is simpler and more natural than reported speech. There is no elaboration of details either in the narration of events or in the characterization. No details are given of the famine in Judah or of the journey of Elimelech and his family to Moab. Instead we have the bald statement, 'In the days when the judges ruled there was a famine in the land, and a certain man of Bethlehem in Judah went to sojourn in the country of Moab, he and his wife and his two sons' (i. 1). Though the story is a love-story there is no direct reference to love in it. There are no descriptions of the actors in the story and no attempt is made at analysis of character. Effective use is made of contrast. Elimelech and his family leave Bethlehem in a time of famine and Naomi, accompanied by Ruth, returns when she hears 'that the Lord had visited his people and given them food' (i. 6). Henceforth she desires to be called not Naomi ('pleasant') but Mara ('bitter') for she went away full and the Lord had brought her back empty (i. 20f.). The poverty of Naomi and Ruth is contrasted with the wealth of Boaz, and the keenness of Boaz to marry Ruth with the indifference of the nearer kinsman. At times the prose becomes rhythmical and rises to the level of poetry. Poetical rhythm is obvious in Ruth's words to Naomi, 'Entreat me not to leave you, or to return from following you; for where you go I will go, and where you lodge, I will lodge; your people shall be my people, and your God my God; where you die I will die, and there will I be buried' (i. 16). It is apparent in Naomi's words to the women of Bethlehem, 'I went away full, and the Lord has brought me back empty' (i. 21); and in those of Boaz to Ruth, 'The Lord recompense you for what you have done, and a full reward be given you by the Lord, the God of Israel, under whose wings you have come to take refuge!' (ii. 12).

Conclusion

The story, with its idyllic setting, its peaceful, pastoral atmosphere, its interesting plot, and its simple kindly characters, is told with rare delicacy and grace, and possesses a beauty and a charm which have captured the imaginations of people, especially poets and artists, in every age, for everyone delights in a love-story, especially when it is beautifully told. It is no wonder that Goethe speaks of it as 'the loveliest little thing that has come down to us of all the epics and idylls of the past'.

CHAPTER XIII

LAMENTATIONS

TITLE AND PLACE IN CANON

THE title of the book in the Hebrew Canon is 'Ekah' ('How!'), the word which commences the first, second and fourth of the five poems to which the five chapters correspond. In the Talmud the book is named after its contents, 'Qinoth' ('Dirges'), and this term in translation is found in the Septuagint ('Threnoi') and in the Vulgate ('Threni'). The versions usually add 'of Jeremiah'.

In the Hebrew Canon the book is the third of the five Megilloth or Rolls. In the Septuagint and practically all the versions it comes immediately after Jeremiah.

STRUCTURE

The book comprises five poems corresponding to the five chapters. The first four poems are alphabetical acrostics. Each of the first two poems contains twenty-two three-lined stanzas, each beginning with the appropriate letter of the Hebrew alphabet. The third poem consists of sixty-six single lines (or verses) grouped in threes, each of the three lines in the same group beginning with the same letter, with the result that there are three 'aleph' lines, three 'beth' lines, etc. In the fourth poem the structure is similar to that of the first except that each stanza has two lines only. The fifth poem contains twenty-two lines (or verses) but they are not arranged alphabetically.

The order of the Hebrew alphabet in the first poem is slightly different from that in the other four. In the first poem the letters are placed in their usual order, whereas in the second, third and fourth poems the letter 'Pe', usually the seventeenth, precedes the letter 'ayin', usually the sixteenth. This letter order is found elsewhere in the Old Testament, showing that it was once regarded as the correct order.

The metre used in the first four poems is the 'Qinah' or 'Dirge'.

In this metre each line (or verse) usually contains five accents with a pause after the third group of syllables, so that the rhythm is 3:2 (with an occasional 2:2), the unequal division giving the metre 'a plaintive, melancholy cadence', which can sometimes be traced, even in translation. The metre of the fifth poem is 3:3.

The combination of the artificial acrostic form with the deep emotional content of the poems has roused much discussion. It has been suggested that the acrostic form was adopted because of the magical power of the letters. It is, however, very unlikely that in the sixth century B.C. devout Jews would attribute magical power to letters. A more commonly held view is that the acrostic form was a pedagogic device to aid the memory. Gottwald claims that although facility in memorization may have played a part in the adoption of the acrostic form, its main purpose was 'to encourage completeness in the expression of grief, the confession of sin, and the instilling of hope'.[1]

CLASSIFICATION

The laments which make up Lamentations can be classified according to literary types. The first, second and fourth laments reveal the characteristics of the funeral dirge, the third is an individual lament and the fifth a communal lament. The laments, however, are not pure but are a blend of literary types. For example, elements of the individual lament appear in i. 9c, 11c, 12–16 and of the communal lament in iii. 40–47 and iv. 17–22. According to Gottwald, 'it would be better to recognize that in chapters one and two there is a polarization between the individual sufferings of the people and the collective personified suffering of Jerusalem. Both the funeral song and individual lament as formal types are employed here and there, but always in the communal sense.'[2]

Opinions differ regarding the type to which the third lament belongs. Some scholars think that it is an individual lament based upon the concept of corporate personality, which enables the writer to pass from his own personal sorrows to those of the whole nation. Others consider that the writer is describing not so much his own sufferings as those of Jeremiah. Gottwald calls Lamentations 'a communal lament of mixed types from the sixth century B.C.'.[3]

---

[1] N. K. Gottwald, *Studies in the Book of Lamentations*, 1954, p. 28.
[2] *Ibid.*, p. 37.
[3] *Ibid.*, p. 42.

AUTHORSHIP

An ancient tradition ascribes the authorship of the book to Jeremiah. In the Septuagint the book opens with the words, 'And it came to pass after Israel was taken captive and Jerusalem made desolate, Jeremiah sat weeping and lamented with this lamentation over Jerusalem and said. . . .' The Talmud, the Church Fathers and the Vulgate also attribute the authorship of the book to Jeremiah. This tradition has now been abandoned by the majority of scholars for the following reasons.

(1) The tradition probably arose from a misunderstanding of 2 Chronicles xxxv. 25 where we read 'Jeremiah also uttered a lament for Josiah; and all the singing men and singing women have spoken of Josiah in their laments to this day. They made these an ordinance in Israel; behold, they are written in the Laments.' An examination of Lamentations, however, shows that it has nothing to do with Josiah, so that it cannot be the same book as that mentioned by the Chronicler, which is no longer extant.

(2) It is true that the book has literary affinities with the prophecies of Jeremiah, but these may be accounted for on the assumption that the author (or authors) of the book was familiar with the prophet's writings and borrowed from them.

(3) In the Hebrew text the book is not ascribed to Jeremiah. Had it been known as the work of the author, his name would surely have been mentioned.

(4) Some of the views embodied in the book are contrary to those held by Jeremiah. It is unlikely that he who claimed to speak by divine inspiration (Jer. i. 1-9), would have said that the prophets of Zion received 'no vision from the Lord' (Lam. ii. 9). He taught that every man was responsible for his own sins (Jer. xxxi. 29f.), but in Lamentations v. 7 we read, 'Our fathers sinned, and are no more; and we bear their iniquities.' He placed no trust in Egypt (Jer. xxxvii. 5-10), but in Lamentations iv. 17 we find the author identifying himself with those who expected help from that country. The prophet classed Zedekiah among the evil-doers whom Yahweh would utterly destroy (Jer. xxiv. 8-10), but in Lamentations iv. 20 he is described as 'the breath of our nostrils'.

(5) It is hard to believe that Jeremiah, who was capable of great intensity of feeling, would have adopted the artificial form of the

acrostic, which impedes the free development of thought, for the expression of his inconsolable grief over the destruction of Jerusalem.

(6) The alphabetical order of the first chapter differs slightly from that of the second, third and fourth chapters, suggesting that the chapters are the work of more than one author.

(7) Considerations of language and style are against Jeremiah's authorship. The book contains a large number of words not found in the writings of Jeremiah. The style of the five chapters comprising the book is not uniform, suggesting that they are not the work of any one man.

DATE

The question of the date is complicated since it is necessary to fix the time of writing of five chapters. The second and fourth chapters reveal an intimate knowledge of the tragic events associated with the destruction of Jerusalem in 587 B.C., and are perhaps the work of an eyewitness who was influenced by the prophecies of Ezekiel and wrote not many years after the siege and sack of the city.

In the first chapter the fall of the city is past history (i. 7) and is not portrayed with the same vividness and intensity of feeling. There is no reference to the return of the exiles from captivity. It probably belongs to the latter part of the exilic period.

The third chapter presents us with a different problem. It describes the suffering, not of a community but of an individual. It was evidently written in a time of persecution, but there is no explicit reference either to the destruction of Jerusalem or to the Exile. It has literary affinities with Isaiah xl–lxvi and with some of the Psalms of lament in the Psalter.[1] It is artificial in style and contents, and from a literary point of view inferior to the other four chapters. The author perhaps lived in the fourth century B.C. and felt the weight of his country's woe and the tragedy of Jeremiah.

The fifth chapter presents a picture of the sad plight of the Jewish community after the destruction of Jerusalem. A considerable time has elapsed since the catastrophe, for the mountain of Zion is desolate and the jackals walk upon it (v. 18). The poet says, 'Our fathers sinned, and are no more' (v. 7), and asks why the Lord has forsaken His people for such a long time (v. 20). There is no suggestion that

---

[1] Gottwald (*Studies in the Book of Lamentations*, 1954, pp. 42–44) holds that all the chapters in Lamentations have literary affinities with Isaiah xl–lxvi and that both Deutero-Isaiah and Trito-Isaiah were acquainted with the book. He assigns all the chapters to the exilic period and suggests that they formed a single corpus as early as 538 B.C.

they have escaped from beneath the Babylonian yoke. The chapter probably comes from the same period as the first, that is, the latter part of the exilic period.[1]

The book must have been compiled in the post-exilic period, but the exact date of its compilation cannot be determined.

CONTENTS

Outline

Ch. i. The poet laments over the desolation and misery of Zion. The city (personified) takes up the lament, describing her woes, confessing her sins and praying that a similar fate may befall her enemies.

Ch. ii. The poet laments over the ruin wrought by Yahweh in His anger, blaming the prophets for the calamity, and exhorting Zion to appeal to Yahweh for help.

Ch. iii. The poet laments over his own sufferings and those of his compatriots, finds comfort and hope in the assurance of Yahweh's mercy for those who seek Him, confesses his sins, and prays for vengeance on his enemies.

Ch. iv. The poet laments over the fate of the people, the princes, the prophets and priests, and the king, and prophesies the doom of Edom.

Ch. v. The poet prays to Yahweh, laying before Him the sufferings of His people and appealing for a speedy deliverance.

Summary: Ch. i

The poet laments over the solitude and desertion of Zion. The once great city that had received the tribute of other nations is now herself a subject state. Of all those who sought friendly relations with her, there is not one of them to comfort her in her distress. Her friends have betrayed her and become her enemies. The inhabitants of Judaea have gone into exile to escape affliction and servitude. The roads to Zion mourn because no one comes to the appointed feast. Her gates are deserted, her priests sigh for the loss of the Temple and her maidens are afflicted. Yahweh has punished her for her sins; her child-

---

[1] There are wide differences of opinion on the question of the dates of the five chapters. Lohr, followed by Budde, assigns ii and iv to c. 580 B.C., v to c. 550 B.C., i to 540 B.C. and iii to 325 B.C. Cheyne and Ball assign all the chapters to the post-exilic period, while Driver assigns them to the exilic period. Pfeiffer assigns ii and iv to 586–560 B.C., v to c. 530 B.C., i to 516–444 B.C. and iii to the third century B.C. Rowley assigns all the chapters to the exilic period, except perhaps iii which may be post-exilic.

ren have gone into captivity. All her grandeur has vanished and her princes have no strength to flee from their enemies. In her affliction Jerusalem remembers her former happy state. She has sinned grievously and all who honoured her now despise her because of her wickedness. Her sins are now public for all to see and she is heedless of the consequence of her sins. Her adversaries have seized all her treasures and she has seen the heathen enter her sanctuary. Her people have given up their most valuable possessions for food (vv. 1–11).

Jerusalem laments that there is no sorrow like her sorrow, which Yahweh has brought upon her 'on the day of his fierce anger'. He has sent calamities upon her, and bound together her transgressions into a yoke which He has placed on her neck to weigh her down. He has summoned a festival to celebrate the overthrow of the flower of her army, and trodden her down as grapes are trodden in a wine-press. She weeps because the comforter is not present to refresh her soul and because her children are desolate. The poet laments that Zion pleads in vain. Her enemies look upon her with loathing as if she is ceremoniously defiled. The city, resuming her lament, acknowledges that Yahweh is a righteous God and that she has rebelled against Him. Her people have gone into captivity, her allies betrayed her and her priests and elders perished for lack of food. All her enemies are glad because they have heard of her troubles which Yahweh has brought upon her. She prays that He will bring a similar fate upon them because of their wickedness (vv. 12–22).

Ch. ii

The poet laments over the havoc which Yahweh has wrought in the land. He has flung down the beauty of Israel, demolished her homes and fortresses, degraded her king and her princes, taken away her strength, withdrawn His protection from them as they faced the foe and carried destruction into the heart of the nation. In Zion He has destroyed her palaces and strongholds, demolished His own sanctuary, abolished feast and sabbath and spurned aside in indignation king and priest alike. He has discarded His own altar and scorned the sanctuary. The enemy has raised the shout of triumph in the sanctuary. Yahweh was determined to destroy the walls of Zion. He made rampart and wall lament and totter; her gates have sunk into the ground. Her king and her princes are in exile; there is no priestly instruction and her prophets have no vision from Yahweh. The elders of Zion are now silent and her maidens hang their heads (vv. 1–10).

The poet laments over the children who die of starvation. He cannot point to any other nation that has suffered a like calamity, and therefore cannot comfort her with the thought that she is not alone in her grief. The prophets have lulled the people into a false sense of security with their worthless visions instead of exposing and rebuking their sins. All her enemies gloat over her downfall, reminding her of the high esteem in which they had held her. They gnash their teeth in rage, and rejoice that what they have hoped for has come to pass. Yahweh has fulfilled His word and destroyed her without pity (vv. 11–17).

The poet calls upon Zion to pray to Yahweh that He may spare her starving children, and that He may remember that the people whom He has afflicted are His chosen people. Women devour their children; priests and prophets are slain in the sanctuary; young and old lie dead in the streets. He has summoned the terrors of war to destroy her (vv. 18–22).

Ch. iii

The poet laments that he has suffered under the rod of Yahweh's anger. He has led him along a dark, unlighted road, turned His hand continually against him, worn away his bodily strength, besieged him, made him dwell in the darkness of death, hemmed him in, burdened him with chains, ignored his prayer, ambushed and torn him like a wild beast, pierced him with arrows and made him a laughing stock to all His people. He has filled him with bitterness and broken his teeth, covered him with ashes, and bereft him of all bliss so that he forgets what it is to prosper. The poet laments that his strength and his hope in Yahweh have gone. His soul is always thinking of his afflictions and is crushed within him (vv. 1–20).

The poet is comforted by the thought of Yahweh's mercies, which are inexhaustible. Yahweh is his allotted portion and therefore he will hope in Him. He is good to those who wait for Him. It is good for a man to wait submissively and uncomplainingly for His salvation, and to bear the yoke of suffering in his youth. He should submit patiently since it has been laid upon him. Yahweh will not cast off men for ever. Though He wounds He will have mercy, so rich is His love. He is loth to pain or grieve the children of men. He does not see fit to treat men cruelly, or to defraud them of their rights, or to condemn them unjustly. Nothing can happen against His will. Calamity and prosperity come in response to His command. Since calamity is His punishment for sin, man has no cause to complain (vv. 21–39).

The poet pleads with his people to scan and search their own lives and to return to Yahweh, lifting up their hearts as well as their heads. They have sinned and Yahweh in His anger has punished them relentlessly. He has covered Himself with a cloud which no prayer can pierce. He has made them the scum and refuse of the world. Their foes all yell against them and dismay and destruction fall upon them. Tears flood the poet's eyes because of the ruin of his people; his eyes stream without ceasing until Yahweh will look down from heaven. They cast him into a dungeon to die, flinging stones at him. Intense distress came upon Him (vv. 40-54).

From the depth of the dungeon the poet called to Yahweh who came at his call and bade him not to fear. Yahweh took his part, saved his life and saw the wrong done to him. The poet prays that Yahweh will vindicate him. Yahweh has seen all the revenge and all the insults which his enemies have plotted against him. Amid all their activities he is the subject of their taunting songs of contempt and triumph. He prays that Yahweh will pursue them in His anger and destroy them (vv. 55-66).

Ch. iv

The poet laments over the fate of the inhabitants of Zion. Her choicest inhabitants are treated as dross. Mothers are as cruel as the ostrich, for they desert their children who vainly beg for bread. Those children who fared on dainties now rot upon the streets, and those who were clad in rich and costly clothing now lie prostrate on ash-heaps. The sin of the people is greater than that of Sodom, that fell in a flash before anyone could wring his hands. Her nobles, who were purer than snow and whiter than milk, are now darker than night, and are so emaciated that no one recognizes them in the street. It were better to die by the sword than by hunger. Mothers, naturally pitiful, have devoured their own offspring (vv. 1-10).

Yahweh has poured out His fury in full measure, and has lit a fire in Zion that has burned her foundations. Neither the kings nor the inhabitants of the earth could believe that the foe could enter the gates of Jerusalem. The calamity is due to the sins of the prophets and the priests who have shed in her the blood of the just. Stained with blood they wander blindly through the streets, and men shrink from them as though they were lepers. They seek refuge in foreign lands but the heathen will not allow them to settle. The anger of Yahweh has scattered them, caring nothing for them, regardless of the priests and heedless of the prophets. The people look in vain for help from Egypt. Foes dog their steps and they cannot walk abroad. Their pursuers hunted them over the mountains and ambushed them in the wilderness. They trapped the king, the very breath of their lives, under whom they believed they would retain their national identity. Edom's triumph will be shortlived for the cup of punishment shall pass to her. The punishment of Zion is accomplished and she shall no more be carried into captivity, but Edom's iniquity shall be punished and her sins laid bare (vv. 11–22).

Ch. v

The poet appeals to Yahweh to consider the plight of the people. Their lands and houses have been handed to strangers. They are fatherless orphans (because the fathers are in exile) and the mothers are like widows. They must beg water and wood in order to obtain food; the yoke on their neck has been made heavy and they toil and have no rest. They have submitted to the Egyptians and the Assyrians to obtain enough bread. They have suffered for the sins of their fathers. Slaves rule over them and they get their bread at the risk of their lives. Their skin is hot with the fever-heat of famine. The women of Zion and Judaea were ravished, princes were tortured and elders dishonoured. Young men were compelled to carry the heavy millstone and children stumbled carrying loads of wood. Elders no longer sit at the gate or young men at their music. The joy of the people is turned into mourning and their honour is brought to the dust. Their hearts are faint and their eyes dim because of the desolation of Zion (vv. 1–18).

The poet asks Yahweh, who endures for ever, why He has forgotten Israel for such a long time, and prays that He may give them repentant hearts, unless He has utterly rejected them (vv. 19–22).

TEACHING

The whole of Lamentations reflects the teaching of the great prophets. The influence of their teaching is seen in its monotheism, its conception of the deity, its preaching of doom as the direct consequence of sin, its exhortation to confession, repentance and submission, its awareness of the spiritual nature of true religion and its hopeful outlook.

Monotheism

Monotheism, though it is not explicitly taught, is taken for granted. There is no mention of the worship of other gods. Yahweh is God alone and reigns as king over the whole world. 'But thou, O Lord, dost reign for ever; thy throne endures to all generations' (v. 19).

God Controls History

Yahweh controls the destinies of nations and of men. He has cast down from heaven to earth the beauty of Israel, destroying her dwellings and fortresses, degrading her king and princes and shattering her might. In Zion He has poured out His fury like fire, destroying her palaces, demolishing His own shrine, abolishing feast and sabbath, spurning king and priest alike, scorning His sanctuary, making rampart and wall lament and totter, and carrying into exile her king and princes (ii. 1–9). He has roused the hostility of other nations against her (i. 17), caused her enemy to rejoice over her downfall and exalted the might of her foes (ii. 17). He has the power to bring the day of retribution upon all her enemies (i. 21). The writer of the third chapter declares that Yahweh is the cause of all his suffering (iii. 1–17). Yahweh is the author of both good and evil. 'Is it not from the mouth of the Most High that good and evil come?' (iii. 38.) His ways are beyond man's comprehension. 'Who has commanded and it came to pass unless the Lord has ordained it?' (iii. 37.)

The Nature of God

Yahweh is a righteous God who demands righteousness of life from His worshippers, rewarding the good and punishing the wicked. He is a just God who does not approve of injustice (iii. 34–36). Though He is just He is also merciful. His mercies are inexhaustible and are new every morning (iii. 22f.). He is good 'to those who wait for him, to the soul that seeks him' (iii. 25). Though He wounds He will have compassion, so rich is His love, 'for he does not willingly afflict or grieve the sons of men' (iii. 33).

Retribution

The theme of the whole book is the doom which has fallen upon Jerusalem as the direct consequence of her sin. Yahweh in His anger has destroyed her Temple, palaces, houses, ramparts, walls and gates, slain many of her inhabitants, carried others into captivity and left the remainder to live in destitution and servitude. No other nation has ever witnessed such a catastrophe; it can only be compared in its magnitude with the vastness of the sea (ii. 13). So terrible is the tragedy of the fall of the city that it is identified with the 'day of Yahweh' (i. 12; ii. 1, 21f.). Her sin is so evident that all who honoured her now despise her (i. 8), and so heinous that it is greater than that of Sodom (iv. 6). Only one national sin, however, is specified, namely the irresponsible leadership of her prophets and priests. The prophets delight in false visions of peace and prosperity and have not warned Zion of her sin (ii. 14), while both prophets and priests have shed the blood of the righteous (iv. 13). The responsibility of the people for their own suffering is acknowledged. 'Woe to us, for we have sinned!' (v. 16.) In verse 7 of the same chapter, however, it is stated that they are paying the penalty for the sins of their fathers. Apparently the writer considers that the people in their suffering are paying the penalty not only for their own sins, but for those of the preceding generations. Yahweh has not only punished Zion for her sin but will also punish the guilt of Edom and lay bare her sins.

> The punishment of your iniquity, O daughter of Zion,
>   is accomplished,
>   he will keep you in exile no longer;
> but your iniquity, O daughter of Edom,
>   he will punish,
>   he will uncover your sins. (iv. 22.)

Confession and Repentance

Stress is laid upon the necessity of confession and repentance. Again and again we come across the confession of sin. Yahweh has punished Zion for her many sins (i. 5, 18, 20, 22; iv. 13). She has become filthy (i. 8); she cannot rest because she has been 'very rebellious' (i. 20). The destruction of Jerusalem is due to 'the sins of the prophets and the iniquities of her priests' (iv. 13). Because the people have sinned the crown has fallen from their head, their heart has become sick and their eyes have grown dim, Mount Zion lies desolate and jackals prowl over it (v. 16–18). The people are exhorted to examine their ways, to confess their sins and to return to Yahweh (iii. 40–42). Repentance is the work not only of man, but also of God. 'Restore us to thyself, O Lord, that we may be restored!' (v. 21.)

Submission to God and the Foe

Man should adopt a submissive attitude towards God and the foe. It is good that a man should wait quietly for the salvation of Yahweh and that he should bear the yoke in his youth. Since it has been laid upon him, he should wait in silence and put his mouth in the dust, for there may be hope for him. He should offer his cheek to the smiter and suffer all the insults of man (iii. 25–30). The patient endurance of suffering does not imply simply resignation or compliance with an inscrutable fate. It is true that suffering is a punishment for sin and should be accepted without a murmur (iii. 39), but it is also part of the divine plan. By the patient endurance of suffering man co-operates with Yahweh in the redemption of mankind (iii. 25–27).

The Spirituality of True Worship

The religion of Yahweh can exist independently of the Temple and its priesthood. Their loss does not mean that Yahweh can no longer be worshipped; the people can still call upon Him for pardon and deliverance. Moreover they are exhorted to lift up their hearts as well as their hands to God in heaven (iii. 41). There is an awareness of the fact that true religion is essentially spiritual in its nature and does not depend on the Temple and the sacrificial system. The book, therefore, has a place in the development of personal religion.

Hope

In the book there sounds, though not loudly or continuously, the note of hope. There is nothing in the prevailing conditions to encourage the people to hope. Jerusalem, with her Temple, palaces, houses, ramparts, walls and gates, is in ruins and many of her inhabitants have been slain. The survivors of the catastrophe are either in exile or living in a state of destitution and servitude amid the ruins of the capital or in the surrounding districts. The hope of the people is based upon their belief in an omnipotent, just and merciful God who controls history. The people are urged to pray in the hope that Yahweh will have mercy upon them and come to their aid. There is the hope that there will be no more exile for them (iv. 22) and that Yahweh will renew their days as of yore (v. 21). In their apparently hopeless condition they can still dream of regaining their freedom, re-establishing the monarchy and the priesthood, reorganizing the Temple worship and recovering their former prosperity.

PERMANENT INFLUENCE

Lamentations is historically important for the information it supplies concerning the siege and sack of Jerusalem of 587 B.C., and the conditions existing in the Jewish community in Palestine during the Exile. As historical records the most important chapters are the second and the fourth, which are probably the work of an eyewitness. Of less importance are the first and fifth chapters, which were probably written in the latter part of the exilic period when the events associated with the siege and destruction of the city had become a dim memory. The third chapter is a personal lament with little or no historical significance.

From i, ii, iv and v we learn that when the Babylonians captured Jerusalem they wrought such havoc that there remained of it little more than a heap of ruins (ii. 2–9; cf. i. 1–4). The inhabitants expected help from Egypt but their hopes were not realized (iv. 17). During the siege children died of starvation (ii. 11f.) or were eaten by their mothers (ii. 20). Priests and elders died as they searched in vain for food (i. 19). The sufferings from famine were so terrible that death by the sword was preferable to death by starvation (iv. 9). Women were ravished, princes tortured and elders dishonoured (v. 11f.). Priests and prophets were slain in the sanctuary and young and old lay dead in the streets (ii. 20f.). The king, under whom they hoped to retain their national identity, was trapped (iv. 20; cf. ii. 9). The prophets and priests, the recognized leaders of the people, were held responsible for the catastrophe because of their sins. They wandered blindly through the streets and were regarded by the people as moral lepers. They fled abroad but found no shelter (iv. 13–16).

The fifth poem is also of importance because of the information it supplies concerning the conditions existing in Palestine during the Exile. Mount Zion lay desolate with jackals prowling over it (v. 15). The lands and houses of the people were in the hands of foreigners (v. 2). The necessaries of life, like water and wood, had to be paid for (v. 4). Slaves, who had risen to high office among the Babylonians, ruled over them (v. 8). Surrender to the enemy had meant endless toil, starvation and dishonour (v. 5, 9f., 16). All that delighted the heart had gone and dancing had been turned into mourning (v. 15).

As literature the book occupies an important position in the development of Hebrew religious poetry. Subsequent writers of laments found in it the perfect mode of expression and so used its imagery and its terminology. 'Indeed the radical change of the religious life of the nation caused by the captivity could not fail to influence the psalmody of the sanctuary more than any other part of the worship: the Book of Lamentations marks an era of profound importance in the religious poetry of Israel, and no collection formed before those dirges were first sung could have been an adequate hymn-book of the Second Temple'.[1]

The book has also influenced the worship of the Christian Church. Passages from it for reading in Holy Week are included in the liturgies of the Roman Catholic Church, the Church of England and the Presbyterian Church of the United States. It seems, however, to have played little part in the preaching ministry of the Church.

LITERARY MERIT

We have already shown that the first four poems are acrostics written in the Qinah metre, while the fifth is an incomplete ascrostic written in the 3:3 metre. This artificial arrangement shows that the poems are not the spontaneous outpourings of distress but the work of conscious art. The poems are written in deep distress but the distress is deeper in some than in others. There is, however, 'none of that wild almost vulgar distress displayed by Hecuba in the tragedy of Euripides, but rather the restrained and measured grief of Moschus in his lament for Bion'.[2]

The poems are probably not the work of a single author, since the order of the letters of the alphabet differ in the first poem from that in the second, third and fourth poems, and the poems vary in quality. The second and fourth poems are by far the best and are perhaps from one hand. The first and fifth poems are somewhat inferior to them, while the third is distinctly the poorest of them all. They are, however, all characterized by graphic description, vivid imagery, felicity of expression and deep feeling, and are worthy to be ranked among the finest productions of the ancient Hebrew literature.

---

[1] W. Robertson Smith, *The Old Testament in the Jewish Church*, 1892, 2nd ed., p. 218.
[2] H. R. Roper, *The Lamentations of Jeremiah*, in Gore's Commentary, 1928, p. 515.

CHAPTER XIV

ECCLESIASTES

TITLE AND PLACE IN CANON

THE Hebrew title of the book is Koheleth, which is a masculine noun with a feminine termination. Jewish rabbis explain the feminine form on the supposition that it denotes personified Wisdom; but since the word refers to a king in Jerusalem, it probably denotes an office or title. The term is generally taken to mean, 'one who convenes or addresses a religious assembly'. In the Septuagint the title of the book is Ecclesiastes = 'Preacher', which is an attempt to express the meaning of the Hebrew word 'Koheleth'. This title was adopted in its Latinized form, 'Concionator', by Jerome in the Vulgate whence it passed over to the English versions. In the Hebrew Scriptures it is the fourth of the five Megilloth or Rolls and is placed immediately after Lamentations. In the Septuagint and the English versions it is found between Proverbs and the Song of Songs.

AUTHORSHIP

The book purports to be the work of Solomon (i. 1), and was accepted as such by Jewish and Christian scholars until the nineteenth century. This ascription is now seen to be impossible for the following reasons.

(1) In i. 12 we have the statement, 'I the Preacher have been king over Israel in Jerusalem'.[1] But Solomon reigned in Jerusalem without a break until the day of his death.

(2) Apparently many generations of Israelites had preceded the

---

[1] According to H. L. Ginsberg (article on 'The Structure and Contents of the Book of Koheleth', in *Wisdom in Israel and in the Ancient Far East*, ed. by M. Noth and D. Winton Thomas, 1955, pp. 148ff.), the Hebrew word 'mlk', translated 'king', means a 'property owner', while W. F. Albright (article on 'Some Canaanite-Phoenician Sources of Hebrew Wisdom', in *Wisdom in Israel and in the Ancient Far East*, ed. by M. Noth and D. Winton Thomas, 1955, p. 15) favours the meaning 'counsellor'.

king in Jerusalem (i. 1–16; ii. 7, 9); but Jerusalem was not captured by the Israelites until the time of David.

(3) The writer sometimes speaks not as a king, but as a subject who is living under an unjust regime. The administration of justice is corrupt and the poor are oppressed to such an extent that death is better than life (iv. 1f.). In the provinces it is impossible to obtain justice owing to the insatiable greed of the officials (v. 8). The king chooses his ministers in an arbitrary fashion, so that fools hold exalted positions and the noble take a lowly seat (x. 5–7). The king's spies are everywhere and no one is safe (x. 20). It is very unlikely that Solomon would have condemned the government for which he himself was responsible.

(4) Solomon's reign could not have been a time of such great literary activity that one could say, 'Of making many books there is no end' (xii. 11).

(5) The condition of anarchy prevailing in the state suggests that the writer lived towards the close of the Persian period or in the Greek period.

(6) The linguistic evidence is decisive against Solomonic authorship. The Hebrew of the book is not that of Solomon's day but of a much later period. 'If', says Delitzsch, 'the book of Koheleth were of Solomonic origin, then there is no history of the Hebrew language.'[1]

The attribution of works of Persian or Greek date to the great men of old is well-known. Moses, David, Solomon and many of the prophets have writings attributed to them in canonical books, apart from the books which were never admitted to the Canon, one of which went as far back as Enoch to find its putative author. Solomon is chosen, partly for his reputed wisdom and in imitation of Proverbs, and partly because his fabulous wealth and his enjoyment of all the world had to offer would make his conclusion that 'all is vanity' all the more telling.

CONTENTS

Outline

Chs. i, ii. The title (i. 1); the ceaseless and aimless toil of man and nature (i. 2–11); the futility of human life (i. 12–ii. 26).

Ch. iii. Everything is ordained (vv. 1–15); man is no better than the beasts (vv. 16–22).

---

[1] F. Delitzsch, *Commentary on the Song of Songs and Ecclesiastes*, trans. 1877, p. 190.

Ch. iv. The evils of oppression (vv. 1–3), rivalry (vv. 4–6) and loneliness (vv. 7–12); the vanity of royal popularity (vv. 13–16).

Ch. v. The need of reality in religion (vv. 1–7); the corruption of government officials (vv. 8f.); the futility of riches (vv. 10–20).

Ch. vi. The frustration of desires and hopes (vv. 1–12).

Ch. vii. The cultivation of what is good for man in life (vv. 1–22); futility of the search for wisdom and a good woman (vv. 23–29).

Ch. viii–ix. 16. The necessity of compromise in dealing with a king (viii. 1–5); man cannot restrain the spirit of man, death, war and moral evil (viii. 6–9); the righteous are soon forgotten while the wicked enjoy honour and long life (viii. 10–15); since the works of God are incomprehensible and death ends all, the best thing a man can do is to enjoy life and work strenuously (viii. 16–ix. 10); rewards are not bestowed upon men according to merit; men are creatures of time and chance (ix. 11f.); wisdom is better than might (ix. 13–16).

Chs. ix. 17–x. 20. A collection of proverbs on wisdom and the consequences of folly (ix. 17–x. 15); the wretched condition of a country under the rule of a feeble king (x. 16–20).

Chs. xi.–xii. 8. Commendation of benevolence, work and the enjoyment of life, even though the future be dark (xi. 1–8); a young man should rejoice in his youth, before the decrepitude of old age overtakes him, and at the same time remember his responsibility to God (xi. 9–xii. 8).

Ch. xii. 9–14. An epilogue praising the Preacher and summing up the argument of the book.

Summary: Chs. i, ii

Koheleth is identified with Solomon (i. 1). All human effort is utterly futile. Generations come and go but the world abides for ever. Sun, moon and rivers pursue a dreary round of repetition and all things are utterly weary. What appears to be new is really the reappearance of the old (i. 2–11). All human enterprises are futile; the crooked cannot be straightened and the defects of life are numberless. Koheleth gained more wisdom than any in Jerusalem and included in his investigations the manifestations of madness and folly. As a result of his investigations, he perceived that increased knowledge only meant more sorrow (i. 12–18). He turned to pleasure but found that it accomplished nothing. He indulged in wine, not allowing indulgence to overcome his judgment. He went in for great works, building houses, planting vineyards, laying out gardens and making pools.

He bought slaves and had large herds and flocks; he amassed silver and gold and secured singers and many mistresses. He grew richer than any before him in Jerusalem and his wisdom never left him. He threw off every restraint and denied himself no pleasure; but when he turned to look at all that he had achieved, he found that it was futile (ii. 1–11). He saw that wisdom is better than folly; the fool cannot see what is plain and obvious to the wise man. But the wise man has no advantage over the fool, for death overtakes both of them and they are forgotten (ii. 12–17). So Koheleth hated life because of its futility; he hated all his laborious efforts, because he would have to leave his possessions to someone who might be a fool or to one who had not toiled for them. A man gets no good from all the toil and strain of his labours (ii. 18–23). There is nothing better for him than to eat and drink and find enjoyment in his toil. To the man who pleases Him God gives wisdom, knowledge and joy; but to the sinner he gives the task of gathering and amassing wealth, only to give it to the man who pleases Him (ii. 24–26).

Ch. iii

Everything has its appointed time and man gains nothing from all his toil (vv. 1–9). God has set every event in its appropriate setting, and has put eternity in man's mind that he may never comprehend His purpose from the beginning to the end. For men there is nothing better than to enjoy themselves as long as they live; it is God's gift to man. Whatever God does endures for ever; nothing can be added to it and nothing can be taken from it. He has made it so that men should stand in awe of Him. Events follow each other in a dreary round of endless repetition (vv. 10–15). Wickedness is prevalent in the courts of justice (and probably in the courts of religion). God is testing men, showing them that they are no better than the beasts and have no advantage over them, for both men and beasts die and return to the dust. No one knows what happens to the spirit of man and the spirit of the beast after death, so the best thing for man is to be happy in his work (vv. 16–22).

Ch. iv

Oppression is rampant in the world; tyrants are in power and the oppressed are in tears with no one to comfort them. The dead are happier than the living, but better than both is the unborn man who has never known the misery of the world (vv. 1–3). Human toil and skill spring from jealousy between man and man and are futile. It is foolish, however, to be lazy for by so doing a man reduces himself to poverty. A modest amount of quietness is better than a life full of toil and futile effort (vv. 4–6). Another futile thing is a lonely man without son or brother, toiling to amass wealth without stopping to ask for whose sake he is toiling and depriving himself of pleasure (vv. 7f.). The co-operation of two persons has its advantages; it means help in time of need, warmth and protection. If two are better than one, three are better still (vv. 9–12). A young man, lowly born and wise, is better than an old and foolish king who will no longer take advice. Such a young man once became king and all the people acclaimed him as their leader, but they soon lost interest in him. The search for fame is futile (vv. 13–16).

Ch. v

Those who go to God's house should go thoughtfully and reverently. God is infinitely great and therefore one's petitions should be brief. Many words mean that a fool is talking. Vows should be kept in all circumstances. Hasty vows should not be made lest God be angry. One should stand in awe of God (vv. 1–7). No surprise should be shown at the sight of the poor being oppressed or right and justice tampered with in the state, for it is due to the insatiable greed of the officials. Each official watches the official beneath him in the hope of receiving part of the money collected from the citizens. The profit of the country's produce is shared by all the officials. On the whole a king is an advantage if he takes an interest in agriculture (vv. 8f.). A lover of money will never be satisfied with his money. The more he gets the more people there are to spend it for him (vv. 10–11). The sleep of the labouring man is sweet, but the surfeit of the rich man will not let him sleep. A wealthy man may lose his wealth in some unlucky venture and gain nothing by all his futile toil (vv. 12–17). It is good and fitting for a man to find enjoyment in his work during his brief life. This is God's ordained plan for man. If he accepts it he will never brood over the brevity of his life, for God keeps him occupied with joy in his heart (vv. 18–20).

Ch. vi

Sometimes God gives a man wealth, possessions and honour without the power to enjoy them. This is a sore misfortune; he is worse off than a still-born child that has never seen the sun or known anything (vv. 1-6). A man toils on to satisfy his hunger but his wants are never satisfied. Neither the wise man nor the poor man has any advantage over the fool. It is better to enjoy one's possessions than to long for the unattainable (vv. 7-9). Man's fate has been determined long ago and he cannot contend with one mightier than himself. No one can tell what is good for man during the few days of his empty life that passes like a shadow (vv. 10-12).

Ch. vii

It is a fine thing to have a good name in life, but the day of death is better than the day of birth. Seriousness is better than frivolity, for the living should bear in mind that death is the end of all men. Grief is better than gaiety for sadness does the soul good. The wise man is at home in the house of mourning and the fool in the house of mirth. It is better to listen to the censure of the wise man than to the song of fools. Oppression makes a wise man foolish and a bribe corrupts the mind. The end of a business is better than its beginning and patience is better than pride. A man should control his anger and should not praise the good old days. Wisdom is as good as an inheritance, for like money it can give protection. No one can straighten what God has made crooked. Both prosperity and adversity come from God to keep man from knowing what is to happen. Koheleth has seen the righteous man perishing by his righteousness and the wicked man prolonging his days by his evil-doing. A man should not be too righteous or too wise, for why should he die before his time. It is better to cling to both good and evil, for he who stands in awe of God shall avoid both extremes. Wisdom is a better protection for the wise than ten rulers of a city. There is not a single righteous man on earth who is free from sin. A man should not listen to all that people say, for he may hear his own slaves cursing him (vv. 1-22). Koheleth has failed to attain wisdom; reality is beyond his grasp. In his search for wisdom and the reason of things he discovered that a seductive woman is more bitter than death. The man who pleases God shall escape her but she will snare the sinner. Koheleth has found one true man in a thousand but never a true woman. God made men upright but they have contrived many a cunning wile (vv. 23-29).

Chs. viii–ix. 16

Wisdom transfigures a rough countenance. A man should obey the king and never thwart him, for his word is supreme and no one dare ask what he means. He who obeys the royal command will never come to harm. The mind of a wise man knows that a time of judgment is coming for all. Just as a man has no power to retain the spirit (or hold the wind in check), or to control the day of his death, or to escape from forced service in war, so he cannot escape from his wickedness (viii. 1–9). The wicked are buried with honour, while the righteous are excluded from the holy place and forgotten in the city. Because sentence on a crime is not executed at once, men are prone to evil practices. Though a sinner may sin repeatedly and flourish, it is those who fear God who are safe, while the wicked man fares ill, passing like a shadow because he does not fear God. In the world righteous men fare as though they are wicked, and wicked men fare as though they are righteous. This is vanity. The best thing for a man to do is to enjoy himself as he toils through the life God gives him (viii. 10–15). The ways of God are beyond man's comprehension. The righteous and the wise with all their works are within His power, but whether He looks upon man with love or hate no one can tell. For all men alike there is one fate. The hearts of men are full of evil and mad desires during their lives, and then they join the dead. Still, while a man lives there is hope, for a live dog is better than a dead lion. A man, therefore, should enjoy life with the woman he loves and throw himself into any work that may appeal to him, for there is no work, or thought, or knowledge or wisdom in Sheol (viii. 16–ix. 10). Rewards are not bestowed upon man according to merit. Death and misfortune happen to all men. No man knows his hour. A poor wise man once saved a small city but no one remembered him. Wisdom is better than strength, but the poor man's wisdom is despised (ix. 11–16).

Chs. ix. 17–x. 20

The words of a wise man spoken in quiet are more acceptable than the shouts of a ring-leader of fools. Wisdom is better than weapons of war but one sinner destroys much good. A little folly mars wisdom and honour. A wise man's sense will keep him straight but a fool's mind leads him wrong. Even on a walk the fool shows lack of sense for he calls everyone a fool. If a ruler's wrath flares up against a man, he should not resign his post but defer to him. A ruler's mistakes are not always intentional. Fools often get high posts from him while the noble take a lowly place. Slaves are seen on horseback and princes walking as slaves. Men should exercise prudence. He who digs a pit may fall into it, and he who breaks a wall down may be bitten by a serpent. He who quarries stones may be injured by them and he who cuts wood may get a wound. Wisdom teaches a man to sharpen a blunt axe instead of putting more strength into his blows; it teaches the snake-charmer to exercise his skill before the serpent bites. The words of a wise man win him favour, but those of a fool ruin him. A fool talks on and on; anyone who asks him the way to the city is weary of his talk before he gets there (ix. 17–x. 15). A land is unfortunate when its king is young and inexperienced and its princes revel in the morning. It is well for a land when its king is nobly born and its princes revel at the right hours, and are stalwart men, not sots. Idleness leads to the ruin of a land. A man should not curse the king or the rich for someone will report his words to them (x. 16–20).

Chs. xi–xii. 8

A man should give freely and some day he will be rewarded. He should help as many as possible and so ensure friends in time of trouble (xi. 1–3). A man is as powerless to alter the conditions of life as he is to alter the weather or to prevent a tree from falling. He who waits till all the conditions of life are favourable will do nothing. Man's ignorance of the mysteries of birth and of the wind shows the impossibility of understanding the ways of God. A man should perform his daily work, taking life as it is and not waiting for ideal conditions that may never arrive. Light is sweet and it is pleasant to be alive. If a man lives many years he should enjoy them, remembering the many dark days that are sure to come. All that comes after death is emptiness (xi. 4–8). A man should make the most of his youth and satisfy his heart's desires, bearing in mind that God will bring him to account. He should banish all worries and keep his body free from pain, for youth and manhood will not last. He should remember his Creator in the days of his youth before the decrepitude of old age and death overtake him (xi. 9–xii. 8).

Moffatt translates xi. 1f., thus, 'Trust your goods far and wide at sea, till you get good returns after a while. Take shares in several ventures; you never know what will go wrong in this world.'

Ch. xii. 9–14

Koheleth was not only a sage; he also taught knowledge to the people, pondering, examining and arranging proverbs with great care, and setting down plainly what was true. The reader is warned against reading anything beyond the collected sayings of the wise.

There is no end to the writing of books and much study is a weariness of the flesh. It is every man's duty to fear God and to keep His commandments, for all human actions will eventually be judged by Him.

UNITY

On the question of the unity of the book there is no unanimity of opinion. Some scholars accept the entire or almost the entire book as a literary unit, but others reject without any reservations the theory of unity of authorship, chiefly on the following grounds.

(1) The main theme is the futility of life and the aimlessness of existence, but apart from the first two chapters there is little evidence of any systematic development of thought. There is, in fact, often such confusion of thought that it is difficult to follow the argument.

(2) The book contains many abrupt transitions of thought. For example, in vii. 19 we are told that wisdom gives strength, and in the following verse that a perfectly righteous man cannot be found. Chapters ix. 17–x. 15 consist of a series of proverbs on various subjects.

(3) There are many contradictory ideas in the book. A few examples will suffice to show this.

And I applied my mind to know wisdom and to know madness and folly. I perceived that this also is but a striving after wind. (i. 17.)

Then I saw that wisdom excels folly as light excels darkness. (ii. 13.)

What has a man from all the toil and strain with which he toils beneath the sun? (ii. 22.)

So I saw that there is nothing better than that a man should enjoy his work, for that is his lot. (iii. 22.)

There is nothing better for a man than that he should eat and drink, and find enjoyment in his toil. (ii. 24.)

It is better to go to the house of mourning than to go to the house of feasting. (vii. 2.)

For the fate of the sons of men and the fate of beasts is the same; as one dies, so dies the other. They all have the same breath, and man has no advantage over the beasts; for all is vanity. All go to one place, all are from the dust and all turn to dust again. (iii. 19f.)

I said in my heart, God will judge the righteous and the wicked, for he has appointed a time for every matter, and for every work. (iii. 17.)

And I thought the dead who are already dead more fortunate than the living who are still alive. (iv. 2.)

But he who is joined with all the living has hope, for a living dog is better than a dead lion. (ix. 4.)

There is a vanity which takes place on earth, that there are righteous men to whom it happens according to the deeds of the wicked, and there are wicked men to whom it happens according to the deeds of the righteous. (viii. 14.)

Though a sinner does evil a hundred times and prolongs his life, yet I know that it will be well with those who fear God, because they fear before him; but it will not be well with the wicked, neither will he prolong his days like a shadow because he does not fear before God. (viii. 12f.)

Several theories have been advanced to account for the absence of the orderly arrangement of thought, the abrupt transitions of thought and the inconsistencies in the book. According to Galling, the book is a collection of thirty-seven separate proverbs from two to fifteen lines long, loosely strung together. It has no uniform theme and no logical structure. It contains the casual jottings of the author who sometimes quotes a current maxim to correct it by a critical appeal to the facts of life and to his own interpretation of them.[1] The view of Gordis is that the book is a unity, the appearance to the contrary being due to the author's habit of quoting a conventional maxim and then commenting on it.[2]

Some scholars consider that the book contains the reflections of a single author in varying moods by turns an optimist and a pessimist. 'The spiritual journey is not along a straight road, but winds backwards and forwards. Hence the apparent contradictions and repetitions which are frequently met with. They are natural and inevitable as mood succeeds mood, and doubts temporarily stifled, reassert themselves.'[3] Bickell, impressed by the absence of orderly arrangement, suggests that by a series of accidents the leaves of the work, which was in book form, became dislocated and were put together again by an editor who was ignorant of the true order. Before the leaves had been displaced, a hostile reader had made alterations in the text, and after-

---

[1] K. Galling, 'Kohelet-Studien', Z.A.W., 1, 1932, pp. 276–299. 'Stand und Aufgabe der Kohelet-Forschung', T.R., vi, 1934, pp. 355–373. 'Der Prediger; in Die fünf Megilloth', H.A.T., i. 18, 1940, pp. 47–90.

[2] G. Gordis, *The Wisdom of Koheleth, A Translation with a Commentary and an Introductory Essay*, 1950, pp. 9–20.

[3] A. C. Cohen, 'Commentary on "Ecclesiastes"' in *The Five Megilloth*, 1952, p. 107.

wards two other editors had made further alterations.[1] Williams thinks that the lack of orderly arrangement is due to the fact that Koheleth recorded his thoughts unsystematically and died before he could arrange them properly. A pupil made a few additions (i. 1f.; iii. 17; viii. 11–13; xi. 9b; xii. 1a, 9–14) to bring out what he thought were his master's beliefs.[2] Siegfried finds in the book the work of at least nine different persons, namely, a philosopher who was influenced by Greek thought, a Sadducee with epicurean tendencies, a wise man (hakam), a pious orthodox Jew (hasid), a collector of maxims, a first redactor who edited the book adding i. 1 and xii. 8, and three redactors who added xii. 9–14 (9f. + 11f. + 13f.).[3] According to McNeile[4] and Barton,[5] the book was worked over by two persons— a wisdom writer (hakam), who added a series of didactic passages in defence of wisdom, and a pious orthodox Jew (hasid) who inserted statements on the duty of fearing God and in the certainty of the judgment. The parts attributed by McNeile and Barton are as follows:

Passages attributed to the hakam

By McNeile: iv. 5, 9–12; vi. 7, 9a; vii. 1a, 4–6, 7–12, 19; viii. 1; ix. 17–x. 3; x. 8–11, 12–15, 18f.; xii. 11f.

By Barton: iv. 5; v. 3, 7a; vii. 1a, 3, 5, 6–9, 11f., 19; viii. 1; ix. 17f.; x. 1–3, 8–14a, 15, 18f.

Passages attributed to the hasid

By McNeile: ii. 26ab; iii. 14b, 17; iv. 17–v. 6; vii. 18b, 26b, 29; viii. 2b, 3a, 5, 6a, 11–13; xi. 9b; xii. 1a, 13f.

By Barton: ii. 26; iii. 17; vii. 18b., 26b., 29; viii. 2b, 3a, 5, 6a, 11–13; xi. 9b; xii. 1a, 13 (from the words 'fear God') and 14.

To-day the prevailing tendency is to regard the book as the work of one mind in varying moods, except for a few minor additions. Ranston considers that the only certain later additions are: iii. 17; xi. 9c; xii. 1a, 13f.[6] Eissfeldt finds the following interpolations: ii. 26; iii. 17; vii. 26b; viii. 5, 12b, 13a; xi. 9b; xii. 7b, 12.[7]

---

[1] G. Bickell, *Der Prediger über den Wert des Daseins*, 1884.
[2] A. L. Williams, *Ecclesiastes*, 1922.
[3] C. Siegfried, 'Prediger und Hoheslied' in *Handkommentar zum Alten Testament*, 1898, pp. 2ff.
[4] A. H. McNeile, *An Introduction to Ecclesiastes*, 1904.
[5] G. A. Barton, *A Critical and Exegetical Commentary on Ecclesiastes*, 1908.
[6] H. Ranston, *The Old Testament Wisdom Books*, 1930, p. 265.
[7] O. Eissfeldt, *Einleitung in das alte Testament*, 1934, p. 582.

In our opinion the absence of the orderly arrangement of thought, the abrupt transitions of thought, and the inconsistencies are too obvious to be explained except by a redactor, but the simplest theory of redaction, which is adequate for explanation, is the best, and that is to assume a single orthodox redactor who inserted the passages relative to the fear of God and the judgment. Where the contradictions do not come from the orthodox interpolator, each consists of a few words taken out of a pessimistic passage. If these contexts are taken into account, we see that the passages in which the few apparently less pessimistic words occur are as consistent with the thesis that all is vanity as their apparent opposites.

FOREIGN INFLUENCE

The question of the relation of Ecclesiastes to foreign thought has roused much discussion in recent years and it still continues. Some scholars profess to find in the book traces of dependence upon the Egyptian and Babylonian Wisdom writings, especially the former. It is claimed, for example, that there are similarities of thought and even of expression between the book and the Egyptian *Song of the Harper*, *The Dialogue of the Misanthrope with his Soul*, *The Teaching of Ptahhotep* and *The Teaching of Amen-em-ope*, and between the book and the Babylonian *Gilgamish Epic* and *The Dialogue of Pessimism*.[1] There is, however, no proof of any direct connexion between the book and the Egyptian and Babylonian writings. The similarities of thought may be explained on the supposition that the same problems occupied the minds of men in different countries and that sometimes they reached the same conclusions. As regards the similarities of expression they are explicable on the assumption that certain phrases employed in these writings had passed into Palestinian speech. Some scholars find in the book traces of the Stoic and Epicurean philosophies. The Stoic doctrine of 'cycles' according to which history shows no sign of progress but only moves in endless recurring cycles is said to be reflected in i. 1–11. The doctrine of living in accordance with nature is supposed to be set out in iii. 1–8. The ideas that evil is the necessary accompaniment of the good (vii. 14), folly is madness (i. 17; ii. 12; vii. 25; ix. 3), life with all its strivings is futile (i. 2–4; ii. 1–23), and men are at the mercy

---

[1] See G. A. Barton, *A Critical and Exegetical Commentary on Ecclesiastes*, 1908; A. L. Williams, *Ecclesiastes*, 1922; S. Langdon, *The Babylonian Wisdom*, 1923; P. Humbert, *Recherches sur les sources égyptiennes de la Littérature Sapientiale d'Israël*, 1929.

of chance (ix. 11f.) are also said to belong to the same school of thought. The influence of Epicureanism on Koheleth is said to be seen in his belief that man is no better than the beasts and that death for both means extinction (iii. 18-20), in his exhortation to enjoy the pleasures of life (ii. 24; iii. 12, 22; v. 18f.), and in his idea of tranquil happiness (v. 18-20).

Ranston produces evidence to prove that the book is dependent not upon the works of the higher philosophers, but upon those of certain early Greek gnomic writers, expecially Theognis of Megara (c. 520 B.C.). He does not think that Koheleth obtained his knowledge directly from the works of Theognis, but that he gathered material from among people who were familiar with his thought.[1]

Others, including Driver and Peake, think that Koheleth was familiar with Greek philosophical ideas but did not adopt those of any particular school. He was, however, influenced by the Greek spirit, which is revealed by his appeal to men's reason and judgment, and by his universalistic outlook which is concerned with man everywhere.

In our opinion the influence of Greek philosophical thought upon the book is unmistakable. The two Greek ideas which we think can be detected in it are the idea of God as the unknown physical power behind the universe and the attribution of a man's good or bad fortune to Chance. We have to find what Koheleth has to say about God apart from any insertions by the orthodox interpolator. God has given everything its appointed time and has put eternity (or 'the world') in man's heart that he may never comprehend His purpose from the beginning to the end (iii. 1-11). Man's fate was fixed long ago; he cannot argue with one mightier than himself and lavish talk about it is mere folly. Man is unable to grasp the truth of all that God does in the world. He may labour in ceaseless quest for it by day and night but he will never attain it (viii. 16f.). The righteous and the wise and all their doings are within the power of God. Will He love them? Will He hate them? None can tell (ix. 1). For all alike there is one fate (ix. 2f.).

There is nothing similar to this in any eastern religion; the gods of the Middle East are all personal beings whose favour can be won. Though Koheleth does not overtly say that God is an impersonal cause, we feel that he is acquainted with Aristotle's God, who (or rather 'which') is the unknowable physical power which sets the world

[1] H. Ranston, *Ecclesiastes and the Early Greek Wisdom Literature*, 1925, p. 61; *The Old Testament Wisdom Books*, 1930, pp. 255-264.

in motion. We have absolute determinism, absolute unchangeableness and a cyclic round of impersonal orderings.

With the loss of faith in the Olympian gods, the Greeks came to believe in Chance which was eventually deified under the name of 'Tyche'. Aristophanes accused the Sophists of his day of having set aside the gods and substituted for them Chance; and probably the charge was true. According to the author of Ecclesiastes, the affairs of human life are ruled by Chance. 'Again I saw that under the sun the race is not to the swift, nor the battle to the strong, nor bread to the wise, nor riches to the intelligent, nor favour to the men of skill; but time and chance happen to them all' (ix. 11). This is an attitude not only contrary to all Hebrew thought, but to all thought in the religions of the Near East. Gods might be won over by good deeds, or bribed by sacrifices, or twisted by magic. There was always some way of dealing with them personally but nothing can be done with Chance. It is an attitude which revived tremendously among the troops in the First World War. Their fate seemed to depend on an impersonal, unapproachable fate.

Those who reject the theory of the influence of Greek philosophical thought upon Ecclesiastes or hesitate to accept it, do so chiefly for the following reasons. (1) The evidence advanced to prove Greek influence is not convincing. (2) There are fundamental differences between the teaching of Koheleth and that of the Greek philosophers. (3) The similarities of thought and expression are due to the fact that all were engaged on the same problems and occasionally reached the same conclusions, and to the fact that with the spread of Greek culture consequent upon Alexander's conquests, Greek philosophical terminology had become current coin.

According to Albright, Ecclesiastes betrays Phoenician influence in spelling, morphology, syntax, vocabulary and content.[1]

DATE

The date of composition of the book cannot be precisely determined. The conditions of anarchy prevailing in the state (iii. 16; iv. 1-3, 13-16; x. 16f.) suggest that the book was written towards the close of the Persian period or in the Greek period. The linguistic evidence shows that it has many affinities with the latest Hebrew such as that of

[1] W. F. Albright, article on 'Some Canaanite-Phoenician Sources of Hebrew Wisdom' in *Wisdom in Israel and in the Ancient Near East*, ed. by M. Noth and D. Winton Thomas, 1955, pp. 6-15.

Chronicles-Ezra-Nehemiah (c. 300–250 B.C.), and Esther (c. 180–114 B.C.), and that it contains terms and grammatical constructions which are common in Mishnaic Hebrew. It also contains many Aramaisms, two Persian words ('pardes' ii. 5; 'pithgam' viii. 11) and perhaps a few Graecisms. It has been suggested that the 'poor wise man', mentioned in ix. 14–16 refers to Archimedes and the siege of Syracuse (212 B.C.), and that the king mentioned in iv. 13–16 and x. 16 is an allusion to the accession of Ptolemy v in 203 B.C. These alleged references to historical events are too vague to be of any value. It has been assumed that Ben Sirach in 'Ecclesiasticus' (c. 180 B.C.) shows acquaintance with the book, but the parallels are too uncertain to draw any definite conclusions from them. The book was probably written before the outburst of religious faith and patriotic fervour caused by the oppression of Antiochus iv Epiphanes (175–163 B.C.). The resignation of Koheleth is not compatible with the active spirit of the Maccabees, or with the heroic faith in the divine purpose for the world found in Daniel. Scraps of the Hebrew text of the book discovered at Qumran have been dated in the first half of the second century B.C. We shall not be far wrong in fixing the date between 250 and 200 B.C.

KOHELETH: HIS LIFE AND CHARACTER

Little is known of the author who wrote under the name of Koheleth. He was evidently a Jew living in or near Jerusalem, for he was an eye-witness of events which occurred in the holy place (viii. 10). Some scholars infer from xi. 1–6 that he was a corn-merchant with a home in Alexandria. It has also been suggested that he was a doctor, or a high official, or a member of a high-priestly family, or a Sadducee. He had great wealth and had used it for his personal gratification, building houses, planting vineyards, laying out gardens and parks and buying slaves. He had large herds and flocks, larger than any before him in Jerusalem, had amassed silver and gold and secured singers and many mistresses (ii. 4–8). His domestic life seems to have been a tragedy, for he had discovered something more bitter than death— a woman who entangled men and whose hands were fetters (vii. 26). At the time when he wrote his book he was no longer young for he looked back upon the pleasures of youth and early manhood. The passage on old age (xii. 2–7) could only have been written by one who was conscious of the failure of his physical powers. Intellectually, he was one of the most original thinkers in the Old Testament. He was not prepared to accept anything on authority: observation and experience led him to challenge the established doctrines of his day.

The character of Koheleth is not one to be admired. For many years he had led a self-indulgent life, striving to satisfy all the desires of his heart. There is not a trace of altruism in the whole of his book. No mention is made of any good deeds he had ever done, and there are no regrets for the wasted years. 'Koheleth never found life', says Kent, 'because he never lost it'.[1] His selfish policy and his distrust of his fellow men won him no friends. He had rarely found a true man and never a faithful woman (vii. 27). Though he distrusted his fellow men he apparently longed for human companionship, for he tells us that two are better than one and that a threefold cord is not quickly broken (iv. 9–12). It would be wrong, however, to condemn him as a complete hedonist. Even when he was pursuing a life of selfish indulgence he never relinquished his wisdom (ii. 9). He never recommended the pursuit of pleasure for its own sake. To seek pleasure was as foolish as to seek anything else (ii. 1f.). He never recommended a life of debauchery, for he had learned from bitter experience that a woman who entangled men was 'more bitter than death' (vii. 26). The pleasures which he thought men should enjoy were the simple pleasures of eating and drinking and of marriage, combined with strenuous labour (ix. 7–9).

Koheleth was a pessimist. His book begins and ends with the words, 'Vanity of vanities! All is vanity' (i. 2; xii. 8). All things in nature and in human history move in monotonous cycles, giving one the impression of utter weariness (i. 4–10). All men's efforts—his pursuit of wisdom (i. 12–18; vii. 23f.), pleasure (ii. 1–11), labour and riches (ii. 18–20; v. 10–16; vi. 1–6)—are futile. 'I have seen everything that is done under the sun; and behold, all is vanity and a striving after wind' (i. 14). Man cannot alter his destiny since all his actions, both good and bad, have been preordained (iii. 1–9), and since he cannot contend with one (i.e. God) stronger than himself (vi. 10). It is useless for him to strive for a better social order for, 'what has been done is what will be done, and there is nothing new under the sun' (i. 9). No distinction is made between the lot of the righteous and the lot of the wicked (vii. 15; viii. 14). Man cannot avert the last calamity—death (viii. 8). He dies like the beast and his body returns to dust (iii. 19f.), while his shade descends to Sheol, where 'there is no work, or thought, or knowledge, or wisdom' (ix. 10).

[1] C. F. Kent, *The Growth and Contents of the Old Testament*, 1926, p. 273.

With such a pessimistic view of the world and of life it is not surprising that Koheleth came to hate life and all its labours (ii. 17-23). The day of death is better than the day of birth (vii. 1); the dead already in their graves are happier than the living that are still alive, and happier than both of them is the unborn man, who has not seen the evil deeds that are done in the world (iv. 2f.). He was not, however, a confirmed pessimist. Sometimes he could see the brighter side of life. While there is life there is hope; life under any condition is better than death. 'But he who is joined with all the living has hope, for a living dog is better than a dead lion' (ix. 4). The world is a beautiful place in which to live (iii. 11). 'Light is sweet, and it is pleasant for the eyes to behold the sun' (xi. 7).

Assuming that Koheleth was not the author of the passages relating to the fear of God and the judgment, we may conclude that religion had little place in his life. The God whom he recognized was the impersonal Power behind all phenomena, rather than a personal God who is mindful of man and cares for him, and whose steadfast love endures for ever. No man could have a living faith in God who found in nature and in human life only the weariness of endless repetition. His belief meant no more than intellectual assent which had no power to bring him into any personal relation with God or to effect his character. It did not involve any attitude of dependence, or trust or love towards God, or any desire to serve Him. Unlike most of his fellow-countrymen he apparently had no deep sense of sin, no desire for forgiveness, no longing for fellowship with the divine, and no touch of that rapturous joy which thrilled the heart of the Psalmist who sang,

> Because thy steadfast love is better than life,
>   my lips will praise thee.
> So I will bless thee as long as I live;
>   I will lift up my hands and call on thy name.
>   (Ps. lxiii. 4.)[1]

---

[1] There are wide differences of opinion on the character of Koheleth. Some scholars, like Taylor, regard him as a stoic, and others, like Plumptre, Cheyne and Tyler, as an epicurean. Dillon thinks that he was a peculiar mixture of pessimism and epicureanism, and Driver that he was not a pessimist in the modern sense of the term and never abandoned his belief in God. Jastrow considers that he was non-religious rather than irreligious, an easy-going dilettante in philosophy and a gentle cynic, and Odeberg that he was not a hedonist or a confirmed pessimist, or an infidel, but that God was the centre of his life. Zimmerli declares that we must guard against making Koheleth into a pious soul who treads the path of the biblical believer. H. W. Robinson holds that he can be described as both pessimistic and agnostic but not as atheistic, while T. H. Robinson calls

TEACHING

The Nature and Work of God

Koheleth does not doubt the existence of God. He has, however, lost the belief in a personal Being, which inspired the prophets and the psalmists and has come to believe in an inscrutable and irresistible cosmic force. He never uses the personal term 'Yahweh' for God but 'Elohim' or 'the Elohim', the omnipotent Creator and Controller of the world, who dwells in a remote heaven and is unconcerned with the affairs of mankind. The world is so constituted that the order and time of events are fixed (iii. 1–8) and all things in nature and in human history move in an endless succession of cycles (i. 4–10). All good things—food, drink, riches, happiness and the power to enjoy life are His gifts (iii. 13; v. 18–20; viii. 15; ix. 7). Many of the evils in society also come from Him (i. 13; iii. 10f.; v. 6). Whatever He does endures for ever; nothing can be added to it and nothing taken from it (iii. 14). 'What is crooked cannot be made straight, and what is lacking cannot be numbered' (i. 15). His ways are beyond man's comprehension (iii. 11).

God gives life to man (xii. 7) and fixes the length of his days on earth (v. 18; viii. 15; ix. 9), allotting to each his work (i. 13; iii. 10) and his pleasures (ii. 24; iii. 12f.; v. 18). Wealth, possessions and honour are also His gifts, but sometimes the power to enjoy them is denied him (vi. 1f.). He has put eternity in man's mind, so that he cannot fathom His purpose from the beginning to the end (iii. 11).

Man

Man, who is created by God, is morally weak and prone to sin. 'Surely there is not a righteous man on earth who does good and never sins' (vii. 20). His heart is full of evil, and madness is in his heart while he lives (ix. 3). He cannot comprehend the purpose of God (iii. 11) nor can he enter into intimate communion with Him. He should enter the house of God, not carelessly but thoughtfully and reverently, 'Guard your steps when you go to the house of God; to draw near to listen is better than to offer the sacrifice of fools, for they do not know that

---

his book 'in a sense one of the most pessimistic in general literature'. Bea maintains that he was no sceptic or pessimist, or epicurean, but a man with a firm belief in God who recognized the limitations of his own knowledge in regard to life's problems and its difficulties.

they are doing evil. Be not rash with your mouth, nor let your heart be hasty to utter words before God, for God is in heaven and you upon earth; therefore let your words be few' (v. 1f.). He does not know what is really good for him during the few days of his empty life that passes like a shadow (vi. 12). Since industry and skill spring from jealousy between man and man, and idleness reduces a man to penury, it is better to adopt the golden mean between work and idleness, for a modest amount of quietness is better than a life full of toil and futile effort (iv. 4–6). He should not go to extremes, for it is just as reprehensible to be too righteous and too wise as it is to be too wicked and too foolish (vii. 16f.). A poor, wise young man is better than an old and foolish king who will not take advice. The former may become king and be hailed as a leader, though a future generation may lose interest in him (iv. 13–16). In his dealings with the king and the rich a man should act with caution lest he should be betrayed. 'Even in your thoughts, do not curse the king, nor in your bedchamber curse the rich; for a bird of the air will carry your voice, or some winged creature tell the matter' (x. 20). He should not long for the good old days believing that they were better than the present (vii. 10). As he goes through life he should realize the value of comradeship (iv. 9, 12), and of a good reputation (vii. 1), practise benevolence and cultivate seriousness rather than levity (vii. 2–4). Since he cannot alter his destiny (iii. 14) and death and Sheol await him (ix. 10), the only wise thing for him to do is to live as joyfully as possible (ii. 24; iii. 12, 22; v. 18–20; viii. 15; ix. 7–9; xi. 8–9a).

Wisdom

Wisdom has certain advantages. It gives strength 'more than ten rulers that are in a city' (vii. 19) and is better than weapons of war (ix. 18). It puts eyes into a man's head, enabling him to see where he is going; it makes all the difference between walking in darkness and light (ii. 13f.). Like money it is a protection, preserving the life of him who has it (vii. 12). It transfigures the countenance, taking the hardness out of it (viii. 1).

Wisdom has its limitations. It is not honoured for its own sake. The wisdom of a poor man may save a city in a time of crisis but afterwards no one remembers him (ix. 14–16). Wisdom cannot grasp the truth of all that God is doing in the world (vii. 23f.; viii. 16f.). It can sometimes be destroyed by a little folly (x. 1). The search for it leads to sorrow and is a mere striving after wind (i. 12–17; ii. 18–23), for ultimately it confers no benefit on its possessor. The wise man dies like the fool and is forgotten (ii. 14-17; vi. 8).

Riches

Riches are the gift of God (v. 19), but sometimes they are bestowed upon a man without the power to enjoy them (vi. 1f.). Wealth amassed with toil and care does not bring satisfaction. A lonely man without son or brother, toiling on to make money, is never satisfied with his riches, and never stops to ask for whose benefit he is toiling and depriving himself of pleasure (iv. 7f.). The more a man gains the more there are to spend it for him; he himself gets no more than the sight of it. The pursuit of wealth brings care and anxiety. The man who labours with his hands enjoys sound refreshing sleep, but the over-abundant wealth of the rich man keeps him awake (v. 11f.). Wealth is not permanent. It may be lost in some unlucky venture and the owner of it has nothing to leave to his son. A man cannot take his wealth with him at death. 'As he came from his mother's womb he shall go again, naked as he came, and shall take nothing for his toil, which he may carry away in his hand' (v. 15). Moreover, he knows that he must leave his wealth to someone who has not toiled for it and may be a fool (ii. 18-21).

Retribution

Koheleth rejects the belief in retribution. Observation and experience prove that the righteous are not invariably rewarded and the wicked punished. God appears to be indifferent to moral distinctions. In the world which He has created injustice rules and might not right prevails. The wicked occupy positions of power and oppress the poor, causing such suffering that death is better than life (iii. 16; iv. 1-3; v. 8). Success is not governed by justice but by chance. 'Again I saw that under the sun the race is not to the swift, nor the battle to the strong, nor bread to the wise, nor riches to the intelligent, nor favour to the men of skill, but time and chance happen to them all' (ix. 11). Since all men's actions, both good and bad, have been predetermined he cannot alter his destiny. The just and the wise and all their doings are within the power of God, but He acts so capriciously that they do not know whether He loves or hates them (ix. 1). The righteous man perishes by his righteousness and the wicked man flourishes upon his evil (vii. 15). Righteous men fare as though they were wicked and wicked men as though they were righteous (viii. 14). The same fate comes to all, 'to the righteous and the wicked, to the good and the evil, to the clean and the unclean, to him who sacrifices and to him who does not sacrifice. As is the good man, so is the sinner; and he who swears is as he who shuns an oath' (ix. 2). There is no hope of a future life beyond the grave in which justice may be done, for man, like the beast, dies and returns to dust (iii. 19f.).

The Future Life

Koheleth has no conception of personal immortality. He holds firmly the current view that at death the shade of man descends to Sheol. He is never tired of describing the inevitability of death and the dreary existence that awaits him beyond the grave. Man shares the same fate as the beasts, 'All go to one place; all are from the dust and all turn to dust again' (iii. 20). Death reduces all men to the same level. Both the wise man and the fool die and are forgotten (ii. 14-16). The dead know nothing and have no more reward for their labour (ix. 5). Their love, their hate and their enmity have perished, and they have no share in anything that goes on in the world (ix. 6). In Sheol, 'there is no work or thought or knowledge or wisdom' (ix. 10). The days of darkness there are many (xi. 8) and there is no return (iii. 22).

In one passage Koheleth expresses doubt as to what happens to the spirit of man and that of the beast at death. 'Who knows whether the spirit of man goes upward and the spirit of the beast goes down to the earth?' (iii. 21). But in xii. 7 he declares categorically that the dust returns once more to the earth and the spirit to God who gave it. The spirit (ruach) is not the soul which the Greeks thought could at death escape from the prison of the body and be truly free, but an impersonal principle of life which is lent by God to man and beast and withdrawn by Him at death. There is no thought of personal immortality.

PERMANENT INFLUENCE

Historically, Ecclesiastes has some importance as affording information on the political conditions existing in Palestine towards the close of the third century B.C. The country was evidently groaning under a despotism. The administration of justice was corrupt (iii. 16), the poor were oppressed (iv. 1-3) and the king's spies were everywhere (x. 20).

From the religious point of view the book shows the unexpected existence of a negation of religion among the Jews in the very period when our attention would otherwise be directed almost entirely to the growth of the higher elements in Judaism, which made it a possible prelude to Christianity—belief in a holy, righteous, just, merciful and loving God, in the existence of a power of evil, in the advent of the judgment and the kingdom of God, and in the resurrection of the body and the immortality of the soul. We think of the Jews as inherently a religious people and are perplexed by the existence of Karl Marx and an intense anti-religious communism among the Jews of eastern Europe. In Ecclesiastes we see their spiritual ancestor.

The teaching of the book, if followed, would tend to paralyse all human effort, kill idealism and rob life of its joy. 'It puts the logic of a non-Christian position with tremendous force to all who feel keenly the misery of the world. More vividly than anything else in the Old Testament it shows how imperious was the necessity for the revelation of God in Christ.'[1] Of all attacks ever made on religion, it is the least likely to attract followers. Its influence has been and is almost nil.

LITERARY MERIT

On the question of the literary merit of the book opinions differ widely. Jastrow speaks of the author's great literary skill and Delitzsch of his eloquence. According to McNeile, the author's intense originality raised him above the literary level of his day. Under the stress of keen disappointment and indignation at the wrongs of the world he gave to his style 'a stinging sarcasm, a tendency to epigram, a moan in it which is unique in Hebrew literature.'[2] Cheyne speaks of the author's 'loose notes' and Galling of 'casual jottings'. Burkitt declares that there is no literary charm in the book, that the style is neither correct nor natural, and that the 'crabbed and unnatural lingo' suggests that the book is a translation from the Arabic.[3]

The book is written partly in prose and partly in poetry, the former predominating. Occasionally the prose rises to the level of poetry. The style is for the most part smooth, dignified and sometimes imaginative. Frequent use is made of figures of speech, such as simile (ii. 13; vii. 6; viii. 13), metaphor (ii. 14; v. 17; x. 20) and exclamation (ii. 16; x. 16) and of the literary devices of the rhetorical question

---
[1] A. S. Peake, *The Problem of Suffering in the Old Testament*, 1904, p. 135.
[2] A. H. McNeile, *Introduction in Ecclesiastes*, 1904, p. 32.
[3] F. C. Burkitt, *Journal of Theological Studies*, xxiii. 1922, 22–25. The theory that *Ecclesiastes* is a translation from the Aramaic has won little support. There are at least certain practical portions (i. 2–8; iii. 1–8; xi. 9–xii. 7) which do not read like translations. It is probable that Koheleth thought and spoke in Aramaic and wrote in Hebrew.

(i. 10; ii. 25; viii. 1), repetition (i. 2; iii. 2–8) and contrast (vii. 1; ix. 1–5; xi. 7f.). He has the power to express his maxims in epigrammatic form (iv. 6; v. 12; x. 6) and to coin pithy phrases (i. 7; v. 10; vi. 9), so that they are easily remembered and often pass current on the lips of people who know nothing of their origin. The passage depicting old age and death (xii. 2–7), with its rich symbolism, pathos and compassion is worthy to be ranked among the world's great literature. The young man is exhorted to rejoice in his youth, to banish all worries from his mind, and to keep his body free from pain before the evil days come, 'before the sun and the light, and the moon, and the stars are darkened, and the clouds return after the rain; in the day when the keepers of the house tremble, and the strong men are bent, and the grinders cease because they are few, and those that look through the windows are dimmed, and the doors on the street are shut; when the sound of the grinding is low, and one rises up at the voice of a bird, and all the daughters of song are brought low; they are afraid also of what is high, and terrors are in the way; the almond tree blossoms, the grasshopper drags itself along and desire fails; because man goes to his long home, and the mourners go about the streets; before the silver cord is snapped, or the golden bowl is broken, or the pitcher is broken at the fountain, or the wheel broken at the cistern, and the dust returns to the earth as it was and the spirit returns to God who gave it.'

CHAPTER XV

ESTHER

TITLE AND PLACE IN CANON

ESTHER receives its name from the principal character of the narrative. In the Hebrew Scriptures it stands in the third division of the Canon and is the last of the five 'Megilloth' or 'Rolls'. In the Septuagint it usually stands after the historical books (or after the poetical books) before the prophetic books, while in the English Bible it is found between the historical and the poetical books.

CANONICITY

From the time of its publication until long after the Canon was finally fixed at the Synod of Jamnia in A.D. 90, the canonicity of Esther was not universally accepted among the Jews. As late as the third century A.D. we find the Jewish Rabbi, Samuel, saying, 'Esther does not defile the hands', that is, it is not sufficiently sacred to require the washing of the hands after reading it. According to Bentzen,[1] those who rejected it did so not on moral grounds, but because the Feast of Purim, which was specially enjoined in ix. 21–29, was contrary to the principle that the Law of Moses was complete, and that, therefore, no prophet after Moses could introduce any new festival (Lev. xxvii. 34). Those who accepted the book overcame the difficulty by declaring that the book had been revealed to Moses on Mount Sinai, but had not been written down until the time of Esther and Mordecai.

Opposition to the book gradually died down, and in the course of time it acquired immense popularity among the Jews. It became known as 'The Megillah', that is, 'The Roll', surpassing in excellence the other four 'Rolls', and was even coupled with the law as of supreme importance. Its popularity is due mainly to the fact that Haman, the villain of the story, is regarded as the prototype of all the persecutors

[1] A. Bentzen, *Introduction to the Old Testament*, vol. II, 1948, pp. 30f.

of the Jewish people, and that his downfall helps to keep alive in their hearts the hope of ultimate deliverance from all their sufferings.

When the book passed into the Christian Church it seems to have been entirely ignored by the early Christian Fathers. It was omitted from some of the earlier lists of the sacred Scriptures, but finally declared to be canonical at the Council of Carthage in A.D. 397. The reason for its tardy recognition is quite understandable. It breathes the spirit of hatred and revenge, and is further removed from the spirit of the Gospel than any other book in the Old Testament. In the hour of triumph the Jews slew over 75,000 of their enemies and afterwards, 'they rested, and made that a day of feasting and gladness' (ix. 17f.). From the beginning to the end of the story there is no mention of the name of God or of prayer. It is true that the Jews are saved from a fearful massacre, but Yahweh is not represented as intervening to save them. Even if it is said that Divine Providence and the law of retribution are implied, it seems strange that a blood-thirsty tale of hatred and revenge should be necessary to teach these things.

The book has never become popular in the Christian Church. At the Reformation Luther declared his hostility to it and wished that it did not exist. In recent times Paton has said, 'The book is so conspicuously lacking in religion that it should never have been included in the Canon of the Old Testament.'[1] Bishop Gore, however, sees some good in it. Of it he wrote, 'The divinest element in the book is perhaps to be found in the profound sense of the indestructibility of Israel, and the duty of an Israelite to maintain the cause of his people at whatever risk. It was this probably that caused its final inclusion in the Canon.'[2]

AUTHORSHIP

The authorship of Esther is unknown. The Talmud (Baba Bathra, 15a) ascribes it to the Men of the Great Synagogue,[3] and the Rabbis and many Christian scholars on the basis of ix. 20, 32 ascribe it to Mordecai. Most scholars now accept Kuenen's view that the Great Synagogue is unhistorical, while the book mentioned in ix. 20, 32 may

---

[1] L. B. Paton, *I.C.C.*, 1908, p. 97.
[2] *A New Commentary of Holy Scripture*, ed. by Charles Gore, 1928, p. 305.
[3] The men of the 'Great Synagogue' or the 'Great Assembly' was a term applied to a college of learned scribes, supposed to have been founded by Ezra (cf. Neh. viii–x). They were credited with the composition of Ezekiel, Daniel, Esther and the *Twelve Minor Prophets*, with the introduction of the feast of Purim, and the fixing of the Eighteen Benedictions and other prayers. There is, however, no evidence that such an institution as the Great Synagogue ever existed.

not be our Esther. All that can be said on the subject is that the author was probably a Jew who had gained some knowledge of the Persian empire.

PURPOSE

The main purpose of Esther was to explain the origin of the Jewish festival of Purim, which had no religious significance and no basis in the law but which had become very popular among the Jews. There is, however, some doubt about the origin of the festival as indicated in the book. The word 'Pur' which is used in connexion with the festival presents a difficulty. In iii. 7 we read that 'they cast Pur, that is the lot, before Haman day after day; and they cast it month after month till the twelfth month, which is the month of Adar' (in order to find an auspicious date for the massacre of the Jews). In ix. 26 it is stated that 'they called these days Purim after the term Pur' (the Hebrew plural termination 'im' is added). The fact that the author felt it necessary to explain the word 'Pur' ('lot') by its Hebrew equivalent suggests that the festival Purim was originally a pagan festival. No Persian word with the meaning of 'lot' has been traced; the word puru'um or puru has been discovered in Assyrian texts with the meaning of 'lot' or 'stone'.[1] Moreover the casting of lots plays a very minor part in the story and is unlikely to have given its name to the festival

Several theories have been advanced to explain the origin of the festival. According to Jensen, the story is based on a Babylonian myth. Esther is the Babylonian goddess Ishtar, Mordecai the Babylonian god Marduk, Haman the Elamite god Humman, and Vashti the Elamite goddess Mashti. The story represents the triumph of the Babylonian god Marduk over the ancient deities of the Elamites.[2] Lewy identifies the festival of Purim with the Persian festival called Farvardigan, celebrated in honour of the dead.[3] Pfeiffer suggests that the book is 'fiction pure and simple' and that the author invented both the feast of Purim and its name to express the ardent patriotism of the Jews and their hatred of the heathen in the time of Hyrcanus.[4] All such theories are interesting but unconvincing.

---

[1] W. F. Albright, 'Some Recent Archaeological Publications', *B.A.S.O.R.*, No. 67, p. 37; J. Lewy, 'Old Assyrian puru'um and purum', *Revue Hittite et Asianique*, V, 1939, 117–24; E. F. Weidner, 'Die assyrischen Eponymen,' *Archiv für Orientforschung*, xiii, 1941, 308b.
[2] P. Jensen, 'Elamitische Eigennamen,' *W.Z.K.M.*, 1892, pp. 47ff.
[3] J. Lewy, *H.U.C.A.*, xiv. 1939, pp. 127–151.
[4] R. H. Pfeiffer, *Introduction to the Old Testament*, 1948, p. 745.

Another purpose of the book was to exalt the Jews and to foster the spirit of patriotism among them at a time when they were struggling for their independence and the preservation of their religion and way of life. Of all the maidens in Persia a Jewess is chosen to be queen (ii. 17). Haman can never succeed against Mordecai because the latter belongs to the Jewish race (vi. 13). Mordecai is promoted to the post of grand vizier, and an account of his greatness is written 'in the Book of the Chronicles of the kings of Media and Persia' (x. 2). The Jews find favour with the king, for we read that they 'had light and gladness and joy and honour' (viii. 16). Many pagans became Jews, 'for the fear of the Jews had fallen upon them' (viii. 17). Without the loss of a single casualty they slew over 75,000 of their enemies (ix. 6–10, 16).

CONTENTS
Outline

Ch. i. The royal feast and Vashti's disobedience and deposition.

Ch. ii. Esther's elevation to the rank of queen and Mordecai's discovery of a conspiracy.

Ch. iii. The promotion of Mordecai and the plot against the Jews.

Ch. iv. Esther's resolve to save the Jews.

Ch. v. The opposing plans of Esther and Haman.

Ch. vi. Mordecai is rewarded by the king.

Ch. vii. The downfall of Haman.

Ch. viii. The triumph of the Jews.

Ch. ix. The revenge of the Jews and the institution of the Feast of Purim.

Ch. x. The greatness of Ahasuerus and Mordecai.

Summary: Ch. i

Ahasuerus (i.e. Xerxes I, 486–465 B.C.) who reigned 'from India to Ethiopia' gives a great feast for 180 days in his palace at Susa to the principal men of his kingdom. A second feast follows for seven days for the citizens of Susa (vv. 1–8). Vashti, his queen, gives a similar feast to the women of the court. On the seventh day of the feast the king commands Vashti to appear before his guests in order that they may see her beauty, but she refuses to obey the command (vv. 9–12). The king consults his wise men as to what punishment should be inflicted upon her, and one, Memucan, recommends that she shall be deposed and deprived of her royal revenues, because she has not only

ESTHER   245

defied the king, but has set a bad example to all other wives by disobeying his command (vv. 13–20). The king agrees to do this, and sends instructions to all the provinces that every man is to be master in his own house (vv. 21f.).

Ch. ii

Before long the king regrets his deposition of Vashti. The chamberlain proposes a plan for the selection of another queen. All the beautiful maidens of the provinces should be brought to Susa for the royal inspection. The proposal pleases the king and he acts accordingly (vv. 1–4). It happens that there is living at Susa a Benjamite Jew, named Mordecai, and he has under his care his cousin, Esther (or Hadassah), who is beautiful. With other maidens she is placed in the harem in charge of Hegai, who shows her special favour (vv. 5–9). Esther conceals her nationality although Mordecai inquires daily after her welfare (vv. 10f.). After a year's beauty treatment each one of the maidens is brought before the king and becomes one of his concubines. Four years after Vashti's deposition Esther's turn comes. The king loves her more than all the other maidens and makes her queen instead of Vashti. A great feast is held to commemorate the occasion (vv. 12–18). Shortly after the marriage Mordecai, through Esther, reveals to the king a plot on the part of two of the court chamberlains to assassinate him. An enquiry is held and the two conspirators are hanged, but Mordecai receives no reward (vv. 19–23).

Ch. iii

A new favourite now appears on the scene, one Haman, who is made vizier. The king orders all his servants to do obeisance to him but Mordecai refuses (vv. 1–5). Haman, hearing of his refusal and discovering that he is a Jew, resolves to destroy all the Jews in the kingdom. To determine the most auspicious day for the proposed massacre he has a lot (Pur) cast, and the lot falls on the thirteenth day of the twelfth month, Adar. He then reports to the king that a certain people (i.e. the Jews) scattered throughout the kingdom have their own laws and do not observe the royal decrees, and promises to pay into the treasury 10,000 silver talents if they are destroyed. The king places his signet ring on Haman's hand, and tells him to keep the money and do as he thinks fit (vv. 6–11). A decree is drafted and sent to all the satraps and governors, commanding that on the thirteenth day of the twelfth month, Adar, all the Jews are to be destroyed and their goods confiscated (vv. 12–15).

Ch. iv

On hearing of the decree, Mordecai and all the Jews throughout the kingdom mourn bitterly (vv. 1–3). Mordecai sends Esther a copy of the decree and begs her to intercede with the king for the people. Esther replies that no one can enter the presence-chamber without a summons under the penalty of death, unless the king signifies his favour to that person by holding out to him the golden sceptre. Mordecai rebukes her for shrinking from the perilous task and she finally decides to go to the king at the risk of her life (vv. 4–17).

Ch. v

Esther, having gained the king's favour and obtained from him a promise to grant her request, invites him and Haman to a banquet (vv. 1–5). When they are seated she invites them to another banquet on the morrow (vv. 6–8). Haman is delighted at the apparent sign of the queen's favour, but his happiness is marred by the sight of Mordecai who shows his contempt for him. His wife and friends suggest that he should build a gallows fifty cubits high and that he should persuade the king to have Mordecai hanged upon it (vv. 9–14)

Ch. vi

That night the king, unable to sleep, orders the archives of the kingdom to be read to him. From them he learns of Mordecai's discovery of a plot to assassinate him, and is told that Mordecai has not been rewarded for his service. When early in the morning Haman arrives to obtain permission to hang Mordecai, the king asks him what should be done to the man whom the king delights to honour. Haman, thinking that the king is referring to him, answers that the man should be clad in the royal apparel, mounted on the royal steed, crowned and led through the streets of the city in triumph. Thereupon the king orders him to bestow those honours on Mordecai, and this is done (vv. 1–11). Haman, deeply humiliated, returns home to tell his wife and friends what has happened to him. From his wise men and his wife he receives no comfort, for he is told that in his struggle with Mordecai he is bound to be defeated. In the midst of these forebodings the king's chamberlains come to escort him to the queen's second banquet (vv. 12–14).

Ch. vii

During the banquet the king reminds Esther that she has not yet made her request. She thereupon begs him to save her and her people from the destruction which threatens them. The king asks who has brought that danger upon them and is told that it is Haman (vv. 1–6). The king rises in his wrath and goes into the garden, and Haman stays to plead with the queen for his life. Returning and finding Haman prostrate on the couch where the queen is sitting, he utters a coarse jest, and orders that he shall be hanged on the gallows which he has prepared for Mordecai (vv. 7–10).

Ch. viii

The king gives Esther the property of Haman, and bestows upon Mordecai the signet ring which he had taken from Haman (vv. 1f.). The queen now begs the king to revoke the decree drawn up by Haman for the destruction of the Jews. As the Persian law does not permit the revocation of a decree, the king authorizes Mordecai to issue a decree, permitting the Jews on the 13th of Adar to bear arms in self defence and to destroy all who may attack them (vv. 3–14). Mordecai is clad in royal robes and the Jews throughout the kingdom rejoice. Many heathen, in view of the coming conflict, become proselytes to the Jewish faith (vv. 15–17).

Ch. ix

On the 13th of Adar on which the original royal decree had been planned to take effect, the Jews in all the provinces gather together, and with the assistance of the local officials massacre their enemies (vv. 1–5). At Susa they slay 500 men, including the sons of Haman (vv. 6–10). The king grants Esther's request to continue the slaughter for another day, and so on the 14th day of Adar 300 more men are slain (vv. 11–15). In the provinces on the 13th day of Adar they slay 75,000 men and observe the 14th day as a day of rejoicing. But at Susa after two days' slaughter, they observe the 15th day as a day of rejoicing (vv. 16–19). Mordecai sends letters to all the provinces, instructing the Jews to observe annually for ever the 14th and 15th of Adar as days of feasting and gladness and for sending portions one to another, and gifts to the poor. The two days' feast is called 'Purim' because of the lot of 'Pur', which Haman had caused to be cast in order to find the most auspicious date for the destruction of the Jews. Esther also enjoins the observance of the feast (vv. 20–32).

Ch. x

Ahasuerus imposes a tribute on his subjects. A full account of the might and greatness of both Ahasuerus and Mordecai is recorded in the royal archives of Media and Persia. Mordecai seeks the welfare of his fellow-countrymen and is beloved by them (vv. 1–3).

THE GREEK VERSION (SEPTUAGINT)

The Greek version of Esther contains six passages, comprising 107 verses, which are not in the Hebrew Text. In the Vulgate these additions are placed together at the end of the canonical Esther, while in the revised version of the Aprocrypha they are collected under the title, 'The Rest of the Chapters of the Book of Esther which are found neither in the Hebrew, nor in the Chaldee'. In the Revised Standard Version they bear the title, 'The Additions to the Book of Esther'.

The following is an outline of the additions in the Septuagint, according to the versification of the Vulgate.

A. xi. 2–xii. 6 (before i. 1 in the Septuagint). Dream of Mordecai and his discovery of the plot against the king for which he is rewarded.

B. xiii. 1–7 (after iii. 13 in the Septuagint). Copy of the decree of Artaxerxes (i.e. Xerxes) against the Jews.

C. xiii. 8–xiv. 19 (after iv. 17 in the Septuagint). Prayer of Mordecai (xiii. 8–18) and Prayer of Esther (xiv. 1–19).

D. xv. 1–16 (immediately after C in the Septuagint). Esther enters the king's presence and falls down in a faint, whereupon she is comforted by the king with loving words.

E. xvi. 1–24 (after viii. 12 in the Septuagint). An edict of Artaxerxes (i.e. Xerxes) in favour of the Jews.

F. x. 4–xi. 1 (after x. 3 in the Septuagint). Interpretation of Mordecai's dream. The last verse is a note stating that a Greek translation of the Letter of Purim was brought to Egypt in the fourth year of the reign of Ptolemy and Cleopatra.

Some scholars maintain that the Greek version of Esther is a translation of a much larger Hebrew or Aramaic original, but the weight of evidence is against the theory. There is no trace of any such original. The Additions show no sign of having been translated from Hebrew or Aramaic; they contradict the Hebrew text in so many particulars that they cannot be regarded as an integral part of the book. The Greek style of the Additions is different from that of the main translation, indicating that they must be the work of a different person. Josephus made use of the Greek text, but evidently did not know of two of the additions, so that they could not have been in all the Greek texts.

The main object of the Additions was to give a religious note to what was otherwise a purely secular story in which the divine name was never mentioned. In the Additions reference is made to the name of God whenever possible, and prayers are put in the mouths of Esther and Mordecai.

UNITY

The unity of the book is disputed. Some scholars reject the authenticity of the passage, ix. 20–x. 3, on the following grounds.

(1) The style of the passage differs from that of the rest of the book.

(2) There are inconsistencies and contradictions between the passage and the previous narrative. According to ix. 16–19, the Jews in the capital of Susa celebrated the feast of Purim on the fifteenth day of Adar, and those residing in the provinces on the fourteenth day of the same month. But according to ix. 20–22, Mordecai ordered that the feast should be held on both the fourteenth and the fifteenth day of Adar. According to ix. 17, 19, the feast of Purim was a time 'of feasting and gladness', whereas, according to ix. 31, Mordecai and Esther commanded that it should be a time of fasting and lamenting. In vii. 10 and viii. 7 we are told that Haman and his sons were hanged on different days, but in ix. 25 it is assumed that they were hanged on the same day. Some scholars maintain that the passage was derived from an earlier Purim source and placed at the end of the book by the author, and others that it was added subsequently by a later editor.

The arguments advanced for the rejection of the passage, ix. 20–x. 3, are not conclusive. The author's characteristic style is found throughout the book, the so-called differences in the disputed passage being due to the change of subject matter. In iii. 7 we read the lot Pur was cast before Haman day after day and month after month 'till the twelfth month, which is the month of Adar'. It is quite natural, therefore, that the author should later refer to the feast of Purim. 'For Haman the Agagite, the son of Hammedatha, the enemy of all the Jews, had plotted against the Jews to destroy them, and had cast Pur, that is the lot, to crush and destroy them' (ix. 24). Moreover, the author's purpose was to account for the different customs of his day regarding the celebration of the Feast of Purim. Accordingly, he first explained the origin of observing the feast on different dates. Then he showed how a two-day feast was legalized by Mordecai's letter (ix. 20), by the Jews' acceptance of the feast as a tradition (ix. 23, 27f.) and by a letter of confirmation sent out jointly by Esther and Mordecai (ix. 29–32). The inaccuracy regarding the hanging of Haman and his sons was probably due to the compression of the account of Haman's plot written in the brief compass of two lines. Finally, the passage ix. 20–x. 3 (except for v. 30) is found in the Septuagint which probably appeared within a hundred years of the publication of the book.

DATE

The date of Esther cannot be accurately determined. At the time of writing the Persian Empire had disappeared and was no more than a dim memory (i. 1, 13f.; viii. 8). The book contains Aramaisms and late Hebrew words and constructions which point unmistakably to a late period. The language appears to be that of a person who spoke Aramaic but found difficulty in expressing himself in the medium of classical Hebrew. In the great Hymn of Praise to the Fathers in Ecclesiasticus xliv–xlix (c. 180 B.C.) no mention is made of Mordecai. It is, therefore, probable that the book was unknown to the author, Ben Sirach, otherwise he would surely have made some reference to it. The book is first mentioned in 2 Maccabees xv. 36 (c. 50 B.C.) where we read, 'And they all decreed by public vote never to let this day go unobserved, but to celebrate the thirteenth day of the twelfth month—which is called Adar in the Syrian language—the day before Mordecai's day'. The day to which reference is made is 'Nicanor's day', that is, the anniversary of a striking Jewish victory over the Syrian general of that name in 161 B.C., so that the 'day of Mordecai' was the 14th of Adar. In 1 Maccabees vii. 49 (c. 100 B.C.) we learn that 'Nicanor's day' was to be celebrated annually on the 13th of Adar, but no reference is made to the 'day of Mordecai'. Thus the Feast of Purim was not well established till about the middle of the first century B.C. The note to 'The Additions to the Book of Esther' claims that the book was brought to Egypt by Dositheus in the fourth year of Ptolemy and Cleopatra (probably 114 B.C.) after being translated by Lysimachus (xi. 1). If the note is authentic, the book must have been written before 114 B.C. Unfortunately, however, the note is suspect.

From the above data we conclude that the book was probably written between 180–114 B.C. It is perhaps, possible to fix the date with

ESTHER

greater precision. The intense national pride, fanatical exclusiveness and fierce hatred of the Jews which the book reveals, suggest a period of bitter persecution followed by a signal triumph. The period which best suits the conditions is that of the Maccabaean revolt against the Seleucid dynasty. Hence the book was perhaps written about 150 B.C.[1]

HISTORICITY

Until recent times Esther was regarded both by orthodox Jews and Christians as a record of actual events which took place in the reign of the Persian king, Ahasuerus (i.e. Xerxes I, 486–465 B.C.). Even the Christian scholar, Driver, declared that the story was within the limits of historical possibility.[2] Several reasons were advanced in support of the theory. The book itself purports to be a record of actual events; the Persian king was a real historical figure; tension between Jews and Gentiles actually existed in that period; the author was evidently familiar with Persian customs and institutions—with banquet customs (i. 6–8; v. 5f.), royal edicts (iv. 11; viii. 9), the royal harem (ii. 8, 12–18), and palace intrigues (ii. 21–23; vii. 9f.).

To-day, however, the majority of scholars are agreed that the book is not a record of actual events but a work of fiction. The evidence for this theory is overwhelming. The fact that the book contains a certain amount of accurate local colour does not necessarily prove that it is a record of actual events. The author could easily have obtained the information at second hand. The book contains several historical inaccuracies. The queen of Ahasuerus (Xerxes I) was neither Vashti nor Esther, but Amestris, the daughter of a Persian general. Esther could not have been queen, for, according to Herodotus, the king was bound to choose his consort from one of the seven noble Persian families. The number of provinces in the Persian empire was under 30, not 127, as in Esther i. 1, viii. 9.

Numerous details of the story are highly improbable, if not actually incredible. Mordecai is said to have been deported from Jerusalem to Babylon in the reign of Jehoiachin that is, in 598 B.C. (ii. 6), so that

---

[1] A. E. Morris ('The Purpose of the Book of Esther,' *E.T.*, xlii., 1930, pp. 124–128) places the book in the early years of the reign of Antiochus Epiphanes (175–163 B.C.), on the ground that the author advocates a policy of co-operation with the conqueror before he set out to destroy the Jewish religion. R. H. Pfeiffer (*Introduction to the Old Testament*, 1948, p. 742), suggests that the book was probably written about 125 B.C. in the reign of John Hyrcanus (135–104 B.C.) because such forcible conversions to Judaism, alluded to in viii. 17, are unknown before his time.

[2] S. R. Driver, *An Introduction to the Literature of the Old Testament*, 9th ed., 1913, p. 482.

he must have been 125 years old when in the twelfth year of Xerxes I (474 B.C.) he became grand vizier (viii. 2; cf. iii. 7). The fact that Esther was a Jewess was to be kept secret (ii. 10, 20), yet everyone knew that Mordecai was a Jew (ii. 5). He admitted his nationality and refused to bow down before Haman because he was a Jew (iii. 1–6). It is very unlikely that either an Agagite (Amalekite) or a Jew would have been appointed to the post of grand vizier (iii. 1; viii. 1f.).

Exaggeration, which is characteristic of imaginative fiction, is much in evidence throughout the narrative. We are told that the royal feast lasted 180 days (i. 1–4), that many fair young virgins imported from all the provinces of the kingdom were given a year's beauty treatment (ii. 2–12), that the gallows on which Haman was hanged was 50 cubits high, and that the Jews slew over 75,000 of their enemies (ix. 6, 16).

The story reads more like a romance than a history. The incidents have evidently been carefully arranged for the sake of dramatic effect. It is impossible to believe they could have happened in the same order in real life. There is also the ancient story-teller's trick of contrasted characters in Mordecai and Haman. Poetic justice, which rarely occurs in real life, is very prominent in the story. Haman had the right to demand reverence from Mordecai, but in the end it was Haman who had to do reverence to Mordecai. Haman built a gallows on which to hang Mordecai, but instead he was hanged on it himself. The Jews were to be massacred on a certain day, but instead they massacred their opponents.

PERMANENT INFLUENCE

Historically, Esther has little to commend it. The amount of knowledge which it supplies concerning the Persian empire is negligible. It cannot be regarded as a true reflection of the moral and spiritual condition of the Jewish people in the second century B.C. The whole nation cannot be condemned because one of its members wrote a book practically devoid of any moral or religious content and breathing a spirit of hatred and revenge. It must not be forgotten that if the post-exilic period produced Esther it also produced Ruth and Jonah.

LITERARY MERIT

As literature Esther possesses considerable merit. It has an intricate plot which is a masterpiece of technical construction. The reader's interest is roused at the beginning of the story with an account of a six-month banquet given by the Persian king, Ahasuerus, 'for all his princes and servants' (i. 3) and is held to the end with an account of the exaltation of Mordecai, who, from being a captive ranks next to the king, and is a great man among the Jews and popular among all his fellow-countrymen (x. 3).

The characters, with the exception of the queen, Vashti, are vividly portrayed. The king is a typical eastern tyrant, arrogant, capricious, cruel and merciless. He commands his queen, Vashti, to appear before his guests to display her beauty and deposes her for refusing to obey him (i. 9–22). He issues an edict for the destruction of all the Jews in the kingdom and immediately afterwards sits down to drink with Haman (iii. 10–16). He exalts Haman (iii. 1) and shortly afterwards orders him to be hanged (vii. 10). To please Esther he grants her request for a second day's massacre of the enemies of the Jews at Susa, and 300 more men lose their lives (ix. 11–15).

Vashti is a dim, shadowy figure. Nothing is told about her except that she has the courage to refuse to obey the commands of the king and is deposed.

Haman's chief characteristics are vanity, cruelty and cowardice. Because Mordecai refuses to bow down to him, he schemes to destroy all the Jews in the kingdom (iii. 5f.). He longs to be the cynosure of every eye (vi. 6–9), and laments when his wife and all his friends tell him that if Mordecai is a Jew, he will not prevail against him (vi. 12f.). When Esther denounces him to the king, he prostrates himself in abject fear before her.

Esther is not a very pleasant character. It is true that she possesses beauty and charm, which win for her the favour of Hegai who has charge of the women (ii. 8f.), and the love of the king (ii. 17); but she is a narrow-minded nationalist with a deep hatred of all foreigners. She contrives to bring about the downfall of Haman (vii.), and requests the king to order a second day's massacre of the enemies of the Jews at Susa. She even asks that the dead bodies of Haman's ten sons shall be hanged on the gallows (ix. 13). There is, however, a touch of nobility in the words which she utters when she finally decides to enter the presence of the king to plead the cause of her fellow-countrymen. 'Go, gather all the Jews to be found in Susa, and hold a fast on my behalf, and neither eat nor drink for three days, night or day. I and my maids will also fast as you do. Then I will go to the king, though it is against the law; and if I perish, I perish' (iv. 16).

Mordecai is by far the noblest character in the book. He stands out as a brave dignified figure, with a great love of his own people, a deep sense of responsibility and a warm heart. Though he is under no legal obligation, he brings up Esther after the death of her parents as his own child (ii. 7). He becomes deeply attached to her, walking every day 'in front of the court of the harem to learn how Esther was and how she fared' (ii. 11). He uncovers a plot against the king (ii. 21f.) and thwarts Haman's scheme to destroy all the Jews in the kingdom (vii. 3–10). He becomes the grand vizier and is accounted great among the Jews, 'for he sought the welfare of his people and spoke peace to all his people' (x. 3).

The style of the book is undistinguished. It lacks the simplicity, directness, conciseness and charm of that of the narratives of the classical period of Hebrew prose. Its chief characteristics are vividness and vigour of expression. The author is fond of elaboration and leaves little to the imagination. Detailed descriptions are given of the king's palace (i. 6f.), Esther's life in the harem (ii. 9–14), Mordecai's kingly robes (viii. 15) and the writing and dispatch of the edict, authorizing the Jews to defend their lives and destroy any armed force that might attack them, and to plunder their goods (viii. 9–12). In the development of the plot skilful use is made of vigorous and natural dialogue (iv. 10–16; v. 3–8). Throughout the story use is made of the literary device of dramatic irony (iii. 12–15 and viii. 9–14; vi. 1–11; vii. 9f.).

Esther, with its elaborate details, especially in the introductory chapter, its complex plot, and its subtle characterization, belongs to a late stage in the evolution of the art of Hebrew story-writing. 'It is indeed', says Hudson, 'by far the most advanced example of narrative to be found in the Old Testament'.[1]

---

[1] W. H. Hudson in his article on 'The Bible as Literature', in *Peake's Commentary*, 1919, p. 22.

CHAPTER XVI

DANIEL

TITLE AND PLACE IN CANON

THE book bears as its title the name of the person who is the hero of the stories in the first half (i–vi) and the recipient of the visions in the second half of the book. In the Septuagint, the Vulgate and the English versions it stands after Ezekiel, as the fourth of the 'Major Prophets'. In the Hebrew Canon it is placed among the 'Writings', between Esther and Ezra-Nehemiah. The chief reasons suggested for its exclusion from the 'Major Prophets' are that, (1) Daniel was not a professional prophet, and (2) he exercised the gift outside Palestine. Neither of these two reasons is convincing. Amos repudiated the charge that he was a professional prophet (Am. vii. 14), while both Ezekiel and the author of Jonah exercised their gift outside Palestine. If, however, the book was written in the Maccabaean Period, as it is generally thought (see p. 272) this fact alone would account for its position among the 'Writings' since the collection of the works of the prophets was completed by about 200 B.C.

CONTENTS

The book falls naturally into two parts, namely, (a) Chs. i–vi, which form a collection of stories about Daniel and his companions, and (b) Chs. vii–xii, recording the visions and revelations given to Daniel by God.[1]

Outline: Chapters i–vi

Ch. i. The capture of Jerusalem by Nebuchadrezzar, the deportation of Daniel and his companions to Babylon and their education for the king's service.

Ch. ii. The dream of a great image and a stone, Daniel's interpretation and his subsequent promotion.

---

[1] Some scholars divide the book at the end of vi., and others divide it at the end of vii.

Ch. iii. The erection of a golden image on the plain of Dura, the refusal of Daniel's companions to worship it and their deliverance from the fiery furnace.

Ch. iv. Nebuchadrezzar's dream of a great tree and Daniel's interpretation.

Ch. v. The writing on the wall and its interpretation.

Ch. vi. Daniel in the den of lions.

Chapters vii–xii

Ch. vii. The vision of the four great beasts.

Ch. viii. The vision of the ram and the he-goat.

Ch. ix. Daniel's prayer and confession of the nation's sins, and the angel Gabriel's explanation of Jeremiah's 'seventy weeks'.

Chs. x–xi. 1. A vision concerning the latter times.

Chs. xi. 2–xii. 4. A summary of history from the beginning of the Persian era to the time of Antiochus IV, Epiphanes, the deliverance of Israel and the resurrection of the martyred Jews and apostates, the former to everlasting life and the latter to everlasting punishment.

Ch. xii. 5–13. The time of the end. Daniel is assured that after his death he will rise again 'at the end of the days'.

Summary: Chs. i–vi

Ch. i. In the third year of the reign of Jehoiakim, Nebuchadrezzar captured Jerusalem and deported a number of Jews to Babylon. Among the captives were Daniel and his three companions, Hananiah, Mishael and Azariah, who were instructed in the learning and language of the Chaldeans and educated for the king's service. Their names were changed, Daniel to Belteshazzar, Hananiah to Shadrach, Mishael to Meshach and Azariah to Abednego (vv. 1–7). The four young men refused to defile themselves by eating the king's food, and Daniel persuaded the steward to allow them to adopt a vegetarian diet, on which they throve so well that at the end of ten days they appeared fairer and fatter 'than all the youths who ate the king's rich food' (vv. 8–16). At the end of three years their education was complete, and they were introduced to the king who found that they were all distinguished for wisdom and understanding, Daniel especially being gifted with 'understanding in all visions and dreams' (vv. 17–21).

Ch. ii. Nebuchadrezzar in the second year of his reign had a dream, but in the morning he could not recall its details. In his difficulty he sent for the magicians and enchanters to see if they could reveal it, but they could not. Their failure infuriated the king, who ordered that all the wise men of Babylon, including Daniel and his companions, should be destroyed (vv. 1–13). Daniel asked for an opportunity to tell the king his dream (vv. 14–16). The dream and its interpretation were revealed to Daniel in a vision of the night and he sang a psalm of thanksgiving (vv. 17–23). Brought before the king, he reported that he (i.e. the king) had seen a great image, the head of gold, the breast and arms of silver, the belly and thighs of brass, the legs of iron, and the feet of iron and clay mixed. A stone, 'cut out without hands' smote the feet of the image, which thereupon broke up, while the stone became a great mountain and filled the earth (vv. 24–36). Then Daniel proceeded to give the interpretation of the dream. The great image was a pictorial representation of the course of history. Four kingdoms would succeed each other and would be finally destroyed by God's eternal kingdom before which all earthly powers would ultimately fall (vv. 37–45). Nebuchadrezzar worshipped Daniel, and made him governor of Babylon and prefect over all the magicians. At Daniel's request his companions were put in charge of the business of the province of Babylon, but Daniel himself remained at the court (vv. 46–49).

The golden head of the image represents the Babylonian kingdom, the silver breast and arms that of the Medes, the brass belly and thighs that of the Persians, and the iron legs that of the Greeks set up by Alexander the Great. The mixture of iron and clay in the feet represents the division of Alexander's empire on his death and the rise of the two rival kingdoms of the Ptolemies in Egypt and the Seleucids in Syria. The stone represents the Messianic kingdom which is to destroy the other kingdoms. Four of the kingdoms, therefore, belonged to the past and the fifth is the ideal kingdom of the future.

Ch. iii. Nebuchadrezzar set up a great gold image on the plain of Dura and at the time of its dedication ordered all the people to worship it (vv. 1–7). Daniel's three companions refused to comply with the order and were reported to the king, who ordered them to be brought before him. When they were given another chance, they declared that they would not serve his gods or worship the image which he had set up (vv. 8–18). They were at once bound and cast into the burning fiery furnace, heated seven times hotter than usual (vv. 19–23). To his astonishment the king beheld them walking unhurt in the midst of the fire in the company of a fourth whose aspect was like that of 'a son of the gods' (vv. 24f.). He approached the furnace and ordered the three men to come out. When they emerged from the furnace, he found that they had suffered no injury and that even their garments remained unsinged, whereupon he acknowledged their God and promoted them to a higher position in the administration of the province of Babylon (vv. 26-30).

Ch. iv. Nebuchadrezzar declared that it seemed good to him to make known the signal acts of the Most High God in dealing with him (vv. 1-3). He reported that in a dream he had seen a gigantic tree growing up to heaven and giving protection and sustenance to all. Suddenly a holy one from heaven appeared and commanded that it should be cut down, leaving only a stump in the ground. By a swift transition the tree became a human being, who was to share the grass of the field with the beasts and whose heart was to be changed into that of a beast. The dream was told to the magicians but they could not interpret it (vv. 4-18). Daniel, after some natural hesitation, made known to the king the meaning of the dream. The tree was the king himself, who, because of his pride, would be afflicted with madness and would live for seven years like the beasts of the field. Daniel exhorted the king to repent by practising justice and showing mercy to the poor (vv. 19-27). While the king was boasting of Babylon's greatness, he became mad and was driven from human beings to dwell with the beasts of the field (vv. 28-33).[1] At the end of the period his reason was restored and he was re-established on the throne, whereupon he praised, extolled and honoured the king of Heaven (vv. 34-37).

Ch. v. Belshazzar, king of Babylon, made a great feast for a thousand of his nobles, his wives and the women of his harem. During its course he sent for the sacred vessels which had been brought from the Temple of Jerusalem by his father, Nebuchadrezzar, that he and his guests might drink from them (vv. 1-4). Suddenly a hand appeared, writing on the wall a secret writing which the wise men of Babylon could not interpret (vv. 5-8). At the suggestion of the Queen, Daniel was summoned. After rebuking the king for his arrogance and impiety

---

[1] Among the Dead Sea Scrolls is a fragment, written in Aramaic, containing 'The Prayer of Nabonidus', from which we learn that Nabonidus was struck with a malignant disease for seven years by the decree of the Most High God, and became unlike men. It has been suggested that the author of *Daniel* transferred the illness from Nabonidus to Nebuchadrezzar. (For a translation of the fragment see J. T. Milik, *Ten Years of Discovery in the Wilderness of Judaea*, Eng. trans., 1959, pp. 36f.

he read the writing—'Mene, Mene, Tekel, and Parsin'—and told him that his days were numbered, and that his kingdom would be divided and given to the Medes and Persians (vv. 9–28). Daniel was honoured, and that same night Belshazzar was murdered and his throne seized by Darius the Mede (vv. 29–31).

There are two forms of the writing on the wall. In the inscription we find, 'Mene, Mene, Tekel, and Parsin' (v. 25), and in the interpretation, 'Mene, Tekel, Peres' (vv. 26–28). The term 'Peres' may be explained as the substitution of the singular for the plural, together with the omission of the connecting particle 'U' = 'and'. Daniel interpreted the words as 'numbered, weighed, divided'. Another suggestion which is widely accepted, is that the terms are the names of three weights, 'a mina', 'a shekel', and 'a half-mina'.

Ch. vi. Darius appointed 120 satraps over his kingdom under three presidents, one of whom was Daniel, who distinguished himself more than all the presidents and satraps, so that the king thought of setting him over the whole realm (vv. 1–3). Filled with jealousy, the other officials induced the king to issue an irrevocable decree, forbidding petition to any god or man other than himself for thirty days on pain of being cast into the den of lions (vv. 4–9). Daniel, however, still continued to pray to the God of Israel three times a day with his face toward Jerusalem. This was reported to the king who most unwillingly ordered him to be cast into the den of lions (vv. 10–18). On the morrow, Daniel was found to be alive and unhurt, whereupon the king ordered him to be brought out of the den, and the men who had plotted his downfall, together with their families, to be flung to the lions instead. They were instantly devoured (vv. 19–24). The king then issued a decree throughout all the dominions, commanding his subjects to fear and tremble before the God of Daniel (vv. 25–28).

Chs. vii–xii

Ch. vii. In the first year of Belshazzar's reign Daniel saw in a vision four beasts emerging from the sea—the first a lion with eagle's wings, the second a bear, the third a leopard with four wings and four heads, and the fourth an unknown beast, 'terrible and exceedingly strong', having ten horns. As Daniel watched the horns, there arose among them another small horn which uprooted three of the original horns (vv. 1–8). A great assize was held with the 'ancient of days' as judge, and judgment was pronounced upon the beasts. The fourth beast was slain and its body destroyed by fire. The lives of the other three beasts were prolonged for a time, but they were deprived of their dominions. A figure in human form appeared 'with the clouds of heaven' and received from the 'ancient of days' an everlasting dominion (vv. 9-14). An angel gave Daniel the interpretation of the vision. The four beasts were four kingdoms, but the saints of the Most High would receive the kingdom and hold it for ever. The fourth beast was a fourth kingdom, which would be different from all other kingdoms, crushing and shattering the whole earth. The ten horns were ten kings who would rise out of this kingdom. The little horn was an eleventh king, who would overthrow three kings and persecute the saints of the Most High for three-and-a-half years. Then the kingdom would be destroyed, and all the kingdoms under heaven given to the saints of the Most High—a people whose kingdom would be an everlasting kingdom, to be served and obeyed by all dominions. Daniel was alarmed but kept everything in mind (vv. 15-28).

The identification of the four kingdoms is much discussed and various identifications have been suggested. The four beasts probably represent the Babylonian, Median, Persian and Greek empires, the ten horns of the fourth beast ten Seleucid kings, the little horn Antiochus IV Epiphanes (175-163 B.C.), and the three horns rooted out, Seleucus IV, Heliodorus, and Demetrius.

Ch. viii. In the third year of Belshazzar's reign Daniel had another vision. A ram with two horns appeared and made conquests in all directions. Then a he-goat with a conspicuous horn between his eyes appeared from the west and overthrew the ram (vv. 1-7). Then the goat magnified himself mightily, but at the height of his power his large horn was broken, and four others came up in its place pointing to the four winds of heaven. From one of these emerged a small horn, which, growing in power, advanced in the direction of the south, the east and the fair land of Palestine. The daily sacrifices were suppressed, the sanctuary was desecrated and the true religion was beaten down for 1,150 days (vv. 8-14).

The vision was interpreted to Daniel by the angel Gabriel. The vision related to the crisis at the close of the age. The two horns of the ram were the kingdoms of Media and Persia; the he-goat was the kingdom of Greece, and the large horn between his eyes the first king of Greece. The four horns, which rose in place of the broken horn, were four kingdoms which would rise out of the Greek nation, but with less power. In the later period of their power there would arise a king who would be defiant and crafty. He would prosper in his policy, gaining great power, not by force of arms but by craft, and destroying his powerful foes and the holy people; but in the end he would be broken by no human hand (vv. 15–25). Daniel was told to keep the vision secret for it related to the future. So astonished was he by the disclosure that he was ill for some days. He could not understand it (vv. 26f.).

The ram with the two horns represents the joint kingdom of the Medes and the Persians. The he-goat represents Alexander the Great, and the later four horns represent the four kingdoms into which Alexander's empire was divided at his death in 323 B.C. The small horn represents Antiochus IV Epiphanes, (175–163 B.C.), who desecrated the Temple and caused the suspension of the services for over three years.

Ch. ix. In the first year of the reign of Darius (here called the son of Xerxes) Daniel, perplexed by the thought that Israel had not been delivered from captivity, though Jeremiah had prophesied that the Exile would last for seventy years (Jer. xxv. 11f.; xxix. 10), found the cause in the sins of the past, made humble confession before Yahweh on behalf of the people and pleaded for the restoration of Jerusalem (vv. 1–19). His prayer was heard and Gabriel came by divine command to reveal to him the meaning of the prophecy (vv. 20–23). The seventy years were really seventy weeks of years (i.e. 490 years), divided up into three unequal periods. The first period would last seven weeks (i.e. 49 years) and run from the utterance of the prophecy to the commencement of the work of restoration and the advent of the 'anointed one'. During the second period of 62 weeks (i.e. 434 years) the restoration would be carried out; the period would end with the cutting off of the 'anointed one' and with the coming of a time of desolation. During the third period of one week (i.e. 7 years) persecution would arise, and for half that time the sacrifices would cease, but it would end in the destruction of the oppressor (vv. 24–27).

The prayer (vv. 4–19) is regarded by some scholars as an interpolation on the ground that it does not fit its present context.

Many interpretations of the 'seventy weeks' (vv. 24–27), have been suggested, but none has won universal agreement. The 70 weeks, that is, 490 years, probably covers the period from the beginning of the Exile in 587 B.C. to the death of Antiochus IV Epiphanes in 163 B.C. This period actually covers only 424 years—a discrepancy of 66 years, probably due to the writer's lack of sufficient chronological data. The first period of 7 weeks, that is, 49 years, probably extends from 587 B.C. to the Edict of Cyrus in 538 B.C., and the second period of 62 weeks, that is, 434 years from 538 B.C. to the murder of the High Priest, Onias III, in 171 B.C.,—a discrepancy of 67 years. The period of one week, that is, seven years is divided into two equal portions. During the first 3½ years, Antiochus IV Epiphanes favoured the renegade Jews, and during the second 3½ years, he desecrated the Temple and suspended the sacrifices.

Chs. x–xi. 1. In the third year of Cyrus, king of Persia, Daniel had a vision while he was standing on the banks of the Tigris. An angel appeared to him and told him that he had been stopped from coming to him by the guardian angel of Persia, until Michael, the guardian angel of Israel, had come to his assistance, and that he had come to let him know what would befall his people at the end of the ages (x. 1–14). Daniel was overcome by the vision, but the angel strengthened him and told him that he (the angel) and Michael would have a long contest on behalf of Israel, first with the guardian angel of Persia, and then with the guardian angel of Greece (x. 15–xi. 1).

Chs. xi. 2–xii. 4. The angel told Daniel the truth concerning the future. Three kings would arise in Persia, and then a fourth richer than them all, who would rouse all the realms of Greece to conflict. But a mighty king would arise who would do according as he pleased. When he came to power his kingdom would be shattered. It would not pass to his posterity but would be divided among his four generals and others (xi. 2–4). A fairly accurate account is given of the conflict between Egypt (the kingdom of the south) and Syria (the kingdom of the north) during the period preceding the reign of Antiochus IV Epiphanes (xi. 5–20). This is followed by an account of the reign of Antiochus which is given in greater detail. We are told of his seizure of the throne, his deposition and murder of the High Priest, Onias III, his two campaigns against Egypt, his cruel persecution of the faithful Jews and his favouring of the apostates, his desecration of the Temple, his assumption of divinity, his disregard of all gods but Zeus and his assignment of honours and rewards to his partisans. Here history ends and prophecy begins (xi. 21–39). Antiochus will conquer Egypt, Libya and Ethiopia and die in Palestine (xi. 40–45). After the death of the tyrant, Michael, the defender of Israel would come, and a period of bitter trouble would ensue. The faithful, whose names were written in the book of life, would be delivered, and many of the dead would awake, 'some (i.e. the faithful martyrs) to everlasting life, and some

DANIEL

(i.e. the apostates) to shame and everlasting contempt'. Daniel was to keep all this a close secret till the crisis at the end (xii. 1–4).

The three kings (xi. 2) are probably Cyrus (539–530 B.C.), Cambyses (530–522 B.C.) and Darius I (522–486 B.C.) and the fourth (xi. 2) Xerxes I (486–465 B.C.) who invaded Greece. The 'mighty king' (xi. 3) is Alexander the Great. After the death of Alexander his dominions were divided among his four generals, the two chief divisions being Egypt, ruled by the Ptolemies and Syria governed by the Seleucids.

Ch. xii. 5–13. Two angels were seen standing on the banks of the river, and one of them asked the narrating angel (described in x. 5f.) how long it would be till those marvels happened. The answer was $3\frac{1}{2}$ years, and that when the tyrant was destroyed the end would come (vv. 5–7). Daniel did not understand, and asked what was to be the final issue, but further explanation was refused. It was enough to know that from the suspension of the sacrifices in the Temple and the setting up of the 'abomination that makes desolate' would be 1,290 days (or 1,335 days). He would rest in the grave and rise to take his allotted place 'at the end of the days' (vv. 8–13).

In viii. 14 it is stated that the daily sacrifices would be suspended for 2,300 evenings and mornings (i.e. for 1,150 days). This number does not correspond to the $3\frac{1}{2}$ years of vii. 25 and xii. 7. It is possible that one or other of the numbers is a later insertion. If the number 2,300 evenings and mornings was added after the rededication of the Temple, it is probably correct. In this case the interval would be about 3 years and 2 months, and the $3\frac{1}{2}$ years would not be exact. As regards the numbers 1,290 and 1,335 days mentioned in xii. 11 and xii. 12 respectively, no satisfactory explanation has been found for the additional 45 days. Charles suggests that xii. 11f. are later insertions.

Ch. xii. 11–13 are regarded by some scholars as a later addition.

ADDITIONS

Additions to Daniel are found in two Greek versions—The Septuagint, but only in the Codex Chisianus, and Theodotion's revision of the Septuagint. Other versions of less importance are the Vulgate, the Syriac version (Peshitta) and the Syro-Hexaplaric version. The chief additions are the following.

(1) *The Song of the Three Holy Children.* This follows immediately after Daniel iii. 23 in the Septuagint and the Vulgate, and consists

of the prayer of Azarias, the heating of the fiery furnace, and the song or hymn of praise of the three children.

(2) The History of Susanna. This precedes Daniel i. 1 in the Septuagint and appears as ch. xiii in the Vulgate. In the story a good woman, Susanna, refused to lie with two Jewish elders as she was preparing to bathe in her garden pool. They accused her of adultery with an imaginary youth and she was condemned to death. But Daniel proved that the accusation was false and the two guilty elders were put to death.

(3) Bel and the Dragon. These two stories follow immediately after Daniel xii. 13 in the Septuagint and are xiv in the Vulgate.

The Story of Bel. Cyrus, king of Persia, worshipped the god Bel, who was supplied daily with a large quantity of food and wine. Daniel refused to worship the idol, declaring that it was made of clay and brass and never ate or drank anything. He proved that the priests and their families ate the food provided for the god, and the king ordered them to be put to death. Daniel destroyed the idol and his temple.

The Story of the Dragon. The Babylonians worshipped a great dragon. When the king asked Daniel to worship it, he refused and undertook to slay the animal without sword or staff. The dragon burst asunder when given a concoction of pitch, hair and fat. The Babylonians, incensed at the death of their god, accused the king of being a Jew, and Daniel was thrown into a den of lions where he remained unharmed for six days. On the seventh day he was released, and those who sought to destroy him were thrown into the den of lions and 'devoured in a moment' before his face.

The original language of the Additions is uncertain. As regards 'The Song of the Three Holy Children', it is thought by some scholars that the prayer of Azarias and the song or hymn were written in Hebrew, the language of prayers and hymns, and that the narrative portion was written in Aramaic. Some believe that all the three parts were written in Aramaic, and others that only the prayer and the hymn were written in that language. As regards 'The History of Susanna' and 'Bel and the Dragon', it is usually held that the original language was Greek. The date of Additions cannot be precisely determined. The Additions are interesting as legends but they possess no historical value. They were regarded as inspired Scripture by the early Church but were later relegated to the Apocrypha.

DANIEL

PURPOSE

The book was written to encourage the faithful who were suffering persecution under Antiochus IV Epiphanes, by assuring them of the greatness of the God of Israel, of His intervention in the struggle on their behalf, of their ultimate deliverance from the power of their oppressor and of the establishment in the near future of the kingdom of God on earth. Throughout the book God is exalted. All the kingdoms of the earth were under the control of the 'God of heaven' (ii. 18), who removed and set up kings and revealed deep and mysterious things (ii. 21f.). The stone, which smote the great image and became a great mountain filling the whole earth, was the work of His hands (ii. 34f.). It was He who decreed that Nebuchadrezzar should be driven from among men, and made to dwell with the beasts of the field until he knew that the Most High ruled the kingdom of men and gave it to whomsoever He pleased (iv. 25). When Belshazzar, with his lords, wives and concubines drank wine from the sacred vessels taken from the house of God in Jerusalem, the fingers of a man's hand wrote his doom on the wall of the palace (v. 5), and 'that very night Belshazzar the Chaldean king was slain' (v. 30).

The kings of the earth acknowledged His greatness. 'Truly', said Nebuchadrezzar to Daniel, 'your God is God of gods and Lord of kings, and a revealer of mysteries' (ii. 47). Belshazzar acknowledged His greatness when he honoured Daniel, clothing him with purple, putting a gold chain about his neck and making him the third ruler in the kingdom (v. 29). Darius issued a decree commanding that all men in the royal dominion should tremble and fear before the God of Daniel (vi. 25).

It was trust in God that enabled Daniel and his three friends to keep the faith. They refused to defile themselves by eating the king's rich food or by drinking his wine (i. 8). Daniel's three friends refused to worship the golden image set up on the plain of Dura, declaring, 'O Nebuchadrezzar, we have no need to answer to you in this matter. If it be so, our God whom we serve is able to deliver us from the burning fiery furnace; and he will deliver us out of your hand, O king. But if not, be it known to you, O king, that we will not serve your gods, or worship the golden image which you have set up' (iii.16–18). When Darius issued a decree commanding that no one should pray to any god or man for thirty days, except to himself (vi. 6–9), Daniel 'went to his house where he had windows in his upper chamber open towards

Jerusalem; and he got down upon his knees three times a day and prayed and gave thanks before his God, as he had done previously (vi. 10).

God rewarded Daniel and his three friends for putting their trust in Him. He gave them better health 'than all the youths who ate the king's rich food' (i. 15). He sent His angel and delivered the three young men from the burning fiery furnace because they 'yielded up their bodies rather than serve and worship any god except their own God' (iii. 28). He sent His angel and delivered Daniel from the lions' mouths because he was found blameless before Him (vi. 22). Many of the faithful would pay for their loyalty with their lives but God would raise them from the dust to everlasting life (xii. 2).

Finally, God, who was carrying out His eternal purpose in the world, had already destroyed three great kingdoms (the Babylonian, Median and Persian). 'At the time of the end' He would destroy the fourth kingdom (the Greek) and bring in the fifth kingdom—that of the 'saints of the Most High', (vii. 27) symbolized by 'one like a son of man' coming with the clouds of heaven (vii. 13). All peoples, nations and languages would serve Him and His kingdom would endure for ever (vii. 14).

SOURCES

It is unlikely that the book is entirely original, but the sources from which the author derived a certain amount of material cannot be determined with certainty. The author himself mentions only one of his sources, namely Jeremiah (xxv. 11f.; xxix. 10; cf. Dan. ix. 2). Attempts have been made to identify the prototype of the story. There are references in Ezekiel to Daniel who was apparently renowned for his wisdom and righteousness (Ezek. xiv. 14, 20; xxviii. 3). The fact that he is mentioned along with Noah and Job suggests that he was not a younger contemporary of the prophet but a figure of the remote past. Among the Ras Shamra tablets of the fourteenth century B.C. have been found some containing a legend of Daniel or Dan'el, who appears to have been an ancient king who lived before the fourteenth century B.C. He is not portrayed as a wise and righteous man as in Ezekiel, but as one who dispensed judgment in the gate and protected the widow and the orphan. It is probable that the Daniel of the legend is the figure mentioned in Ezekiel. It is quite possible, too, that the author of Daniel borrowed the name of the legendary figure for his own hero, whom he, however, located not in the remote past but in the early years of the sixth century B.C. It is also quite possible that stories about the ancient sage were transmitted orally from generation to generation until they were finally fixed in writing, and that our author was familiar with them and utilized some of the material in them when he came to write his own book, at the same time combining with it traditional stories about Nebuchadrezzar and his successors.

It is thought by some writers that some of the material contained in the visions was derived from Babylonian and Persian mythology.

UNITY

In recent years many scholars have advanced the theory that the book is not a literary unit. Among the exponents of this view, the prevailing opinion seems to be that it is the work of at least two authors, one living in the third century B.C. and the other in the Maccabaean age. The main arguments adduced in support of this view are the following:

(1) The first part of the book consists of simple stories in the third person and the second part of elaborate visions in the first person.

(2) There is no reference in the first part to Antiochus IV Epiphanes, while in the second part he occupies a permanent position.

(3) In the first part the scene is laid in Babylon and in the second part it is laid in Palestine, 'the sumptuous barbaric scenery' of the former contrasting with the 'arid scenery' of the latter.[1]

(4) The book is written partly in Aramaic (ii. 4b–vii. 28) and partly in Hebrew (i–ii. 4a; viii–xii).

The arguments which are put forward in support of this theory are not convincing. The inclusion of narratives in the third person and visions in the first person in the same book is no proof of dual authorship. Prose narratives in the third person and prose narratives in the first person together with oracular poetry can be found in the works of the prophets. Although there is no reference to Antiochus IV Epiphanes in the first part, it contains a clear indication of the same age in the Greek terms used. These are the names of musical instruments, one of which, 'sumphonia', is nowhere met in Greek literature as the name of an instrument before the second century B.C., and there it is mentioned in connexion with the festivities of Antiochus IV

[1] J. A. Montgomery, *A Critical and Exegetical Commentary on the Book of Daniel*, 1927, p. 90.

Epiphanes.[1] The Babylonian background of the first part is the creation of the author's imagination rather than the description of an eye-witness, 'and is scarcely more accurate than the picture of Nineveh in the Book of Jonah, penned long after the city had ceased to exist, and certainly less accurate than the Persian background of the Book of Esther'.[2] The division of the book on grounds of language does not coincide with the division into stories and visions.

The two parts of the book have certain characteristeristics which, in our opinion, indicate uniformity of authorship. It is generally agreed that viii–xii belong to the Maccabaean period. Ch. vii is linked by its language to ii since the Aramaic portion of the book extends from ii. 4b to vii. 28, and by its ideas and its reference to the advent of the Messianic Age to the later chapters. The same historical inaccuracies regarding Belshazzar and Darius the Mede are found in both parts of the book. Darius the Mede stands between Belshazzar and Cyrus in v. 30–vi. 28, and ix. 1–xi. 1 and a Median empire stands between the Babylonian and the Persian in ii and vii. The trials of the persecution under Antiochus IV Epiphanes to which the visions lead up are reflected in the trials endured by Daniel and his friends. The style of both parts of the book is more or less uniform throughout. It is true that the prayer in ix. 4–19 is written in a different style, but it is probably based on earlier literary models. Finally, the same message of encouragement and hope is to be found in both the stories and the visions.

THE BOOK'S BILINGUAL CHARACTER

The book is written partly in Hebrew (i–ii. 4a; viii–xii) and partly in Aramaic (ii. 4b–vii. 28). Several theories have been advanced to account for its bilingual character but none of them is convincing. Of these theories the following may be mentioned:

(1) The author began to write in Hebrew and then at ii. 4b changed to Aramaic, intending to complete the work in that language, but when he reached the end of vii he realized that Hebrew was better suited for his purpose.

(2) The first part of the book (i–vi) was originally written in Aramaic by an author living in the third century B.C. The second part of the book (vii–xii) was written by another author living in the

---

[1] H. H. Rowley, article on 'The Unity of Daniel' in *The Servant of the Lord*, 1952, p. 264.
[2] R. H. Pfeiffer, *Introduction to the Old Testament*, 1948, p. 763.

Maccabaean period. He wrote viii–xii in Hebrew, translating i–ii. 4a into the same language, and composing vii in Aramaic in order to weld the two parts of the book together.

(3) The book was originally written in Aramaic, but before it was included in the Canon, part of it had to be translated into the sacred language, Hebrew. Chs. ii. 4b–vii. 28 were left in the original language, because in ii. 4a we have the words (in the Masoretic text of the Old Testament), 'Then the Chaldeans said to the king in Aramaic'. The author let the Chaldeans speak in what he supposed was their own language.

(4) The entire work was originally written in Hebrew, but part of it was lost, and the gaps were filled with material derived from an Aramaic translation which had already been prepared for popular circulation.

(5) The stories in i–vi, based on popular traditions, were issued separately in Aramaic during the struggle with Hellenism and achieved an immediate success. Then the author of the stories wrote the first vision (vii), also in Aramaic, and issued it in the name of Daniel as an indication that it came from the author of the stories about Daniel. Later, the same author wrote the visions in viii–xii in Hebrew, which he regarded as more suitable for this less popular type of literature. Finally, he collected his stories and visions in a bilingual work, and rewrote the section i–ii. 4a in Hebrew, the language of the later sections (viii–xii), in order to make it serve as an introduction to the whole.

DATE

The traditional view that the book was written by Daniel, the hero of the book, who was taken prisoner by Nebuchadrezzar to Babylon in the reign of Jehoiakim (609–598 B.C.) is no longer tenable, for there is overwhelming evidence to show that it belongs to the Maccabaean period of revolt against Antiochus IV Epiphanes (175–163 B.C.). Among the considerations that have led scholars to this conclusion are the following:

(1) In the Hebrew Canon the book is not included in the collection called the Prophets, which was completed about 200 B.C., but in the Writings. Had the work existed before 200 B.C. it is reasonable to suppose that it would have been placed among the Prophets.

(2) In Ecclesiasticus xliv–xlix (c. 180 B.C.) Ben Sirach gives a list of the Jewish worthies, Isaiah, Jeremiah, Ezekiel and the Twelve

Minor Prophets, but has apparently never heard of Daniel. The earliest references to the book are found in The Sibyline Oracles III. 381–400 (c. 140 B.C.–A.D. 125) and in I Maccabees ii. 59f. (c. 100 B.C.) Fragments of the text of Daniel found at Qumran have been dated in the early first century B.C. These facts suggest that the book was produced before the middle of the second century B.C.

(3) The linguistic characteristics of the book point to a date considerably later than the sixth century B.C. The book, apart from the apocryphal additions, is written partly in Aramaic (ii. 4b–vii. 28) and partly in Hebrew (i–ii 4a; viii–xii). The Aramaic sections are not written in sixth-century Aramaic, but in Aramaic which can be definitely dated later than the fifth century B.C. The Hebrew is late and inferior to that written say by Deutero-Isaiah, in the sixth century. The text contains some fifteen Persian loan words which suggest a long period of Persian influence. There are also three Greek words, including one, 'sumphonia' which does not seem to be used in the required sense before the second century B.C.

(4) The book contains many historical inaccuracies which a sixth-century writer would not have made. Among the historical inaccuracies are the following:

(a) Nebuchadrezzar is said to have captured Jerusalem in the third year of the reign of Jehoiakim (i. 1f.); but no capture of Jerusalem during Jehoiakim's reign by Nebuchadrezzar is recorded in 2 Kings xxiii. 36–xxiv. 6.

(b) Belshazzar is described as the son and successor of Nebuchadrezzar (v. 2, 11, 13, 18, 22; vii. 1; viii. 1). He was, however, the son of Nabonidus, and was not king but regent during the absence of his father in Tema in Arabia.

(c) Darius the Mede is represented as receiving the kingdom after the conquest of Babylon (v. 31; vi. 28; ix. 1; xi. 1). But according to all other authorities Cyrus was the immediate successor of Nabonidus, the last king of Babylon. There is, therefore, no room for an intervening king.

(d) According to Daniel's interpretation, the image (ii) and the beasts (vii, viii) represent four empires—the Babylonian, the Median, the Persian and the Greek. But the Median empire did not stand between the Babylonian and the Persian empires. Cyrus deposed the king of the Medes and absorbed his empire before he conquered Babylon.

(e) The term Chaldean (ii. 2; v. 7) to denote a priestly class of 'wise men' is an anachronism. The term originally meant a citizen of the Babylonian kingdom, and in this sense only it is found in the Old Testament outside Daniel. It was not used to denote a priestly class of 'wise men' until after the fall of the Babylonian empire.

(f) It is improbable that Daniel, a strict Jew, would have consented to become a member of the class of Chaldean 'wise-men', or that he would have been admitted by the 'wise-men' themselves (ii. 13, 48).

(5) The message of the stories in the first half of the book is appropriate to the Maccabaean age. Daniel and his friends refused to defile themselves by eating the king's rich food and by drinking his wine (i). Antiochus sought to compel the Jews to eat unclean food. The story of the image destroyed by a stone which became 'a great mountain and filled the whole earth' (ii), would inspire the faithful Jews to continue the struggle in the hope of their ultimate deliverance and of the advent of the kingdom of God. The three youths, Shadrach, Meshach and Abednego, refused to worship the golden image set up on the plain of Dura (iii). Antiochus erected an altar to the Olympian Zeus on the altar of burnt offering in the Temple, and commanded that sacrifices should be offered to idols both there and in the cities of Judah. According to Daniel, Nebuchadrezzar's dream of a great tree that was hewn down meant that for seven years the king would be insane and live like a beast (iv). Antiochus was sometimes called 'Epimanes' (madman). The story of Belshazzar, who drank wine from the sacred vessels taken from the house of God in Jerusalem and read his doom written by the fingers of a man's hand on the wall of his palace (v), reminded the Jews that divine vengeance would fall upon Antiochus who had profaned the Temple vessels. Daniel refused to obey the decree forbidding for thirty days all petitions to any god or man except the king, and continued to pray to Yahweh three times a day facing towards Jerusalem (vi). Antiochus claimed to be an incarnate god and called himself 'Epiphanes' ('God made manifest' or 'Illustrious').

The visions in the second half of the book are really historical surveys all leading up to the Maccabaean age. The author has a fairly accurate knowledge of events from the days of Alexander the Great to the desecration of the Temple by Antiochus IV Epiphanes. He apparently knows of Alexander's conquests (viii. 6–8; x. 20; xi. 3f.), and of the division of his empire into four kingdoms after his death in 323 B.C. (viii. 8, 22; xi. 4), and of the rivalry between the Ptolemies of Egypt and the Seleucids of Syria (xi. 5–20). He is particularly interested in the relations between Antiochus and the Jews and records the events of his reign in considerable detail. In vii. 8, 24–26 the 'little horn' is no other than Antiochus whose kingdom would be destroyed. In viii. 9–12 he is again portrayed as the 'little horn, which grew exceedingly great toward the south, toward the east and toward the glorious land', desecrated the sanctuary and suppressed the sacrifices. The survey of history in xi culminates in an account of the reign of Antiochus and of his persecution of the Jews (vv. 21–39). In v. 31 there is a direct reference to the setting up of 'the abomination that makes desolate'. In vv. 40–45 the author predicts that after a successful campaign in Egypt, Libya and Ethiopia, Antiochus would meet his doom in Palestine. He is ignorant of the fact that Antiochus died in Persia in 163 B.C.

(6) In ix. 24 we are told that 'seventy weeks of years' were to elapse before Israel was restored and the everlasting kingdom established. The chronology of the 'seventy weeks of years' is obscure, but it is generally agreed that they culminate in the Maccabaean period. Moreover the sacrifices are to be suppressed for half a week (ix. 27), 'a time, two times, and half a time' (vii. 25; xii. 7), that is, $3\frac{1}{2}$ years, or 2,300 'evenings and mornings' (viii. 14), that is, 1,150 days, or 1,290 days (xii. 11), or 1,335 days (xii. 12). These figures do not agree, but they probably indicate a period of about $3\frac{1}{2}$ years. We know that the sacrifices in the Temple were suppressed for just over $3\frac{1}{2}$ years.

From the evidence we conclude that Daniel must have been composed in the reign of Antiochus IV Epiphanes. The date, however, may be fixed with greater precision. The author knew of the setting up of the heathen altar in the Temple in 167 B.C. (cf. 1 Macc. i, 54; 2 Macc. vi. 1f.), but he apparently had no knowledge of the rededication of the sanctuary in December 164 B.C. (cf. 1 Macc. iv. 52) or of the death of Antiochus in 163 B.C. which he predicted. The book, therefore, must have been composed after the desecration of the Temple in 167 B.C. and before its rededication in December 164 B.C.[1]

TEACHING

God

Stress is laid upon the transcendence of God. Yahweh is the only God: all the gods of the heathen are mere idols of silver, gold, bronze,

---

[1] Bickermann (*Der Gott der Makkabäer*, 1937, p. 144) attempts to fix the date still more precisely. He alleges that the author of Daniel knew nothing of an edict of the Syrian government (quoted in 2 Macc. xi. 20) putting an end to persecution and issued in April, 164 B.C., or of the campaign in the East begun by Antiochus early in 165 B.C. Hence the book must have been composed in 166 or 165 B.C.

iron, wood and stone, 'which do not see, or hear or know' (v. 23). He is the 'God of Heaven' (ii. 19), the God of wisdom and might who changes times and seasons, removes and sets up kings, gives wisdom to the wise and knowledge to the intelligent, and reveals deep and mysterious things (ii. 20–22), the 'God of gods and Lord of kings' (ii. 47), the 'Most High God who works great signs and mighty wonders' (iv. 3; cf. vi. 27), the 'King of heaven' whose works are right and whose ways are just (iv. 37), the 'living God' who delivers His servants (vi. 20–22) and the 'great and terrible God' (ix. 4). He dwells in heaven apart from mankind (ii. 28) and works in the world through angelic intermediaries (iii. 28; iv. 13–17; vi. 22; viii. 16; ix. 21–27; x. 10f.; xii. 5–13). He is righteous, loving and merciful (ix. 4–19) and is swift to answer the prayers of His servants. His dominion is an everlasting dominion, and before Him all the inhabitants of the earth are accounted as nothing. He does as He pleases in the host of heaven and among the inhabitants of the earth. None can interfere with Him or ask Him what He is doing (iv. 34f.).

The kingdom of God

The central thought of the book is the ultimate triumph of the kingdom of God. He was carrying out His purpose in history. After the destruction of the four great kingdoms—the Babylonian, Median, Persian and Greek—represented by a great image made of different materials (ii. 31–33) and by the four great beasts that 'came up out of the sea, different from one another' (vii. 2–8), the God of heaven would set up a fifth kingdom—a kingdom of righteousness—which would embrace the whole world and endure for ever (vii. 9–14). The sovereignty of this kingdom would be given to the saints of the Most High (vii. 27), represented by the stone which 'became a great mountain and filled the whole earth' (ii. 35), and by one 'like a son of man' (vii. 13).

Angelology

The book shows a development in the doctrine of angels. In the pre-exilic period angels are rarely mentioned, and when they are, they are for the most part theophanic, that is, they are really the deity appearing in human form. In the post-exilic period the emphasis laid upon the divine transcendence led to the idea that the deity was far removed from man, and that intermediaries were necessary as channels of communication. Hence Yahweh no longer spoke directly to man but only through angels. The later Greek period saw a striking development of the doctrine of angels. Names were given to them and certain functions assigned to them. In Daniel, angels are present to interpret Daniel's visions (vii. 16; viii. 16). Names are ascribed to angels for the first time in the Old Testament. Reference is made to the angels Gabriel (viii. 16; ix. 21) and Michael (x. 13, 20f.; xii. 1). For the first time we find the doctrine of guardian angels. Michael is represented as being the guardian angel of Israel (x. 13, 20f.; xii. 1), and the 'princes', the guardian angels of Persia and Greece, are mentioned (x. 20). For the first time distinctions in rank appear among the angels. Michael is described as 'one of the chief princes' (x. 13) and as the 'great prince' (xii. 1). Doubtless, the ascription of names to the angels, the definition of their functions and their division into orders were due to Persian influence.

The Resurrection

The book shows a development of thought on the resurrection. Speaking generally we may say that the doctrine of the resurrection had no place in the religious thought of Israel before the Exile. It was believed that at death the shade of man passed to the underworld of Sheol, the abode of both the righteous and the wicked, and there was no moral distinction between them. The firm establishment of monotheism and the growing awareness of the worth of the individual through communion with Yahweh, gradually destroyed the primitive belief in Sheol and led to the doctrine of the resurrection. At first, however, there was no idea of a universal resurrection to judgment. In Ezekiel's vision of the dry bones the prophet had in mind not the resurrection of individual Israelites, but the restoration of the nation from the death of the Exile to renewed life in Palestine (Ezek. xxxvii. 11f.). A prophecy in the apocalyptic section of Isaiah (xxiv–xxvii), which is almost certainly older than Daniel, speaks of the resurrection of the body, but it is conceived as the sole prerogative of the righteous Israelites (xxvi. 19). The resurrection of the wicked is categorically denied (xxvi. 14).

It is in Daniel that we find for the first time the idea of the resurrection of both the righteous and the wicked. 'And many of those who sleep in the dust of the earth shall awake, some to everlasting life, and some to shame and everlasting contempt' (xii. 3). The author's teaching was born in the fires of persecution. He was led to believe that Yahweh, a righteous God, would not deny His martyrs a share in the eternal kingdom, nor would He allow those who had been disloyal to Him to escape punishment for their sins. He would raise both the martyrs and the apostates from the dead and recompense them for the deeds done in life. The resurrection, however, would not be universal. Apparently it would be confined to the martyrs and apostates of Israel. The author thought that it would take place in the immediate future and that it would be to life on earth. The idea of the resurrection is sometimes traced to the influence of a Persian Zoroastrianism, but it is difficult, however, to accept this theory since the idea of the resurrection in Daniel differs from that in Zoroastrian sources. In the former there is no thought of a universal resurrection such as is found in the latter.

Son of Man

In the book appears the term 'son of man' which later became so familiar to readers of the New Testament. Originally it was a poetic synonym for 'man', and in this sense is frequently used in Ezekiel to indicate the prophet himself. 'Son of man, stand upon your feet, and I will speak with you' (Ezek. ii. 1). In Daniel the expression 'son of man' is applied to a human figure who is symbolical of the kingdom of God or the saints as invested with the authority of the kingdom (vii. 13f., 18). (For the later application of the term see p. 277).[1]

Prayer, Fasting and the Observance of the Law

Stress is laid upon prayer, fasting and the observance of the Law. Daniel was a man of prayer. He told his three companions to ask the 'God of heaven' to be merciful and to reveal the mystery of Nebuchadrezzar's dream (ii. 17f.). It was his custom to pray three times a day in his upper chamber which had windows 'open toward Jerusalem' (vi. 10). It would appear that the banks of rivers were also used for private devotions and that revelations were received there (viii. 2; x. 4; xii. 5). Prayer was accompanied with fasting. Distressed by the

[1] Scholars are not agreed as to the identification of the figure 'like a son of man'. To T. W. Manson (*The Teaching of Jesus*, 2nd ed., 1935, pp. 227ff.) the figure represents the kingdom of God on earth—the community of the saints of the Most High. W. O. E. Oesterley (*The Jews and Judaism during the Greek Period*, 1941, pp. 152ff.), thinks that the figure is a leader of the kingdom comparable to the figure of the Messiah. Albright (*From the Stone Age to Christianity*, 2nd ed., 1947, pp. 378f.) maintains that the figure is a pre-existent heavenly being 'created by God before the creation of the world in order to appear as Messiah in the fulness of time'. T. F. Glasson (*The Second Advent*, 2nd ed., pp. 15ff.) holds that Daniel vii is dependent upon 1 Enoch xiv and that the figure is Enoch.

non-fulfilment of Jeremiah's prophecy concerning the restoration of the Jews from exile (Jer. xxv. 11f.; xxix. 10), Daniel prayed to God 'with fasting and sackcloth and ashes' (ix. 3). His final vision came to him after fasting for three weeks (x. 3). Daniel and his friends refused to defile themselves by partaking of Nebuchadrezzar's rich food and throve on a diet of vegetables and water (i. 8–16). To partake of the king's food would have involved the risk of eating food which was forbidden by the Law, or which had not been slaughtered according to the provisions of the Law, or which had been offered in sacrifice to idols (cf. Lev. xi. 2–43; Deut. iv. 3–24). Daniel prayed every day at the times prescribed by the Law, namely, the time of the morning burnt offering, the ninth hour (i.e. 3 p.m.), and at sunset (vi. 10; cf. Ps. lv. 17).

PERMANENT INFLUENCE

The book has had a profound influence on Jewish and Christian literature. It is to this book that we owe most of the features, which, with many variations, reappear time after time in later apocalypses. As we have already indicated, this type of literature was popular in Palestine, especially in Galilee, in the first century A.D. It was against this apocalyptic background that John the Baptist proclaimed the immediate advent of the judgment and the kingdom of God, and it was in an atmosphere charged with these expectations that Jesus proclaimed His message. Some of the ideas contained in the apocalyptic writings are reflected in His teaching and in the Epistles, while The Revelation with the exception of the charges to the seven churches of Asia at the beginning (Rev. i. 4–iii. 22), is entirely apocalyptic.

The book played a considerable part in the later development of the doctrine of the resurrection. In it for the first time in Hebrew literature the doctrine is stated as a dogma. It was not commonly held in the author's own day, but in the apocalyptic writings composed between the Maccabaean Age and the New Testament times, the doctrine was developed in one form or another. It became an article of faith of the Pharisees but was rejected by the Sadducees as having no biblical authority. It was taken for granted by Christ and the Apostles and became a fundamental doctrine of the Christian faith. In the New Testament, as in the apocalyptic writings, it appears in different forms, among which the thought of eternal bliss in heaven and everlasting punishment in hell has secured the firmest hold on Christian people.

The ascription of names to angels and the definition of their functions led to the introduction of an elaborate angelic hierarchy into Christian literature and thought. In the New Testament there are good and bad angels. Reference is made to the good angels Gabriel (Lk. i. 19, 26) and Michael (Jude 9; Rev. xii. 7) and to the bad angels Satan (Lk. x. 18; Acts v. 3; Rom. xvi. 20), Beelzebub (Mk. iii. 22; Mt. x. 25), and Belial (2 Cor. vi. 15). Angels perform many functions. They worship God in heaven (e.g. Rev. v. 11f.; vii. 11f.; viii. 1-4) and on earth (Lk. ii. 13f.), and will attend on the Son at the last judgment (e.g. Mk. viii. 38; 1 Thess. iv. 16; Rev. iii. 5). They are sent forth to serve for the benefit of those who are to inherit salvation (Heb. i. 14). They deliver God's messages to men (e.g. Mt. i. 20; Acts xii. 7-11; Rev. xxii. 6), help them in their worship (Rev. viii. 3f.), fight for them against evil (e.g. Jude 9; Rev. xii. 7f.; xix. 14) and at death carry away the righteous souls to a place of rest (Lk. xvi. 22). They assisted at the giving of the Law (Acts vii. 53; Gal. iii. 19; Heb. ii. 2). The Christian fathers greatly elaborated the angelic hierarchy. Dionysius the Areopagite (c. A.D. 500) divided the angels into three divisions with three subdivisions in each, namely, (1) thrones, cherubim and seraphim, (2) powers, lordships and might, (3) angels, archangels and principalities.

The use of the term 'Son of man', which is used in the New Testament as a Messianic title for our Lord, derives its origin from this book. As we have already indicated, the term 'Son of man' is applied to a human figure who represents the kingdom of God or the saints as invested with the authority of the kingdom (vii. 13f., 18). He was quite distinct from the Messiah. It is probable, however, that by the beginning of the Christian era the term had been individualized and that it stood for a divinely appointed leader who would establish the kingdom of God. This identification of the 'Son of man' with the Messiah was largely due to 1 Enoch, especially to the section of it called 'The Similitudes' (xxxvii-lxxi), in which the term 'Son of man' was applied to a pre-existent heavenly being who would judge both men and angels. Our Lord frequently identified Himself with the Messiah when He was speaking of His ultimate triumph as Redeemer and Judge (e.g. Mt. xvi. 27f.; xix. 28; xxiv. 30). He rejected the conception of the Messiah as a warrior king and identified Himself with the Suffering Servant of Deutero-Isaiah (xlii. 1-4; xlix. 1-6; l. 4-9; lii. 13-liii. 12)—a conception which is never found in the apocalyptic writings. 'For the Son of man also came not to be served but to serve, and to give his life a ransom for many' (Mk. x. 45).

Thus He identified Himself with the figures of the 'Son of man', the 'Messiah' and the 'Suffering Servant'.[1]

The conception of the eventual establishment of the kingdom of God on earth set a noble ideal before men, and paved the way for the development of the more spiritual conceptions of that kingdom which we find in the later Jewish apocalypses and in the New Testament writings.

Finally, though the book contains many historical inaccuracies and the dream of the establishment of the kingdom of God has not been realized, it nevertheless contains an enduring message for mankind. The idea that history is not a meaningless series of disconnected events but an orderly progress towards a predetermined goal, and that it is not controlled by chance, or by an impersonal power, but by the will of an omnipotent, wise, just and merciful God, who will finally triumph over the forces of evil and establish His kingdom on earth, combined with the stories of courage and loyalty in the face of persecution, has been a source of comfort, strength and inspiration to people down to the present day.

LITERARY MERIT

The book is not a work of great literary merit. It is far inferior to the matchless stories of the pre-exilic period of Hebrew literature and to those of Ruth, Jonah and Esther of the post-exilic period.[2] The stories in the first part of the book—those of the image made of different materials (ii), the great idol set up on the plain of Dura, the burning fiery furnace with the three men walking in it guarded by one 'like a son of the gods' (iii), the great tree that reached to heaven and was hewn down (iv), Belshazzar's feast and the appearance of the fingers of a man's hand that wrote on the wall of the king's palace (v), and Daniel in the den of lions (vi)—have nothing to commend them except the fact that they are tales of the marvellous which have captured the imagination of people, especially children, in all ages, and are among the most appreciated in the Old Testament.

---

[1] For a discussion of the term 'Son of Man', see H. H. Rowley, *The Rediscovery of the Old Testament*, 1945, pp. 189–191, 195f. *The Relevance of Apocalyptic*, 2nd ed., 1947, pp. 28–31; *The Faith of Israel*, 1956, pp. 194–197, 199f.

[2] The literature of the Old Testament is divided into two periods, namely, (1) the Classical Period (also known as the Pre-exilic or Golden Period), and (2) the Romantic Period (also known as the Post-exilic or Silver Period). To the first period belongs the literature composed between 1,000 B.C., or in certain instances even earlier, and the beginning of the Exile in 587 B.C. To the second period belongs the literature composed during and after the Exile. Daniel belongs to the second period.

They owe their popularity solely to the fact that they appeal to the love of the marvellous which is in us all. The characters in them—Daniel and his three companions, the three kings, Nebuchadrezzar, Belshazzar and Darius, and the Chaldean wise men—are not clearly defined, the dialogue is often pompous and ceremonious and the scenery mere stage setting. The visions in the second part of the book—those of the four great beasts (vii), the ram and the he-goat (viii), the time of restoration (ix), the conflict between the kings of the north and the south (x; xi) and 'the time of the end' (xii)—are obscure, dull and uninteresting.

Apart from the definitely apocalyptic portions, the style of the book is commonplace, possessing few of those qualities which lend distinction to the writings of some of his predecessors in the prophetic ministry. In the apocalyptic portions the author is carried away by the thought of the resurrection and the final judgment and employs a more elevated style. The style of the passage on the resurrection is dignified, if not majestic. 'And many of those who sleep in the dust of the earth shall awake, some to everlasting life, and some to shame and everlasting contempt. And those who are wise shall shine like the brightness of the firmament; and those who turn many to righteousness, like the stars for ever and ever' (xii. 2f.). There is an epic grandeur in the description of the final judgment and the coming of one 'like a son of man' (vii. 9–14).

It was these descriptions of the resurrection, the final judgment, and the coming of one 'like a son of man' that captured the imagination of the author of The Revelation, and which more than any other portion of the Old Testament enabled him to describe the last judgment and the holy city, the new Jerusalem, 'coming down out of heaven from God' (Rev. xx. 11–xxii. 5).

CHAPTER XVII

1 AND 2 CHRONICLES

TITLE AND PLACE IN CANON

IN the Hebrew manuscripts the two books form a single work. The present division is adopted from the Septuagint and the Vulgate. The Hebrew name for the single volume is *Dibre hayyamim*, which means literally, 'The Things of the Days', that is, 'The events of past times'. In the Septuagint the title is *Paraleipomena*, or 'the things omitted', a reference due to the fact that the translators viewed the work as a supplement to Samuel and Kings. The Vulgate, following the Septuagint, has the title *Paraleipomena, primus and secundus*, but Jerome in his 'Prologus Galeatus' suggested the Latin title, *Chronicum totius historiae divinae*, meaning, 'Chronicle of the Whole of Sacred History'. It is from this that the title in our version is derived.

In the Hebrew Canon the two books are placed at the end of the Writings. In the English versions they appear immediately after Kings, an arrangement due to the influence of the Septuagint through the Vulgate.

CHRONICLES AND EZRA-NEHEMIAH

There is almost universal acceptance of the view that 1 and 2 Chronicles, and Ezra-Nehemiah originally formed a single continuous work. The reasons for this conclusion are as follows:

(1) The last two verses of 2 Chronicles (xxxvi. 22f.), which record the opening sentences of the decree of Cyrus, are the introduction to Ezra (i. 1–3a), but in the former work the last sentence is incomplete, whereas in the latter the whole of the decree is recorded. The repetition is probably due to the fact that Ezra-Nehemiah was admitted to the Canon first, since it was viewed as the continuation of the history of Israel, while Chronicles was only supplementary to Samuel and Kings. At a later period Chronicles was admitted, presumably because of its distinctive point of view, and the last two verses (2 Chron. xxxvi. 22f.)

were added to the tragic account of the national disorder in order to make the work end on a more hopeful note. The decree of Cyrus marked the termination of the Captivity and gave promise of a glorious future for the nation.

(2) Both books reveal a love of genealogies and statistics and an intense interest in the Temple and its worship.

(3) Except where the author is quoting from older works the same late Hebrew language and the same distinctive literary peculiarities that mark the style of Chronicles are found throughout Ezra-Nehemiah.

The author of this single work is generally called 'The Chronicler', his name being unknown to us.

CONTENTS

The work may be divided into four parts as follows.

1 *Chronicles*

Chs. i-ix. An outline of history from Adam to Saul given chiefly in the form of genealogies.
Chs. x-xxix. The death of Saul and the reign of David.

2 *Chronicles*

Chs. i-ix. The reign of Solomon.
Chs. x-xxxvi. The history of Judah from Rehoboam to the decree of Cyrus.[1]

AIM

Opinions differ regarding the Chronicler's aim in writing the book. Welch considers that the chief aim of the Chronicler was to persuade Israel and Judah to forget their antagonism to each other and to dwell together in peace and amity. In support of this view he maintains that although the Chronicler practically ignored the Northern Kingdom because of its rebellion against the Davidic dynasty, which had been ordained by Yahweh, he, nevertheless, had a certain sympathy with the people of that kingdom. He shows that they had once acknowledged the Davidic dynasty, and that they belonged to the same race and worshipped the same God as the people of Judah. They had flocked to the coronation of David in their thousands (1 Chron. xii. 23-37). The ark, an Ephraimitic symbol, was an essential feature of the Judaean Temple. After the disruption of the monarchy, those in the Northern Kingdom

[1] For a summary of the two books the reader should consult the larger commentaries.

who remained loyal to the religion of Yahweh, resorted to Jerusalem for sacrifice (2 Chron. xi. 13–16). Some even forsook their country and found a home in Judah (2 Chron. xv. 9). In the reign of Ahaz the people of Israel conquered Judah, taking many captives and much spoil, but on being rebuked by a prophet, they sent the captives home loaded with the stolen property (2 Chron. xxviii. 8–15). In the reigns of Hezekiah and Josiah people from Israel came to Jerusalem to keep the Passover (2 Chron. xxx. 18; xxxv. 18).[1] Elmslie also holds this view. He writes, 'Opposed to that horrid, petty antagonism, the Chronicler wrote, showing in a picture the goodness of brotherhood and reunion. He urged as the will of God that there should be one Hebrew people. He implored quarrelsome men to forget the ancient enmities and to see in God-fearing Israelites their brethren.'[2] Pfeiffer sees no sign of any attempt to heal the division between the Jews and the Samaritans. In his opinion one of the chief aims of the Chronicler was to defend the legitimacy of the Temple at Jerusalem against the claim of the Samaritans that the Temple on Mount Gerizim was the place which Yahweh had chosen for his dwelling place. He hated and despised them. They were aliens and apostates on whom the divine wrath rested because of their abominations. 'Just as the Chronicler under the guise of the kingdom of Judah depicts the idealized Jewish community of his time, so, behind the mask of the ancient kingdom of Israel he portrayed the detested Samaritan community.'[3]

THE CHRONICLER AS A HISTORIAN

The Chronicler was not a historian in the modern sense of the term. The word 'history' comes from a Greek word, 'historia', meaning 'knowledge gained by investigation'. History is as much an exact science as Physics and Chemistry and demands the scientific method of approach. The real historian is one who, in his search for truth, collects his material, sifts it carefully, separating fact from fiction, the relevant from the irrelevant, and then draws his own conclusions. The Chronicler was not a scientific investigator. He did not set out to write an accurate and impartial account of the history of Judah, but to write it in such a way as to prove the validity of his own religious views, the chief of which seem to have been the following:

[1] A. C. Welch, *Post Exilic Judaism*, 1935, pp. 185–207.
[2] W. A. L. Elmslie, article on Chronicles in *The Interpreter's Bible*, vol. III, 1954, pp. 344f.
[3] R. H. Pfeiffer, *Introduction to the Old Testament*, 1948, pp. 810f.

(1) Yahweh was the one eternal God who reigned supreme in heaven and 'over all the kingdoms of the nations' (2 Chron. xx. 6). All things in heaven and earth belonged to Him (1 Chron. xxix. 11f.). His eyes ran to and fro throughout the whole earth (2 Chron. xvi. 9). He searched all hearts, and understood every plan and thought (1 Chron. xxviii. 9). To Him belonged 'the greatness, and the power, and the glory, and the victory, and the majesty' (1 Chron. xxix. 11).

(2) Yahweh was a righteous God who demanded from His worshippers obedience to His commandments which had been given once for all to Moses on Mount Sinai (1 Chron. xxviii. 7; 2 Chron. vii. 17f.; xxiii. 18; xxx. 16; xxxv. 12).

(3) Man had little influence upon the course of history. It was Yahweh who determined events and defeated the enemies of Judah (1 Chron. x. 13f.; xxviii. 1–7; 2 Chron. xiii. 1–20; xiv. 1–13; xx. 1–29).

(4) Yahweh was a just God who rewarded the righteous and punished the wicked (2 Chron. xii. 1–12; xvi. 7–12; xx. 35–37; xxi. 4–19; xxii. 23f.; xxv. 14–28; xxvi. 16–20; xxvii. 1–6).

(5) The Jews were the chosen people of Yahweh. Whoever fought against them fought against Him (2 Chron. xiii. 12). Apostates would be destroyed (1 Chron. xxviii. 9; 2 Chron. xv. 13). If, however, they humbled themselves and turned from their wicked ways Yahweh would hear from heaven, forgive their sin and heal their land (2 Chron. vii. 14; xxx. 9).

(6) Judah was the true Church (2 Chron. xiii. 4–12). The northern tribes, by their rejection of the Davidic dynasty and by their apostasy, had forfeited their right to belong to the true Church. 'Yahweh is not with Israel, with all these Ephraimites' (2 Chron. xxv. 7). Those, however, who returned to Yahweh, could rejoin the true Church (2 Chron. xv. 9; xix. 4; xxx. 10–21; xxxv. 17f.).

(7) Foreigners were outside the covenant and were for the most part objects of Yahweh's wrath, apparently existing only to be conquered by the righteous kings of Judah like David (1 Chron. xviii–xx) and Jotham (2 Chron. xxvii).

(8) The Temple was an essential element in true religion. It was Yahweh and not David or Solomon, who had ordained that the Temple should be built (1 Chron. xxviii. 2–6), and who had designed it, prescribed its furniture and organized its personnel (1 Chron. xxviii. 11–20). He would listen to the prayers made in the Temple. 'For now I have chosen and consecrated this house that my name may be there

for ever; my eyes and my heart will be there for all time' (2 Chron. vii. 16).

(9) Yahweh had ordained that Jerusalem should be the religious centre for all Jews (2 Chron. vi. 5f.).

To the Chronicler, Judah 'is nothing more than an ecclesiastical state, and his narrative as a whole may best be designated as the "Ecclesiastical History of Judah and the Temple".'[1]

HISTORY OF THE JEWISH MONARCHY ACCORDING TO SAMUEL AND KINGS

The United Monarchy c. 1020–922 B.C.

Saul (c. 1020–1000 B.C.) came into prominence at Jabesh-Gilead in Transjordan, where he rallied forces from the whole of Israel to repel an attack by the Ammonites whom he utterly defeated (1 Sam. xi). The victory established his prestige and authority. Later, after defeating the Philistines at Michmash (1 Sam. xiii–xiv), he was recognized as king of Israel. Next came his conquest of the Amalekites and his quarrel with Samuel (1 Sam. xv). From then onwards a gradual change took place in Saul. It is said that 'the Spirit of the Lord departed from Saul, and an evil spirit from the Lord tormented him' (1 Sam. xvi. 14). The end came with his defeat by the Philistines in the battle of Mount Gilboa, when he either committed suicide (1 Sam. xxxi. 4f.) or was slain by an Amalekite (2 Sam. i. 2–10).

On the death of Saul, David ascended the throne and reigned for about forty years (c. 1000–961 B.C.)—for seven years at Hebron and for the remainder of the time at Jerusalem. During his reign he established the monarchy and organized the loosely knit tribes into a military and political whole. Saul had inaugurated the monarchy, but was king only in the sense that he could rally all the people at call against the foe. David carried on the work he began, and under his leadership the monarchy reached the zenith of its prosperity and influence. He defeated the Philistines in two battles in the valley of Rephaim (2 Sam. v. 17–25), captured Jerusalem (2 Sam. v. 6–10) and established a strong central government there, reduced Edom, Moab, Ammon and Syria, and made a peace treaty with the king of Tyre. The whole country from Dan to Beersheba recognized his authority.

David exercised a powerful influence upon the religious life of the

---

[1] C. F. Kent, *The Growth and Contents of the Old Testament*, 1926, p. 72.

nation. The Ark—the visible symbol of Yahweh's presence and favour—was brought from Kiriath-jearim to Jerusalem and installed in a tent-shrine erected for the purpose (2 Sam. vi) thus aiding the centralization of the worship of Yahweh. Though he did not build the Temple he collected materials for it. Assuming that he wrote some of the Psalms in the Psalter, he quickened the religious life of the people and permanently enriched Israel's 'service of praise'.

On the death of David, a younger son, Solomon, became king (c. 961–922 B.C.). He began his reign by removing all possible rivals: Adonijah and Joab were put to death and Abiathar banished to his home at Anathoth. Soon after his accession he formed an alliance with Egypt and married Pharaoh's daughter. He fortified Hazor, Megiddo, Gezer, Beth-horon and Tamar and strengthened his army by developing the chariot arm. He embarked upon numerous building projects. In addition to the Temple he built the 'House of the Forest of Lebanon' which served as a treasure house and armoury, the Hall of Pillars, an assembly room, a judgment hall where affairs of state were transacted and a palace for Pharaoh's daughter (1 Kgs. vi, vii.). To provide a labour force for his numerous projects he resorted to enforced labour (1 Kgs. ix. 20–22). To raise money he engaged in trade and commerce, virtually becoming the first great Israelite merchant (1 Kgs. x. 22, 29). His income, however, was not sufficient and he was forced to cede to Hiram, king of Tyre, in return for gold, territory in the north (1 Kgs. ix. 11–14).

In his religious policy he is represented as falling away from the high standard set by David. We are told that he married numerous foreign women who induced him to forsake Yahweh and worship idols. 'For when Solomon was old his wives turned away his heart after other gods; and his heart was not wholly true to the Lord his God, as was the heart of David his father' (1 Kgs. xi. 4).

The Divided Monarchy 922–587 B.C.

On the death of Solomon, his son Rehoboam was accepted as king in Judah without incident, but when he went to Shechem to be acclaimed king of Israel by the northern representatives, he was met with the demand that the burdens inflicted upon them by Solomon should be relaxed. He foolishly rejected their demands and they announced their secession from the state. The northern tribes found a leader in Jeroboam, a former royal officer, who had been under suspicion and had found refuge in Egypt, and he was accordingly elected king.

Henceforth, the Hebrew people were divided into two kingdoms, known generally as Israel and Judah (1 Kgs. xii. 1-20; 2 Chron. x).

Jeroboam rebuilt Shechem and made it his capital. To prevent his subjects from going to Jerusalem to worship Yahweh he established two sanctuaries, one at Bethel in the south and the other at Dan in the north. At these sanctuaries Yahweh was worshipped in the form of a bull (1 Kgs. xii. 26-33). These acts made the separation of the two kingdoms complete.

The two kingdoms existed side by side, with either hostile or friendly relations for two hundred years. In 745 B.C., Tiglath-pileser III, king of Assyria (745-727 B.C.), embarked upon a career of conquest and both Israel and Judah were compelled to pay tribute. In 724 B.C., Hoshea, king of Israel (732-724 B.C.), probably relying on the promise of Egyptian assistance, rebelled but he was immediately captured and Samaria besieged. The city held out for over two years but in the end it was taken and destroyed (722 B.C.).

Judah survived the downfall of its more powerful rival for 135 years. Hezekiah (715-687 B.C.) made an unsuccessful attempt to throw off the Assyrian yoke but failed and was compelled to pay a heavy tribute (2 Kgs. xviii. 13-16). Sometime during his reign he initiated a religious reformation, removing the high places, breaking the pillars, cutting down the sacred poles and destroying the bronze serpent, called Nehushtan, said to have been made by Moses (2 Kgs. xviii. 4).

Hezekiah was succeeded by his son, Manasseh (687-642 B.C.). According to both Kings and the Assyrian records, he was a loyal vassal of Assyria throughout his reign. In the sphere of religion he reversed the policy of Hezekiah, restoring the high places, erecting altars to Baal and placing an image of Astarte in the Temple, worshipping the stars, practising divination and sorcery, and offering human sacrifice (2 Kgs. xxi. 3-7).

On the death of Manasseh in 642 B.C. he was succeeded by his son, Amon, who followed in the ways of his father. After a brief reign of two years (642-640 B.C.) he was murdered by his courtiers. The 'people of the land' executed the assassins and placed his eight-year-old son, Josiah, on the throne (2 Kgs. xxi. 24).

Josiah's reign (c. 640-609 B.C.) coincided with the decline and fall of the Assyrian empire. Already Psammeticus I, the Pharaoh of Egypt (663-609 B.C.), had succeeded in throwing off the Assyrian supremacy (c. 653 B.C.). About 630 B.C. a horde of barbarians from the north and north-east, known to the Greeks as Cimmerians and Scythians, invaded western Asia ranging as far as the Egyptian frontier, intent on plunder rather than conquest. Under a Chaldean prince, Nabopolassar (625-605 B.C.), the Babylonians recovered their independence and a few years later they formed an alliance with the Medes with the object of destroying Nineveh. In 612 B.C. the city fell before the combined forces. The Assyrians continued the struggle from Harran but this also was captured by the allies in 610 B.C. They continued to fight on and an Egyptian army under the Pharaoh, Neco (609-593 B.C.), came to their assistance but he was defeated by the Babylonians at Carchemish in 605 B.C.

The decline and fall of Assyria had a profound effect upon Judah. Josiah took advantage of the growing weakness of Assyria to assert his independence and to carry through a religious reformation, in accordance with the 'book of the law', said to have been discovered in the Temple, and commonly identified with the central portion of Deuteronomy (xii-xxvi). The various idolatrous objects and vessels were removed from the Temple and all the votaries of impure rites ejected. Moloch worship was abolished and the valley of Topheth defiled. The cult of the heavenly bodies was put down by burning the chariots of the sun and destroying the altars on the roofs. The high places were removed and the idolatrous priests slain. Worship was centralized at Jerusalem (2 Kgs. xxiii. 1-24). His reforms, however, were not permanent, for after his death there was a return to the old heathen practices (Ezek. viii). In 609 B.C. he met his death trying to stop Neco, the Pharaoh of Egypt, from marching to the assistance of the Assyrians (2 Kgs. xxiii. 29f.).

The people now chose as their king, Josiah's second son, Jehoahaz (609 B.C.), but three months later, Neco deposed him and placed Jehoiakim, his elder brother, on the throne (2 Kgs. xxiii. 33f.). He erected magnificent buildings, making use of forced labour and reintroduced the pagan cults which Josiah had removed (Jer. xxii. 13-19). After the battle of Carchemish he transferred his allegiance to the Babylonians, but encouraged by their defeat by the Egyptians in 601 B.C., he rebelled. The Babylonians marched against him but he died either before Jerusalem was besieged or shortly after the siege began. His son, Jehoiachin, who succeeded him, surrendered after a resistance of three months (598 B.C.), and his family and the leading citizens were deported to Babylon (2 Kgs. xxiv. 14-16). Another son of Josiah, namely, Mattaniah, was placed on the throne of Judah and his name changed to Zedekiah.

Zedekiah (598–587 B.C.) was a weak character, quite unfitted to deal with the difficult situation which confronted him. There was constant unrest in the land, and in 589 B.C. he rebelled against his overlord. Jerusalem was invested and after a siege of over two years taken and destroyed (587 B.C.), while the king and the leading citizens were deported to Babylon (2 Kgs. xxv. 11f.). Gedaliah was appointed governor but was murdered by Ishmael, a descendant of David. Many Judaeans fled to Egypt for fear of Nebuchadrezzar's vengeance for the murder of his governor and took the prophet Jeremiah with them against his will (2 Kgs. xxv. 22–26). In 562 B.C., Jehoiachin was liberated from prison by Evil-merodach (Amel-Marduk), son and successor of Nebuchadrezzar, and given a fixed allowance from the royal exchequer (2 Kgs. xxv. 27–30).

THE CHRONICLER'S TREATMENT OF THE HISTORY OF JUDAH

As we have already indicated, the Chronicler approached the history of Judah with preconceived ideas, determined to find not the truth, but what he himself conceived to be the truth. Accordingly, he selected the historical facts which suited his purpose. Whenever he found that his canonical sources conflicted with his own views he did not hesitate to modify the former by a process of idealization, omission, alteration and addition. Only a few of these can be mentioned by way of illustration.

Idealization

He idealized his heroes, David and Solomon. Of the twenty-nine chapters of 1 Chronicles nineteen are devoted to David. As king he led an almost blameless life, committing no sin except that of numbering the people (1 Chron. xxi. 1–8). No reference was made to his adultery with Bathsheba or to the murder of Uriah. He devoted himself almost entirely to ecclesiastical matters. His great ambition was to build 'the house of the Lord God'. Whereas in 2 Samuel xxiv. 24 he paid Araunah fifty shekels of silver for the ground on which the Temple was afterwards built, in 1 Chronicles xxi. 25 he paid 600 shekels of gold for it. For the building of the Temple he collected 'a hundred thousand talents of gold, a million talents of silver and bronze and iron beyond weighing' (1 Chron. xxii. 14). Not content with providing money and material, he drew up a plan of the Temple and organized its services (1 Chron. xxiii–xxvi). Just as Moses received the plan and specifications for the ark and tabernacle on Mount Sinai so David, received those for the Temple from the hand of Yahweh (1 Chron. xxviii. 16). It was he who dreamt of the Temple's future greatness. 'Solomon my son is young and inexperienced, and the house that is to be built for the Lord must be exceedingly magnificent, of fame and glory throughout all lands' (1 Chron. xxii. 5). He was a monotheist centuries before the doctrine of monotheism was explicitly taught by Deutero-Isaiah towards the close of the Exile (1 Chron. xvii. 20). In 1 Kings ii. 5-9 we are told that at the close of his life he urged Solomon to murder Joab and Shimei, but in 1 Chronicles xxix we have a beautiful prayer in which he thanked Yahweh for all His goodness (1 Chron. xxix. 10-13). Finally 'he died in a good old age, full of days riches and honour' (1 Chron. xxix. 28).

Similarly Solomon was depicted as an ideal king. There were no dark stains on his character. No reference was made to the intrigues by which he gained the throne, or of his marriage with foreign women save that with Pharaoh's daughter, or of his employment of forced labour, or of his idolatry in later life and of the anger of Yahweh, who declared that He would tear the kingdom out of the hand of his son and give it to his servant. From the beginning to the end of his reign Yahweh was with him. He was given great repute in sight of all Israel, and such royal majesty was bestowed upon him as had not been on any king before him in Israel (1 Chron. xxix. 25). David and Solomon were idealized evidently because the Chronicler felt that since they were responsible for the building of the Temple, they must have been devoted servants of Yahweh and could not have done anything dishonourable.

The military forces of kings were magnified. To David's coronation came about 340,000 men of war 'arrayed in battle order' (1 Chron. xii. 38). Abijah had 400,000 'picked men' and Jeroboam 800,000 'picked mighty warriors' (2 Chron. xiii. 3). Asa had 580,000 'mighty men of valour' (2 Chron. xiv. 8) and Jehoshaphat over 1,000,000, in addition to those stationed in the fortified cities of Judah (2 Chron. xvii. 10-19). Uzziah had an army of 307,500 'who could make war with mighty power, to help the king against the enemy' (2 Chron. xxvi. 13).

Great victories were won by reliance upon the help of Yahweh. Abijah defeated Jeroboam and slew 500,000 of his men. 'Thus the men of Israel were subdued at that time, and the men of Judah prevailed, because they relied upon the Lord, the God of their fathers' (2 Chron. xiii. 18). Asa wiped out to the last man an Ethiopian army of a million men. 'So the Lord defeated the Ethiopians before Asa and before Judah, and the Ethiopians fled. Asa and the people that were with him pursued them as far as Gerar, and the Ethiopians fell until none remained alive; for they were broken before the Lord and his army' (2 Chron. xiv. 12f.). In the reign of Jehoshaphat an attacking army of Ammonites and Moabites was annihilated without the king having to strike a blow, for they destroyed one another. 'And the fear of God came upon all the kingdoms of the countries when they heard that the Lord had fought against the enemies of Israel' (2 Chron. xx. 29). Neither courage in battle nor strategy decided the issue; God alone vanquished the enemy.

The worship of the Temple was perfectly organized. Its organization was not the result of gradual development through the centuries, but entirely the work of David who had written it down under the inspiration of Yahweh (1 Chron. xxviii. 19). Two orders of priests were recognized, namely, the priests and the Levites. The priests derived their authority from their hereditary descent from Aaron. Holding such authority and forming a close corporation, they controlled the entire ritual of the sanctuary and settled all disputes. They were divided into twenty-four courses, each of which took its turn in attending to the public work of the Temple. 'These had as their appointed duty in their service to come into the house of the Lord according to the procedure established for them by Aaron their father, as the Lord God of Israel had commanded him' (1 Chron. xxiv. 19). In addition to their sacrificial work they taught the Law in the cities of Judah (2 Chron. xvii. 7-9) and administered justice in the court of appeal in Jerusalem (2 Chron. xix. 8). At the head of the priesthood was the High Priest, who occupied a position of great influence and authority. The High Priest, Jehoiada, crowned Joash, had Athaliah slain, and was the virtual ruler under Joash until his death when 'they buried him in the city of David among the kings because he had done good in Israel and toward God and his house' (2 Chron. xxiv. 15). Kings were not allowed to exercise the priestly functions. Uzziah claimed the right to burn incense on the altar of incense in the sanctuary and was smitten with leprosy (2 Chron. xxvi. 16-21).

The Levites, who had been degraded to the performance of subordinate duties in the Temple, were given greater prominence than the priests.[1] Of the 38,000 Levites, thirty-years-old and upward, 24,000

---

[1] According to the Deuteronomic Code, there was no distinction between the priests and the Levites. Every Levite had the right to exercise the priestly functions. When, however, the high places were abolished in the reign of Josiah, the country priests were

had 'charge of the work in the house of the Lord', 6,000 were officers and judges, 4,000 gatekeepers and 4,000 singers and musicians. They were organized in three divisions corresponding to the sons of Levi-Gershom, Kohath and Merari (1 Chron. xxiii. 2-6). Only the Levites were allowed to carry the Ark, 'for the Lord chose them to carry the ark of the Lord and to minister to him for ever' (1 Chron. xv. 2; cf. 2 Chron. v. 4). They assisted 'the sons of Aaron their brethren' in the service of the Temple, looking after the courts and chambers, cleansing all holy things, caring for the shew-bread (1 Chron. xxiii. 28f.), killing the passover lamb and handing the blood to the priests (2 Chron. xxx. 16f.; xxxv. 6), ministering before the Ark of Yahweh and leading the congregation in prayer and praise (1 Chron. xvi. 4). After the disruption of the monarchy, the Levites left their lands in the north and came to Judah and Jerusalem, 'because Jeroboam and his sons cast them out from serving as priests of the Lord' (2 Chron. xi. 14-17). Jehoshaphat sent certain princes, nine Levites and two priests throughout Judah to teach the Law (2 Chron. xvii. 7f.). According to 2 Kings xi. 4, the High Priest, Jehoiada, brought the Carites and a military guard into the Temple in order to protect the young king Joash; but according to 2 Chronicles xxiii. 6, Jehoiada gave orders that no one except the priests and ministering Levites were to enter the Temple. The Levites were to guard the king and whoever entered the Temple was to be slain (2 Chron. xxiii. 7). In the first year of his reign, Hezekiah opened the doors of the Temple which had been closed by his predecessor, Ahaz, and summoned the priests and the Levites. Addressing the Levites he ordered them to sanctify themselves and the Temple, and reminded them that they should not neglect their duties since Yahweh had chosen them 'to stand in his presence, to minister to him, and to be his ministers and burn incense to him' (2 Chron. xxix. 11). The Levites took part, along with the priests, in the cleansing of the Temple (2 Chron. xxix. 12-19) and in the celebration of the Passover (2 Chron. xxx. 13-27). In the reign of Josiah they co-operated

permitted to receive the allowance of food due to them as priests but they were not allowed to exercise the priestly functions. In Ezekiel's ideal community the right was confined to the descendants of Zadok, while the Levites, who were charged with apostasy and idolatry, were degraded to the discharge of menial tasks in the sanctuary, which had hitherto been discharged by uncircumcised aliens (Ezek. xliv. 9-14). In the Priestly Code the priesthood was confined to the sons of Aaron (Lev. viii). The Levites were forbidden to come near the altar or its sacred vessels: they were regarded as servants of the priests leaving the latter free for the ministry (Num. iv. 19-33; xviii. 1-7). Apparently, the object of the Chronicler in extolling the Levites was to raise their status to the level of that of the priests.

wholeheartedly in the work of repairing the Temple (2 Chron. xxxiv. 9–13) and in the celebration of the Passover (2 Chron. xxxv. 1–19). Some of the Levites are represented as performing the functions of the scribes (1 Chron. xxiv. 6; 2 Chron. xxxiv. 13), and even of the prophets (2 Chron. xx. 14–17).

The singers and musicians, who were reckoned as Levites, were also given great prominence. They were mentioned in connexion with the removal of the ark from the house of Obed-edom to the tent of meeting in Jerusalem (1 Chron. xv, xvi) and from the tent of meeting to the Temple (2 Chron. v. 11–14), with the dedication of the Temple (2 Chron. vii. 6), the coronation of Joash (2 Chron. xxiii. 12f.). and the celebration of the Passover in the reigns of Hezekiah and Josiah (2 Chron. xxx. 21; xxxv. 15).

In addition to the priests, Levites, singers and musicians, mention was made of the doorkeepers who were also included among the Levites. They were divided into twenty-four watches under their respective chiefs and set at the four points of the compass round the Temple (1 Chron. xxvi. 1–19).[1]

Omissions

Many incidents recorded in the canonical sources which seemed to him unimportant, or unworthy of his heroes, or disconcerting to his own view of history, were passed over in silence. As we have already shown, no mention was made of incidents which would reflect adversely on the characters of David and Solomon. No reference was made to the Northern Kingdom except where it was in some way connected with Judah. The people by rejecting the divinely appointed Davidic dynasty and by their apostasy had rejected Yahweh, and had, therefore, forfeited their right to belong to the true Israel. Nothing was said about the tribute paid by Hezekiah to the king of Assyria (cf. 2 Kgs. xviii. 14–16), since the Chronicler did not like to think that Judah, which he conceived as a theocracy and a mighty nation, had ever been a tributary state.

---

[1] Reference was also made to the Nethinim (R.S.V. 'temple servants') in 1 Chronicles ix. 2. They were probably originally slaves taken in war and given by David and the princes to the Levites (Ezra viii. 20), or non-Israelite slaves employed by Solomon in his building operations (Ezra ii. 55, 58; Neh. vii. 57, 60; xi. 3). They performed such distasteful tasks as carrying water, removing waste, and cleansing sacred vessels. After the Exile, when separation from the Temple had removed the stigma of lowly service, they were first called Nethinim and came to be reckoned as Levites.

Alterations

Often historical facts were altered. According to 2 Samuel viii. 18, David's sons were priests, but since the Law debarred them from the priesthood, the Chronicler made them 'chief officials in the service of the king' (1 Chron. xviii. 17). In 2 Samuel xxi. 19 it was Elhanan who slew Goliath, but in 1 Chronicles xx. 5 Elhanan slew the brother of Goliath. The Chronicler altered the story in 2 Samuel because it dimmed the glory of David. In 1 Kings viii. 22 Solomon offered his dedicatory prayer before the altar, the place reserved for the priests, but in 2 Chronicles vi. 13 he stood on a raised platform erected in the court. According to 2 Kings xvi. 5–16, Rezin, king of Syria, and Pekah, king of Israel, waged war on Jerusalem but failed to capture it. Ahaz appealed for help to Tiglath-pileser, king of Assyria, and sent a present of treasure to win his support. Tiglath-pileser accepted it as tribute, marched against Damascus and captured it. Ahaz appeared before his suzerain at Damascus, and being impressed by the altar there, sent a copy of it to Urijah, the priest at Jerusalem, with orders to make one like it. On his return he ordered the altar to be used regularly for offering sacrifices. According to 2 Chronicles xxviii. 5–25, Rezin and Pekah invaded Judah separately, each defeating Ahaz with great slaughter. Ahaz appealed for help to the Assyrian king but it was in vain. There is no mention of his visit to Damascus or of the altar there. In his distress, Ahaz sacrificed to the gods of Damascus and closed the doors of the Temple. The Chronicler probably reconstructed the history of the Syro-Ephraimitic War in order to emphasize the punishment of Ahaz on account of his unfaithfulness to Yahweh.

Additions

Over half the material in Chronicles is not derived from canonical sources. This material consists partly of passages inserted in them by way of expansion. In 1 Kings xiv. 25–28 we are told that in the reign of Rehoboam, Shishak, king of Egypt, invaded Judah, captured Jerusalem and took away the treasures of the Temple and of the king's house and all the gold shields which Solomon had made. The Chronicler added the additional information, that on the people's repentance, Rehoboam was told by the prophet Shemaiah, that Shishak would not destroy them (2 Chron. xii. 2–12). It is recorded in 1 Kings xv. 7 that there was war between Abijam, king of Judah, and Jeroboam I, king of Israel, but no details are given. In 2 Chronicles xiii. 3–19 a vivid account is given of the war between the two kingdoms. According to 2 Kings xxi. 16, Manasseh 'shed very much innocent blood, till he had filled Jerusalem from one end to another, beside the sin which he made Judah to sin so that they did what was evil in the sight of the Lord.' No mention is made of any punishment meted out to him or of any repentance. In 2 Chronicles xxxiii. 10-13 we are given the additional information that, because of his sin, Manasseh was carried in fetters to Babylon, and that when he repented he was restored to his kingdom. The description of the celebration of the Passover after Josiah's reformation, given in 2 Chronicles xxxv. 1-19, is much fuller than that given in 2 Kings xxiii. 21-23. In 2 Kings xxiii. 29 it is recorded that Josiah was slain at Megiddo by Neco, king of Egypt, but in 2 Chronicles xxxv. 22 we are told that he was killed because he refused to listen to the divine warning that came to him through the Egyptian king.

SOURCES

The main source of Chronicles is the canonical books from Genesis to Kings (with the possible exception of Ruth), from which the Chronicler derived about half of his material. In addition to this source he must have had access to other material, for he refers the reader to a large number of sources in which further information on the topics with which he deals may be found. These may be classified as (1) historical and (2) prophetic.

Historical Sources

(1) The Book of the Kings of Israel and Judah (2 Chron. xxvii. 7; xxxvi. 8).

(2) The Book of the Kings of Judah and Israel (2 Chron. xvi. 11; xxv. 26; xxviii. 26; xxxii. 32).

(3) The Book of the Kings of Israel (2 Chron. xx. 34).

(4) The Chronicles of the Kings of Israel (2 Chron. xxiii. 18).

(5) The Commentary (Midrash)[1] on the Book of the Kings (2 Chron. xxiv. 27).

Prophetic Sources

(6) The Chronicles of Samuel the Seer (1 Chron. xxix. 29).

(7) The Chronicles of Nathan the Prophet (1 Chron. xxix. 29; 2 Chron. ix. 29).

[1] The term 'Midrash' is common in post-biblical literature. It comes from a Hebrew root meaning 'to search out', 'to investigate', to 'explore,' and is used to denote an edifying religious story or an exposition intended to bring out the implied or the hidden meaning of a scriptural passage. It is doubtful if the term is used in its later sense in Chronicles. Here it may mean simply 'study', 'enquiry', 'work'.

(8) The Chronicles of Gad the Seer (1 Chron. xxix. 29).
(9) The Chronicles of Shemaiah the Prophet and of Iddo the Seer (2 Chron. xii. 15).
(10) The Commentary (Midrash) of the prophet Iddo (2 Chron. xiii. 22.
(11) The Chronicles of Jehu the son of Hanani, which are recorded in the Book of the Kings of Israel (2 Chron. xx. 34).
(12) The Chronicles of the Seers (2 Chron. xxxiii. 19).
(13) The Prophecy of Ahijah the Shilonite (2 Chron. ix. 29).
(14) The Visions of Iddo the Seer concerning Jeroboam the son of Nebat (2 Chron. ix. 29).
(15) The Acts of Uzziah written by Isaiah the prophet the son of Amoz (2 Chron. xxvi. 22).
(16) The Vision of Isaiah the prophet, the son of Amoz in the Book of the Kings of Judah and Israel (2 Chron. xxxii. 32).

In addition to the above-mentioned sources, there are passing references to works of a different type. These are the following:

(17) A genealogical register of the sons of Gad (1 Chron. v. 11–16).[1]
(18) The writing from the hand of the Lord, concerning the plan of the Temple (1 Chron. xxviii. 19).
(19) The Directions of David king of Israel, and the Directions of Solomon his son, outlining the organization of the Levites (2 Chron. xxxv. 4).
(20) The Lamentations for Josiah by Jeremiah and others (2 Chron. xxxv. 25).

It is probable that the historical sources mentioned formed part of a single work which is usually called, *The Midrash of the Book of the Kings*. It is clear that this work was not identical with canonical Kings, for it contained material which is not mentioned in the latter book. No mention is made in canonical Kings of the genealogies (1 Chron. ix. 1), or of the wars of Jotham (2 Chron. xxvii. 7), or of the prayer of Manasseh (2 Chron. xxxiii. 18), or of the acts and 'abominations' of Jehoiakim (2 Chron. xxxvi. 8). This Midrash seems to have been an expanded version of canonical Kings.

Probably, too, the prophetic sources mentioned formed part of *The Midrash of the Book of the Kings*. This is suggested by the facts that (1) one of the prophetic sources mentioned is called 'The Midrash of the prophet Iddo', (2) it is specially stated in 2 Chronicles xx. 34

[1] Some of the genealogies and lists of names in 1 Chronicles i–ix were probably derived from the Temple records.

that 'the rest of the acts of Jehoshaphat, from first to last, are written in the chronicles of Jehu, the son of Hanani, which are recorded in the Book of the Kings of Israel', and in 2 Chronicles xxxii. 32 that 'the rest of the Acts of Hezekiah, and his good deeds, behold, they are written in the vision of Isaiah the prophet, the son of Amoz, in the Book of the Kings of Judah and Israel'.

It is highly probable that the Chronicler used two main sources, namely, the canonical books from Genesis to Kings (with the possible exception of Ruth) and a single work covering the history of Israel and Judah.

In style and thought the parts of Chronicles derived from non-canonical sources resemble the Chronicler's own compositions. Driver maintains that if these parts are excerpts from the Midrash they must have been composed at a date scarcely earlier than that of Chronicles itself, and by an author writing in a similar style and with a similar aim. Opposed to this view are those who argue that there could not have been two compilers writing about the same time and in a similar style, and that the parts of Chronicles derived from non-canonical sources must be the invention of the Chronicler himself.[1] It is more likely, however, that some of the material at least was derived from the Midrash and rewritten by the Chronicler in his own distinctive style and from his own view point. It is possible, too, that some of the material was derived from written sources no longer extant and from oral traditions.

DATE

Chronicles must have been written after the Exile because (1) the narrative is brought down to 'the first year of Cyrus king of Persia' (539–530 B.C.), (2) the language stamps it as belonging to the late post-exilic period, (3) it is the last book in the Writings, the third division of the Hebrew Canon. If we accept the view that Chronicles and Ezra-Nehemiah originally formed a single work and that Ezra arrived in Palestine in 458 B.C., it must have been written after Nehemiah's second visit to Palestine in 433 B.C. (Neh. xiii. 6, 7). If, however, we accept the view that Ezra arrived in Palestine in 397 B.C., it must have been written after that date. In 1 Chronicles iii. 19–24 the geneal-

---

[1] R. H. Pfeiffer (*Introduction to the Old Testament*, 1948, pp. 805f.) denies that the Midrash ever existed. 'When', he says, 'the midrashic ghost source of the Chronicler has been relegated to the limbo of illusions where it rightly belongs, critics will cease to regard the Chronicler as a mere compiler or redactor and recognize, with Professor Torrey, that he is a writer of great originality, vivid imagination, and granite convictions'.

ogy of David's family is brought down to the sixth generation after Zerubbabel (in the Septuagint the eleventh), so that the work could not have been produced earlier than about 370 B.C.[1] (counting twenty-five years to a generation). In 1 Chronicles xxix. 7 mention is made of the daric, a Persian coin named after Darius I (522–486 B.C.); its circulation in Palestine suggests the close of the Persian period (539–331 B.C.). In 2 Chronicles xxxvi. 23 Cyrus is referred to as 'king of Persia', implying that the Persian empire no longer existed. In Haggai, Zechariah, the sources of Ezra-Nehemiah and the Elephantine Papyri we find simply the title of 'the king'. This brings us down to the Greek period (331–63 B.C.). In Nehemiah xii. 11 we find the name of Jaddua, who, according to Josephus, was High Priest in the days of Alexander the Great (d. 323 B.C.). His death is recorded as having taken place soon after that of Alexander. This brings us down to the close of the fourth century B.C. We shall not be far wrong if we assign Chronicles to the period 300–250 B.C. Oesterley and Robinson advocate the date 350 B.C. and possibly later,[2] while H. W. Robinson prefers 300–250 B.C.,[3] Rowley about 300 B.C.,[4] and Pfeiffer about 250 B.C.[5]

Several scholars maintain that the composition of the book extended over a period of a number of years and that it was the work of more than one compiler. Rothstein and Hänel distinguish two editions, the first written soon after 432 B.C., showing the influence of D., and the second about 400 B.C. showing the influence of P., while some additions were made later.[6] G. von Rad also distinguishes two editions, the first written about 400 B.C. under the influence of P., and the second written about 350 B.C. under the influence of D.[7] Welch, who denies the unity of authorship of Chronicles and Ezra-Nehemiah, holds the view that a first edition of Chronicles (except i–ix)[8] was produced about 520

---

[1] Some scholars reject the evidence afforded by 1 Chron. iii. 19–24, and Neh. xii. 11; xiii. 6f. on the ground that they are later insertions.
[2] W. O. E. Oesterley and T. H. Robinson, *An Introduction to the Books of the Old Testament*, 1934, p. 112.
[3] H. W. Robinson, *The Old Testament: Its Making and Meaning*, 1937, p. 71.
[4] H. H. Rowley, *The Growth of the Old Testament*, 1950, p. 165.
[5] R. H. Pfeiffer, *Introduction to the Old Testament*, 1948, p. 812.
[6] J. W. Rothstein and J. Hänel, 'Das erste Buch der Chronik', *K.A.T.*, 1927, pp. 43, 46f.
[7] G. von Rad, *Das Geschichtsbild des Chronistischen Werkes*, 1930.
[8] A. C. Welch maintains that 1 Chronicles i–ix and 2 Chronicles xxxvi. 22f., have no integral relation to the rest of the material and are a later addition. According to G. von Rad, the nine chapters and two verses were not written as an introduction or to connect David with the past of Israel. They are a collection of loose material like that which now forms an appendix to David's life at the close of 2 Samuel.

B.C., followed some time later by a second edition showing the influence of P.[1] These views have not won wide acceptance.

PERMANENT INFLUENCE

Chronicles is of little historical value. Judged as a history of Judah, it is neither accurate nor impartial, and must, therefore, be read with the greatest caution. In recent years there has been a tendency to give more credit to the Chronicler's own contributions when they do not appear to be dictated by his own theories. Some scholars cite passages which seem to them to bear the stamp of truth. This is mere conjecture and in no way constitutes proof. If, as Torrey suggests, the Chronicler was a writer of great originality, vivid imagination and granite convictions,[2] he would have found no difficulty in clothing fiction with the air of reality. According to Albright, the historical accuracy of the Chronicler has been recognized increasingly by archaeologists, and there is not the slightest reason to suspect his account as a whole, though there may be exaggerations in detail. In our opinion, the evidence which he advances in support of this view is inadequate.[3] Chronicles doubtless contains elements of truth, but it is, nevertheless, substantially a complete misrepresentation of history.

Chronicles is of more value in the sphere of religion, though it is not great. Monotheism is stressed (1 Chron. xxix. 10–19) and idolatry condemned (1 Chron. xiv. 12; 2 Chron. xiv. 3f.). Religion is defined

---

[1] A. C. Welch, *Post-exilic Judaism*, 1935, pp. 185ff. *The Work of the Chronicler*, 1939, pp. 1–9, 122–160.

[2] C. C. Torrey, *Ezra Studies*, 1910, pp. 208–251.

[3] Albright supplies the following evidence in support of his views.

Both Syria and Palestine were noted for their musicians in the Near East. Though this does not prove that David organized the first religious music in Israel, it does prove that Hebrew Temple music was recognized in Israel as going back to early times (*Archaeology and the Religion of Israel*, 1951, pp. 125–129).

According to 2 Chronicles vi. 13, Solomon, at the dedication of the Temple, stood upon a bronze platform, five cubits long, five cubits wide and three cubits high, and spread forth his hands towards heaven. In a limestone stela found at Ugarit in 1932, a king is shown praying to the storm-god Baal. He is standing on a chest or tub, apparently of metal, and provided with a lid. His hands are upraised in the attitude of prayer. The account in Chronicles refers to the same practice (*Archaeology and the Religion of Israel*, 1951, pp. 152–154).

In the account of the invasion of Judah by Shishak, king of Egypt, given in 2 Chronicles xii. 2–12, we are told that his army consisted of Libyans, Sukkiim and Ethiopians, and that he captured the fortified cities of Judah. Excavations have shown that the Sukkiim were foreign troops in Egyptian service, and that the towns of Tell Beit Mirsim and Bethshemesh were destroyed about the time of the invasion (c. 918 B.C.) (Article on 'Archaeology of Palestine' in *The Old Testament and Modern Study*, ed. by H. H. Rowley, 1951, p. 18).

in terms of ritual and ceremonies. Only in one passage do we find a more spiritual conception of religion. In 2 Chronicles xxx. 18f., it is recorded that a multitude of people had not purified themselves, yet they ate the passover otherwise than as prescribed, for Hezekiah had prayed for them saying 'The good Lord pardon everyone who sets his heart to seek God, the Lord God of his fathers, even though not according to the sanctuary's rules of cleanness'. The moral demands of God are not stressed as in the prophetic books. Though kings are frequently mentioned nothing is said about their duty to govern well. The sins for which they were punished were, corrupting worship, seeking other gods, depending on foreign alliances and in one case summoning a physician instead of seeking Yahweh (2 Chron. xvi. 12). The necessity of Temple worship is stressed, but the people are not exhorted to come unto the presence of Yahweh with clean hands and a pure heart. Emphasis is placed upon the validity of the Priesthood, but no mention is made of the moral responsibilities of the ministry. The orthodox view concerning the moral order of the world is accepted without question. The reward of goodness is prosperity, and prosperity is an unfailing proof of goodness. Similarly the punishment of sin is adversity, and adversity is a sure proof of sin. Chronicles reveals the attitude of certain Jewish circles towards religion in the late post-exilic period. We see their dedication to the Law, their love of liturgical worship, and their deep conviction of the relationship of Yahweh and the course of history, especially in the covenant-relationship between Him and Israel.

LITERARY MERIT

The style of the Chronicler is distinctive but undistinguished. As regards the vocabulary of the book, it contains many Aramaic forms and later words and expressions. The ease, grace and fluency of the earlier writers has gone, and in its place is a style that is often laboured and uncouth, suggesting either that the language is in decay or that the author has an imperfect command of it. Sometimes, however, the style is enlivened by the introduction of vivid details. The men of war who came to the coronation of David at Hebron stayed three days, 'eating and drinking, for the brethren had made preparations for them' (1 Chron. xii. 39). David had it in his heart 'to build a house of rest for the ark of the covenant of the Lord, and for the footstool of our God' (1 Chron. xxviii. 2). On his death, Asa was laid on a bier 'which had been filled with various kinds of spices prepared by the perfumer's art; and they made a very great fire in his honour' (2 Chron. xvi. 14). Occasionally, we find an apt simile. Benaiah slew an Egyptian who had in his hand 'a spear like a weaver's beam' (1 Chron. xi. 23). From the Gadites there joined David in the wilderness, 'mighty and experienced warriors, expert with shield and spear, whose faces were like the faces of lions, and who were swift as gazelles upon the mountains' (1 Chron. xii. 8). It may be, as Oesterley suggests,[1] that David's prayer of thanksgiving recorded in 1 Chronicles xxix. 10-19, was based upon some form of prayer in the Temple Liturgy, but if it came from the pen of the Chronicler, it shows that he could, when the occasion demanded, rise to the height of the sublime. 'Thine O Lord, is the greatness, and the power, and the glory, and the victory, and the majesty; for all that is in the heavens and in the earth is thine; thine is the kingdom, O Lord, and thou art exalted as head above all. Both riches and honour come from thee, and thou rulest over all. In thy hand is power and might; and in thy hand it is to make great and to give strength to all. And now we thank thee, our God, and praise thy glorious name. But who am I, and what is my people, that we should be able thus to offer willingly? For all things come from thee and of thy own have we given thee. For we are strangers before thee, and sojourners, as all our fathers were; our days on the earth are like a shadow, and there is no abiding' (1 Chron. xxix. 11-15).

[1] W. O. E. Oesterley, article on 1 and 2 Chronicles in Peake's *Commentary on the Bible*, 1919, p. 318.

CHAPTER XVIII

EZRA AND NEHEMIAH

TITLE AND PLACE IN CANON

EZRA and Nehemiah are so called because of the prominence given in them to the two Jewish patriots and reformers whose names they bear, and because they embody extracts from their personal diaries. Although in the English versions, Ezra and Nehemiah constitute two books, they are really sections of one book and we shall treat them as such. In the ancient Hebrew manuscripts they are united in one volume, and it was not till the fifteenth century A.D. that the division into two books was introduced. In the Septuagint they are joined together under the title, 2 Esdras, while in the Vulgate they appear separately, Ezra as 1 Esdras and Nehemiah as 2 Esdras. As we have already pointed out (see p. 280), there are strong reasons for thinking that Chronicles, together with Ezra-Nehemiah, originally formed a single volume. In the Hebrew Canon, Ezra-Nehemiah immediately precedes Chronicles, probably because it was considered more valuable and was therefore the first to be regarded as authoritative Scripture. That in the English versions Chronicles stands immediately after Kings and before Ezra-Nehemiah, is due to the influence of the Vulgate.

CONTENTS

The book relates the history of the Jews during the period 538–433 B.C. (or 538–397 B.C.)[1] that is, from the return of the Jewish exiles from Babylon, to the second visit of Nehemiah to Jerusalem. It may be divided into four sections, thus:

---

[1] According to the Chronicler, Ezra came to Jerusalem 'in the seventh year of Artaxerxes the king' (Ezra vii. 7) and Nehemiah 'in the twentieth year of King Artaxerxes' (Neh. ii. 1). The traditional order depends on the assumption that both these references refer to Artaxerxes I (465–424 B.C.). It is now generally agreed that Ezra and Nehemiah were not contemporaries, that Nehemiah came to Jerusalem in 445 B.C. in the reign of Artaxerxes I, and Ezra in 397 B.C. in the reign of Artaxerxes II (404–358 B.C.).

(1) Ezra i–vi. The return of the exiles and the rebuilding of the Temple (538–516 B.C.).
(2) Ezra vii–x. The activities of Ezra (458 B.C. or 397 B.C.).
(3) Nehemiah i–xii. Nehemiah's administration of Judah in the first part of his governorship (445–433 B.C.).
(4) Nehemiah xiii. Nehemiah's reforms in the second part of his governorship after his return from Babylon in 433 B.C.[1]

These sections may be summarized as follows:

Ezra i–vi

Ch. i. In the first year of his reign, Cyrus, king of Persia, issued a decree allowing the Jewish exiles in Babylon to return to Jerusalem. Many of them returned under the leadership of Shesh-bazzar.

Ch. ii. The chapter contains a list of the exiles who returned, and a report of their contributions to the Temple treasury.

This list occurs with slight variations in Nehemiah vii. 6–73a.

Ch. iii. In the seventh month of the same year they set up the altar and observed the Feast of Booths (vv. 1–6). In the second month of the second year of their coming to Jerusalem, they laid the foundations of the Temple amid mingled joy and tears (vv. 7–13).

According to Haggai i. 1–15, the foundations of the Temple were not laid until the second year of the reign of Darius I (520 B.C.).

Ch. iv. The enemies of Judah and Benjamin (chiefly Samaritans) asked permission to assist in the work of rebuilding the Temple but their request was refused. A feud arose and work stopped until the second year of the reign of Darius I (vv. 1–5, 24). Their enemies wrote to Artaxerxes, the king, informing him that if the Jews were allowed to rebuild the wall of Jerusalem they would rebel against him and that he would lose all his possessions in the province 'Beyond the River' (i.e. west of the Euphrates). Artaxerxes ordered the work on the wall to cease (vv. 6–23).

According to Oesterley and Robinson (*History of Israel*, 1932, vol. II. p. 152), the account of the Samaritan opposition to the rebuilding of the Temple, given in vv. 1–5, 24, is a pure fiction of the compiler. Verses 6 and 7 are isolated fragments, the first referring to a letter written to Xerxes (486–465 B.C.), and the second to a letter written by Mithredath and others to

---

[1] How long Nehemiah's second term of office lasted is not known.

Artaxerxes I (465–424 B.C.). The letter and the reply, given in vv. 8–23, refer not to the Temple but to the city wall and belongs to a much later period. It is obviously out of place and probably refers to some unauthorized attempt to fortify Jerusalem prior to the coming of Nehemiah.

Ch. v. Encouraged by the prophets Haggai and Zechariah, the Jews, under the leadership of Zerubbabel and Jeshua, started again to build the Temple (vv. 1f.). Tattenai, the governor, and his associates demanded to know from whom they had received the order to resume work and were referred to the decree of Cyrus as authorizing their undertaking (vv. 3–6). Their explanation was sent to Darius with the request that search might be made for the decree in question (vv. 7–17).

Ch. vi. Darius ordered a search of the archives to be made and the original decree was found at Ecbatana, whereupon he issued an order, allowing work on the Temple to proceed and commanding Tattenai and his associates to provide aid in money for expenses and cattle, that the Jews might offer 'pleasing sacrifices to the god of heaven and pray for the life of the king and his sons' (vv. 1–12). The Temple was completed and dedicated in the sixth year of the reign of Darius (516 B.C.). Afterwards the Passover was celebrated (vv. 13–22).

Ezra vii–x

Ch. vii. In the seventh year of Artaxerxes, Ezra, accompanied by a number of other Jews, including priests, Levites, singers, gatekeepers and Temple servants came to Jerusalem with the express purpose of teaching the Law and enforcing it (vv. 1–10). He carried with him a letter authorizing him to take to Jerusalem any Jews who might wish to accompany him, to appoint magistrates and judges to enforce the Law under severe penalties, to convey the silver and gold, and the vessels—the free-will offerings of the king and his counsellors, the Babylonians and the Jewish exiles—for the service of the house of God. Furthermore, the letter freed all the priests, Levites, singers, gatekeepers and Temple servants from the payment of tribute, custom or toll (vv. 11–26). Ezra blessed God and gathered the leading exiles to accompany him to Jerusalem (vv. 27f.).

Ch. viii. The chapter opens with a list of the exiles who returned (vv. 1–14). Ezra mustered them at Ahava and inspected them. Finding no Levites among them, he sent messengers to Iddo, the leader of the Jewish settlement at Casiphia, who persuaded 38 Levites and 220 of their servants to join him (vv. 15–20). Ezra proclaimed a fast and entreated divine assistance (vv. 21–23). Then, after putting the free-will offerings in charge of chosen priests and Levites, he and his companions set out and reached Jerusalem safely (vv. 24–32). They handed over to the Temple authorities the free-will offerings, offered sacrifices for all Israel, and delivered to the king's satraps and to the governors of the province, 'Beyond the River', the king's commissions (vv. 33–36).

Ch. ix. On learning that the Jews had married foreign wives, Ezra rent his garments and mantle, pulled his hair from his head and beard and sat appalled till the evening, when he rose, fell on his knees and made a solemn confession of sin in the name of the people (vv. 1–15).

Ch. x. The prayer stirred the people to repentance, and one of them, named Shecaniah, proposed that they should make a covenant with God to put away their foreign wives and their children (vv. 1–5). Ezra then induced the people to swear to do this. A national assembly was summoned, at which, in spite of some opposition, it was agreed that the mixed marriages should be dissolved. A special commission was appointed to examine the individual offenders. Within three months it reported that 113 men had contracted foreign marriages. Among them were seventeen priests, together with Levites, singers and gatekeepers (vv. 6–44).

Nehemiah i–xii

Ch. i. Nehemiah, cupbearer to Artaxerxes, king of Persia, informed of the miserable condition of the inhabitants of Jerusalem and the ruined state of its wall, fasted and prayed, confessing in the name of the people their utter corruption and appealing to God for help (vv. 1–11).

Ch. ii. His troubled countenance attracted the attention of the king who encouraged him to ask a favour. This he did, requesting permission to rebuild the city. The king complied with his request and granted him leave of absence for a set period. He was furnished with letters of safe conduct to show to the governors of the province 'Beyond the River', and with a letter enjoining Asaph, the keeper of the king's forest, to provide him with timber for the projected work (vv. 1–8). He set out with an armed escort, delivered the letters of safe conduct to the governors and reached Jerusalem safely. His arrival roused the opposition of Sanballat and Tobiah, who were greatly displeased that he had come to promote the welfare of the Jews (vv. 9–11). With a few attendants he inspected the wall secretly by night. He then called the leaders of the people together, told them that he had received the royal permission to rebuild the wall and urged them to begin the work at once. His appeal met with an immediate response and the work of reconstruction was taken in hand (vv. 12–18). The decision to rebuild the wall roused the scorn of Sanballat and his allies, who insinuated that Nehemiah and his followers planned to rebel against the king of Persia. Nehemiah declared that God would prosper the work, and that they had no share or claim in Jerusalem or proof of any past connexion with the city (vv. 19f.).

Ch. iii. The chapter gives the groups that rebuilt the wall and the portion of the wall that each group repaired.

Ch. iv. Sanballat and his allies ridiculed what they considered to be the feeble efforts of the Jews, but the work continued and the wall raised to half its height all round (vv. 1–6). When Sanballat and his allies heard that the breaches were beginning to be closed, they were extremely angry and planned a combined attack upon Jerusalem, but the Jews set a guard for protection against them day and night. Those who lived on the borders of Samaria brought news again and again that their enemies were gathering against them from all quarters (vv. 7–12). Nehemiah stationed the people by families, armed with swords, spears and bows, and exhorted the nobles and their officials to fight for their kinsfolk, sons, daughters, wives and homes (vv. 13f.). When their enemies heard that their plan was known they called off the attack. After that half of Nehemiah's servants worked on construction and half stood on guard. The labourers were armed, each working with one hand and holding a weapon in the other. The masons worked with their swords girded at their side. A trumpeter stood by Nehemiah ready to sound the call to arms. All Jews were to sleep in the city at night in order to guard it and to be ready for work at once in the morning (vv. 15–23).

Ch. v. A loud outcry arose among the common people against the wealthy classes, because some of them had been compelled to mortgage their lands and property to buy food, and to sell their children into slavery to pay the king's tribute (vv. 1–5). Nehemiah summoned an assembly and induced the offenders to remit the interest they had charged, and to restore the property which they had taken in pledge (vv. 6–13). Nehemiah recounted his own generosity. During his tenure of office he had refused to impose the usual tax for the governor's support, had not bought the land of the poor but had worked with them in building the wall, and had fed daily at his table 150 Jews and officials in addition to Jewish immigrants from the surrounding nations (vv. 14–19).

This chapter seems out of place here as it breaks the connexion between iv and vi. It would appear that Nehemiah had been governor for some twelve years when the events recorded took place (Neh. v. 14).

Ch. vi. When Sanballat and his allies heard that there was no breach left in the wall, they proposed a private conference with Nehemiah four times in the hope of assassinating him or seizing his person, but each time Nehemiah refused on the ground that he could not find time because he was doing a great work (vv. 1-4). Next, Sanballat sent an open letter to Nehemiah, suggesting that the Jews intended to rebel against Persia and that he intended to make himself king, and proposing a conference to discuss the charges. Nehemiah denied the charges, declaring that they were the invention of Sanballat (vv. 5-9). Again, Sanballat and Tobiah hired a prophet, Shemaiah by name, to urge Nehemiah to take refuge in the Temple as his life was in danger. Nehemiah refused to comply with the suggestion on the ground that such a course of action would weaken his influence with the people, cause him to violate the sanctity of the Temple, and imply a consciousness of guilt (vv. 10-14). The wall was completed in fifty-two days (vv. 15f.). During the building operations the nobles of Judah engaged in treasonable correspondence with Tobiah (vv. 17-19).

Ch. vii. 1-73a. Nehemiah placed Jerusalem in charge of his brother, Hanani, and Hananiah, the governor of the castle, and gave orders that the gates were only to be opened during the hours of full daylight (vv. 1-4). Nehemiah resolved to take a census of the people, and found a record of all those who had returned from exile with Zerubbabel (vv. 5-73a).

The list in vv. 6-73a is reproduced, with slight changes in the order, in *Ezra* ii. 1-70. It must have come originally from the archives in Jerusalem.

Ch. vii. 73b-viii. 18. At a national assembly held on the first day of the seventh month Ezra read to the people from the book of the Law, and thirteen Levites explained the meaning of it so that the people understood what was read. Ezra and the Levites rebuked them for their demonstrations of grief on a day that was holy (vii. 73b-viii. 12). The next day a small group of leading men met to study the Law. It was found that there was a law, which enjoined the observance of the Feast of Booths (or Tabernacles) in the seventh month. So the people made booths of branches and observed the Feast for the first time since the days of 'Jeshua the son of Nun'. During the seven days of the Feast (from the 15th to the 22nd of the month Tishri) the Law was read portion by portion. On the eighth day a solemn assembly was held (viii. 13-18).

Many scholars regard the reference to Nehemiah in viii. 9 as an interpolation by the Chronicler. The statement in viii. 17 that the Feast of Booths was observed for the first time since the days of 'Jeshua the son of Nun' is incorrect. It had been observed by Solomon (2 Chron. vii. 8; viii. 13) and by Zerubbabel (Ezra iii. 4.).

Ch. ix. On the 24th day of the month (two days after the Feast) the people separated themselves from all foreigners, and devoted three hours to reading the Law and three hours to confession and worship. The chosen Levites exhorted them to stand and bless Yahweh (vv. 1-5). Then followed a long prayer which was a summary of Yahweh's dealings with Israel from the call of Abraham to its present state of servitude (vv. 6-37).

The Hebrew version does not state by whom the long prayer in vv. 6-37 was spoken. In the Septuagint version it is assigned to Ezra, but it is probably a late insertion.

Chs. ix. 38-x. 39. A covenant was drawn up and sealed by Nehemiah and representative priests, Levites and chiefs, and the rest of the people took an oath binding themselves to be true to the Law, to abstain from intermarrying with the heathen, to observe the Sabbath, to remit all debts incurred during the sabbatical year, to contribute one third of a shekel annually for the maintenance of the Temple, to bring wood for the altar, and to pay tithes and first fruits.

Ezra's name does not appear in the list of those who sealed the covenant. If Nehemiah came to Jerusalem in 445 B.C. and Ezra in 397 B.C., the former could not have sealed it. The name 'Nehemiah' may be a late insertion. Apparently some kind of a document was drawn up and sealed, binding the people to observe the Law. Noth (*The History of Israel*, 1958, p. 328) suggests that Nehemiah x is closely connected with Nehemiah xiii. 'Its connexion with Neh. xiii would suggest that Nehemiah ultimately pledged the responsible men in the province of Judah to carry out his instructions by means of a written declaration; and this declaration was preserved in Jerusalem and finally came to the notice of the late Chronicler.'

Ch. xi. As Jerusalem was sparsely populated, it was decided that one-tenth of the whole population of the province (chosen by lot) should live in the capital (vv. 1f.). Lists of Judaeans, Benjamites, priests, Levites and gatekeepers dwelling in Jerusalem (vv. 3-19), of the inhabitants of other Judaean towns, including the Nethinim (vv. 20f.), of the chiefs of the Levites and of civil authorities in Jerusalem (22-24), and of the villages occupied by the Jews (vv. 25-36).

Ch. xii. Lists of the priests and Levites who returned with Zerubbabel (vv. 1-9); the High Priests from Jeshua to Jaddua (vv. 10f.), the heads of priestly houses in the time of the High Priest, Joiakim, the son of Jeshua (vv. 12-21); the heads of Levitical houses (vv. 22-26). The walls were dedicated, great sacrifices were offered and the people rejoiced (vv. 27-43). At the same time officers were appointed to superintend the chambers of the Temple set apart for the storing of the contributions, the first fruits and the tithes, and to collect from every town and village the legal provision for the maintenance of the priests and the Levites (vv. 44-47).

The natural place for the narrative recorded in vv. 27-43 would appear to be immediately after vi. 15. It has evidently become misplaced. It is based on the memoirs of Nehemiah as may be seen from vv. 31, 38, 40. The reference to 'Ezra the scribe' as the leader of one of the two processions in v. 36 is probably a late insertion. Verses 44-47 are regarded by many as a late insertion by the Chronicler. They could not have come from the memoirs of Nehemiah since the names of Zerubbabel and Nehemiah are mentioned together.

Chapter xiii

On learning that there was a law (Deut. xxiii. 3-5) excluding the Ammonites and Moabites from the assembly of God for ever, the people excluded from Israel all those of foreign descent (vv. 1-3).

These verses are probably an isolated fragment inserted here as an introduction to the episode which follows (vv. 4-9), and giving the general principle which governed the action of Nehemiah. The fact that the exclusion was not undertaken by Nehemiah shows that the verses were not taken from his memoirs.

During Nehemiah's absence at the Persian court, Eliashib, the High Priest, who was in some way related to Tobiah, had permitted the latter to occupy a large room in the Temple, which had been

EZRA AND NEHEMIAH 309

previously used for the storage of the offerings. On his return to Jerusalem, Nehemiah threw all his household furniture out of the room, purified it and restored it to its proper use (vv. 4-9). Finding that the tithes had not been paid to the Levites and that they had been compelled to leave Jerusalem to earn their livelihood by cultivating their lands, he remonstrated with the officials, summoned the Levites back to perform their proper duties in the Temple, and appointed treasurers over the storehouses to superintend the collection of the tithes and their distribution to the priests and Levites (vv. 10-14). Discovering that men were treading their winepresses and bringing their produce into Jerusalem for sale on the Sabbath, and that Tyrian merchants, who lived in the city, were bringing in fish and other wares for the same purpose, he closed the market and kept the gates shut throughout the day (vv. 15-22). He banned foreign marriages and expelled the grandson of Eliashib from Jerusalem, evidently because he had married a foreign wife (vv. 23-30). Finally, he made provision for the supply of wood for the Temple (v. 31).

Nehemiah was governor of Judah for twelve years (Neh. v. 4), but it does not necessarily follow that he was in residence for the whole of the period. His first visit was probably a brief one—a matter of months rather than of years (Neh. ii. 6). After the rebuilding of the wall, he entrusted the government of the city to his brother, Hanani, and Hananiah, the governor of the castle (Neh. vii. 2), as if he meant to return to the Persian king. His religious reforms, mentioned in Nehemiah xiii were probably carried out on his return to Jerusalem in 433 B.C. after a more or less considerable absence in Babylon. It might not have been his first absence.

A COMPILATION

That the book is not a literary unit but a compilation is clear from the following considerations:

(1) The narrative does not read continuously. Apart from brief references to the opposition of the Samaritans to the rebuilding of the Temple (Ezra iv. 1-5), and the interruption of the work from the return of the Exiles in 538 B.C. to the second year of Darius in 520 B.C. (Ezra iv. 24), we are told nothing of the period 538-520 B.C. Except for the misplaced passage (Ezra iv. 8-23), which breaks the connexion between vv. 5 and 24, the narrative passes over in silence a long period, extending from the completion of the Temple and the celebration of the Passover in 516 B.C. (Ezra vi. 16-22), to the arrival of Ezra in

Jerusalem in 458 B.C. (Ezra vii. 1–6), (or to that of Nehemiah in 445 B.C.–Neh. ii. 1). The activity of the two reformers is confined to three particular years, namely, 458, 445 and 433 B.C. (or 445, 433 and 397 B.C.). These gaps in the history of the period 538–458 B.C. (or 538–397 B.C.), and the concentration on certain points of time in the period 458–433 B.C. (or 445–397 B.C.) suggest that the compiler's knowledge of the period 538–433 B.C. (or 538–397 B.C.) was inadequate owing to the meagreness of the information at his disposal.

(2) The narrative changes frequently from the third to the first person and vice versa. A writer may occasionally vary the person of his composition, but frequent changes indicate that he is making use of quotations from other works.

(3) Although the greater part of the book is written in Hebrew, a large section is written in Aramaic. It is obvious that a writer would not change from one language to another in composing his work unless he was quoting verbatim from sources.

(4) A long list of names with slight variations occurs in Ezra ii. 1–70, and Nehemiah vii. 6–73a, suggesting that the author took it from two different sources.

(5) The style is not uniform throughout the work, a sure sign of its compilatory character. In some parts it is distinctive, revealing the personalities of the writers: other parts show much less force and originality, and at the same time exhibit close affinities with the style of the Chronicler.

(6) The work covers the events of the period 538–433 B.C. (or 538–397 B.C.). If it is agreed that it was written in the period 300–250 B.C., it is obvious that the writer could not have had personal knowledge of the events which he described, and must have obtained his information at secondhand from his 'Authorities'.

SOURCES

The chief sources utilized in the composition of the book are the following:

(1) *The Ezra Memoirs.* These are extracts taken from a record kept by Ezra himself and written in the first person. They are found in Ezra vii. 27f.; viii. 1–34; ix. 1–15. There are some passages which, though they are not extracts, seem to be based on the same record and are written in the third person. These are Ezra vii. 1–10; x, and Nehemiah vii. 73b–ix. 57.

The authenticity of the Ezra Memoirs are not universally recognized. It is alleged by some scholars that their style, whether written in the first or third person, has close affinity with that of the Chronicler. The use of the first person is merely a literary device to give greater vividness to the narrative. Torrey rejects them on the ground that they are the invention of the Chronicler, who created the character of Ezra in order to make him the mouthpiece of his own views.[1] Albright admits that the Chronicler is the author of the whole of the Ezra narrative, but believes not that he is a purely fictitious character but the Chronicler himself.[2] According to Hölscher, Ezra is a purely legendary figure still unknown to Ben Sirach in 180 B.C. (Ecclus. xlix. 11–13).[3] Pfeiffer speaks of the 'spurious memoirs of Ezra patterned after Nehemiah's'. He believes that the Chronicler is probably the author of them, but that Ezra is not necessarily a purely fictitious character. He may well have been a devout Jew living in Jerusalem in the days of Nehemiah whose name was remembered in later generations. The Chronicler apparently selected him for the roll of founder of the guild of the scribes and concocted his fictitious biography.[4] Ahlemann holds that the Ezra memoirs were written with great skill by a surviving contemporary of Ezra (458 B.C.), still alive in the years 430–420 B.C. His object in writing them was to exalt the priest, Ezra, over the layman Nehemiah.[5] According to Welch, Nehemiah ix. is not the work of Ezra or Nehemiah. It consists of a litany written for the worship of Northern Israel on the occasion of a day of fasting, confession and prayer shortly after 722 B.C.[6]

These views have won little support. The general consensus of opinion among scholars is that the Ezra Memoirs are genuine. We do not accept the view, held by some scholars, that the whole of Ezra is a pure fabrication and that Ezra, the man, existed only in the Chronicler's imagination. Such a view is not in accordance with the trend of Jewish thought. Their traditions always contain a core of truth: it is practically certain that Ezra was a real historical character. 'The probability', says Snaith, 'is that Ezra was indeed a real person who came to Jerusalem and did substantially what the Chronicler says he did'.[7]

[1] C. C. Torrey, *Ezra Studies*, 1910, pp. 238–248.
[2] W. F. Albright, *J.B.L.* 40., 1921, pp. 104–124.
[3] G. Hölscher, *Geschichte der israelitischen und judischen Religion*, 1922, p. 140.
[4] R. H. Pfeiffer, *Introduction to the Old Testament*, 1948, p. 283.
[5] F. Ahlemann, 'Zur Esra-Quelle', *Z.A.W.*, N.F. xviii., 1942–3, pp. 77–98.
[6] A. C. Welch, *Post-Exilic Judaism*, 1935, pp. 26–45.
[7] N. H. Snaith, 'The Historical Books' in *The Old Testament and Modern Study*, ed. by H. H. Rowley, 1951, p. 113.

(2) The Nehemiah Memoirs. These are extracts taken verbatim from a personal record of Nehemiah and contained in Nehemiah i-vii. 5; xi. 1f.; xiii. 4–31. As in the case of Ezra there are passages which, while they are not extracts, are apparently based on the same record. These are Nehemiah xii. 27–43; xiii. 1–3. The genuineness of the Memoirs is almost universally recognized though their extent is disputed. According to Mowinckel, they are memorials, a type familiar in the ancient Near East. By placing them in the Temple he sought to preserve the memory of his own great deeds and of the wickedness of his foes.[1] It is generally agreed that the Memoirs formed an integral part of the original work, but Granild,[2] who is followed by Bentzen,[3] maintains that they were not used by the Chronicler, but that they were inserted later by a post-Chronist editor who inserted all the Aramaic, and wished to give Nehemiah rather than Ezra the credit for the foundation of post-exilic Jewry. Welch alleges that Nehemiah x. was written before the Edict of Cyrus in 538 B.C., being the report of a compact made between the Israelites of Judaea and Northern Israel who still remained in Palestine after the destruction of Jerusalem in 587 B.C.[4] The object of the compact was to preserve their religion and their national identity.

(3) Aramaic Sections. These are Ezra iv. 8b – vi. 18 and vii. 12 – 26, which purport to be official documents sent to and from the Persian king. They are the following:

(a) A letter written by the opponents of the Jews to Artaxerxes with the object of preventing the rebuilding of the wall of Jerusalem (iv. 11–16).
(b) The king's reply to (a), forbidding the fortification of the city (iv. 17–22).
(c) A letter from the governor, Tattenai, to Darius, reporting the rebuilding of the Temple and inquiring if the Jews really had permission to undertake the work (v. 7–17).
(d) The king's decree confirming the decree of Cyrus discovered in the archives at Ecbatana (vi. 3–12).
(e) A decree of Artaxerxes authorizing Ezra and his company to go to Jerusalem (vii. 12–26).

---

[1] S. Mowinckel, *Stadtholderen Nehemia*, 1916, pp. 89–159.
[2] E. Granild, *Ezrabogens literaere Genesis undersogt med Henblik paa et efterkronistik Indgreb*, 1949.
[3] A. Bentzen, *Introduction to the Old Testament*, vol. II, 1949, p. 210.
[4] A. C. Welch, *Post-Exilic Judaism*, 1935, pp. 69–86.

The remainder of the Aramaic sections are by the compiler himself. The authenticity of the Letters is generally recognized but doubts have been cast upon the genuineness of the Decrees, chiefly because of their style which closely resembles that of the Chronicler and because of their Jewish colouring. Some scholars, notably Wellhausen, Torrey, Hölscher and Pfeiffer go further, and reject both the Letters and the Decrees as being spurious. It is possible, however, that the Chronicler worked over the documents, imprinting upon them the stamp of his own distinctive style, or that the documents were drafted by Ezra and other Jews, and submitted for approval or modification to the Persian authorities.

(4) Lists. These are mostly the names of persons (e.g. Ezra ii. 1–67; viii. 1–14; Neh. xi. 3–36; xii. 1–26). They are generally regarded with suspicion and considered to be the product of the Chronicler's imagination. Some of them, however, were probably copied from records preserved in the Temple. It is highly probable that the Temple had a library like that associated with the temple of Baal at Ugarit where official documents were preserved.

HISTORICAL PROBLEMS

It is obvious, even to the casual reader, that the book contains many inconsistencies, inaccuracies, misplacements and improbabilities which naturally rouse suspicion. Of these the following may be mentioned:

(1) The edict of Cyrus authorizing the return of the Jewish exiles is produced twice, once in Hebrew (Ezra i. 2–4) and once in Aramaic (Ezra vi. 3–5), but there are great differences between the two. According to the Hebrew version, Yahweh, 'the God of Heaven', commanded Cyrus to build the Temple in Jerusalem. Moreover the king decreed that his Babylonian subjects should contribute towards its cost. According to the Aramaic version, Cyrus himself ordered the Temple to be built, giving exact details concerning its dimensions and its walls. It was to be built at the expense of the royal house, and all the gold and silver vessels removed from the first temple by Nebuchadrezzar were to be returned. In the Hebrew version, Cyrus is made to use the language of a worshipper of Yahweh, and the return of the exiles is represented as a special dispensation of Providence. We know from the cylinder of Cyrus, however, that Cyrus was a worshipper of the Babylonian god, Marduk, and that after the capture of Babylon

he adopted a conciliatory policy and allowed exiled peoples to return to their own land. Cyrus, therefore, was not a monotheist, nor were the Jewish exiles specially favoured in being allowed to return to Palestine. Moreover it is very unlikely that Cyrus would have compelled his Babylonian subjects to contribute to the cost of the Temple.

The edict of Darius (Ezra vi. 6-12) confirmed that of Cyrus and directed Tattenai, the governor of the province, 'Beyond the River', to allow the building of the Temple to proceed, and to grant aid in money from the royal treasury and cattle for the daily sacrifices. Further, prayers were to be offered for the king and his sons. It is hard to believe that Darius would have allowed the Jews to draw from the royal treasury unlimited sums of money for the building of the Temple.

The edict of Artaxerxes I (Ezra vii. 12-26) allowed Ezra, together with all those Jews, who of their own free will wished to accompany him, to go to Jerusalem to investigate the conditions there according to the law of his God, and empowered him to appoint magistrates and judges to enforce the law. He was authorized to convey to Jerusalem the silver and gold and the vessels—the free-will offerings of the king and his counsellors, the Babylonians and the Jewish exiles—for the service of the house of God, and to draw additional supplies from the royal treasury in Babylon and the royal treasuries west of the Euphrates. The priests, Levites, singers, doorkeepers and other servants of the Temple were to be exempt from taxation. Here again it is incredible that Artaxerxes should have conferred such wide powers upon Ezra, or that he should have provided him with such vast sums of money for the Temple.

It is clear that these three edicts, issued by the Persian authorities, have a strong Jewish colouring. Moreover the literary characteristics of all three are similar to those of Chronicles. Two questions might be asked concerning them, namely, (1) Are they genuine documents or forgeries? and (2) Assuming that they are genuine, have they been modified, and if so, to what extent? No definite answer can be given to either question.

(2) We do not know for certain under whose leadership the Jewish exiles returned and commenced to rebuild the Temple. According to Ezra iii. 8-13, Zerubbabel and Jeshua took the lead, but in Ezra v. 1f. Zerubbabel and Jeshua are stimulated to undertake the task by the preaching of Haggai and Zechariah, while in Ezra v. 16 we are expressly told that the foundations were laid by Shesh-bazzar.

(3) According to Ezra iii. 8–13, iv. 1–4, the foundations of the Temple were laid in the second year of the Return, but further work upon it was checked by the hostility of the Samaritans—a people of mixed race and religion—until the second year of the reign of Darius I (520 B.C.). According to the books of the prophets Haggai and Zechariah (the author of i–viii), the rebuilding of the Temple did not start until the second year of the reign of Darius I. There is no mention in them of any Return, or of any previous attempts at rebuilding the Temple, or of any hostility of the Samaritans.[1] The cleavage, in fact, between Jews and Samaritans did not come until the time of Ezra and Nehemiah. As the books of Haggai and Zechariah are contemporary documents they carry the greater weight.

(4) The Chronicler had only vague ideas on the chronology of the Persian kings. He seems to have been unaware that Cambyses (530–522 B.C.) succeeded Cyrus on the Persian throne, and connected Artaxerxes I (465–424 B.C.) with the building of the Temple completed in 516 B.C. In Ezra vi. 14 we read, 'And the elders of the Jews built and prospered, through the prophesying of Haggai the prophet and Zechariah the son of Iddo. They finished their building by command of the God of Israel and by decree of Cyrus and Darius and Artaxerxes, king of Persia; and this house was finished on the third day of the month of Adar, in the sixth year of the reign of Darius the king.'

(5) In Ezra vii. 1–5 we have the genealogy of Ezra which represents him as the son of Seraiah, the High Priest, who, according to 2 Kings xxv. 18–21, was slain by Nebuchadrezzar in 587 B.C. This would make Ezra about 129 years old when he arrived in Jerusalem in 458 B.C. (or 190 years old if he arrived in 397 B.C.).

(6) Ezra ii gives a long list of the names of returned exiles, and this is produced with slight variations in Nehemiah vii. A scrutiny of the list shows that it contains not only the names of persons but also of localities, together with references to the exclusion of certain people from the priesthood as unclean, and to 'the whole assembly', suggesting that it really represents a census of the inhabitants of Judaea,

---

[1] In Haggai ii. 2–4 both the returned exiles ('the remnant of the people') and those who had not been in exile ('the people of the land') are encouraged to rebuild the Temple. Haggai addresses himself in the first place, not to the returned exiles but to the people who had remained in Palestine. The reasons of the Chronicler for representing the two classes as being in hostility were probably his hatred of the Samaritans, and his dislike of the idea that they had any part in the rebuilding of the Temple. The truth would seem to be that the work was begun by 'the people of the land', who were soon joined by the returned exiles.

which the Chronicler mistook for a list of the returned exiles. It would appear also that he took the list from two different documents.

(7) Ezra iv. 8–23 is clearly not in its right position. Ezra iv. 1–5 describes how the 'adversaries of Judah and Benjamin', being refused permission to assist in the work of rebuilding the Temple, thwarted them all through the reign of Cyrus down to the reign of Darius. Ezra iv. 8–23 deals with the interruption of the work of rebuilding of the city walls caused by the enemies of the Jews, who wrote to the Persian authorities, misrepresenting the action as rebellion.[1] This latter passage breaks the continuity of the story of the rebuilding of the Temple.

(8) It has generally been assumed that Ezra preceded Nehemiah in Jerusalem, and that when the latter arrived they continued together as joint leaders. According to Ezra vii. 7, Ezra arrived in Jerusalem in the seventh year of the reign of Artaxerxes, while Nehemiah ii. 1 gives Nehemiah's arrival as in the twentieth year of the reign of Artaxerxes. On the assumption that in both cases Artaxerxes I (465–424 B.C.) is the king mentioned, Ezra arrived in Jerusalem in 458 B.C. and Nehemiah in 445 B.C. so that they must have been contemporaries. But there are good reasons for thinking that Ezra followed Nehemiah many years later, in the reign of Artaxerxes II (404–358 B.C.). The reasons for holding this view are as follows:

(a) Nehemiah found Jerusalem almost uninhabited and subsequently took steps to repopulate it (Neh. vii. 4; xi. 1f.). When Ezra arrived in the city he found a settled and ordered life (Ezra ix. 4; x. 1).

(b) Nehemiah found the defences of Jerusalem destroyed (Neh. i. 3; ii. 13, 17), whereas Ezra thanked God that the walls of the city had been built (Ezra ix. 9).

(c) If Ezra arrived in Jerusalem in 458 B.C., it is hard to believe that Nehemiah, thirteen years later, would have made no reference to the fact.

(d) It is strange that of all the ardent reformers who came from Babylon with Ezra (Ezra. viii. 1–14) not one of them is mentioned as helping Nehemiah in the task of building the city walls (Neh. iii).

(e) Nehemiah prohibited mixed marriages for the future (Neh. xiii. 23–31), whereas Ezra not only banned such marriages but also insisted that Jews should divorce their foreign wives (Ezra ix, x). It is more likely that the harsher policy came later.

---

[1] Verses 6 and 7 are isolated fragments.

(f) Nehemiah was a contemporary of the High Priest, Eliashib (Neh. iii. 1, 21f.; xiii. 4, 7, 28), whereas Ezra was a contemporary of the High Priest, Jehohanan, the grandson of Eliashib (Ezra x. 6).[1] According to the Elephantine Papyri, Jehohanan was High Priest in Jerusalem in 408 B.C., under Darius II (423–404 B.C.). This evidence indicates that Ezra was active under Artaxerxes II (404–358 B.C.).

(g) It is extremely unlikely that there would be two leaders at once exercising similar powers in such a small community.

These are some of the problems which confront scholars in their enquiries into the authenticity of Ezra-Nehemiah. They are practically insoluble and therefore general agreement cannot be expected. 'All things considered', says Bentzen, 'the books (i.e. Ezra-Nehemiah) are so complex and confused that it is very difficult to arrive at certain and sure views concerning them and their different components'.[2]

CHARACTERS OF EZRA AND NEHEMIAH

Ezra

Ezra was a man of strong religious convictions. His conception of God reflects the teaching of the great prophets. Ethical monotheism was evidently taken for granted. Yahweh was the only God, the Creator of the world, the Preserver of all things, and the Controller of history. An absolutely righteous being, He demanded from men obedience to His moral demands and rewarded them according to their works. 'The hand of our God is for good upon all that seek him, and the power of his wrath is against all that forsake him' (Ezra viii. 22). Though He was just, He was merciful, for He had punished His people less than their iniquities deserved and had saved a remnant (Ezra ix. 13). He had not forsaken them in their bondage, but had shown them kindness in the sight of the kings of Persia to grant them sustenance in their bondage, to set up the house of God, to repair its ruins, and to enjoy His protection in Judah and Jerusalem (Ezra ix. 9). Ezra found courage in the thought that God was with him to protect and guide him. 'I took courage, for the hand of the Lord my God was upon me, and I gathered leading men from Israel to go up with me' (Ezra vii. 28). Before setting out for Jerusalem from the river Ahava he proclaimed a fast, that the returning exiles might humble themselves before their God, that they might obtain from Him a straight,

---

[1] In Ezra x. 6 Jehohanan (also known as Johanan) is called 'the son of Eliashib', but 'son' here means 'grandson', as in Genesis xxix. 5.
[2] A. Bentzen, *Introduction to the Old Testament*, vol. II, 1948, p. 210.

safe course for themselves, their children and their goods (Ezra viii. 21). 'So we fasted and besought our God for this, and he listened to our entreaty' (Ezra viii. 23). On the journey the hand of their God was upon them, and he delivered them from the enemy and from ambushes by the way (Ezra viii. 31).

He seems to have lived in the fear of Yahweh. At the thought of the faithlessness of the people he rent his clothes, sat appalled, wept and cast himself down before the house of God (Ezra ix. 1-5; x. 1). He was anxious to settle the question of mixed marriages, lest the anger of Yahweh might destroy the people until 'there should be no remnant, nor any to escape' (Ezra ix. 14). Like the majority of his fellow-countrymen he had a deep consciousness of sin. Because of his own sins and those of the nation, he was ashamed and blushed to lift up his face to God (Ezra ix. 6). 'Behold, we are before thee in our guilt, for none can stand before thee because of this' (Ezra ix. 15). He exhorted the people to confess their sins to Yahweh, the God of their fathers, and to do His will (Ezra x. 11).

To him the Law was not a burden or a restriction but a delight. The day on which he proclaimed it to the people was a day for rejoicing, and not for mourning and weeping, 'for the joy of the Lord is your strength' (Neh. viii. 10). One of the finest traits in his character was his thought for the poor. He exhorted the people amid their rejoicing to 'send portions to him for whom nothing was prepared' (Neh. viii. 10).

The Temple with its sacrificial system was dear to him. He blessed Yahweh, who had inspired the king of Persia 'to beautify the house of the Lord which is in Jerusalem' (Ezra vii. 27). Finding that no Levites had volunteered to accompany him to Jerusalem, he succeeded in getting 38 Levites together with 220 Temple servants to join him that they might become 'ministers for the house of our God' (Ezra viii. 15-20). The priests to whom he entrusted the silver and gold, and the vessels—the freewill offerings of the king and his seven counsellors and of the Jews in Babylon—for conveyance to the house of God at Jerusalem, were 'holy to the Lord', as was also the treasure (Ezra viii. 24-30). Immediately on his arrival at Jerusalem he and his company 'offered burnt offerings to the God of Israel' (Ezra viii. 35). On hearing that the Jews had married foreign wives, he prostrated himself before the house of God (Ezra x. 1).

He, however, was not an admirable figure. He was intolerant in spirit and lacking in human kindness. His treatment of the foreign wives and their children was harsh in the extreme, and could be justified only by the conviction that there was no other way of preserving the identity of the nation and of saving the religion of Yahweh.

For a long time after his death he was not regarded as a national figure. Ben Sirach does not include his name in the roll of Jewish heroes (Ecclus. xlix) at the beginning of the second century B.C. In later Jewish tradition, however, he was magnified beyond reason. He was represented as the founder of the Great Synagogue [1] as having written all the sacred books which had been destroyed when Nebuchadrezzar captured Jerusalem, and as having closed the Canon.

Nehemiah

Nehemiah was a devoted servant of Yahweh, 'the great and terrible God who keeps covenant and steadfast love with those who love him and keep his commandments' (Neh. i. 5), and regarded Him with reverential awe (Neh. i. 11; v. 15). He was a firm believer in divine guidance. The good hand of God was upon him (Neh. ii. 8, 18). God had put it into his mind to rebuild the wall of Jerusalem (Neh. ii. 12) and it was with His help that the work was accomplished (Neh. vi. 16). It was He who had frustrated the plans of Sanballat and his allies (Neh. iv. 15); in the day of battle He would fight for His people (Neh. iv. 20). At the dedication of the wall He had made them rejoice with great joy (Neh. xii. 43).

He was a man of prayer, calling upon God not only at definite times during the day, but also in the midst of his work (Neh. ii. 4; iv. 4; v. 19; vi. 9, 14; xiii. 14). Though he sought the help of God he did not relax his efforts. He looked for no catastrophic intervention of God in history. To his mind the duty of the faithful was not to wait for such a supernatural event, but to act in the present, though with the help of God. His attitude is summed up in the words, 'And we prayed to our God, and set a guard as a protection against them day and night' (Neh. iv. 9).

His words and actions show that he held the Temple in the greatest veneration, regarding it as central in the religious life of the nation. On his second visit to Jerusalem he drove out Tobiah the Ammonite from one of its chambers, purified it and 'brought back thither the vessels of the house of God, with the cereal offering and the frankincense' (Neh. xiii. 6–9). It grieved him to think how the Temple had been forsaken, and adopted such measures as were required for the

---

[1] For an account of the Great Synagogue, see note on p. 242.

better organization of its services (Neh. xiii. 10–14). Having vindicated its sanctity and restored its worship, he prayed, 'Remember me, O my God, concerning this, and wipe not out my good deeds that I have done for the house of my God and for his service' (Neh. xiii. 14).

He was an ardent patriot, being one of those Jews living in Babylon who could not forget the land of their fathers (Neh. ii. 3). He was smitten with grief when he heard of the state of affairs in Jerusalem and prayed to the 'God of heaven' for assistance and guidance (Neh. i. 1–4; ii. 1–5). The great purpose of his life was to rebuild the wall of Jerusalem, and to prevent the absorption of the Jews by the surrounding nations and the contamination of their religion by the introduction of foreign cults. He had the power to rouse the spirit of patriotism in others. The people responded immediately to his appeal to rebuild the wall of Jerusalem (Neh. ii. 18). So great was the response that voluntary workers from the provincial towns joined in the work (Neh. iii).

He was essentially a man of action, bold and resolute. Once he had started on a project he never relaxed his efforts until he had achieved his purpose. Ridicule (Neh. iv. 1–3), armed opposition (Neh. iv. 7–12) and intrigue (Neh. vi. 1–19) were all tried by Sanballat and his supporters to prevent the rebuilding of the wall, but they were all in vain. In spite of opposition, Nehemiah pressed on with the work. Though he was bold and resolute he was at the same time wise and prudent. His wisdom and prudence frustrated all the efforts of his enemies to retard the work on the wall and to capture him.

He was a man of wide human sympathies. He listened sympathetically to the complaints of the poor and strove to alleviate their sufferings (Neh. v. 6–18).

His temperament was emotional and impulsive. When he heard of the wretched condition of the inhabitants of Jerusalem and the defenceless state of the city, he wept, mourned, fasted and prayed (Neh. i. 4), and went about his duties at the court with a sad countenance (Neh. ii. 1–3). In his wrath he threw all the household furniture of Tobiah out of one of the chambers in the Temple (Neh. xiii. 8). He contended with those who had married foreign wives, 'and cursed them and beat some of them and pulled out their hair' (Neh. xiii. 25). He drove from his presence one of the sons of Jehoiada, apparently, because he refused to put away his foreign wife (Neh. xiii. 28).

There were, however, certain defects in his character. He was too much of the dictator, with the result that he could not win the wholehearted support of all the people. As soon as his strong arm was removed the old abuses reappeared. If he could sympathize with the poor and show generosity of spirit, he could also hate and call down curses upon those who opposed him. He prayed that Sanballat and Tobiah might be given up to be plundered and that their sins might not be blotted out (Neh. iv. 5; cf. vi. 14). He cursed those who had married women of Ashdod, Ammon and Moab (Neh. xiii. 25). Finally, he was intolerant in spirit though not to the same extent as Ezra. He laid down the principle that Jews and Gentiles were to be for ever separated. To Sanballat and his supporters he declared, 'The God of heaven will make us prosper, and we his servants will arise and build; but you have no portion or right or memorial in Jerusalem' (Neh. ii. 20). In the pursuit of his policy he banned mixed marriages (Neh. xiii. 23–27).

In spite of his faults he is one of the noblest characters in the Old Testament. Ben Sirach in Ecclesiasticus xlix. 13 includes his name among the famous men in the nation's past.

PERMANENT INFLUENCE

The book is valuable as being our main source for the history of the period 538–433 B.C. (or 397 B.C.). At first sight it seems to give a fairly comprehensive account of the history of the period, but a close study of it shows that it is but the merest outline. As we have already shown (see pp. 309f.), it is not a continuous historical record. The political, social and economic conditions of the country receive scant attention. The Chronicler's chief concern is with the religion of the nation, so he concentrates on such matters as the building of the Temple, and the organization of its worship, the inculcation of the Law, the celebration of the Feasts and the prohibition of heathen marriages. The two parts of the book do not have the same historical significance. The Ezra narrative describes very briefly the return of the Jews from captivity in Babylon, the rebuilding and dedication of the Temple, the abortive attempt to rebuild the wall of Jerusalem, the opposition of the people of the land to their building operations, the coming of Ezra to Jerusalem and the expulsion of foreign wives. A good deal of this material is of doubtful authenticity and needs to be accepted with great caution. The Nehemiah narrative describes, also very briefly, the coming of Nehemiah to Jerusalem, the rebuilding of the wall of Jerusalem in spite of the opposition of Sanballat and his allies, the promulgation of the Law, the celebration of the Feast of Booths, the sealing of the covenant, the dedication of the walls and the removal of abuses. Most of this material is authentic and can be accepted without hesitation. The Nehemiah Memoirs are, in fact, among the most accurate documents in the Old Testament. The light shed by both narratives may at best be dim, but, nevertheless, it does help to dispel the darkness of one of the most important epochs of Jewish history.

The book sheds light upon conditions in Judah in the early post-exilic period, especially in the days of Nehemiah and Ezra. The Jews were the descendants of those who had been deported to Babylon by Nebuchadrezzar and allowed to return in the first year of the reign of Cyrus, king of Persia (Ezra i. 3; cf. Neh. i. 1–3). Judah was not an independent state but was incorporated in the Persian empire, being part of the great satrapy, called 'Beyond the River' (Ezra iv. 11; Neh. ii. 7), which included Syria, Phoenicia, Palestine and Cyprus. It was under the control of a satrap or governor (Ezra v. 3), who was responsible to the central government at Susa. Under the satrap were minor governors, those of Samaria (Neh. ii. 9f.) and Judah (Neh. ii. 4–8; v. 14) being responsible to the satrap of the whole province.

The Jews were surrounded by peoples who feared that the former might throw off the Persian yoke and become a strong independent state. On the north were the Samaritans, on the west the Ashdodites (the Philistines), on the east the Ammonites and Moabites, and on the south the Arabians. From the day of their return from captivity the Jews had never lived in complete isolation from their neighbours. Intermarriage took place on an increasing scale. Nehemiah discovered that Jews had married women of Ashdod, Ammon and Moab, that a generation was growing up that could not speak Hebrew, and that Jehoiada, the grandson of Eliashib, the High Priest, had married the daughter of Sanballat, the Horonite (Neh. xiii. 23–28). In the days of Ezra investigations showed that 113 Jews had married foreign wives (Ezra x. 10–44). There was thus a danger that the Jews might ultimately lose their national identity.

The territory occupied by the Jews seems to have been small—probably not more than twenty or thirty miles in length and breadth. In the days of Nehemiah the chief occupation of the people was agriculture, the main crops being corn, grapes, olives and figs (Neh. v. 11; x. 37; xiii. 15). Country produce was brought into Jerusalem on asses and sold in the market, while merchants from Tyre, who lived in the city, traded in fish and other wares (Neh. xiii. 6). The majority of the people found it difficult to wrest a living from the soil.

The poorer members of the community had been compelled to sell their lands and property, and in some cases to sell their children into slavery, to buy food and to pay the 'king's tax'. The rate of interest charged on the loans by their richer neighbours aggravated the distress and was a source of bitterness and class hatred (Neh. v. 1–5).

By the middle of the fifth century B.C. religion among the Jews was at a low ebb. The old enthusiasm for the Temple and its sacrificial system, which the prophets Haggai and Zechariah had roused in the hearts of the people, had died out. The sanctity of the building was violated (Neh. xiii. 5); the tithes were no longer paid and the Levites had to earn their living by cultivating their lands (Neh. xiii. 10). In addition the observance of the seventh day as a day of rest had fallen into disuse (Neh. xiii. 10) and timber was not provided for the sacrificial fires (Neh. xiii. 31). There was a danger that the religion of Yahweh might become contaminated and ultimately die out through the introduction of the idolatrous worship and immoral practices of the surrounding nations.

The book tells us a little about the work of the two reformers, Nehemiah and Ezra. Nehemiah was both a political and a religious reformer, but primarily the former. During his governorship he rebuilt the wall of Jerusalem, increased the population of the city and made it the religious centre for all Jews, abolished certain abuses in public worship and carried out the most urgent social reforms. In addition, he separated the Jews from the surrounding peoples by prohibiting foreign marriages and enforced the strict observance of the Sabbath. Though he was an advocate of the strictest religious purity, he was not greatly concerned with the reform of the inner life of the community. This came with the arrival of Ezra in Jerusalem.

Ezra's work was entirely religious. The great purpose of his life was the promotion among his countrymen of a fuller knowledge and a stricter observance of the Law. The first problem which engaged his attention was that of mixed marriages (Ezra ix, x). As we have already indicated, he adopted sterner measures than Nehemiah, not only prohibiting such marriages for the future, but also insisting that all those who had married foreign women should divorce them (Ezra x. 3, 11, 44). His main work, however, was the enforcement of the Law which was destined to exercise a profound influence upon Jewish life and thought. It was Ezra who made the Jews 'the people of the Book' and created Judaism as we know it to-day.

LITERARY MERIT

From the literary point of view Nehemiah's Memoirs are superior to the other parts of the book. Nehemiah does not rank among the great writers of the Old Testament. Unlike the great prophets he has no poetical gifts. We shall look in vain in his Memoirs for flights of imagination, graphic descriptions, imagery drawn from nature, apt figures of speech and striking contrasts. He is not a conscious literary artist striving to produce a work of outstanding merit. As befits a man of action his style is characterized by simplicity, lucidity, conciseness and vigour. There is no attempt made at ornamentation. A good example of his style may be seen in the following passage. 'Then I said to them, "You see the trouble we are in, how Jerusalem lies in ruins with its gates burned. Come, let us build the wall of Jerusalem, that we may no longer suffer disgrace." And I told them of the hand of my God which had been upon me for good, and also of the words which the king had spoken to me. And they said, "Let us rise up and build. So they strengthened their hands for the good work" '. (Neh. ii. 17f.). He shows a fondness for particular words and phrases, such as, 'my God' (ii. 8; v. 19; xiii. 14), 'nobles and officials' (iv. 14; 19; v. 7), and 'the God of heaven' (i. 4f.; ii. 4, 20). His Memoirs contain late words and idioms which, however, are much less numerous than those which occur in the writings of the Chronicler. His diction and grammar are also more classical than his.

Ezra's style is more akin than Nehemiah's to that of the Chronicler. This is perhaps due partly to the fact that Ezra was a priest who was naturally more conversant than the layman, Nehemiah, with the priestly terminology.

APPENDIX A

THE SECOND TEMPLE

BUILDING AND FURNITURE

The Second Temple was built at the insistence of the two prophets, Haggai and Zechariah, under the leadership of Zerubbabel. The foundation was laid in the second year of the reign of Darius I, i.e. 520 B.C. (Hag. i. 1–15), and the building was completed in the sixth year of his reign, i.e. 516 B.C. (Ezra vi. 15). It may be assumed that it stood on the site of Solomon's Temple and that it followed the same plan. It was built with huge stones with timber joists in the walls (Ezra v. 8); the height of the structure was 60 cubits and its width 60 cubits (Ezra vi. 3), but its length is not given. Like the earlier structure it contained a Holy of Holies and a Holy Place, separated not by a wall but by a veil or curtain (1 Macc. iv. 51). There were two courts—an outer court to which everyone was admitted, and an inner court which only Jews who were in a condition of levitical purity might enter (1 Macc. iv. 38, 48; ix. 54). According to Ben Sirach, the Temple was fortified by 'Simon the High priest, son of Onias' (probably Simon II, c. 225–200 B.C.). In material splendour the Temple was much inferior to that of Solomon. The aged people who remembered the first disparaged it. 'Who is left among you that saw the house in its former glory? How do you see it now? Is it not in your sight as nothing?' (Hag. ii. 3)

The Holy of Holies was empty, for the Ark had evidently been destroyed in 587 B.C. and no attempt had been made to construct a new one. The Holy Place contained the altar of incense, the seven-branched golden lampstand, the table for the shew-bread, various vessels and the curtain separating the Holy of Holies from the Holy Place. In the inner court stood the altar of burnt offering, made of unhewn stones (Ezra iii. 3; 1 Macc. iv. 44–47; cf. Exod. xx. 24).

In 167 B.C., Antiochus IV Epiphanes spoiled and desecrated the Temple, carrying away the sacred furniture and setting up a small altar to Zeus Olympius on the altar of burnt offering. Three years later, Judas Maccabaeus recaptured Jerusalem, tore down the polluted altar, built a new one with other unhewn stones according to the Law, rebuilt the sanctuary and refurnished it, and decorated the façade of the Temple with golden crowns and small shields. Finally, on December 25th, 164 B.C., the Temple was rededicated. 'There was very great gladness among the people, and the reproach of the Gentiles was removed' (1 Macc. iv. 58). With minor alterations and additions the Temple remained as the Maccabaeans left it until it was replaced by the magnificent edifice built by Herod the Great.

WORSHIP

The daily sacrifice (tamid) was offered in the morning and in the evening, or rather in mid-afternoon (Exod. xxix. 39–41; Num. xxviii. 4). At the beginning of the Christian era these times were the third hour (9 a.m.) and the ninth hour (3 p.m.). Before sunrise the priests, who wished to officiate at the morning service, repaired to the chamber Gazith in order to determine by lot those of their number who should officiate. First a priest was chosen by lot to remove the ashes from the altar of burnt offering and to put fresh wood upon it for the approaching sacrifice. This done, lots were drawn to decide who should slay the tamid, who should sprinkle the blood on the altar, who should remove the ashes from the altar of incense, who should trim the lamps, etc.—thirteen lots being drawn in all. At sunrise the lamb to be offered as the tamid was slain, nine priests taking part in the slaying and in the preparation of the victim. Then the officiating priests assembled in the chamber Gazith where the prescribed prayers, the Shema (Deut. vi. 4–9) and the Ten Commandments were recited. Following this, the priests repaired to the Holy Place where incense was burnt on the altar of incense, the worshippers without prostrating themselves in adoration and silent prayer. After the priestly blessing had been pronounced from the steps of the porch, the several parts of the tamid were laid upon the altar and consumed. The burnt-offering ('olah') was accompanied by a meal-offering ('minhah') and a drink-offering ('nesek'). During the offering a cymbal was struck and the choir of the Levites, accompanied by instrumental music, began the Psalm for the day. The Psalm was sung in three portions, and on the completion of each portion, the priests blew three blasts on their trumpets at which the people prostrated themselves and worshipped. With the close of the Psalm the public service ended.

The order of the evening service differed slightly from that of the morning service in that the incense was offered after the burning of the victim instead of before. The lamps, also, on the gold lampstand were lighted at the evening service.

There is no mention of Scripture reading followed by explanation and exhortation, but these doubtless had their place in the service. They seem to be referred to by Josephus in his Antiquities xvi. 43. 'And the seventh day we set apart from labour; it is dedicated to the learning of our customs and laws.'[1]

[1] A detailed description of the daily Temple service is given in the treatise *Tamid* of the Mishnah. Ben Sirach gives a glowing account of 'Simon, the high priest, son of Onias' clad in gorgeous apparel, performing the concluding acts of the service (Ecclus. i. 11–21).

Appendix A

OFFICIALS

High Priest. The High Priest was the spiritual head of the community. From the days of Zerubbabel onward he gradually acquired political authority until he became practically the secular as well as the spiritual head.

Sagan. The Sagan was next in rank to the High Priest. His duty was to maintain order in the Temple.

Priesthood. The Priesthood was divided into twenty-four courses or divisions. These courses took their turn in supplying the necessary members for the services of the Temple.

Singers. The Singers, who were divided into twenty-four courses, conducted the musical portion of the Temple service. They accompanied their singing with instrumental music. In the time of the Chronicler they were reckoned as Levites and traced their descent from Asaph, Heman and Jeduthun or Ethan (1 Chron. xxv. 1–6; cf. xv. 17, 19).

The Doorkeepers. The duty of the doorkeepers was to keep watch at the outer gates of the Temple. They daily set twenty-four watches under their respective chiefs at the four points of the compass around the Temple (1 Chron. xxvi. 1–19; cf. ix. 24–27). In the time of the Chronicler they were reckoned as Levites.

Treasurers. The treasurers had charge of the treasures of the house of God and of the stores of votive offerings (1 Chron. xxvi. 20–28). In the time of the Chronicler they were reckoned as Levites.

Officers and Judges. These managed the external affairs of the Jews (1 Chron. xxvi. 29–32). They probably collected taxes for both civil and ecclesiastical purposes from Jews living outside of Palestine proper.

APPENDIX B

HEBREW MUSIC

ORIGIN AND USES

THE art of music, both vocal and instrumental, was practised by the Hebrew from very early times. The author of Genesis iv. 21 credits Jubal, a descendant of Cain, with being 'the father of all those who play the lyre and pipe'. He may have had in mind the early Hebrew travelling players who were also metal workers and diviners, going from one place to another, playing and repairing as they went. The art, however, doubtless originated with their Semitic ancestors, the nomadic tribes of southern Arabia. Since archaeological research has shown that the Hebrews were influenced by the cultures of the surrounding nations, we can reasonably assume that their music would have affinities with that of Egypt, Babylonia and Assyria.

From ancient Egyptian inscriptions we learn that musicians occupied high positions at the court. Music, both vocal and instrumental, was used on festive occasions, the musicians being men who sang as they played, but they were often accompanied by women who danced as they sang. Music was also employed in religious worship and at the burial of the dead. They had a great variety of instruments, including the tambourine, double-headed drum, kettle-drum, sistrum, trumpet, lute and harp.

In Babylonia and Assyria there is abundant evidence to prove that music played an important part in the lives of the people. They believed that the gods could be worshipped and propitiated by the use of the human voice and musical instruments. Music was employed in the services of the Temple. As early as the nineteenth century B.C., the Babylonians in their religious worship had a complete liturgical service, consisting of from five to twenty-seven psalms, varied with musical interludes. In the course of time, female singers were added to the male, and the conduct of religious music became more elaborate. Since only the Temple officials kept records, we know a good deal about their sacred music but little about their secular music. The Assyrians borrowed largely from the Babylonians in the sphere of religion. During the period 1305–612 B.C. music became more prominent and minstrels were attached to the royal household. They not only performed for the royal household at banquets and on other occasions, but also gave public

Appendix B

performances. They had various kinds of musical instruments including the harp, trumpet, flute and drum.

In the Old Testament there are not many allusions to the music of the Hebrews, though it is clear that it played an important part in their lives, especially in religious worship. They sang unaccompanied and accompanied by musical instruments, often dancing at the same time. In the patriarchal age we find Laban reproaching Jacob with the words, 'Why did you flee secretly and cheat me, and did not tell me, so that I might have sent you away with mirth and songs, with tambourine and lyre' (Gen. xxxi. 27).

According to Philo, the Jewish philosopher of Alexandria, (c. 20 B.C.–A.D. 50), Moses was instructed in the sciences and in music by the Egyptian priests. Moses and the people of Israel celebrated in song the triumph of Yahweh over Pharaoh and his hosts at the Red Sea, while the women, headed by Miriam, celebrated it with a choral dance, beating the time with the timbrel (Exod. xv. 1–21). Deborah celebrated Israel's victory over the Canaanites in song.

> Hear, O kings; give ear, O princes;
> to the Lord I will sing,
> I will make melody to the Lord, the God of
> Israel.   (Jud. v. 3.)

The daughter of Jephthah went out to meet her father, 'with timbrel and with dances', on his return from his victory over the Ammonites (Jud. xi. 34). Samuel told Saul that as he approached Bethel he would meet 'a band of prophets coming down from the high place with harp, tambourine, flute and lyre before them, prophesying' (1 Sam. x. 5). Saul tried to kill David while he played the lyre before him (1 Sam. xviii. 10f.). David 'danced before the Lord with all his might' as the Ark was brought to Jerusalem 'with shouting, and with the sound of the horn' (2 Sam. vi. 14f.). As the prophet, Elisha, listened to the king's minstrel, 'the power of the Lord came upon him' and he prophesied (2 Kgs. iii. 15–19). Jehoshaphat appointed a band of singers to 'sing to the Lord and praise him in holy array as they went before the army' (2 Chron. xx. 21). That songs, accompanied by musical instruments, were employed at their sacred festivals and during the offering of the sacrifices may be inferred from the words of Amos.

> Take away from me the noise of your songs;
> to the melody of your harps I will not listen.
>   (Amos v. 23.)

After the fall of the Northern Kingdom in 722 B.C., the people of the Southern Kingdom retained their love of music. Hebrew musicians were considered worthy to play at the Assyrian court of Sennacherib (705–681 B.C.), as suggested by the account of his third campaign against Judah in 701 B.C., inscribed on the Taylor Prism. Hezekiah was compelled to pay a heavy tribute, part of which was 'his male and female musicians'. When the Jewish captives in Babylon were asked to sing one of the songs of Zion, they hung up their harps on the willows and wept, for they could not sing the Lord's song in a strange land (Ps. cxxxvii. 1–4). When the foundations of the Second Temple were laid, 'the priests in their vestments came forward with trumpets, and the Levites, the sons of Asaph, with cymbals to praise the Lord, according to the directions of David king of Israel' (Ezra iii. 10). In the days of Nehemiah the dedication of the wall of Jerusalem was celebrated 'with thanksgiving and with singing, with cymbals, harps and lyres' (Neh. xii. 27).

The Temple Music

The history of the Temple music, both vocal and instrumental, is obscure. Among the collections of Psalms we find two, one belonging to the Sons of Korah and the other to the Sons of Asaph, while two Psalms are associated with Heman and Ethan. The inference is that there were guilds of singers and that two of them at least had their own collections of Psalms. In the time of the Chronicler we find that there were three guilds of Temple singers, namely, those of the Sons of Asaph, Heman and Jeduthun, who is identified with Ethan (1 Chron. xxv. 1–6; cf. 1 Chron. xv. 17, 19). The Chronicler identifies their members with the Levites and traces their descent from Asaph, Heman and Jeduthun, who had been placed in charge of the music of the Temple by David (1 Chron. xxv. 1), and had officiated at the dedication of Solomon's Temple (2 Chron. v. 12–14). What happened to the sons of Korah, who had originally been 'in charge of the work of the service, keepers of the thresholds of the tent' (1 Chron. ix. 19), and had later become a guild of Temple Singers, as is shown by the Psalms assigned to them, we do not know, but they were probably merged with the guild of Heman, as 1 Chronicles vi. 33–37 and Psalm lxxxviii suggest.

David's part in the organization of the Temple music is in dispute. The current view among scholars is that the Chronicler projected into the past the conditions of his own age, and that the musical guilds were not formally organized until after the Exile. They allege that there is no definite evidence of a special class of singers in the pre-exilic period. It is true that the singers of the Asaph guild are mentioned among the returned exiles in Ezra ii. 41 and Nehemiah vii. 44, from which it might be inferred that the guild was pre-exilic, but the lists of returned exiles are of doubtful authenticity. Albright, however, maintains that there is no reason to question the historical accuracy of the Chronicler, who gave David the credit for organizing the guilds of Temple musicians, for the following reasons: (1) Music was very popular among the Canaanites from very early times and the Hebrews were

APPENDIX B

strongly influenced by it. It is known that singers were employed in the Temples of Ugarit (Ras Shamra) about 1400 B.C. as they were in Solomon's Temple in the tenth century B.C. (2) There is incontrovertible evidence of the antiquity of the Hebrew musical guilds. They can be traced back in some instances to musical families with Canaanite names, which are said to have flourished in the time of David. There are so many indications of David's musical prowess (1 Sam. xvi. 14–23; 2 Sam. vi. 5, 14) that 'scepticism would be thoroughly unwarrantable.'[1]

HEBREW MUSICAL INSTRUMENTS

The chief musical instruments were the following:

Stringed Instruments

Harp. (1) Heb. Kinnor. Probably a small portable lyre or harp. According to Josephus, it had ten strings. It was played with a plectrum (Job xxi. 12; Ps. cxxxvii. 2; Is. v. 12).

(2) Heb. Nebel. Probably a large harp. According to Josephus, it had twelve strings. It was usually played with the fingers (1 Sam. x. 5; Neh. xii. 27; Ps. xxxii. 2).

(3) Heb. Asor. A small instrument of ten strings (Ps. xxxiii. 3; cxliv. 9).

(4) Aram. Kathros. A lyre with four strings (Dan. iii. 5, 7).

Lute. See Harp: Nebel.

Psaltery. (1) Heb. Nebel. See Harp: Nebel.

(2) Aram. Psanterin. An instrument formed of strings tightly stretched by fixed pins and turning screws over a rectangular sounding board or box, and played by striking the strings with hammers (Dan. iii. 5, 7).

Sackbut. Aram. Sabbekha. A kind of harp, variously described as a large harp with many strings and a rich tone, and as a very small harp of high pitch (Dan. iii. 5, 7).

Viol. See Harp: Nebel.

Wind Instruments

Cornet. See Trumpet: Keren and Shophar.

Dulcimer. Aram. Sumponyah. A kind of bagpipe (Dan. iii. 5, 10, 15).

Flute. Aram. Mashrokitha. Variously described as a double flute, a set of Pan-pipes, and an organ. Probably a flute (Dan. iii. 5, 7, 10, 15).

Organ. Heb. Ugabh. Perhaps a bagpipe, or reeds or Pan-pipes (Gen. iv. 21; Ps. cl. 4).

Pipe. Heb. Halil or Chalil. Perhaps a mere tube with holes, played by blowing either into one end or into a hole at the side, or a reed played from a mouthpiece at one end. It was played in coming and going to the high

---

[1] W. F. Albright, *Archaeology and the Religion of Israel*, 1953, pp. 14, 125–128.

place (1 Sam. x. 5), in mourning (Jer. xlviii. 36) and in the festive processions of pilgrims (Is. xxx. 29).

Trumpet. (1) Heb. Keren. The primitive trumpet formed of a ram's horn (Josh. vi. 4; Jud. iii. 27; 1 Sam. xiii. 3). In Daniel iii. 5, 7, 10, 15 it is rendered 'cornet' in A.V. and R.V., and 'horn' in R.S.V.

(2) Heb. Shophar. A long ram's horn straightened by heat, used mainly to rouse warlike or religious enthusiasm (2 Kgs. xi. 14; 1 Chron. xv. 28; Ps. xcviii. 6). In 1 Chronicles xv. 28 and Ps. xcviii. 6 it is rendered 'cornet' in A.V. and R.V., and 'horn' in R.S.V.

(3) Heb. Hasoserah. A long straight metal trumpet used mainly for religious purposes (Num. x. 1–10; Lev. xxv. 8–11).

Percussion Instruments

Timbrel or Tabret. Heb. Toph. A small tambourine-like hand drum, used as a musical accompaniment to mark the rhythm (Gen. xxxi. 27; Exod. xv. 20; 1 Sam. x. 5; 2 Sam. vi. 5).

Cymbals. Heb. Mesiltaim, later Selselim. Of two shapes, one consisting of two flat plates which were clashed together, and the other consisting of two metal cones with short handles, one cone being brought down on top of the other. Used to mark the rhythm (1 Chron. xv. 16, 19, 28; Ezra iii. 10; Neh. xii. 27).

Castenets (or Sistra). Heb. Menaanim. Consisted of two thin metal plates through which were passed rods with loose metal rings at their ends (2 Sam. vi. 5).

Triangles or three-stringed instruments. Heb. Shelishim. Probably triangles, sistra or rattles with only three metal rods run through a bow with a handle (1 Sam. xviii. 6).[1]

CHARACTERISTICS OF HEBREW MUSIC

The music of the Hebrews was probably strident and noisy. We may assume, by analogy with the music of the modern nomadic Arabs, that its chief feature was rhythm and that the melody was secondary. Their melodies would be short, consisting of not more than two or three bars. As a melody was so short it would naturally be repeated again and again in a song. Though the music was, according to modern western standards, at least inharmonious, it appears to have had a powerful effect upon the emotions of the hearers. We read that when David played upon the lyre the evil spirit departed from Saul (1 Sam. xvi. 23), that the sound of the harp, tambourine, flute and lyre induced a state of ecstasy in the band of roving prophets and in Saul (1 Sam. x. 1–10), and that when a minstrel played before Elisha,

---

[1] For an account of Hebrew musical instruments see A. Z. Idelsohn, *Jewish Music in its Historical Development*, 1929, pp. 8–15; *Helps to the Study of the Bible*, O.U.P., 2nd ed., 1932, pp. 118–120; D. Stevens and A. Robertson, *The Pelican History of Music*, vol. I, 'Ancient Forms to Polyphony', 1960, pp. 105–107.

Appendix B

'the power of the Lord came upon him' (2 Kgs. iii. 14f.). Something of the splendour of the ancient Jewish music and its effect upon its hearers may be judged from the account of the dedication of the Temple written by the Chronicler. A hundred and twenty priests blew trumpets and the Levitical singers sang and sounded their instruments 'to make themselves heard in unison in praise and thanksgiving to the Lord, and when the song was raised, with trumpets and cymbals and other musical instruments, in praise to the Lord ... the house, the house of the Lord, was filled with a cloud, so that the priests could not stand to minister because of the cloud, for the glory of the Lord filled the house of God' (2 Chron. v. 11–14).

The music of a people does not remain unchanged from century to century, and that of the Hebrews would be no exception to the rule. Developments would naturally take place in the course of history.

APPENDIX C

THE SAMARITAN SCHISM

ORIGIN OF THE SAMARITANS

AFTER the fall of Samaria in 722 B.C., Sargon, the king of Assyria, transported many of its citizens to Mesopotamia and Media and introduced a new population to take their place (2 Kgs. xvii. 6, 24). Naturally, these foreigners introduced their native customs and beliefs, and together with others brought in later intermarried with the surviving Israelites. A sudden invasion of the territory by lions led them to think that the god of the land was angry, and they appealed to the king of Assyria, who despatched one of the captive priests to teach them 'the law of the god of the land'. He settled in Bethel and the result was a composite worship of Yahweh and foreign deities. 'So they feared the Lord but also served their own gods, after the manner of the nations from among whom they had been carried away' (2 Kgs. xvii. 33). The descendants of these people were called the Samaritans.

GROWTH OF JEWISH-SAMARITAN HOSTILITY

Hostility gradually developed between the Jews and the Samartians, becoming so bitter that Ben Sirach (c. 180 B.C.) places the latter lower than the Philistines and Edomites and refers to them contemptuously as 'the foolish people that dwell in Shechem' (Ecclus. l. 25f.). It is not easy to trace the history of that hostility with any certainty but it must have had its origin in some definite historical fact. The traditional view is that it had its roots in the impurities of race and religion introduced into the northern area by the intermarriage of foreigners, brought there from Mesopotamia and Media, with the surviving Israelites after the fall of Samaria in 722 B.C. It is more probable, however, that the hostility goes back to the time of the Hebrew conquest of Palestine and the years immediately following. There is evidence for thinking that the tribe of Judah did not take part in the main conquest, but were already in southern Palestine when that conquest took place. The lead in the conquest was taken by the tribe of Joseph, which settled in the northern hills; the tribe of Judah did not come into prominence until the time of David. The hostility may, therefore, have had its roots in the jealousy and resentment of Judah. In the reign of Solomon there are signs of antagonism between north and south, and on his death violent hostility broke out.

Appendix C

The ten northern tribes revolted and the kingdom split into two—the kingdom of Israel consisting of the ten northern tribes, and the kingdom of Judah consisting of the two southern tribes. The ostensible reason for the revolt of the ten northern tribes was the oppression of Solomon and the refusal of his son, Rehoboam, to reform the worst abuses of his father's reign. But this alone would apply as much to the south as to the north. It is quite clear, therefore, that hostility must have been brewing for a long time, and that Solomon's oppression gave the north an opportunity, which quite independently of royal oppression, they welcomed to break away from association with the south. Political separation naturally increased the bitterness between the divided kingdoms. It is true that there were occasional alliances and co-operation, but this was usually more or less due to the fact that one side was in the ascendant and was using some compulsion. The opposition throughout was purely political; there is no trace of either racial or religious antagonism.

From the fall of the Northern Kingdom to the close of the Exile there was no marked hostility between the Jews and the Samaritans. On the contrary, there is evidence of co-operation and friendliness (2 Kgs. xxiii. 15-20; 2 Chron. xxx. 18; xxxv. 17-19; Jer. xxxi. 4-6; Ezek. xxxvii. 15-28). On their return to Palestine in 538 B.C. the Jewish exiles settled down to cultivate the land. The Samaritans would naturally regard them with suspicion and dislike since they claimed land which they regarded as their own. According to the Chronicler, hostility showed itself immediately in connexion with the rebuilding of the Temple. The Samaritans approached the Jews with the request to share in the work on the ground that they worshipped the God of the Jews from the time they had entered the land. Their request met with a curt refusal by the Jews, presumably because they regarded the Samaritans as being of mixed race and religion. The refusal of the request caused bitter resentment, and in consequence the Samaritans, by active interference and misrepresentations to the Persian authorities, prevented the completion of the Temple until the reign of Darius I (Ezra iv. 1-5, 24). The two prophets, Haggai and Zechariah, who were contemporary with the events they describe, make no mention of any such interference. We must conclude, therefore, that the whole idea of Samaritan interference in the work of rebuilding the Temple is a fiction of the Chronicler who has allowed his hatred of the Samaritans to cloud his historical sense and his accuracy. The hostility between the Jews and the Samaritans in the post-exilic period did not break out in connexion with the rebuilding of the Temple.

The first clear and convincing evidence of Jewish-Samaritan hostility is seen in the repeated but vain efforts of the Samaritans to prevent the rebuilding of the city wall by Nehemiah. There is, however, good reason to believe that this hostility was purely political and personal. The Samaritans feared the revival of a rival province so close to them, and Sanballat did not welcome a rival governor in Judah, especially one who was a marked favourite of the Persian court. There is nothing to suggest that the hostility originated in racial and religious antagonism. It was not till Nehemiah's second visit to Jerusalem that the question of differences of race and religion between Jews and Samaritans began to appear. According to Nehemiah xiii. 1–3, the people separated from Israel all 'those of foreign descent'. This would include the Samaritans. This passage, however, does not form part of the original text; it has been added by the Chronicler and reflects his own prejudices. In Nehemiah xiii. 4–9 we have an account of Nehemiah's expulsion of Tobiah from the Temple. It seems likely that this was as much on personal grounds, because Tobiah had opposed him in the matter of the building of the city wall, as on the grounds that he was a Samaritan. In Nehemiah xiii. 23–31 we have an account of Nehemiah's prohibition of mixed marriages. His primary objection, however, is not that the Samaritans were of mixed race and religion, but that the children of these unions were forgetting their native tongue (xiii. 24). His chief reason for expelling the grandson of Eliashib, the High Priest, was probably not that he was a Samaritan, but that he had married the daughter of his political rival, Sanballat. Moreover he does not insist on the divorce of foreign wives but bans such marriages in future. Ezra goes further than Nehemiah in the matter of mixed marriages, and not only prohibited such marriages in future but also insisted that the Jews should divorce their foreign wives on the ground that they had broken the commandments of Yahweh by intermarrying with those who had made the land unclean with their abominations (Ezra ix. 10–15). Here the Samaritans are regarded as being religiously unclean.

We conclude that during the period 538–397 B.C. there was no deep racial and religious antagonism between the Jews and the Samaritans. The readiness of the Jews to intermarry and mix with the Samaritans is evidence of the friendly intercourse which must have existed between the two peoples. The letters of the Jewish community at Elephantine in Egypt to Bagoas, the governor of Judaea, and to the sons of the Samaritan governor, Sanballat, written during the period 410–408 B.C., do not reveal any deep cleavage between them. The fact that the Samaritans could accept the Pentateuch as canonical points to the same conclusion.

THE SCHISM

After the time of Nehemiah and Ezra the relations between the Jews and the Samaritans rapidly worsened, and finally the Samaritan congregation separated from Jerusalem and built their own Temple on Mount Gerizim. The date of separation is uncertain. The first certain date of the Samaritans as a separate community is 128 B.C. when John Hyrcanus destroyed the Samaritan Temple. Josephus, who, however, wrote several centuries after the event, states that it had been in existence for 200 years. If this is correct, the schism must have taken place about the middle of the fourth century B.C. We conclude that the schism was of gradual growth. Beginning with

Appendix C

hostility between north and south at the time of the conquest, it took definite shape in the Samaritan opposition to the building of the wall of Jerusalem, and gradually hardened until it culminated about the middle of the fourth century in the building of a separate Temple by the Samaritans on Mount Gerizim. The tradition that the Jewish-Samaritan hostility was caused by the impurities of race and religion, brought about by intermarriage between the northern Israelites and the deportees brought in from various parts of the Assyrian empire after the fall of the Northern Kingdom in 722 B.C., is a pure fiction.

The Jews regarded the Temple on Mount Gerizim with great hostility, because it was an avowed rival of their Temple in Jerusalem. The Samaritans claimed that their Temple was the only legitimate sanctuary of Yahweh, and to support their claim they tampered with the text of the Pentateuch, adding at the end of the Ten Commandments (after Exod. xx. 17) a passage ordering a Temple to be built on Mount Gerizim; and in Deuteronomy xvii. 4, substituting Mount Gerizim for Ebal as the place where the Law was to be inscribed and an altar built. From the time of the destruction of the Temple on Mount Gerizim the Jews and the Samaritans had no dealings with each other. In 108 B.C. Samaria was taken and destroyed by the sons of John Hyrcanus, and the territory of Samaria was incorporated in the Jewish state. In 63 B.C., when Pompey captured Jerusalem, the Samaritans regained their freedom under Roman suzerainty, their land forming part of the Roman province of Syria. Herod, a half-Jew, knowing that he would be likely to find support more readily among the Samaritans, favoured them. He rebuilt the city of Samaria, calling it Sebaste, and bestowed other favours upon them. The support given to Herod by the Samaritans was never forgotten or forgiven by the Jews, their hostility becoming so intense that they avoided the very soil on which the Samaritans trod.

APPENDIX D

PARTICULARISM AND UNIVERSALISM

PARTICULARISM

Definition

By particularism, as we meet with it in the Old Testament, is meant the belief that the Israelites were the chosen people of God and that salvation was offered to them alone. To the Israelites it came to imply their complete separation from the surrounding heathen nations.

Development

The religion of the Israelites is based upon a covenant, said to have been made on Mount Sinai between Yahweh on the one hand and the people on the other. The terms of the covenant are not known. Some scholars think that they are to be found in Exodus xxi–xxiii, and others that they are comprised in the Ten Commandments which we find in Exodus xx. 1–17. According to Jeremiah, the covenant consists of the simple statement, 'Obey my voice, and I will be your God, and you shall be my people; and walk in all the way that I command you, that it may be well with you' (vii. 23). Whatever the terms of the covenant may have been, the fact of the covenant remains without doubt. Henceforth, the Israelites were the people of Yahweh and He was their God. Until the Exile they seem to have had no thought of separating themselves from the surrounding heathen nations. In their conquest of Canaan they did not pursue a policy of extermination. It is true that following the custom of the early Semites they massacred the inhabitants of some towns like Jericho (Jos. vi. 15–21), Ai (Jos. viii. 24–26) and Lachish (Jos. x. 31), but they spared those of other towns, settling down among them, intermarrying with them and even worshipping their gods. 'So the people of Israel dwelt among the Canaanites, the Hittites, the Amorites, the Perizzites, the Hivites and the Jebusites; and they took their daughters to themselves for wives, and their own daughters they gave to their sons; and they served their gods' (Jud. iii. 5).

In the course of time, however, their attitude towards the heathen nations gradually changed. The belief in their election and the teaching of the prophets concerning the glorious future that awaited them at the close of the age, engendered in them a spirit of pride and a feeling of superiority over

Appendix D

other nations. The devoted followers of Yahweh and the ardent patriots among them feared, lest intermarriage might lead to the contamination and ultimately to the loss of their religion by the introduction of alien cults with their idolatrous worship and immoral practices, and of their national identity by the slow process of absorption. Moreover the thought that they, the chosen people of Yahweh, should be compelled to submit to foreign domination was a severe blow to their pride and made them hate their oppressors. Thus pride, fear and hatred turned their thoughts in the direction of separation. The Deuteronomic Code emphasizes the danger of having social and religious intercourse with the heathen nations. Moses is represented as ordering the complete extermination of the Canaanites. 'When the Lord your God brings you into the land which you are entering to take possession of it, and clears away many nations before you, the Hittites, the Girgashites, the Amorites, the Canaanites, the Perizzites, the Hivites, and the Jebusites, seven nations greater and mightier than yourselves, and when the Lord your God gives them over to you, and you defeat them; then you must utterly destroy them; you shall make no covenant with them, and show no mercy to them. You shall not make marriages with them, giving your daughters to their sons, or taking their daughters for your sons. For they would turn away your sons from following me to serve other gods' (vii. 1-4; cf. vii. 16; xx. 15f.). But as we have already indicated, the Israelites did not pursue a policy of extermination in their conquest of Canaan. The Deuteronomic Code reflects a later attitude towards the Canaanites and their religion.

Particularism may be said to have really begun in the exilic period, when the devoted followers of Yahweh and the ardent patriots among the exiles formed themselves into a close-knit society for the purpose of preserving their religion and their national identity. We are told that certain of the elders of Israel were accustomed to assemble in the house of Ezekiel 'to inquire of the Lord' (Ezek. xx. 1; cf. Ezek. viii. 1; xiv. 1). Stress was laid upon sabbath observance (Ezek. xx. 12-21; xxii. 8, 26; xxiii. 38), circumcision (Ezek. xliv. 6-9), and ritual cleanness (Ezek. iv. 14; xxii. 26) as marks of differentiation between Jews and Gentiles. In Ezekiel's New Jerusalem 'no foreigner uncircumcised in heart and flesh' was to be allowed to enter the sanctuary (Ezek. xliv. 9).

In the post-exilic period the policy of separation was pursued with ever-increasing vigour as the danger of losing their religion and their national identity grew. Nehemiah (445 B.C.) banned mixed marriages for the future (Neh. xiii. 23-31), and Ezra not only prohibited intermarriage but also insisted on the divorce of foreign wives already married (Ezra ix. 10-15, 44). The latter also enforced the strict observance of the Law (Ezra vii. 12-26; Neh. viii. 1-8). By these measures Nehemiah and Ezra raised an insurmountable barrier between Jews and Gentiles. From the days of these two reformers particularism became a powerful force in the life of the people.

Influence

Particularism led to the growth of the spirit of intolerance and hatred among the people, which is often revealed in their attitude towards the heathen nations whom they regarded as being outside the covenant and rejected by God. It is evident in some of the Psalms and especially in Esther. The author of Psalm lix declares that Yahweh holds all nations in derision (v. 8), and prays that he will consume them in His wrath, 'till they are no more, that they may know that God rules over Jacob to the ends of the earth' (v. 13). Esther simply breathes the spirit of intolerance and hatred. In the story an edict gave the Jews permission 'to gather and defend their lives, to destroy, to slay, and to annihilate any armed force of any people or province that might attack them, with their children and women, and to plunder their goods upon one day throughout all the provinces of King Ahasuerus, on the thirteenth day of the twelfth month, which is the month of Adar' (viii. 11f.). 'So', we are told, 'the Jews smote all their enemies with the sword, slaughtering and destroying them, and did as they pleased to those who hated them' (ix. 5). Particularism also led to the growth of an intense nationalism which ultimately resulted in the downfall of the state.

The influence of particularism, however, was for good as well as for evil, for it preserved Judaism from complete extinction. Had it never arisen in Babylonia the exiles 'would have been lost to history, and Deutero-Isaiah might never have heard of the faith he was so eager to propagate. And had not others practised it now, Judaism might have been overwhelmed'.[1]

UNIVERSALISM

Definition

By universalism, is meant the belief that salvation is offered to all mankind and not to one particular nation.

Development

Universalism was implicit in the faith of Israel long before any thought that Israel was charged with a mission to carry the religion of Yahweh to the nations arose. God is often represented as supreme not only over Israel, but over all mankind. In the story of the Creation and the Flood He is represented as the Maker of man and the Master of all men. In Genesis xii. 3 we find the words spoken by God to Abraham, 'I will bless those who bless you, and him who curses you I will curse; and by you all the families of the earth will bless themselves' (or, 'in you all the families of the earth will be blessed'). These words are generally taken to mean that Abraham will be so richly blessed that other nations will desire a similar blessing for themselves. Abraham, in fact, has been called to play an important role in the redemption

---

[1] H. H. Rowley, *The Missionary Message of the Old Testament*, 1945, p. 66.

of 'all the families of the earth'. In the account of Elijah's vision on Mount Horeb, Yahweh is represented as being supreme over Syria as well as over Israel (1 Kgs. xix. 9–18). Before the time of Amos it was confidently believed that Yahweh would scatter all the enemies of Israel and give His people great glory. Amos is the first to proclaim that Yahweh would punish both Israel and the surrounding nations for their sins (i, ii). Moreover he ascribes to Yahweh the rule over all the nations (ix. 7). Isaiah declares that Yehweh makes use of heathen nations to punish His people (x. 5f.). Assyria, too, will be punished for her over-weening pride in thinking that she gained her victories by her own strength (x. 12–16). Jeremiah teaches that Yahweh can build up a nation or destroy it according to His will (xviii. 6–10). It is but a short step from the belief that history is under the direction of Yahweh to the belief that all the nations will be saved to worship Him (Is. ii. 2f. and Mic. iv. 1f.; Is. xi. 9 and Hab. ii. 14; Zeph. iii. 9f.; Jer. iii. 17).[1]

In Deutero-Isaiah the doctrine of universalism is for the first time clearly and fully stated. Yahweh is the one and only God.

> Before me no god was formed,
>   nor shall there be any after me.
> I, I am the Lord,
>   and beside me there is no saviour.
>   (xliii. 10f. cf. xliv. 6.)

The reality of idols is denied (xl. 19f.; xli. 7; xlvi. 5–7) and scorn is poured upon the idol-maker (xliv. 9–20). Yahweh is God not only of Israel but of all nations.

> Turn to me and be saved,
>   all the ends of the earth!
> For I am God, and there is no other.
> By myself I have sworn,
>   from my mouth has gone forth in righteousness,
>   a word that shall not return;
> To me every knee shall bow,
>   and every tongue shall swear. (xlv. 22f.)

Deutero-Isaiah does not abandon the thought of Israel's election, Yahweh has chosen her that she might lead the nations to Him.

> I am the Lord, I have called you in
>   righteousness,

---

[1] The authorship and date of these passages is uncertain. Many scholars assign them to the post-exilic period.

> I have taken you by the hand and
> kept you;
> I have given you as a covenant to the people,
> a light to the nations,
> to open the eyes that are blind,
> to bring out the prisoners from the dungeon,
> from the prison those who sit in darkness. (xlii. 6f.)

Israel's mission to the nations is to be fulfilled not so much by active propaganda as by being truly the chosen people of Yahweh and by revealing His greatness by the manner of their lives. Deutero-Isaiah contains the conception of the Servant of Yahweh whose mission it is to convert the nations through his own endurance and undeserved suffering (xlii. 1–4; xlix. 1–6; l. 4–9; lii. 13–liii. 12). Despite his vision of a world-wide salvation, the author of Deutero-Isaiah proclaims to his people that the kings and queens of the world will bow down to them with their faces to the earth and lick the dust of their feet (Is. xlix. 23). In some of the later canonical works, the recognition of the universal worship of Yahweh involves the incorporation of the converted nations in Israel and the elevation of Jerusalem to the spiritual centre of mankind (Is. lvi. 6f.; lx. 10f.; Zech. viii. 20–23; Dan. ii. 44; vii. 27). There is little trace in them of any mission by Israel to the Gentiles.

The author of Jonah rises almost to the same lofty level as Deutero-Isaiah. He teaches that the love of God extends to all nations and even to animals (iv. 11). God is willing to receive and bless all those who repent of their evil ways and turn to Him (iii. 10). Israel is not called upon to convert the nations, though it is implied that it is only through Israel that the nations can be saved.

The prophet, Malachi, gives expression to a different conception of universalism. He reminds the unworthy priests of his day that from east to west Yahweh's name is great among the nations, and that in every place pure offerings are offered in His name (i. 11). He thus recognizes that all sincere worship, wheresoever and by whomsoever offered, is really offered to Yahweh. No mention is made of Israel's mission to the nations, or of the nations flocking to Jerusalem to worship in the Temple or even of the name of Yahweh.

We hear of proselytes to the Jewish faith. Such a proselyte was Ruth who said to her mother-in-law, Naomi, 'Your people shall be my people, and your God my God' (Ruth i. 16). In Trito-Isaiah we read that Yahweh will bring converted foreigners to His holy mountain and make them joyful in His house of prayer (Is. lvi. 6f.). Zechariah sees many nations coming to Jerusalem 'to seek the Lord of hosts in Jerusalem and to entreat the favour of the Lord' (viii. 21).

Appendix D

Influence

Universalism made little impact upon Judaism but its influence upon Christianity was profound. Christ, whose mind was steeped in the Scriptures, must have been familiar with the doctrine. He identified Himself with the Suffering Servant of Deutero-Isaiah (Mk. viii. 31, x. 45). Marvelling at the faith of a centurion, He said to His followers, 'I tell you, many will come from east and west and sit at table with Abraham, Isaac and Jacob in the kingdom of heaven' (Mk. viii. 11). In the parable of the Good Shepherd we read, 'And I have other sheep, that are not of this fold; I must bring them also, and they will heed my voice. So there shall be one flock, one shepherd' (Jn. x. 16). In the 'Third Gospel' and in its sequel, Acts, Luke endeavours to prove that Christ is the Saviour of the whole human race, and to trace the development of Christianity from being a Jewish sect to being a worldwide religion. Paul strove to break down the barriers between Jews and Gentiles. 'There is neither Jew nor Greek, there is neither slave nor free, there is neither male nor female; for you are all one in Christ Jesus' (Gal. iii. 28).

APPENDIX E

ZOROASTER AND ZOROASTRIANISM

Zoroaster: His Life

Of the life of Zoroaster, or to give him the Greek form of the name by which he is known to-day, Zarathustra, nothing definite is known; his existence as a historical person has been frequently challenged. According to sacred legend, he was conducted by an archangel into the presence of the god, Ahura Mazda, who conversed with him at length and revealed his law to him. Those who consider him a historical person describe him as a Mede or Persian who taught under a ruler of Bactria (east Persia) at whose court he had influential friends. He was a married man and had sons and daughters. We do not know when he lived; some authorities place him about 1000 B.C. and some about 800 B.C., while others make him contemporary with Buddha (563–483 B.C.) and Confucius (c. 551–479 B.C.). He appeared on the stage of history as the reformer of the earlier Persian religion, which goes back at least to the fifteenth century B.C., when its influence can be traced in Syria and Palestine. He was a man who had become possessed of a new vision of God which he felt compelled to announce to the world. His teaching exercised great influence both in Iran (Persia) and the surrounding countries. With his exalted ideals he is worthy to be reckoned among those 'prophets which have been since the world began'.

Zoroastrianism

The Sacred Books

The teaching of Zoroaster is preserved in the Zend Avesta (Zend = interpretation), a collection of sacred writings comprising the following parts:

(1) The Yasna: the principal liturgical book, in 72 chapters. It is divided into 3 sections, (1) the introduction (chs. 1–27), consisting mainly of invocations; (2) the Gathas (chs. 28–54), containing the discourses, exhortations and revelations of the prophet, and (3) the Later Yasna (chs. 55–72), consisting of invocations.

(2) The Vispered: a minor liturgical work, in 24 chapters. The word means 'all the chiefs' and refers to the spiritual companions of Ahura Mazda.

(3) The Vendidad: the priestly code.

APPENDIX E

(4) The Yashts: (i.e. Songs of Praise). Consists of invocations of divinities and angels, in 21 chapters.

(5) The Khorda Avesta (i.e. Little Avesta): a collection of shorter prayers designed for the use of priests and laymen, and adapted for the ordinary occurrences of daily life.

The Zend Avesta is only a fragment of a vast literature, the greater part of which perished under the Moslem rule and the tyranny of the Tartars. It was written in the language of ancient Bactria. Between the third and tenth centuries A.D. it was translated into the current Pahlavi and a running commentary added.

In its present form the Zend Avesta belongs to the Sassanian period but it is not of Sassanian origin. The books comprising the collection belong to various dates, some early and some late, but it is generally agreed that the Gathas are the oldest and that they are the work of Zoroaster himself. After the death of the prophet, his teaching was modified, added to and corrupted, so that it is now impossible to state definitely how much of his teaching is embodied in the later writings.

TEACHING

The Doctrine of God

There are two supreme gods in perpetual conflict, namely, Ahura Mazda (later Ormuzd) and Angra Mainyu (later Ahriman), the good and evil powers respectively.[1] Ahura Mazda dwells in light, He is the Lord of Wisdom, the strong and holy One, the all-seeing One, and the all-knowing One. To him is ascribed the creation of the world. He appointed the path of the sun and the stars, established the law by which the moon waxes and wanes, sustains the earth and the clouds so that they do not fall down, created the water and plants, yoked the thunder and the lightning to the wind and the clouds, made light, darkness, sleep and wakefulness, and morning, noon

[1] Opinions differ as to whether Zoroastrianism is a monotheism or a dualism. Many Parsee scholars to-day maintain that it has never been a dualism. Some Christian scholars assert that early Zoroastrianism was monotheistic but that in the course of time it degenerated and became dualistic. J. H. Moulton (*Early Zoroastrianism*, 1913, p. 126) can see no evidence whatever to justify the imputation of dualism. W. O. E. Oesterley (*Hebrew Religion*, rev. ed., 1952, p. 313) holds that Zoroaster taught belief in one God and that his teaching suffered deterioration afterwards, and that 'so far as Zoroaster himself was concerned he was a monotheist'. A. C. Bouquet (*Comparative Religion*, 1941, p. 80), agrees that the later Zoroastrianism is definitely dualistic, but he says, 'It is a serious mistake to treat Zoroastrianism as though it had been of this pattern from the beginning. From the Gathas it is clear that the doctrine of Zarathustra himself was a sublime and distinct monotheism, though below the Supreme Being are satellites or Amesha Spentas, who are of the nature of archangels, and if not exactly creatures, are at any rate inferior divinities, and receive no worship. Later, Persian religion also mentions the god, Mithras, as almost possessing equal honour with Ahuramazda. But it is fair to say that Zarathustra, himself, was as much a monotheist as the second Isaiah.'

and night. In the ethical world he is the creator of law, order and truth. In his struggle against Angra Mainyu he is supported by a host of good spirits (angels) and by a number of archangels, called the 'beneficent immortals' or 'immortal holy ones', (Amesha Spentas), the prototypes of the seven amshaspands of a later date. These are really aspects or attributes of Ahura Mazda that may find a place in the human heart. They are, (1) Vohu Mano, good sense, the principle that works in man inclining him to what is good; (2) Ashem (later Ashem Vahishtem), divine justice; (3) Khshathrem (later Khshathrem Vairim), the power and kingdom of Ahura Mazda; (4) Armaiti, reverence for the divine; (5) Haurvatat, perfection; (6) Ameretat, immortality. Other ministering spirits are Geush Urvan, the defender of animals, Sraosha, obedience, and Ashi, destiny.

Angra Mainyu (the Destroyer) dwells in darkness and is the creator of of all that is evil in the world—harmful animals, noxious weeds, filth, disease, death and the sin of man's heart. Just as Ahura Mazda is supported by a host of good spirits and a number of archangels, so he is supported by a host of evil spirits and a number of archdemons. He is regarded as subordinate to Ahura Mazda and doomed to ultimate extinction.

In the course of time the Amesha Spentas were raised to the rank of gods and new divinities were introduced, in particular, Verethraghna, the angel of victory, and Anahita, the goddess of water.

The Doctrine of Man

The object of the struggle between Ahura Mazda and Angra Mainyu is the soul of man. Man is the creation of Ahura Mazda who, therefore, has the right to call him to account. His supreme duty is the cultivation of good thoughts, good words and good deeds. All our information regarding Zoroastrianism reveals a strong moral element. Its followers looked upon lying as the greatest possible disgrace and getting into debt as the second greatest. That stress was laid upon morality of life may be seen from the Behistun inscription in which Darius I declares, 'On this account Ahura Mazda brought me help ... because I was not wicked, nor was I a liar, nor was I a tyrant, neither I nor any of my line. I have ruled according to righteousness.' The Gathas teach that evil cannot be undone, but may be counterbalanced by a surplus of good works. There is no place for repentance or pardon, or atonement. According to the later sacred writings, repentance, pardon and atonement are possible. Man is endowed with a free will and can choose between good and evil, but choose he must. By a true confession of faith, by his good thoughts, words and deeds, and by keeping pure his body and his soul he strengthens the power of goodness and establishes a claim for reward upon Ahura Mazda. By a false confession of faith, by evil thoughts, words and deeds, and by defilement he increases the power of evil and renders service to Angra Mainyu.

Appendix E

The Doctrine of The Future Life

After death the soul of the righteous or of the wicked as the case may be, lingers near the body in joy or in suffering for three days and three nights. At the dawn of the fourth day it awakens to consciousness of the new life amid a breath of balmy wind fragrant with scents and perfumes, or in the face of a foul, chill blast heavy with a sickening stench. The conscience in the form of a fair maiden or in that of an ugly old woman, then appears and conducts it to the Bridge of Decision (called Cinvat), where a court sits to judge it out of the Book of Life in which all men's thoughts, words and deeds are recorded. The court is presided over by Ahura Mazda, but three judges, Mithra, Sraosha and Rashnu give the decision in accordance with the will of the god. Every soul must cross the bridge, the righteous with the assistance of ministering angels or guided by the fair maiden and the wicked amid the howls of demons and tormenting fiends or led by the ugly old woman. The soul of the righteous finds the passage safe and easy, but to the soul of the wicked the bridge becomes thin as the edge of a razor, so that when half-way across it falls headlong into the depths of hell, there to remain in torment for ever. In the Gathas, the bridge leads to the abode of Ahura Mazda who dwells in the realm of light with all the faithful. In the later sacred writings the further fate of the righteous and the wicked soul unrolls in four stages. The soul of the righteous passes through the paradises of good thoughts, good words and good deeds in the regions of the stars, the moon and the sun respectively, and then enters into the place of 'Eternal Light', the 'House of Song'—the heaven where 'Ormuzd dwells in joy'. The soul of the wicked descends through three courts of evil thoughts, evil words and evil deeds to hell—the 'House of Falsehood', 'the House of the Worst Thought', 'the Worst Life', a place so foul and lonesome, that although the wicked souls are as many and numerous 'as the hairs on a horse's mane' each one reflects, 'I am alone'.

Zoroastrianism teaches the existence of a third place, Hamistaken, designed for those who are neither good nor bad in this life. It is an intermediate place between the earth and the region of the stars, where the soul suffers no other torment than the changes of heat and cold of the seasons, and where it dwells until the resurrection and the final judgment.

Zoroaster predicts the end of the present world order when Ahura Mazda will assemble all his hosts, break the power of evil for ever and establish the one undivided kingdom in heaven and earth. This is called 'the good kingdom' or simply 'the kingdom'. Here the sun will shine for ever, and all the faithful will live a happy life in eternal fellowship with Ahura Mazda and his angels.

In the later sacred writings we find references to the coming of a saviour, a general resurrection, a final judgment and personal immortality. At the close of the last millennium of the world a descendant of the prophet will come as 'Saoshyant' or 'Deliverer' to educate mankind to moral perfection. The dead will be raised, beginning with the first human beings and followed by the rest of mankind. The dead will assume their own bodies and each will recognize his family, relatives and friends. A great assembly of the risen dead will take place. In that assembly everyone will see his own good deeds and his own evil deeds, and the righteous will be separated from the wicked. The wicked will be cast into hell to be tortured for three days while the righteous will taste the joys of heaven. A flood of molten metal will engulf the earth and through it all men will pass and become pure. Cleansed and purified by this fiery ordeal, all, both the righteous and the wicked, will become immortal. Those who died as adults will be restored at the age of forty years and those who died when children at the age of fifteen years. Husband and wife will come together in heaven but there will be no more begetting of children. Angra Mainyu and his evil spirits will be destroyed by fire and the earth restored to its pristine purity. All men will then join in everlasting praise to Ahura Mazda and his archangels.

Throughout all the writings of Zoroastrianism runs the confident belief in the reward of the righteous and the punishment of the wicked, the triumph of goodness and the destruction of evil, the resurrection of the dead, and the advent of 'the good kingdom'.

Worship

The Zoroastrians had Temples and a sacerdotal system. There were no images for they were strictly forbidden. Artaxerxes II (404–358 B.C.) is said to have been the first to erect images of the goddess, Anahita, in Temples in various parts of his dominions about 398 B.C. There is, however, no mention of images of this kind in earlier times. Each Temple contained a fire-chamber, in which burned a sacred fire which was never allowed to die out, which no one might touch or sully with his breath. Fire was not worshipped as such but was merely a symbol of Ahura Mazda. The priests (Athravans, later Magi) formed a hereditary caste, the members of which were alone competent to offer sacrifices and to perform the rites of purification. They educated the young clergy, imposed the penances and exercised a spiritual guardianship and pastoral care of the laity.[1]

[1] For an account of Zoroastrianism see J. W. Waterhouse, *Zoroastrianism*, 1934, and R. C. Zaehner, *The Dawn and Twilight of Zoroastrianism*, 1961.

APPENDIX F

THE INFLUENCE OF PERSIA UPON THE JEWS

THE FOUNDING, ORGANIZATION AND ADMINISTRATION OF THE EMPIRE

In the days of Nebuchadrezzar (605–562 B.C.) two powerful empires, the Median and the Lydian, existed to the east, north and north-west of Babylon, with the river Halys the agreed boundary between them. In 553 B.C. Cyrus, king of Anshan, who had already made himself master of Elam, revolted against his overlord, Astyages, king of Media, and by about 550 B.C. had captured his capital, dethroned him and united the Medes and the Persians under his sway. By 546 B.C. he had captured Sardis, the capital of Lydia, and taken the king, Croesus, prisoner. In 539 B.C. he defeated the Chaldean forces and entered Babylon without opposition. In 525 B.C. his son, Cambyses (530–522 B.C.), conquered Egypt. The organization of this vast empire was undertaken and completed by Darius I (522–486 B.C.). He ruled Egypt and Babylonia directly as king and divided the rest of the empire into twenty satrapies or provinces, each under a satrap or governor—a development of the earlier Assyrian provincial system. Aramaic was made the official language of government, a stamped coinage was introduced throughout the empire, a fleet was organized and a canal dug between the Nile and the Red Sea to provide a sea route between Egypt and Persia.

Under the Persian rule the subject nations enjoyed a considerable measure of self-government as long as they paid their taxes and furnished recruits for the king's forces. The Assyrian and Babylonian policy of deporting subject peoples and suppressing their religions was reversed by Cyrus. The people deported by the Assyrians and Babylonians were as far as practicable restored to their homes, and the images of the gods brought to the capital by the last Babylonian king were restored to their shrines. He issued a decree ordering the restoration of the Temple in Jerusalem and permitting the Jewish exiles to return. His policy was continued by his successors. Cambyses respected the religious traditions of the Egyptians and where necessary restored them. He ordered that the foreign elements which had found their way into the shrine of the goddess, Neith, should be removed, that the divine property should be given to her and to the great gods of Sais as of old, and that all the customary festivals and processions should be celebrated. In 419 B.C. Darius II (423–404 B.C.) issued a decree ordering the Feast of the Passover to be held by the Jewish community in Elephantine. The organization and administrative system established by Darius I survived with minor changes until the conquest of Persia by Alexander the Great.

PERSIAN INFLUENCE UPON THE JEWS

On Administration

Although the Jewish captives in Palestine were allowed to return they were not given their independence. The land was ruled by a governor appointed by the Persian king, who might be a member of their own race, like Zerubbabel or Nehemiah, or himself a Persian. The general policy of the Persian government shows that they enjoyed a considerable measure of self-government. The Persian administration seems to have been on the whole benevolent, if sometimes careless. The governor's main concern was with the preservation of order and the collection of taxes for the imperial exchequer. Provided order was maintained and taxes were paid he took little interest in the life of the community. In the absence of a king the priesthood grew in dignity and power. The prophets, Haggai and Zechariah, speak of Joshua, the High Priest, as though he was the equal of Zerubbabel (Hag. i. 14; ii. 1–9; Zech. iii; iv. 11–14; vi. 9–15). In the course of time the High Priest became virtually, and in some cases officially also, the sacerdotal head of the Church and the secular head of the state. Judah had the right to strike its own coins, which were mostly imitations of Athenian coins but with the addition of the inscription 'Yehud' (i.e. Judah).

On Language

The use of Aramaic as the official language by the Persian government led to its spread throughout Palestine. It is sometimes mistakenly thought that the Jewish exiles in Babylon forgot their native language and adopted Aramaic, which they introduced into Palestine on their return. During the period of the Assyrian and Babylonian empires, Aramaic was the language of trade and diplomacy in Mesopotamia. The introduction into Palestine of foreigners 'from Babylon, Cuthah, Arva, Hamath and Sepharvaim' (2 Kgs. xvii. 24), to whom Aramaic was a familiar language, by the Assyrian king after the fall of Samaria in 722 B.C., provided a powerful stimulus to the spread of that language. From this time onwards bilingualism in the north was probably common. At the close of the eighth century B.C. the people in the south were unacquainted with Aramaic (2 Kgs. xviii. 26) but gradually the language began to spread from the north to the south. When the Jewish exiles returned from Babylon, they probably found the majority of the 'people of the land' were bilingual. For some time Hebrew continued to be used as the medium of expression, but Aramaic continued to spread and finally superseded Hebrew as the language of daily intercourse. In the Maccabaean period Hebrew as a spoken language was almost dead, but it survived and even developed in the schools and among the learned. The Hebrew script of pre-exilic times was replaced by the form of the square characters which was adapted from the Aramaic.

On Judaism

It was not till the Greek period that Persian influence began to play a part in shaping Jewish thought, that is, after the Persian empire had passed away. This was partly because few new Jewish works were produced in the Persian period, and partly because the conquest of the East by Alexander the Great (332–323 B.C.) tended to break down racial barriers so that Persian ideas spread westwards into Palestine. The Persian religion, Zoroastrianism, must have influenced Judaism, because it possessed certain features which reminded the Jews of similar features in their own religion. These were (1) a tendency towards dualism, (2) a tendency towards the formation of organized angelic and demonic hierarchies, and (3) a developing belief in the last judgment and in rewards and punishments after death.[1]

The influence of Zoroastrian dualism can be traced in the apocalyptic writings in which we find the conception of two worlds, namely, a world of righteousness under the rule of God and a world of evil under the lordship of Satan. These two worlds are in perpetual conflict. Dualistic conceptions can be found in 4 Ezra, 1 Enoch, 2 Enoch, The Testaments of the Twelve Patriarchs, The Book of Jubilees and The Assumption of Moses.

The Jews never allowed dualism to destroy their faith in one God. The mystery of evil was not to be explained by blaming a second deity—a god of evil. Deutero-Isaiah, for example, insists that Yahweh alone is the responsible Creator of the world with its light and darkness, its good and evil.

> I form the light and create darkness,
> I make weal and create woe,
> I am the Lord, who does all these things.
> (Is. xlv. 7.)

Dualism gradually decreased in importance in late Judaism and seems to have been rejected by rabbinical circles.

On Angelology and Demonology

The Jews were influenced by the Persian religion, Zoroastrianism, in the spheres of angelology and demonology. From early time they believed in

[1] W. F. Albright, *From the Stone Age to Christianity*, 2nd ed., 1957, p. 361.

good and evil spirits, who came to be called angels and demons or devils. The former were spiritual beings, who were endowed with immortality and dwelt in heaven; the latter were the offspring of the sons of God and the daughters of men, who dwelt upon the earth and brought evil upon it. Prior to the publication of Daniel (c. 167–164 B.C.), Jewish angelology and demonology were inchoate and unorganized. As regards angels they were not divided into orders, nor did they receive personal names or perform definite functions, except in the case of the Satan (the Adversary), who, before he became the embodiment of evil, was one of the sons of God who was entrusted with the task of observing the doings of men and opposing their claims to righteousness in the heavenly court (Job i. 6–12; ii. 1–7; Zech. iii. 1–3). In Daniel, personal names are given to angels and particular functions are assigned to them for the first time. Reference is made to the angel Gabriel (viii. 16; ix. 21) and Michael (x. 13,2 of.; xii. 1). Gabriel interprets Daniel's visions while Michael is the guardian angel of Israel. Since the latter is called 'one of the chief princes' (x. 13) and as 'the great prince who has charge of your people', it would appear that he belonged to a special group in the heavenly hierarchy, thus showing that by this time angels had been divided into orders. In 1 Enoch ix. 1–4 two more angels are mentioned, namely, Uriel and Raphael, and they are implored to act as mediators between God and man. In 1 Enoch xx. 1–8 three more angels are mentioned, namely, Raguel, Saraqâêl and Remiel. 'And these are the names of the holy angels who watch. Uriel, one of the holy angels, who is over the world and over Tartarus. Raphael, one of the holy angels, who is over the spirits of men. Raguel, one of the holy angels, who takes vengeance on the world of the luminaries. Michael, one of the holy angels, to wit, he that is set over the best part of mankind and over chaos. Saraqâêl, one of the holy angels, who is set over the spirits who sin in the spirit. Gabriel, one of the holy angels, who is over Paradise, and the serpents, and the Cherubim. Remiel, one of the holy angels, whom God set over those who rise.' These seven archangels are doubtless to be identified with the Amesha Spentas of Zoroastrianism.[1]

As regards demons, there developed the conception of a host of evil spirits under the command of a sovereign prince who is variously called Satan, Mastema, Azazel, and Beliar or Belial. Some of these evil spirits had names such as Asmodeus (Tobit iii. 8, 17), and those listed along with their leader, Semyaza, in 1 Enoch vi. 7. Their function was to tempt men and lead them into sin, and to oppose the purposes of God.

On Eschatology

Opinions differ regarding the influence of Persia on Jewish eschatology. Oesterley, for example, traces the doctrine of the resurrection to the influence

---

[1] The number of archangels varies from four to seven.

APPENDIX F

of Zoroastrianism.[1] Rowley finds it difficult to accept the theory on the ground that the doctrine is so different in Daniel, in which it is most clearly stated, and in Zoroastrian sources. In the former there is no idea of a universal resurrection such as is found in Zoroastrianism, but only of a selective resurrection. He thinks it more satisfactory to find its origin in the writer's own faith than in this foreign source.[2] Many scholars hold that the conceptions of the division of the history into world periods, the last judgment, and the destruction of the world by fire were taken over from Zoroastrianism.

INFLUENCE OF PERSIAN RULE ON JUDAISM

The two centuries or thereabouts of Persian rule were of the greatest importance to Judaism. This was in no way due to the influence of Zoroastrianism on Judaism, for its influence was not felt until the Greek period and then not to any appreciable extent until the second century B.C. The importance of Persian rule lay in the fact that for about 200 years the Jews enjoyed comparative peace and security, which gave them an opportunity, of which they took full advantage, to develop their religion. They rebuilt the Temple and reorganized its worship, made Jerusalem the religious centre of Jewry, and by prohibiting intermarriage with foreigners and by enforcing the strict observance of the Law, preserved their religion and made the Jews 'the people of a Book'. It was in this period that Judaism acquired the form which has persisted in its essentials down to the present day. Had they not been allowed to return, they would probably have been absorbed by the Babylonians and lost to history. One of the most important things that we owe to the Persians, therefore, was the restoration of the Hebrews to Palestine. 'The Persians thus saved and aided in transmitting to us the great legacy from Hebrew life, which we have in the Old Testament and in the life of the Founder of Christianity.'[3]

---

[1] W. O. E. Oesterley, *Hebrew Religion*, rev. ed., 1937, pp. 395f.
[2] H. H. Rowley, *The Faith of Israel*, 1955, pp. 161, 167f.
[3] J. H. Breasted, *The Conquest of Civilization*, 1926, p. 232.

APPENDIX G

HELLENISM: Its Diffusion throughout the Near East and its Influence upon the Jews

THE GREEK SPIRIT

HELLENISM (or Greek culture), which is the sum total of Greek achievement, is the creation of the Greek spirit, which in turn is the product of the Greek character. The Greek spirit is more easily felt than defined, but we shall not go far astray if our definition takes the form of an enumeration of the chief attributes of the Greeks.

The Greeks were a people who recognized the importance of the individual. In their view he was capable of almost unlimited development, and it was one of their chief aims to discover ways and means of helping him to realize his true potential and to attain the fullest and richest life possible. Hence, they have been rightly called 'humanists', though this designation does not imply that they were humanitarians, for they did not believe in equality or in the inherent sanctity of all life.

Appreciation of the importance of the individual led to an intense love of freedom—freedom not only of body, but also of thought and expression. Perhaps the greatest achievement of the Greeks was the cultivation of the art of thinking. They combined intense curiosity about the nature of things with a firm belief in their own powers of observation and deduction. Their individualism was tempered by a sense of obligation to the community, though it was not so much a case of social conscience as of enlightened self-interest. Unfortunately, however, their sense of obligation to the community often stopped short at the borders of their own city.

The logical corollary to the two ideals of individual freedom and a harmonious social order was democracy. Democracy, however, was never complete. Society was founded upon slavery; foreigners were denied citizenship, and women were disenfranchised, that is, they could not attend the Assembly or hold office.

The Greeks were enthusiastic in their pursuit of Truth. Their chief concern was with man, with the origin and nature of the universe, and with ultimate reality. In their pursuit of Truth they tried to see life steadily and to see it whole, and to describe what they saw in language or in marble without passion and without prejudice.

APPENDIX G

Another attribute of the Greeks was their sensitiveness to beauty. It was a beauty which did not lie in lavish ornament but in the very essence and structure of the object made. Beauty is a characteristic of all Greek art, whether it be a poem, or a vase, or a statue or a Temple. The beauty of their Temples has been called 'frozen music' and 'beauty as seen by the light of eternity'.

Along with a sense of beauty went a love of simplicity. To the Greeks life meant 'plain living and high thinking'. Their towns were small, their houses unpretentious, their dress simple and their diet monotonous. Simplicity was a characteristic of all their works of art. In their literary works there is a strict economy of words, much being left to the imagination of the reader. Their Temples are not lavishly decorated or luxuriously appointed, but are marked by dignity and restraint.

Finally, the Greeks were filled with zest for life. For them to be alive was bliss, for they believed that the best was yet to be and that nothing was impossible to the adventurous spirit. Their great masterpieces have a rare vitality which gives them permanence and endows them with immortality.

It should not be forgotten that there was a dark side to the character of the Greeks. It would seem that they combined artistic and intellectual genius with a large element of savagery. 'Many of them', says Sir Gilbert Murray, 'were sunk in the most degrading superstitions; many practised unnatural vices; in times of great fear some were apt to think that the best "medicine" was a human sacrifice. After that it is hardly worth mentioning that their social structure was largely based on slavery; that they lived in petty little towns, like so many wasps nests, each at war with its next-door neighbour, and half of them at war with themselves.'[1]

THE SPREAD OF HELLENISM THROUGHOUT THE NEAR EAST

Hellenic culture was known in the Near East long before the time of Alexander. Greek traders were familiar in the Near East from the early seventh century, if not earlier. In the sixth century B.C. the coasts of Syria and Palestine were dotted with Greek ports. About 500 B.C. Ionian, Carian and Lydian craftsmen were summoned to Susa (Shushan) by Darius I to decorate the royal palace. In the fifth century B.C. the Near East was flooded with Greek adventurers, mercenaries, scholars and tradesmen, among whom were learned men like Herodotus and Xenophon. 'From the standpoint of material civilization Alexander's conquest only intensified and organized a movement which was already under way.'[2]

Alexander was an enthusiastic supporter of Greek culture believing implicitly in its superiority. In his youth he had been a pupil of Aristotle,

---

[1] Sir Gilbert Murray, Article on 'The Value of Greece to the World' in *The Legacy of Greece*, ed. by R. W. Livingstone, 1921, p. 14.
[2] W. F. Albright, *From the Stone Age to Christianity*, 2nd ed., 1957, p. 338.

the greatest thinker of his age. His imagination was nourished on Homer: his court and camp were the scenes of athletic and dramatic festivals. When he captured and destroyed Thebes he spared the house of Pindar, the great Greek lyric poet. His policy was to break down all racial barriers and to bring about the union of East and West. After his conquest of the Persian empire, he adopted Persian state, dress and customs, compelled thousands of his soldiers to marry eastern wives, married an eastern princess himself, incorporated Persians in his army, trained their youth in Greek culture, promoted their nobility in his service and recognized the religion of conquered peoples. Realizing this policy of fusion must rest upon an economic basis, he fostered trade and commerce, linking the Nile, the Tigris and the Indus with the Mediterranean Sea. At important points on his lines of communication he built towns like Alexandria in Egypt and transferred Greek colonists to them. These towns embodied the chief features of Greek life, such as theatres, amphitheatres, baths and gymnasia, and were not only centres of trade, but also of Greek culture. Men everywhere learnt Greek, which became a universal language.

At the death of Alexander his vast empire, which stretched from the Adriatic to the Indus and from the Caspian Sea to Upper Egypt, collapsed, and his generals fought for the inheritance. The Punjab soon recovered its independence. Ptolemy I Soter (323–285 B.C.) occupied Egypt immediately on the conqueror's death, Macedonia with the suzerainty over Greece eventually fell to Lysimachus and parts of Asia Minor, Syria and Babylonia to Seleucus I Nicator (312–280 B.C.). Ptolemy I Soter founded the museum at Alexandria, which was both a library and a place of study, and attracted the foremost scholars of the day to his court including Zeno, the founder of the Stoic school of philosophy, Epicurus, the founder of the Epicurean school of philosophy, the geometrician, Euclid, the geographer, Eratosthenes, and the mathematician and engineer, Archimedes. His example was more or less followed by Seleucus and his descendants. Many cities were founded and schools established throughout their dominions; lecturers travelled everywhere teaching as they went; books were cheap and multiplied. Thus, the Ptolemies and the Seleucids threw open the world to Greek culture.

INFLUENCE OF HELLENISM UPON THE JEWS

After the conquests of Alexander, Palestine became part of the Hellenistic world and Greek colonists built cities in many districts, especially on the western seaboard, in Galilee, and in the region east of the Jordan. These cities became centres of Greek culture, and it was inevitable that the Jews should feel its influence. At the same time the peculiar genius and character of the Jews were such as to reduce that influence to a minimum. With them tradition was strong and new ideas were not easily accepted. Moreover in spite of the universalistic trend which developed in such writers as Deutero-

Appendix G

Isaiah and the author of Jonah, the whole genius and emphasis of the Jews centred in exclusiveness and separation. They were God's chosen people, and the Gentiles were aliens, outside the covenant. Hence, the influence of Greek culture which was readily accepted by most peoples, met with strong resistance among the Jews. Nevertheless, that influence was so powerful that they could not wholly resist it.

The Greeks do not seem to have imposed their system of government on Palestine. The Greek system was that of the city state, the city being the civic centre of the surrounding districts and the government an annually elected representative council. The Jews did not adopt the Greek system of government but they were undoubtedly influenced by the conciliar idea. From the days of old the large towns of Palestine had formed centres of political life. Under the influence of Hellenism new towns were founded and both these and the older communities were made the basis of the political organization of the country in a far more thorough manner than before.[1]

The influence of the Greek gymnasium had a profound effect upon the young Jewish manhood. In 1 Maccabees i. 11–15 we read, 'In those days (i.e. in the days of Antiochus Epiphanes) lawless men came forth from Israel, and misled many saying, "Let us go and make a covenant with the Gentiles round about us, for since we separated from them many evils have come upon us". This proposal pleased them, and some of the people eagerly went to the king. He authorized them to observe the ordinances of the Gentiles. So they built a gymnasium in Jerusalem, according to Gentile custom, and removed the marks of circumcision, and abandoned the holy covenant. They joined with the Gentiles and sold themselves to do evil.' From 2 Maccabees iv. 9–11 we learn that Jason offered Antiochus Epiphanes a bribe of 440 talents for the office of High Priest, and a further 150 talents 'if permission were given to establish by his authority a gymnasium and a body of youth for it, and to enrol the men of Jerusalem as citizens of Antioch' and that 'when the king assented and Jason came to office, he at once shifted his countrymen over to the Greek way of life.'

Greek influence is perhaps more definitely seen in the sphere of literature. This influence is apparent in both form and content, that is, in the use of the Greek language and in the spread of Greek thought. The Greek language, in its colloquial form (called the Koine) spread throughout the Mediterranean world and was superior to the Hebrew as a medium of expression. It is probable that many Jews in Palestine, especially those belonging to the educated classes, were bilingual, while all the Jews of the Dispersion spoke Greek and used in their synagogues the Septuagint—the Greek translation of the Old Testament Scriptures, made in Alexandria. A large number of Hebraized Greek words found their way into the language of the Jews. According to some scholars, the influence of Greek thought can be traced in

---

[1] W. O. E. Oesterley and T. H. Robinson, *A History of Israel*, 1932, p. 180.

Proverbs, Job and Ecclesiastes. From the middle of the third century B.C. to about A.D. 100 a new Jewish literature sprang up, written in Greek to commend Greek thought to the Jews and to commend Judaism to the Greeks and the wider world. The writer of the third book of *The Sibylline Oracles* has clothed his work in a Greek dress in order to commend Judaism to the Greek world. The object of 4 Maccabees is to show that Greek philosophy is really implicit in the Mosaic Law. The Greek philosopher, Philo, was steeped in Greek philosophy and sought in all his work to harmonize Greek and Hebrew thought.

In the sphere of religion Greek influence was not great. It is probable that the spectacular element in Greek religion—its ritual and its shows and processions—appealed to many Jews, and tended to loosen the ties which bound them to their ancestral faith. In the realm of thought some influence can be traced. In particular, the belief in the immortality of the spirit, as distinct from the hitherto characteristic Jewish belief in the resurrection of the body, came into Judaism from Greek thought. The writer of The Wisdom of Solomon teaches that the soul is immaterial and pre-existent, and that each soul, when born into the world receives a body appropriate to its quality (viii. 20). The body is the prison-house of the soul (ix. 15); at death the soul is released from its prison and the righteous pass to an immediate reward (iv. 7–15). It was the attempt to harmonize the Jewish belief in the resurrection of the body, with the Greek belief in the immortality of the spirit which led to the postulate of an intermediate state in which the body underwent a process of purification. Glasson holds that (1) it is possible that Enoch's journeys into the underworld and through unknown places of the universe, as related in 1 Enoch, were suggested by similar stories of Greek heroes, and that 1 Enoch i–xxxvi could be regarded as the Jewish Nekyia (i.e. accounts of visits to the realm of the dead); (2) the divisions of Sheol and the pictorial elements as they relate to the remote parts of the earth and to the rewards and punishments correspond to similar Greek conceptions; (3) the Orphic conception of transmigration may have been a contributory element in the development of the Jewish doctrine of immortality; (4) the conceptions of the intermediate state and of the conditions after death follow the same pattern among the Greeks and the Jews; (5) there is a similarity between the Greek and Jewish teaching concerning the supernatural beings and the fate and functions of fallen angels; (6) some of the details in the Jewish teaching concerning this age and the age to come may well be derived from Greek sources and from eastern lore mediated through Hellenism.[1]

[1] T. F. Glasson, *Greek Influence in Jewish Eschatology*, 1961.

APPENDIX H

THE LAW

DEFINITION

The word 'law' in the English Bible is the translation of the Hebrew word 'torah' which occurs over 200 times in the Old Testament. The latter word is derived from a verbal root (yarah) meaning 'to throw' or 'to fling', and was used of the casting of lots by which the divine will was determined (Jos. xviii. 6; 1 Sam. xiv. 42). Hence, originally, the noun 'torah' was applied to a decision given by lot, and later to the oral instruction given by the priest or the prophet in the name of Yahweh in response to a particular question posed by the people or by an individual (Is. i. 10; Mic. iii. 11). The term was also applied to the decisions of judges. For example, the prophet and law-giver, Moses, gave 'toroth' (plural of 'torah') in the desert (Exod. xviii. 16, 19) and a court of appeal was established at Jerusalem in later days (Deut. xvii. 8-11; cf. 2 Chron. xix. 8-10).

The term 'torah' was translated 'nomos' = law in the Septuagint, from which it passed into the English Bible. The translation, however, is misleading since it implies that Israel was bound to Yahweh in a relation which was adequately expressed by strict obedience to a code of laws. 'Torah' includes not only ordinances which must be obeyed, but also the whole content of Yahweh's revelation of His nature and purpose.

In the course of time the teaching of the priests and the prophets, and the decisions of the judges were committed to writing, codified and embodied in the Pentateuch, which became known as the 'Torah'.

AUTHORSHIP

According to an ancient Jewish tradition, the 'Torah' was revealed by Yahweh to Moses on Mount Sinai and the latter committed it to writing. The tradition was almost universally accepted by Christians down to the eighteenth century A.D. To-day, however, all competent biblical scholars among Protestant Christians reject the tradition on the following grounds:

(1) The book makes no claim to Mosaic authorship. Moses is only said to have written certain passages (Exod. xvii. 14; xxiv. 4, 7; xxxiv. 27; Num. xxxiii. 2), the laws of Deuteronomy (cf. xxxi. 9), and the Song of

Moses (Deut. xxxi. 19). These passages are not proof of authenticity, but only witness to a tradition the correctness of which cannot be verified.

(2) There are many cases of disagreement in the narratives (e.g. Gen. i–ii. 4a and Gen. ii. 4b–25).

(3) Many of the laws of Deuteronomy differ somewhat from those given on the same subject in the earlier books (e.g. Deut. xii. 14 and Exod. xx. 24; Deut. xvi. 15 and Lev. xxiii. 36; Deut. xviii. 7 and Exod. xxviii. 1).

(4) There are passages which were obviously written long after the entry into Canaan (e.g. Gen. xxxvi. 20–31; Exod. xvi. 35; Deut. xxxiv. 10).

(5) Discrepant statements are found in the use of the divine names (e.g. Exod. vi. 2f. and Gen. xv. 2, 8 and xvi. 2; xxiv. 31).

(6) There are different conceptions of God (e.g. Gen. ii. 4b–25 and Gen. i–ii. 4a; Exod. xxxiii. 11; Deut. iv. 12).

(7) Moses is constantly referred to in the third person and often in eulogistic terms (e.g. Num. xii. 3). Further, Deuteronomy closes with an account of his death and burial (xxxiv. 5–12).

(8) There are marked differences of style in various parts of the Pentateuch. Deuteronomy is marked by a rhetorical and hortatory style. In the other parts of the Pentateuch there are many passages marked by a formal and repetitious style, and others by great simplicity.

Thus we see that the Pentateuch is not the work of a single author or of a single age. It grew by a process of accretion extending over several centuries. It contains a vast body of law which is largely the work of the priests of exilic and post-exilic periods of Israel's history. That this contains a certain amount of early material, some of it going back to the time of Moses, is fairly certain, but it is impossible to distinguish early and late material with any degree of accuracy. Moses was doubtless a legislator, but what laws are to be attributed to him it is impossible to say. According to Bentzen, it is impossible to trace one single element of the law in its present form back to him. Some scholars ascribe to him a portion of the Covenant Code and the two decalogues (in their original form).[1]

SOURCES

Many scholars accept the following documents as sources of the Pentateuch:

(1) The Yahwistic (Jehovistic) document, known as J (c. 850 B.C.).

(2) The Elohistic document, known as E (c. 750 B.C.).

(3) The Deuteronomic Code, known as D (c. 621 B.C.).

(4) The Priestly Code, known as P (late exilic and early post-exilic period).

To these, some scholars, notably Pfeiffer, add a non-Israelite source in Genesis, called S, or Seir, from its place of origin.

---

[1] A. Bentzen, *Introduction to the Old Testament*, vol. I, 1948.

APPENDIX H

COMPILATION

The process of compilation of the sources is a matter of conjecture since there is no record of it. J and E were probably united first and D was added at a later date. Later still the material of JED was fitted into a framework of P. At each editorial stage minor additions and modifications were made by the compiler. The Pentateuch reached its final form about the middle of the fourth century B.C. (According to Pfeiffer, the Source S was inserted into the Pentateuch after P.).[1]

CODES

In the Pentateuch seven distinct codes of law can be identified, thus:

(1) The Covenant Code (Exod. xx. 22–xxiii. 33).
(2) The Ritual Decalogue (Exod. xxiv. 10–26).
(3) The Twelve Curses (Deut. xxvii. 14–26).
(4) The Ten Commandments, in two forms (Exod. xx. 1–17; Deut. v. 6–21).
(5) The Deuteronomic Code (xii–xxvi).
(6) The Holiness Code or H (Lev. xvii–xxvi).
(7) The Priestly Code or P in its legal portions (scattered throughout Genesis, Exodus, Leviticus and Numbers).

FOREIGN INFLUENCE

The laws in the above codes are not entirely original creations. If we compare them with the Babylonian, Assyrian and Hittite Codes and the laws of the Canaanites and Hurrians, we find numerous resemblances in content and in terminology. Between the Hebrew and the Babylonian Codes, especially that of Hammurabi, the resemblances are very striking, indicating some connexion between them. It is now generally agreed that there was no direct borrowing. The Hebrews borrowed some of their laws from the Canaanites who, as the Tell-el-Amarna tablets show, were familiar with Babylonian culture and used the Babylonian cuneiform script. Hence, they must have gained their knowledge of the Babylonian law through the Canaanites. Some of the resemblances between the Hebrew and Babylonian Codes were doubtless due to the fact that the Hebrews, Babylonians and Canaanites, as Semitic peoples, possessed in common a body of Semitic law.

The extent of Hebrew borrowing from the Canaanite laws is a matter of dispute. Alt holds the view that two types of law can be distinguished in the Hebrew Code. Some of the laws begin with the words, 'If a man' or their equivalent, followed by a description of the anti-social act and its appropriate penalty. These constitute a body of law to which he gives the name of

[1] R. H. Pfeiffer, *Z.A.W.*, N.F.7, 1930, pp. 66–73.

'casuistic law', or what in the English legal system is known as 'case law', that is, law as settled by precedent. This body of law, he affirms, was taken over from the Canaanites by the Hebrews on their settlement in Palestine. The remaining laws of the Hebrew Code consist of definite commands or prohibitions and constitute a body of law, called 'apodictic law'. They are based on the decisions of priests or Levites; they are represented as expressing the revealed will of God and are enforced by penalties of a different nature from those which characterize the 'casuistic law'. This body of law, he maintains, the Hebrews brought with them from the desert.[1]

The Hebrews were undoubtedly influenced by Canaanite ritual law. It is obvious that the agricultural feasts—the Feast of Unleavened Bread, the Feast of Weeks, and the Feast of Ingathering—did not originate in the desert but were taken over from the Canaanite religion. Some of the sacrificial practices in the two religions are identical and in nearly all cases the terminology is the same.[2]

The Hebrews were indebted to some extent to the Hurrians for certain elements in their code, and to a very slight degree to the Assyrians and the Hittites.[3]

GROWING IMPORTANCE OF THE LAW

No one ever questioned the tradition that the Law had been given by Yahweh to Moses on Mount Sinai, and that the latter had delivered it to the children of Israel, but it was not observed by those who had inherited it. The prophets warned them repeatedly Yahweh would punish them for refusing to obey His commandments (Amos. ii. 4; Hos. viii. 1; Jer. ix. 13-15). In Ezekiel's view the calamity of the Exile was brought upon them because of their disobedience (Ezek. xxii. 23-31). During the Exile there was a spiritual reformation and the priests turned their attention to the study of the Law. Stress was laid upon Sabbath observance, circumcision and ritual cleanness, and the work of codifying the Law was begun. In 458 B.C. (or 397 B.C.) Ezra took with him to Jersualem 'the book of the law of Moses which the Lord had given to Israel' (Neh. viii. 1) and induced the people to accept its authority for faith and practice. The Law came to be regarded as the complete and final revelation of the will of God and there was no room for the inspiration of the prophet. The result was that the prophets gradually decreased in number until in the Greek period they finally disappeared.

Subsequent to the work of Ezra it was found necessary to adapt the Law to suit the changing needs of the times, and accordingly, side by side with the 'written law', there grew up a vast mass of interpretation which formed

---

[1] A. Alt, *Die Ursprünge des israelitischen Rechts*, 1934.
[2] R. Dussaud, *Les origines cananéennes du sacrifice israélite*, 1921; A. Lods, 'Éléments anciens et éléments modernes dans le rituel du sacrifice israélite,' *R.H.P.R.* viii, 1928, pp. 399ff.
[3] T. J. Meek, *Hebrew Origins*, rev. ed., 1950, p. 81.

APPENDIX H

the 'unwritten law', called in the Gospels 'the tradition of the elders' (Mk. vii. 3, 5; Mt. xv. 2). It was claimed that this law had been handed down in unbroken succession from Moses and that it had a validity equal to that of the 'written law' (Pirke Aboth i. 1f.). Of the 'written law' the 'scribes of the Pharisees' were the exponents (Mk. ii. 16) while the priests and the Sadducees rejected it (Acts iv. 1). The conflict began in the latter part of the second century B.C., in the reign of John Hyrcanus I (134–104 B.C.) and continued until the fall of Jerusalem in A.D. 70. About A.D. 200 the vast mass of interpretation, which had been transmitted orally for centuries, was committed to writing by Rabbi Judah Hanasi (c. A.D. 135–220) in the Mishnah which formed the basis of the later Talmud.

At first the Law was of importance mainly as prescribing the correct way of worshipping Yahweh, and the emphasis fell upon the Temple with its ritual. Gradually, however, the emphasis shifted from the Temple to the Law, until the time came when the latter was venerated for its own sake and praised in the most enthusiastic terms. Its observance was not a burden but a delight (Ps. i. 2). The ordinances of Yahweh were to be desired more than fine gold and were sweeter than honey (Ps. xix. 10). To the author of Ps. cxix the word of Yahweh was a lamp to his feet and a light to his path, and he swore an oath to observe His righteous ordinances (v. 105f.). When the Maccabaean revolt broke out (167 B.C.) the destruction of the 'books of the law' by the command of Antiochus IV was felt keenly (1 Macc. i. 56; iii. 48). The most convincing proof of the shift of emphasis from the Temple to the Law is seen in the fact that after the destruction of the Temple in A.D. 70 Judaism was able to survive on the basis of the Law alone. Since sacrifices could no longer be offered on Mount Zion, the ancient sacrificial worship was replaced by a service of prayer in the synagogue, the study of the Scriptures, and the living of a life in strict accordance with the Law. The Temple had been replaced by the Law and the priest by the Rabbi.

INFLUENCE

On Jewish History

The Law exercised a profound influence on Jewish life and thought. It made the Jews deeply conscious of their separateness from other nations. Yahweh had chosen them 'to be a people for his own possession, out of all the peoples that are on the face of the earth' (Deut. xiv. 2). The whole course of history revolved by His will around the life and destiny of Israel. His people should be holy like Himself. 'You shall be holy, for I the Lord your God am holy' (Lev. xix. 2). No other nation had such a lofty ethical code as that given by Yahweh to Moses on Mount Sinai. 'And what great nation is there that has statutes and ordinances so righteous as all this law which I set before you this day?' (Deut. iv. 8). It was their loyalty to the Law which enabled the Jews to withstand all the attempts of Antiochus IV to destroy their religion and their culture, and to survive the overthrow of their state and the destruction of their holy city, Jerusalem, and their Temple. It was a bond of union uniting all the Jews of the Dispersion with their fellow-countrymen in Palestine. No nation has been so oppressed or so dispersed as the Jewish nation, yet the Jews have preserved their distinctive nationality and their distinctive religion.

The Law fostered in the Jewish community a lofty standard of morality and a rich vein of piety. It provided for almost every situation which could arise between God and man, man and man, and man and animals. There was no distinction between the religious and the secular spheres of life. It dealt not only with such subjects as the appointment of the Temple personnel, the offering of sacrifice and the keeping of the feasts and fasts, but also with such subjects as the punishment of crime, behaviour towards strangers and lepers, the eating of clean and unclean foods and the care of animals. The whole purpose of the Law was to produce a holy nation (Exod. xix. 6).

The reading and study of the Law gave an impetus to synagogue worship. The origin of the synagogue is obscure but it probably goes back to the period of the Babylonian Exile. Deprived of their Temple and in a strange land the Jews had to find another place of worship, so they began to meet in local groups on the Sabbath for prayer and the reading and exposition of the Scriptures. Three times the prophet, Ezekiel, mentioned that the elders of Israel assembled in his house and sat before him to enquire of the Lord (Ezek. viii. 1; xiv. 1; xx. 1-3). In such gatherings as these we may perhaps see the germ of the future synagogue. On the return of the exiles to their native land they restored the Temple and its ritual, but continued to hold the meetings which they had been accustomed to hold in Babylon. It is probable that the Chronicler's description of the reading of the Law by Ezra was inspired by the synagogue practice of the day. In the post-exilic age the synagogue became established as a centre of local worship without sacrificial cultus. By New Testament times it was found not only in Palestine but also in the Dispersion.

During the Exile the work of rewriting the history of Israel and of codifying the Law led to the rise of a class of officials, known as sopherim or scribes, who devoted themselves to the study of the annals and legislation of their race and became the editors, copyists and interpreters of the documents concerned. The word 'sopherim', usually rendered 'scribes' means 'bookmen', because they taught the people out of the 'book of the law'. Ezra was pre-eminent among the scribes. He is described as 'a scribe skilled in the law of Moses' (Ezra vii. 6), who had 'set his heart to study the law of the Lord and to do it, and to teach his statutes and ordinances in Israel' (Ezra vii. 10). He, with certain Levites, not only 'read from the book, from the law of God clearly', but also 'gave the sense, so that the people understood the reading' (Neh. viii. 8). After his death the scribes set themselves the task of carrying on his work of spreading the knowledge of the Law among the people and of interpreting it so that men could apply it to their daily lives. According to tradition, the period of their activity as authoritative teachers ended with Simon the Just about 270 B.C. These early scribes were mainly recruited from the priests. After an interval of about seventy years there arose a body of lay teachers whose names are given in pairs from Jose ben Joezer and Jose ben Johanan (c. 200 B.C.) down to Hillel and Shammai, in the time of Jesus (Pirke Aboth i. 1–12).

The scribes came to occupy a great position in the state. They claimed to be the medium of a revelation which was greater than that made to Moses and the prophets (Mt. xxiii. 2). They demanded a place in the national life next to that of God Himself, and claimed the places of honour at all public functions. By the first century A.D. they had forced their way into the Sanhedrin (Jn. iii, vii; Acts v). Jesus accused them not only of transgressing the commandment of God (Mk. vii. 9–13; Mt. xv. 2–6), but even of shutting the kingdom of heaven against men (Mt. xxiii. 13) by their misinterpretation and misapplication of the Law. Nevertheless, there were among them many of sterling character and of deep learning, like Hillel, Shammai and Gamaliel. Some of them were 'not far from the kingdom of God' (Mk. xii. 34).

The influence of the Law was not wholly good. It was through the provision made for the payment of tithes and dues according to the Law that the priests became the wealthiest class in the community and eventually secured the political power in Jerusalem. It engendered a fierce and intolerant spirit in membership of a righteous community and closed the door to all spiritual fellowship with the Gentiles. It led to the growth of formalism in religion. To many religion came to mean nothing more than the strict observance of a host of petty regulations. The moral demands of the Law were forgotten. Our Lord charged the Pharisees and the scribes with paying tithes of mint, dill and cummin and neglecting the weightier matters of the Law—justice, mercy and faith (Mt. xxiii. 23). To say, however, that all the members of the Jewish community were guilty of formalism would be gross exaggeration. Among them there were many pious souls, who, while they were devoted to the Law, strove to worship Yahweh in spirit and truth.

On the History of Christendom

The Law has exercised an influence upon the history of Christendom. The moral precepts, especially the Decalogue, contained in the Pentateuch have exercised a powerful influence on Christian ethics. The history of the Christian priesthood has been influenced by the Priestly Code and by the Jewish conception of the Priestly Office. During the Middle Ages the influence of the Law on the actual legislation of the peoples of western Europe was not great. The Anglo-Saxon Code, for example, quotes from all the five books of the Pentateuch, but it shows practically no trace of their influence. At the time of the Reformation, however, Christian rulers and reformers were influenced to a greater extent by the Law. Protestant communities frequently embodied some of its precepts in their legislation. A manifesto of the German peasantry, issued in A.D. 1525, declared that all doctors of law should be abolished and that justice should be administered according to the Law of Moses. Luther taught that all Law was embodied in the Decalogue. In some of the American colonies, like Massachusetts and Connecticut, judges were commanded to inflict penalties according to the 'law of God'. Gradually, however, it was superseded by the Common Law of England. The influence of the Law has been both harmful and beneficial. For example, on the one hand from early times supposed witches were burnt at the stake in accordance with the Law, 'You shall not permit a sorceress to live' (Exod. xxii. 18). On the other hand, 'the deep concern of Jewish law for the stranger, the afflicted, the widow and the orphan, its humanitarian measures reaching to the ox that treadeth the corn and to the mother-bird, the concern for the labourer toiling in the vineyard, the hired man awaiting his reward, the poor debtor—all this has given inspiration as well as aid and comfort to reformers, even when their proposed Bills copied none of the phraseology of the Bible'.[1]

NOTES: THE MISHNAH

The Mishnah (Heb. = 'to repeat', then 'to learn or to teach by repetition') is based on the work of Rabbi Judah Hanasi (c. A.D. 135–220) which in turn is based on various collections of oral laws made by Hillel and other eminent lawyers. It has two main divisions, namely, (1) Halakhah, containing the whole of the 'unwritten law' which was legally binding, and (2) Haggadah, the whole of the non-legal matter, such as homilies and stories about biblical saints and heroes. The Mishnah consists of sixty-three tractates and is divided into six sections, dealing with (1) agriculture, (2) festivals, (3) women (betrothal, marriage, divorce, etc.), (4) injuries, including an important tractate on the constitution of the Sanhedrin and its rules of procedure, (5) holy things (various types of sacrifices) and (6) laws of purification. At an early stage it was recognized that a fence had to be put round the Law so that it would be impossible for anyone to transgress it. The object of the Mishnah was to provide such a fence.

THE TALMUD

The Talmud (Aramaic = 'instruction') is a vast commentary on the Mishnah. Often the term applies to both the Mishnah and the commentary on it. It exists in two versions, namely, the Palestinian or Jerusalem Talmud and the Babylonian Talmud. The Babylonian Talmud extends over thirty-nine of the Mishnah tractates, and much of it originated in Tiberias in the school of Rabbi Johanan (c. A.D. 199–279). The Babylonian Talmud was

---

[1] N. Isaacs, 'The Influence of Judaism on Western Law', in *The Legacy of Israel*, ed. by E. R. Bevan and C. Singer, 1927, p. 383.

Appendix H

compiled by a succession of scholars, headed by Rabbi Ashi (c. A.D. 352–427), president of the Jewish academy of Sura in Babylonia. Additions to both of these Talmuds were constantly being made. The Palestinian Talmud was not finally closed until the end of the fourth century A.D., and the Babylonian Talmud not until the beginning of the sixth century A.D. The Talmud is also called the 'Gemara'. To the orthodox Jews, who believe that the oral law, preserved in the Talmud, was given to Moses on Mount Sinai, the Talmud is as authoritative as the Scriptures.

APPENDIX I

THE DEAD SEA SCROLLS

QUMRAN CAVES

IN the spring of 1947 a Bedouin goatherd of the Ta'amireh tribe, seeking a lost goat near the Wadi Qumran at the north-west end of the Dead Sea, accidentally discovered a cave containing a number of ancient Jewish scrolls. Subsequently, five of these scrolls (really four, since two were severed halves of one original scroll) were acquired by the Syrian Orthodox Monastery of St Mark in the Old City of Jerusalem and three of them by the Hebrew University. In 1955 the former were bought by the State of Israel which now owned all the scrolls discovered in the cave in 1947. The scrolls comprised the following works:

(1) A practically complete Hebrew manuscript of Isaiah.
(2) A commentary on the first two chapters of Habbakuk, also in Hebrew.
(3) The *Manual of Discipline* of the sect which once owned the scrolls, also in Hebrew.
(4) An expanded Aramaic version of Genesis v–xv.
(5) A collection of hymns of thanksgiving. They closely resemble the Psalms of the Old Testament, but considered as literature they are for the most part inferior to them.
(6) *The War of the Sons of Light against the Sons of Darkness*. The Sons of Light are defined as the tribes of Levi, Judah and Benjamin, and the Sons of Darkness as the Edomites, Moabites, Ammonites, Philistines and the Kittim. The work seems to be not a narrative of an actual war but an apocalyptic vision.
(7) A fragmentary manuscript of Isaiah.

The last three works are in Hebrew.

Later, several hundred fragments were discovered in the same cave. These included portions of biblical books in Hebrew—Genesis, Exodus, Leviticus, Deuteronomy, Judges, Samuel, Psalms, Isaiah, Ezekiel and Daniel. There were also fragments of non-biblical books—commentaries on Micah, Zephaniah and Psalms, apocryphal works like Jubilees, Noah and The Testament of Levi, works dealing with the life and worship of a religious community, etc.

APPENDIX I

The search for more manuscripts has continued. About eleven caves in the Qumran area have so far yielded important material. These caves are designated by numbers. The cave where the original discoveries were made is known as Cave 1 or 1 Q, where Q stands for Qumran, and the others are numbered Cave 2, Cave 3 and so on.

In Cave 3 two scrolls of copper were discovered, but they could not be unrolled because the copper was completely oxidized. In 1956 they were taken to the laboratories of the Manchester School of Technology where they were successfully cut into strips and deciphered. They proved to be an inventory of sacred treasures buried in places as far apart as Mount Gerizim and Hebron, but mostly in the vicinities of Jerusalem and Qumran.

The most sensational discovery was that of many thousands of manuscript fragments in Cave 4. These had once constituted about 330 separate books, ninety of which were parts of the Bible. Every book except Esther is represented, some several times over. In addition to biblical fragments, the cave has yielded fragments of several commentaries, and fragments of The Manual of Discipline, Tobit, Jubilees, Enoch, The Testament of Levi, various apocalyptic works and hymns. In addition, fragments of the Zadokite Work have been found. The Zadokite Work was discovered in 1896 in the genizah of the ancient Karaite synagogue in Cairo and published by Schechter in 1910. It comprises two fragmentary documents, one consisting of a series of admonitions and the other of a collection of laws, produced within a community that claimed to be the true spiritual descendants of Zadok. For this reason it is frequently described as the Zadokite Work, and the community that produced it has been called the community of the Zadokites or the New Covenanters. The work is also known as the Damascus Document, because it was produced within a community that 'entered into the New Covenant in the land of Damascus'. The two fragmentary documents were written between the tenth and twelfth centuries A.D., but the precise date of their composition cannot be determined. The discovery of further fragments of the documents in the Qumran caves and the study of The Manual of Discipline, also found in the same caves, prove conclusively that the community referred to in the Zadokite Work is identical with that described in The Manual of Discipline. Some scholars believe that the phrase 'the land of Damascus' is used figuratively for Qumran. Milik (*Two Years of Discovery in the Wilderness of Judaea*, trans. from the French, 1959, p. 38), assigns the oldest of the manuscripts to the period 75–50 B.C.

In 1956 an eleventh cave was discovered by Bedouins, probably comparable in importance to Caves 1 and 4. It is known that at least four scrolls —Leviticus, Psalms, an Aramaic translation of Job and a pseudepigraphic work on the New Jerusalem—were found, together with hundreds of fragments.

DATING THE SCROLLS

From the first announcement of the discoveries made in the Qumran caves controversy has raged over the dating of the manuscripts. The consensus of opinion now seems to be that they were written within the period 200 B.C.–A.D. 68.

MURABBA'AT

In 1952 excavations were carried out in the caves in the neighbourhood of the Wadi Murabba'at, about eleven miles south of the Wadi Qumran. Traces were found of five periods of human occupation, but it is from the Roman period that the most interesting material has come. There were two letters written by Simon Bar Cochba (here named Ben Kosebah),[1] the leader of the second Jewish revolt against the Romans A.D. 132–135, some Greek and Aramaic documents belonging to the second century A.D., fragments of Genesis, Exodus, Deuteronomy and Isaiah and a complete phylactery. More recently, there has come from Murabba'at a scroll of the Minor Prophets in Hebrew, from the middle of Joel to the beginning of Zechariah, belonging to the second century A.D. The Murabba'at discoveries seem to have no connexion with those made in the Qumran caves.

AN UNKNOWN SOURCE

In 1952 the Bedouins produced another group of manuscripts from a region of the Dead Sea which has never been revealed. Among these manuscripts were a letter in Hebrew addressed to Simon Ben-Kosebah, some Nabataean and Jewish papyri of business and marriage contracts, and fragments of a Greek version of the Minor Prophets, which differs from the Septuagint version and will have a profound effect on future Septuagint studies.

KHIRBET MIRD

From a ruined Christian monastery at Khirbet Mird, not far from Bethlehem, the Bedouins in 1952 unearthed further manuscripts of great interest. These included papyrus fragments of private letters in Arabic, a Syriac letter, a fragment of the *Andromache* of Euripides, and some Old and New Testament fragments in Greek. In 1953 further fragments of the same type were brought to light. All the documents are much later than those coming from Qumran or Murabba'at and are dated between the fifth and sixth centuries of our era.

NAHAL HEVER

Excavations carried out in 1960 and 1961 in a large cave in Nahal Hever near Engedi, have led to the discovery of a large number of papyri. Among

---

[1] 'Ben' is Hebrew for 'son', and 'bar' is the corresponding Aramaic word.

them are eleven letters from Bar Cochba (Ben Kosebah): four in Hebrew, nine in Aramaic and two in Greek, and five documents: three in Hebrew and two in Aramaic, all of which shed light on several important aspects of the period of Bar Cochba's rule. There are also thirty-six documents, written partly in Greek, partly in Aramaic or in a combination of the two, as well as in Nabataean, which shed light on many phases of life in Judaea and the Dead Sea area on the eve of Bar Cochba's revolt.

THE KHIRBET QUMRAN SETTLEMENT

On the north side of the Wadi Qumran, nearly three quarters of a mile from the Dead Sea, lie the ruins of Khirbet Qumran from which the manuscripts found in the caves of the Qumran area undoubtedly came. It comprised a main building about 120 feet long and ninety feet wide, constructed of large undressed stones, with a strong tower at the north-west corner. It had a dining-room and kitchens, a dormitory, a dyer's shop, a laundry, a pottery factory, potters' kilns, workshops, stables, two swimming baths or baptistries and a scriptorium. Two inkstands, one of bronze and the other of clay were discovered, the former still containing dried ink made from lampblack and glue. Potsherds were found on which scribes had practised their penmanship. The monastery had an elaborately organized water supply, which came by aqueduct from a branch of the Wadi Qumran.

To the east of the building is the cemetery containing about 1,100 graves some of which have been opened. The bodies were laid out in parallel rows lying north and south with the head to the south. They were not placed in coffins or accompanied by funeral offerings. Each body was placed face upwards in a small mortuary chamber at the bottom of a trench. The entrance to the chamber was covered with a layer of unbaked bricks or a flat stone, the trench filled in, and the burial marked on the surface by two upright stones with a row of pebbles between them. Skeletons of women as well as men were found in the cemetery, suggesting that if the monastery was occupied by Essenes, there must have been an order of Essenes which practised matrimony, as distinct from all the other Essenes who were celibate.

Excavations show that the site was occupied by a religious community from the end of the second century B.C. to A.D. 68. In 1951 a jar was found, precisely like those found in the caves, together with a number of coins dating from the first century of our era. Later excavations have brought to light several hundred coins starting in the reign of John Hyrcanus (134–104 B.C.) and continuing without interruption to A.D. 68.

Excavations show that the building was damaged by an earthquake, which has been identified with that which devastated Judaea in 31 B.C. From the presence of a thick layer of black ash it can be deduced that the building was destroyed by fire, probably in A.D. 68. After its destruction it was partly rebuilt and occupied by a Roman garrison until about A.D. 90

when it was apparently abandoned. In the second Jewish revolt (A.D. 132–135) it was occupied for a short time by members of the insurgent forces.

THE KHIRBET QUMRAN LIBRARY

The manuscripts discovered in the Qumran caves represented over 500 books, some of them in a fairly good state of preservation but the majority in a fragmentary condition. They had formed a large library, not a genizah where badly damaged books were stored before being discarded. During the first Jewish revolt against the Romans (A.D. 66–70) the members of the community hid their manuscripts in the caves, hoping to recover them in happier times. Their hopes, however, were not realized, for their monastery was destroyed by the Romans, probably in A.D. 68, and they were either killed or dispersed, never to return.

THE KHIRBET QUMRAN COMMUNITY

Origin and Teaching

It is probable that the Qumran community originated among the Hasidim of the second century B.C., more especially those who were opposed to the Hasmonaean priest-kings. Under the leadership of the Teacher of Righteousness they went out into the wilderness to live there as a society of 'volunteers of holiness' dedicated to the study and practice of the Law. By this means they believed that they would prepare the way for the coming of the kingdom of God, which would be heralded by the appearance of a prophet and of the two 'anointed ones of Aaron and Israel', that is, of two Messiahs, one an Aaronic High Priest and the other a Davidic King. At the close of the present age it would fall to them to execute judgment upon the Gentile oppressors of God's people and on the leaders of Israel who had led their fellow countrymen astray. In the kingdom of God they would form the nucleus of the new Israel. They believed that by their devotion to the Law, their patient endurance of suffering, and their submission to severe discipline they would be accepted by God as an atonement for the sins of the nation. They saw themselves in the role of the Suffering Servant in Isaiah lii. 13–liii. 12. In their eyes the only legitimate high-priestly family was the house of Zadok which had been deposed by Antiochus IV Epiphanes. They looked forward to the day when a High Priest of the house of Zadok would once again offer up sacrifices to God in a purified Temple. They were embued with the spirit of the canonical prophets, whose works are all represented in the manuscripts recovered from the caves. It is from the prophets that the great ethical impulse came which moved the sectarians to promote justice and righteousness among men. They believed that the prophets, by divine inspiration and command, had foretold the things that were to happen at the end of the present age, but that it had not been revealed to them when the end would come. This knowledge was revealed to the leader, the Teacher of Righteousness, who communicated it to his disciples. In their hymns of thanksgiving the latter praised God for revealing to them His wonderful mysteries. They called themselves the saints of the Most High, the holy people of the covenant, the poor of the flock, the sons of light, the men of truth, the elect of God, and the community of Israel and Aaron.

Persecution

There are several references to the persecution of the Teacher of Righteousness by the Wicked Priest. On one occasion, we are told, he persecuted the Teacher 'in the house of his exile' on the day of atonement. The members of the community believed that God would raise up the Kittim, probably the Romans, to punish the Wicked Priest and his associates. It has been suggested by some scholars that the Wicked Priest was Alexander Jannaeus, king and High Priest of the Jews (104–76 B.C.), and that the Teacher of Righteousness was Onias, the righteous, who, according to Josephus, was stoned to death in 65 B.C. Some, however, think that the Teacher of Righteousness was Onias III, the last legitimate High Priest of the house of Zadok, who was deposed by Antiochus IV Epiphanes. The Wicked Priest would then be his rival, Menelaus, who usurped the sacred office and procured his assassination. If these identifications are correct, the Kittim would be not the Romans, but the Seleucids who were Greeks.

Admission of Members

Candidates for admission to the community spent a year as postulants to prove their worth. If found suitable they served two years as novices before being admitted to full membership of the community. The main features of the initiatory ceremony were the taking of a solemn vow to return to the Law of Moses and to shun all contact with ungodly men, and the pronouncement of blessings by the priests and curses by the Levites. Women as well as men might be admitted to the community. When novices became full members, they had to place all their wordly possessions in the common stock from which they received back only the bare necessities of life.

Organization

The organization of the community was hierarchical. It was governed by a supreme council of twelve laymen and three priests. There was also a general assembly called 'the session of the many', in which every man was placed according to his rank and had the right to speak and vote. There were also 'cells' consisting of ten persons with a priest as president. Legislative and judicial authority belonged by right to the Sons of Aaron, but matters involving both judicial and executive authority were referred to 'the session of the many'. Over each company into which the community was divided was an inspector, and over them all a chief inspector to see that discipline was maintained. The members of the community ate their meals together, worshipped together and deliberated in council together. There is some evidence for thinking that they partook periodically of a sacred meal, consisting of bread and wine, and were presided over by a priest.

SIGNIFICANCE OF THE DEAD SEA SCROLLS

As we have already indicated (see pp. 43f.), the Dead Sea Scrolls are important for the textual criticism of the Old Testament and for the fixing of the dates of certain books with greater accuracy. They are also important for the study of Hebrew palaeography. Four scripts can be distinguished, namely, (1) the Palaeo-Hebrew (or Phoenician) script, (2) the square-letter script of the Hebrew book-hand, (3) the cursive script and (4) a mixed script of book-hand forms and cursive forms. From the manuscripts we learn that the Palaeo-Hebrew script was used for copying the Scriptures, especially the Pentateuch, and for legends and coins, the square-letter script for copying the Scriptures, the cursive script for legal documents and the mixed script for letters and ossuaries. The Palaeo-Hebrew script changed little until the beginning of the Christian era when a rapid development took place, the last stage being reached in the early years of the second century A.D. After the second Jewish revolt against the Romans it ceased to be used by the Jews, but among the Samaritans it continued to be used down to the present day. Four stages can be traced in the evolution of the square script—the archaic, the Hasmonaean, the Herodian and the ornamental. The cursive script assumed its fully developed form in the first century A.D. This type of script is rather rare at Qumran, but at Murabba'at it is largely used in private documents. After the second Jewish revolt it fell into disuse.

The Dead Sea scrolls are also important for the study of Christian origins, but our concern is with the Old Testament.

APPENDIX J

CHRONOLOGICAL TABLES

TABLE I
THE UNITED MONARCHY C. 1020–922 B.C.

	B.C.
Saul	c. 1020–1000
David	c. 1000–961
Solomon	c. 961–922

TABLE II
THE DIVIDED MONARCHY 922–587 B.C.

ISRAEL	B.C.	JUDAH	B.C.
Jeroboam I	922–901	Rehoboam	922–915
Nadab	901–900	Abijam	915–913
Baasha	900–877	Asa	913–873
Elah	877–876	Jehoshaphat	873–849
Zimri	876	Jehoram	849–842
Omri	876–869	Ahaziah	842
Ahab	869–850	Athaliah	842–837
Ahaziah	850–849	Jehoash	837–800
Jehoram	849–842	Amaziah	800–783
Jehu	842–815	Azariah (Uzziah)	783–742
Jehoahaz	815–801	Jotham (regent)	750–742
Jehoash	801–786	Jotham (king)	742–735
Jeroboam II	786–746	Ahaz	735–715
Zechariah	746–745	Hezekiah	715–687
Shallum	745	Manasseh	687–642
Menahem	745–738	Amon	642–640
Pekahiah	738–737	Josiah	640–609
Pekah	737–732	Jehoahaz (Shallum)	609
Hoshea	732–724	Jehoiakim (Eliakim)	609–598
Fall of Samaria	722	Jehoiachin (Jeconiah)	598
		Zedekiah (Mattaniah)	598–587
		Fall of Jerusalem	587

TABLE III
BABYLONIAN KINGS 625–539 B.C.

	B.C.
Nabopolassar	625–605
Nebuchadrezzar	605–562
Amel-Marduk (Evil-Merodach)	562–560
Nergal-shar-usur (Neriglissar)	560–556
Labashi-Marduk	556
Nabu-naid (Nabonidus)	556–539
Fall of Babylon	539

TABLE IV
PERSIAN KINGS 539–331 B.C.

	B.C.
Cyrus (counting from conquest of Babylon)	539–530
Cambyses	530–522
Darius I	522–486
Xerxes I (Ahasuerus)	486–465
Artaxerxes I (Longimanus)	465–424
Xerxes II	424–423
Darius II	423–404
Artaxerxes II (Mnemon)	404–358
Artaxerxes III (Ochus)	358–338
Arses	338–336
Darius III (Codomannus)	336–331
Alexander conquers Persian Empire	331

TABLE V
THE PTOLEMIES (EGYPT)

	B.C.
Ptolemy I (Soter)	323–283
Ptolemy II (Philadelphus)	(285) 283–246
Ptolemy III (Euergetes)	246–221
Ptolemy IV (Philopator)	221–203
Ptolemy V (Epiphanes)	203–181
Ptolemy VI (Philometor)	181–164
Ptolemy VII (Euergetes) Joint ruler with Philometor	170–164
Ptolemy VII (Euergetes) Sole king	164–146
Ptolemies continue until Egypt becomes a Roman province in	30

TABLE VI
THE SELEUCIDS (SYRIA)

	B.C.
Seleucus I (Nicator)	312–280
Antiochus I (Soter)	280–261
Antiochus II	261–247
Seleucus II	247–226
Seleucus III	226–223
Antiochus III (the Great)	223–187
Seleucus IV	187–175
Antiochus IV (Epiphanes)	175–163
Antiochus V (Eupator)	163–162
Demetrius I	162–150
Alexander Balas, a usurper	150–145
Antiochus VI	145–142
Demetrius II	142–139
Antiochus VII (Sidetes)	139–129

TABLE VII
EVENTS IN JEWISH HISTORY 538–63 B.C.

	B.C.
Return of the Exiles	538
Building of the Second Temple	520–516
Dedication of Second Temple	516
Nehemiah's governorship	445–433
Return of Ezra	397
Samaritan Schism	350
Conquest of Palestine by Alexander	331
Palestine under the Ptolemies	312
Palestine passes to Seleucids	198
Profanation of Temple	167
Revolt under Judas Maccabaeus	167
Rededication of Temple	164
Death of Judas Maccabaeus	160
Jonathan	160–142
Simon	142–134
John Hyrcanus I	134–104
Aristobulus I	104–103
Alexander Jannaeus	103–76
Alexandra	76–67
Civil War between Hyrcanus II and Aristobulus II	67–63
Pompey conquers Jerusalem and Palestine becomes a Roman province	63

APPENDIX K

BIBLIOGRAPHY

The following bibliography makes no claim to be exhaustive. It is simply a collection of relevant works from a great volume of literature, and is designed primarily as a guide to those who wish to make a more extended study of the Writings. Foreign works have been included for those whose reading is not restricted to English.

Chapter I
THE CANON OF THE OLD TESTAMENT

BUHL, F., *Canon and Text of the Old Testament*, 1892.
FILSON, E. F., *Which Books belong to the Bible? A Study of the Canon*, 1957.
RYLE, H. E., *The Canon of the Old Testament*, 2nd ed., 1895.
ZEITLIN, S., *An Historical Study of the Canonization of the Hebrew Scriptures*, 1933.

Chapter II
HISTORICAL BACKGROUND

GENERAL WORKS

ALBRIGHT, W. F., *From the Stone Age to Christianity*, rev. ed., 1957.
BRIGHT, J., *A History of Israel*, 1960.
NOTH, M., *The History of Israel*, 2nd Eng. ed., 1960.
OESTERLEY, W. O. E., and ROBINSON, T. H., *A History of Israel*, 2 vols., 1932.
OLMSTEAD, A. T., *History of the Persian Empire*, 1949.
ROBINSON, H. W., *The History of Israel: its Facts and Factors*, 1938.
SNAITH, N. H., *The Jews from Cyrus to Herod*, 1949.
WHITLEY, C. F., *The Exilic Age*, 1957.

SPECIAL STUDIES

BEVAN, E. R., *Jerusalem under the High Priests*, 1904.
BOX, G. H., *Judaism in the Greek Period*, 1932.
CHARLES, R. H., *Religious Development between the Old and the New Testaments*, 1914.

MOORE, G. F., *Judaism in the First Centuries of the Christian Era*, 3 vols., 1927–1930.
OESTERLEY, W. O. E., *The Jews and Judaism during the Greek Period: the background of Christianity*, 1941.
ROBINSON, H. W., *Inspiration and Revelation in the Old Testament*, 1946.
ROWLEY, H. H., *The Faith of Israel*, 1956: 'Sanballat and the Samaritan Temple,' reprinted from B.J.R.L., No. 1, 1955, pp. 166–198.
WELCH, A. C., *Post-Exilic Judaism*, 1935.
WRIGHT, G. E., *The Old Testament against its Environment*, 1950.

Chapter III
ARCHAEOLOGY

ALBRIGHT, W. F., *The Archaeology of Palestine*, 1951.
ALLEGRO, J. M., *The Dead Sea Scrolls*, rev. ed., 1958.
BRUCE, F. F., *Second Thoughts on the Dead Sea Scrolls*, 1956.
BURROWS, M., *What mean these Stones?* 1941.
COWLEY, A., *Aramaic Papyri of the Fifth Century B.C.*, 1923.
DRIVER, G. R., *Aramaic Documents of the Fifth Century B.C.*, 1957.
MILIK, J. T., *Ten Years of Discovery in the Wilderness of Judaea*, trans. from the French, 1959.
PARROT, A., *The Temple of Jerusalem*, trans. from the French, 1957.
PRITCHARD, J. B., *Ancient Near Eastern Texts relating to the Old Testament*, 1950.
REIFENBERG, A., *Ancient Jewish Coins*, 2nd rev. ed., 1947.
THOMAS, D. W., *Documents from Old Testament Times*, 1958.
WISEMAN, D. J., *Illustrations from Biblical Archaeology*, 1958.
WRIGHT, G. E., *Biblical Archaeology*, 1957.

Chapter IV
APOCALYPTIC LITERATURE

BURKITT, F. C., *Jewish and Christian Apocalypses*, 1914.
CHARLES, R. H., (ed.), *The Apocrypha and Pseudepigrapha of the Old Testament*, 2 vols., 1913.
FROST, S. B., *Old Testament Apocalyptic: its Origin and Growth*, 1952.
ROWLEY, H. H., *The Relevance of Apocalyptic*, 2nd ed., 1947.

SPECIAL STUDIES

JONGE, M. DE, *The Testaments of the Twelve Patriarchs*, 1953.
PHILONENKO, M., *Les interpolations chrétiennes des Testaments des douze Patriarches et les manuscrits de Qoumrân*, 1960.

Chapter V
WISDOM LITERATURE

English

BAUMGARTNER, W., Article on *The Wisdom Literature* in *The Old Testament and Modern Study*, ed. by H. H. Rowley, 1951.
NOTH, M., and THOMAS, D. W., *Wisdom in Israel and in the Ancient Near East*, 1955.
OESTERLEY, W. O. E., *The Wisdom of Egypt and the Old Testament*, 1927.
RANKIN, O. S., *Israel's Wisdom Literature: its Bearing on Theology and the History of Religion*, 1936.
RANSTON, H., *The Old Testament Wisdom Books and their Teaching*, 1930.

Foreign

HUMBERT, P., *Recherches sur les sources égyptiennes de la littérature sapientiale d'Israël*, 1929.

Chapter VI
THE FORMS AND CHARACTERISTICS OF HEBREW POETRY

BURNEY, C. F., *The Poetry of our Lord*, 1925.
GORDON, A. R., *The Poetry of the Old Testament*, 1912.
GRAY, G. B., *The Forms of Hebrew Poetry*, 1915.
MACDONALD, D. B., *The Hebrew Literary Genius*, 1933.
ROBINSON, T. H., *The Poetry of the Old Testament*, 1947.
SANDS, P. C., *Literary Genius of the Old Testament*, 1924.

Chapters VII and VIII
PSALMS
COMMENTARIES

English

BARNES, W. C., 1931; BRIGGS, I. C. C., 1906–7; BUTTENWIESER, 1938; LESLIE, 1949; OESTERLEY, 1939; KIRKPATRICK, Camb.B., 1902, repr. 1939; articles in one-volume commentaries on the Bible.

Foreign

BAETHGEN, H. K., 3rd ed., 1904; DUHM, 2nd ed., 1922; GUNKEL, H. K., 1926; GUNKEL and BEGRICH, 1933; KITTEL, K. A. T., 5th and 6th ed., 1929; MOWINCKEL, 1921–4; SCHMIDT, H. A. T., 1934.

SPECIAL STUDIES

English

GUNKEL, H., *What remains of the Old Testament*, Eng. trans., 1927.
JOHNSON, A. R., Article on 'The Psalms' in *The Old Testament and Modern Study*, ed. by H. H. Rowley, 1951; *Sacral Kingship in Ancient Israel*, 1955.

Appendix K

OESTERLEY, W. O. E., *A Fresh Approach to the Psalms*, 1937.
PATERSON, J., *The Praises of Israel*, 1950.
PATON, J. H., *Canaanite Parallels in the Book of Psalms*, 1944.
PETERS, J. P., *The Psalms as Liturgies*, 1922.
SIMPSON, D. C. (ed.), *The Psalmists*, 1926.
SMITH, J. M. P., *The Religion of the Psalms*, 1922.
SNAITH, N. H., *Studies in the Psalter*, 1934.
WIDENGREN, G., *The Accadian and Hebrew Psalms of Lamentation as Religious Documents*, 1937.

Foreign

LÖHR, M., 'Psalmenstudien', B.W.A.T., N.F., Heft 3, 1922.
QUELL, G., 'Das Kultische Problem der Psalmen', B.W.A.T., N.F., Heft 11, 1926.
WEISER, A., *Die Psalmen ausgewählt übersetzt und erklärt*, 2nd ed., 1939.

Chapter IX
PROVERBS
COMMENTARIES

English

OESTERLEY, W. C., 1929; TOY, I. C. C., 1899; articles in one-volume commentaries on the Bible.

Foreign

FRANKENBERG, H. K., 1898; GEMSER, H. A. T., 1937; WILDEBOER, 1897.

SPECIAL STUDIES

English

ELMSLIE, W. A. L., *Studies in Life from Jewish Proverbs*, 1917.
OESTERLEY, W. O. E., *The Wisdom of Egypt and the Old Testament*, 1927.
RANKIN, O. S., *Israel's Wisdom Literature: its Bearing on Theology and the History of Religion*, 1936.
RANSTON, H., *The Old Testament Wisdom Books and their Teaching*, 1930.

Foreign

BAUMGARTNER, W., *Israelitische und altorientalische Weisheit*, 1933.
DUESBERG, H., *Les Scribes inspirés; Introduction aux livres sapientiaux de la Bible*, 1938–39.
FICHTNER, J., 'Die altorientalische Weisheit in ihrer israelitisch-jüdischen Auspragung', B.Z.A.W., LXII, 1933.
GRESSMANN, H., *Israels Spruchweisheit im Zusammenhang der Weltliteratur*, 1925.

Chapter X
JOB
COMMENTARIES

English

DRIVER and GRAY, I. C. C., 1921; PEAKE, Cent.B., 1905; STRACHAN, 1913; articles in one-volume commentaries on the Bible.

Foreign

BUDDE, H. K., 2nd ed., 1913; DHORME, 1926; DUHM, K. H. C., 1897; HÖLSCHER, rev. ed., 1952; KONIG, 1929.

SPECIAL STUDIES

English

EERDMANS, B. D., *Studies in Job*, 1939.
JASTROW, M., *The Book of Job; its Origin, Growth and Interpretation*, 1920.
KRAELING, E. G., *The Book of the Ways of God*, 1938.
MCFADYEN, J. E., *The Problem of Pain: a Study of the Book of Job*, 1917.
PEAKE, A. S., *The Problem of Suffering in the Old Testament*, 1904.
ROBINSON, H. W., *The Cross of Job*, 1916.
ROBINSON, T. H., *Poetry and Poets in the Old Testament*, 1947; *Job and his Friends*, 1954.
STEVENSON, W. B., *The Poem of Job*, 1947.

Foreign

BAUMGÄRTEL, F., 'Der Hiobdialog', B.W.A.N.T., IV. 9, 1933.
LINDBLOM, J., 'La Composition du livre de Job', *Bull. de la Soc. Royale des Lettres de Lund* (1944–45, III), 1945.

Chapter XI
THE SONG OF SONGS
COMMENTARIES

English

HARPER, Camb.B., 1902; JASTROW, 1921; LEHRMAN in *The Five Megilloth*, 2nd ed., 1952; MARTIN, Cent.B., 1908; OESTERLEY, 1936; POUGET and GUITTON, trans. from the French, 1948; WATERMAN, 1948; articles in one-volume commentaries on the Bible.

Foreign

BUDDE in 'Die fünf Megillot', K. H. C., 1898; DELITZSCH, 1875; EWALD, 1826; GORDIS, 1954; HALLER in 'Die fünf Megilloth,' H. A. T., 1940; HAUPT, 1907; HAZAN, 1936; RENAN, 1860; ROTHSTEIN, 1893; SIEGFRIED, H. K., 1898; STAERK, 2nd ed., 1920; WITTEKINDT, 1926.

APPENDIX K

SPECIAL STUDIES

English

CANNON, W. W., *The Song of Songs*, C.U.P. 1913.
MEEK, T. J., 'Canticles and the Tammuz Cult', A.J.S.L., xxxix, 1922-23.
ROWLEY, H. H., 'Interpretation of the Song of Songs', in *The Servant of the Lord and other Essays on the Old Testament*, 1952.
SNAITH, N. H., *The Song of Songs: The Dance of the Virgins*, A.J.S.L., L, 1933-34, pp. 129-142.
SCHOFF, W. H., *The Song of Songs: a Symposium*, 1924.

Foreign

WETZSTEIN, J. G., *Die Syrische Dreschtafel*, 1873.

Chapter XII
RUTH

COMMENTARIES

English

COOKE, Camb.B., 1913; LEHRMAN in *The Five Megilloth*, 2nd ed., 1952; THATCHER, Camb.B., 1904; articles in one-volume Commentaries on the Bible.

Foreign

BERTHOLET, K. H. C., 1898; HALLER in *Die fünf Megilloth*, H.A.T., 1940; NOWACK in *Die fünf Megilloth*, 1902.

SPECIAL STUDIES

English

BURROWS, M., 'The Oriental Background of Hebrew Levirate Marriage', B.A.S.O.R., No. 77, 1940; 'Levirate Marriage in Israel', J.B.L., LIX, 1940.
ROBERTSON, E., 'The Plot of the Book of Ruth', B.J.R.L., XXXII. 2, 1949-50, pp. 207-228.
ROWLEY, H. H., 'The Marriage of Ruth' in *The Servant of the Lord and other Essays on the Old Testament*, pp. 163-186.
STAPLES, W. E., 'The Book of Ruth', A.J.S.L., LIV, 1937, pp. 145-157.

Foreign

GUNKEL, H., 'Ruth' in *Reden und Aufsätze*, 1913, pp. 65-92.
HUMBERT, P., 'Art et leçon de l'histoire de Ruth' in R.Th.Ph., N.S., XXVI, 1938, pp. 257-286.

Chapter XIII
LAMENTATIONS

COMMENTARIES

English

GOLDMAN in *The Five Megilloth*, 2nd ed., 1952; PEAKE, Cent.B., 1910–12; STREANE, Camb.B., 1913; articles in one-volume Commentaries on the Bible.

Foreign

HALLER in 'Die fünf Megilloth', H.A.T., 1940; LÖHR, H. K., 2nd ed., 1907; RUDOLF, K.A.T., 1939.

SPECIAL STUDIES

English

GOTTWALD, N. K., *Studies in the Book of Lamentations*, 1954.

Chapter XIV
ECCLESIASTES

COMMENTARIES

English

BARTON, I. C. C., 1908; MARTIN, Cent.B., 1908; REICHART and COHEN in *The Five Megilloth*, 2nd ed., 1952; WILLIAMS, Camb.B., 1922; articles in one-volume Commentaries on the Bible.

Foreign

GALLING in 'Die fünf Megilloth', H.A.T., 1940; HERTZBERG, K.A.T., 1932; ODEBERG, 1929; PODECHARD, 1912.

SPECIAL STUDIES

English

GINSBERG, H. L., *Studies in Koheleth*, 1950.

GORDIS, R., *The Wisdom of Koheleth: A New Translation with a Commentary and an Introductory Essay*, rev. ed., 1950; *Koheleth: the Man and his World*, 2nd ed., 1955.

RANSTON, H. *Ecclesiastes and the Early Greek Wisdom Literature*, 1925.

Foreign

CAUSSE, A., 'Sagesse égyptienne et sagesse juive' in R.H.P.R., IX, 1929, pp. 149–169.

HUMBERT, P., *Recherches sur les sources égyptiennes de la littérature sapientiale d'Israël*, 1929.

RENAN, E., *L'Ecclésiaste*, 1882.

Chapter XV
ESTHER
COMMENTARIES

English

DAVIES, Cent.B., 1909; GOLDMAN in *The Five Megilloth*, 2nd ed., 1952; PATON, I.C.C., 1908; STREANE, Camb.B., 1907; articles in one-volume Commentaries on the Bible.

Foreign

HALLER, H.A.T., 1940.

SPECIAL STUDIES

English

HOSCHANDER, J., *The Book of Esther in the Light of History*, 1923.
MORRIS, A. E., 'The Purpose of the Book of Esther', E.T., XLII, 1930–31; pp. 124–128.

Foreign

STRIEDL, H., 'Untersuchung zur Syntax und Stilistik des hebräischen Buches Esther', Z.A.W., 1937, pp. 73–108.

Chapter XVI
DANIEL
COMMENTARIES

English

CHARLES (O.U.P.) 1929; DRIVER, Camb.B., 1900; MONTGOMERY, I.C.C. 1927; articles in one-volume Commentaries on the Bible.

Foreign

BENTZEN, H.A.T., 1957.

SPECIAL STUDIES

English

GINSBERG, H. L., *Studies in Daniel*, 1948.
ROWLEY, H. H., 'The Unity of the Book of Daniel' in *The Servant of the Lord and other Essays on the Old Testament*, 1952, pp. 237–268; *Darius the Mede and the Four World Empires in the Book of Daniel*. A Historical Study of Contemporary Theories, 1935.
TORREY, C. C., 'Notes on the Aramaic Parts of Daniel', T.C.A., XV, 1909, pp. 241–282.
WELCH, A. C., *Visions of the End*, 1922.

Foreign

BAUMGARTNER, W., 'Ein Vierteljahrhundert Danielforchung', Th.R., N.F., XI, 1939, pp. 59–83, 125–144, 201–228.
BICKERMANN, E., *Der Gott der Makkabäer*, 1937.
HÖLSCHER, G., 'Die Entstehung des Buches Daniel', T.S.K., XCII, 1919, pp. 113–128.
NOTH, M., 'Zur Komposition des Buches Daniel', T.S.K., XCVIII–XCIX, 1926, pp. 143–163.
NYBERG, H. S., 'Daniel' in S.B.U., I, 1948, col. 345.

Chapter XVII
1 and 2 CHRONICLES
COMMENTARIES

English

CURTIS and MADSEN, I.C.C., 1910; ELMSLIE, Camb.B., 1916; HARVEY-JELLIE, Cent.B., 1906; articles in one-volume Commentaries on the Bible.

Foreign

KITTEL, H. K., 1902; VON RAD, B.W.A.N.T., 1930; ROTHSTEIN-HÄNEL, K.A.T., 1927; RUDOLF, H.A.T., 1955.

SPECIAL STUDIES

English

ALBRIGHT, W. F., 'The Date and Personality of the Chronicler', J.B.L., XL, 1921, pp. 104–124.
WELCH, A. C., *The Work of the Chronicler*, 1939.

Chapter XVIII
EZRA-NEHEMIAH
COMMENTARIES

English

BATTEN, I.C.C., 1913; DAVIES, Cent.B., 1909; RYLE, Camb.B., 1893; articles in one-volume Commentaries on the Bible.

Foreign

BERTHOLET, K.H.C., 1902; GALLING, A.T.D., 1954; HÖLSCHER, H.S.A.T., 1923; RUDOLF, H.A.T., 1949; SCHNIEDER, H.S.A.Tes., 1959.

SPECIAL STUDIES

English

ROWLEY, H. H., 'The Chronological Order of Ezra-Nehemiah' in *The Servant of the Lord and other Essays on the Old Testament*, 1952, pp.

131–159; 'Nehemiah's Mission and its Background', reprinted from B.J.R.L., XXXVII, No. 2, 1955, pp. 528–561.
SNAITH, N. H., 'The Date of Ezra's Arrival in Jerusalem', Z.A.W., 63, 1951, pp. 53–66.
TORREY, C. C., *Ezra Studies*, 1910.
WRIGHT, J. S., *The Date of Ezra's coming to Jerusalem*, 2nd. ed., 1958.

Foreign

GRANILD, S., *Ezrabogens literaere Genesis, undersogt med Henblik paa et efterkronistik Indgreb*, 1949.
MOWINCKEL, S., *Stadtholderen Nehemia*, 1916.
SCHAEDER, H. H., *Ezra der Schreiber*, 1930.

INDEX OF SUBJECTS

Abaddon, 140, 143
Abiathar, 285
Acrostics, 86, 204f., 206f.
Adasa, 34
Adonijah, 285
Ahasuerus, 244ff., 253
Ahaz, 282
Akkad, 25, 39
Alexander the Great, 17, 31f.
Alexander, Jannaeus, 35, 373
Alexander, 35
Alexandria, 18, 32
Amasis, 24
Amel-Marduk, 21 n., 37, 288
Ammon(ites), 20f., 195, 284, 322
Amon, 286
Amos, 58f., 158
Angelology, 172, 273f., 276f., 351f.
Anthropomorphism, 112 n.
Anathoth, 285
Anath-bethel, 40
Anshan, 24
Antiochus III (the Great), 33
Antiochus IV (Epiphanes), 33
Antiochus VII (Sidetes), 34
Antipater, 35f.
Apocalyptic Literature, meaning of, 45; date and place of composition and cause of decline, 45f.; list of books, 46–49; origin and development of apocalyptic, 49–53; prophecy and apocalyptic, 53–55; characteristics of, 55–59; permanent influence of, 59–62
Apocrypha, 18f.
Aramaic, 350f.
Archaeology, 37–44
Aristobulus I, 35
Aristobulus II, 35f.
Ark, 285, 291f.
Arsames, 41
Artaxerxes I, 11, 28, 301 n., 314–316
Artaxerxes II, 29, 301 n., 316
Artaxerxes III, 31
Asham-bethel, 40
Ashdod(ites), 322
Assyria(ns), 158, 286f.
Astyages, 24

Ataq-el-Emir, 42
Azekah, 37

Baal-peor, 120
Babylon(ians), 20f., 22–25, 29, 31f., 37–39, 216
Bagoas, 40f.
Bar-Cochba, 370f.
Beersheba, 35
Behemoth, 156f., 165
Belshazzar, 24, 38, 265, 268, 270
Bethel, 22, 286, 329
Beth-ha-Midrash, 66
Beth-horon, 285
Beth-shemish, 37
Bethzur, 43
Boaz, character of, 202

Cairo, 22
Cambyses, 22, 26, 40
Canon, O. T., definition of, 11; conception of, 11f.; contents of 12f.; theories of origin, 13f.; theories of growth, 14; formation of, 14–17; fixation of, 17; the Greek, 18
Carchemish, 287
Chronicler, the, 26, 39, 282–284, 288
Chronicles, Book of, title and place in Canon, 280; Chronicles and Ezra-Nehemiah, 280f.; contents of, 281; aim of, 281f.; the Chronicler as a historian, 282–284; history of the Jewish Monarchy according to Samuel and Kings, 284–288; the Chronicler's treatment of the history of Judah 288–294; sources of, 294–296; date of, 296–298; permanent influence of, 298f.; Literary merit of, 299f.
Cicilian Gates, 32
Circumcision, 23, 33
Codex Alexandrinus, 95
Coins, Jewish, 31
Confession and Repentance, 214
Council of Jamnia, 14, 17
Council of Trent, 18
Croesus, 24, 349
Cosmology, 111

Index of Subjects

Cyrus, 24–26, 38f., 270, 297, 313f.
Cyrus Cylinder, 38f., 313f.

Dan, 35, 286
Daniel, Book of, title and place in Canon, 255; contents of, 255–263; additions to, 263f.; purpose of, 265f.; sources of, 266f.; unity of, 267f.; bilingual character of, 268f.; date of, 269–272; teaching of, 271–276; permanent influence of, 276–278; literary merit of, 278f.
Daric, 42, 297
Darius, I, 25, 27, 265f., 314f.
David, 104–106, 284f., 288f., 290–293
Day of Yahweh, 49, 123
Dead Sea Scrolls, 43f., 258 n., 368–374
Debir, 37
Deborah, song of, 91, 107
Delaiah, 41
Deutero-Isaiah, 23f., 55, 160, 207 n., 341f.
Deuteronomic Code, 158, 339, 360f.
Divided Monarchy, the, 285–288
Divisions of Jewry, 21–25
Doorkeepers, 292, 327
Dositheus, 250
Dragon, the, 111
Drinking Songs, 79

Ecbatana, 27, 303
Ecclesiastes, title and place in Canon, 218; authorship of, 218f.; contents of, 219–226; unity of, 226–229; foreign influences in, 229–231; date of, 234; teaching of, 235–238; permanent influence of, 238f.; literary merit of, 239f.
Edom(ites), 20f., 42, 90, 284
Egypt, 20, 22, 32, 39–41, 42, 107f., 216, 287
Elasa, 34
Elephantine (Yeb), 22, 39f., 317
Eliashib, 29, 317
Enthronement Psalms, 103f.
Esaglia, 24 n.
Eschatology, influence of Persian religion on, 325f.
Esther, Book of, title and place in Canon, 241; canonicity, 241f.; purpose of, 243; the Greek version of, 248f.; unity of, 249f.; date of, 250f.; historicity of, 251f.; permanent influence of, 252; literary merit of, 252f.
Esther, character of, 253f.
Ethics, in proverbs, 142; in Job, 173

Evil-Merodach, *see* Amel-Marduk
Ezekiel, 23f.
Ezra, life and character of, 29–31, 317–319
Ezra and Nehemiah, Book of, title and place in Canon, 301; contents of, 301–309; a compilation, 309f.; sources of, 310–313; historical problems in, 313–317; permanent influence of, 321–322; literary merit of, 324

Fasting, 275f.
Farvardigan, feast of, 243

Galilee, 21
Gaugamela, 32
Gazara (Gezer), 34
Gedaliah, 20, 22, 37, 288
Gehenna, 51, 56
Gentiles, 56f.
Gerizim, 15, 31, 282, 337
Gezer, 41, 43, 285
Gilboa, 284
Gobryas, 24
God, 111–115, 140f., 213, 235
Granicus, 31f.
Great Synagogue, the, 14, 242
Greeks, 351f.
Greek philosophy, 32, 70–72, 229–231
Gutium, 24

Haggai, 25–27, 315 n.
Haman, character of, 253
Hanani, 28
Hananiah (and Nehemiah), 28
Hananiah (Elephantine), 40
Haram-bethel, 40
Harran, 38, 167 n., 287
Hasidim, 33
Hazor, 285
Hebron, 42, 284
Heliodorus, 33
Hellenism, 354–358
Hezekiah, 68, 137, 286
Hilkiah, 15
Hiram, 285
History, unity of, 57 f.
Hope, 215
Hosea, 54, 158
Hoshea, 286
Huldah, 15
Humman (god), 243
Hymns of praise, 102f.
Hyrcania, 31

Index of Subjects

Hyrcanus I, 15, 34f.
Hyrcanus II, 35f.

Idumaea, 35, 42
Imprecatory Psalms, 126
Individual Psalms of Thanksgiving, 103f.
Individualism, 61, 73f., 158–160
Isaiah, 52, 54, 58, 158
Immortality, 120–122, 143, 173f., 238
Ishmael, 20, 288
Ishtar, 21, 243
Ishtar Gate, 38
Israel, 21, 50
Issus, 32
Ituraea, 35

Jaddua, 297, 308
Jamnia, Council of, 14, 17, 18, 241
Jashar, Book of, 78
Jason, 33
Jehoahaz, 287
Jehohanan, 317
Jehoiachin, 21, 37f., 288
Jehoiada, 29, 322
Jehoiakim, 287
Jeremiah, 16, 20, 24, 50, 58, 288
Jeroboam, 285f.
Jerusalem, 13, 16, 20f., 28–31, 34, 284, 287
Jewry, divisions of, 21–25
Jeshua, or Joshua, (the High Priest), 25f., 314
Joab, 289
Job, Book of, title and place in Canon, 147; contents of, 147–157; literary form of, 157f.; purpose of, 158–161; unity of, 161–165; confusions in, 165f.; foreign influences in, 166f.; date of, 167–169; historicity of, 169; life of author, 170f.; teaching of, 171–174; permanent influence of, literary merit of, 176–178
Joel, 55
Johanan (son of Kareah), 20
Johanan (High Priest), 40
John Hyrcanus, *see* Hyrcanus I
Jonathan (brother of Judas Maccabaeus), 34
Joppa, 34
Josiah, 286f.
Judah, tribe of, 334f.
Judah, kingdom of, 37, 286–288
Judah, province of, 20f., 28, 31, 36, 322f.
Judaism, 144, 174f., 351–353

Judas Maccabaeus, 34, 325f.
Judgment, 50f., 61, 123, 279

Kingdoms, the four, 257, 260
Kingdom of God, 54, 273, 278
Kiriath-jearim, 285
Koheleth, life and character of, 232–234

Lachish, 37
Lamentations, title and place in Canon, 204; structure of, 204f.; classification of, 205; authorship of, 206f.; date of, 207f.; contents of, 208–212; teaching of, 212–215; permanent influence of, 216f.; literary merit of, 217
Laments, 79; of the community, 103, 205; of the individual, 103, 205
Law, the, 12f., 119f., 276, 359–367
Leviathan, 111, 156f., 165
Levites, 30f., 290–292, 323
Logos, 77
Lydia(ns), 24, 42
Lysimachus, 250

Maccabees, the, 33–36
Malachi, 27f.
Man, 115f., 125f., 141, 172f.
Manasseh, 286, 294
Marisa, 42
Massoretic text, 43, 85
Marduk, 24, 39, 243
Mashti (goddess), 243
Mattathias, 34
Medeba, 35
Media, 24, 270
Megiddo, 285
Megilloth, 13
Menelaus, 33
Messianic hope, 74
Messiah, 52, 124
Metre (see Rhythm), 83
Micah, 54, 158
Michmash, 34, 284
Midrash, 294 n.
Millennium, doctrine of, 62
Mishnah, 17, 127, 366
Mizpah, 20, 37
Moab(ites), 20, 195f., 284, 322
Modein, 34
Monotheism, 23, 66f., 112, 137, 140f., 171, 213
Mordecai, character of, 254
Moses, 11, 80, 359f., 366

Murashu tablets, 22, 41
Music, Hebrew, 329-333
Mythology, 59

Nabataeans, 35
Nabonidus (Nabunaid), 24, 38, 258 n., 270
Nabonidus Chronicle, 38
Nabopolassar, 287
Nannar (Sin), 214
Naomi, character of, 201
Nash papyrus, 43
Nathan, 68
Nationalism, 56f.
Nebuchadrezzar, 21 n., 24f., 265, 270
Nebuzaradan, 20
Neco, 287
Negeb, 37
Nehemiah, life and character of, 28f., 319-321
Nethinim, 292 n.
New Year's Festival, 104, 109, 123
Nicanor's Day, 250
Nile, 108, 170
Nineveh, 287
Nippur, 41, 167
Northern Kingdom, the, 281f., 283, 285f.

Obadiah, 55
Onias III, 33, 262
Opis, 24

Particularism, 338-340
Penitential Psalms, 126
Pentateuch (see Torah),
Persepolis, 32
Persia(ns), 24-31, 41f., 349
Peshitta, 147
Pharisees, 33, 35
Philistia(ines), 21, 284
Phoenicia(ns), 21, 32
Pilgrim Psalms, 102, 104
Poetry, Hebrew, origin of, 78-80; parallelism, 80-83; rhythm or metre, 83-85; rhyme, 85; strophes or stanzas, 85f.; acrostics, 86; literary characteristics of, 86-94
Prophets, the, 15f., 76, 216
Proverbs, title and place in Canon, 131; contents of, 131-136; authorship of, 136-138; date of, 138f.; pupils of the sages, 139f.; teaching of, 140-143; permanent influence of, 144; literary merit of, 145f.

Psalms, title and place in Canon, 95; title of individual Psalms, 95-97; divisions of the book, 99f.; growth of the book, 100-102; classification of types, 102-104; authorship of, 104-106; foreign influence on, 107-109; Temple worship, 109f.; teaching of, 111-122; eschatology in, 122-124; permanent influence of, 124-128; literary merit of, 128-130
Pseudonymity, 58
Ptolemy I (Soter), 32
Ptolemy II (Philadelphus), 18, 42
Ptolemy V, 232
Purim, Feast of, 17, 241, 249f.

Qinah, 84, 204

Rabbis, 12, 45, 76
Rehoboam, 285
Rephaim, 284
Resurrection, the, 52f., 60f., 274f., 276
Retribution, 75, 118f., 141f., 158f., 173, 213f., 237f.
Return, the, 25f.
Rhyme, 85
Rhythm, 83-86
Riches, 237
Ritual cleanness, 23
Rome, 55
Royal Psalms, 103
Ruth, character of, 201f.
Ruth, Book of, title and position in Canon, 194; date of, 194f.; purpose of, 195-197; contents of, 197-199; unity of, 199; historicity of, 199f.; permanent influence of, 200; literary merit of, 200-203

Sabbath observance, 23, 33
Sacrifice, 74f.
Sadducees, 35
Samaga, 35
Samaria (city), 35, 43
Samaria (province), 21, 37
Samaritan schism, 334-337
Samaritans, 322
Sanballat, 28f.
Sardis, 24
Satan, the, 168f., 172
Saul, 284
Seleucids, 33
Seleucus I Nicator, 32
Seleucus IV Philipator, 33
Septuagint, 18

INDEX OF SUBJECTS

Seventy weeks, 261f., 272
Shechem, 35, 285
Shelemiah, 41
Shema, 43
Sheol, 52, 75, 120f., 140, 143, 160, 173f.
Shesh-bazzar, 26, 314
Simon (brother of Judas Maccabaeus), 34
Sin and forgiveness, 117
Singers, the, 30, 292, 327
Solomon, 68, 73, 136–138, 190, 285
Son of man, 275, 277f.
Sophists, the, 231
Spirituality of true worship, 215
Stoicism, 229f.
Submission, 215
Sumer(ia), 25, 59
Susa, 28, 32, 249
Symbolism, 58f.
Synagogue, the, 13, 17
Syria(ns), 32, 35, 55, 284

Talmud, 12, 206, 366f.
Tamar (mother of Perez and Zerah), 196
Tamar (a fortress), 285
Tammuz Adonis Cult, 189f.
Tattenai, 27
Taunt Songs, 79
Taurus Mountains, 32
Tema, 24, 38
Teman, 73
Temple (the first), 20f., 23, 284ff., 288f., 290–292
Temple (the second), 25–27, 33f., 38f., 282, 315, 325–327
Temple (Elephantine), 22, 40f.
Temple servants, 30, 292
The Song of Songs, title and place in Canon, 179; canonicity of, 179f.; contents of, 180–185; interpretation of, 186–190; authorship and date of, 190f.; permanent influence of, 191; literary merit of, 191–193
Thirty-nine Articles, 19
Tiglath-pileser III, 286
Tigris, 24
Tirzah, 190
Tobiah, 28f., 43, 308f., 320
Torah, 359–367

Trans-Jordan, 21
Trent, Council of, 18
Trito-Isaiah, 27, 55, 207 n.
Tryphon, 34
Tyre, 32, 285, 322

Ugaritic texts, 108f.
United Monarchy, the, 284f.
Universalism, 23, 56f., 340–343

Vashti, character of, 253
Volksbuch, 162f.
Vulgate, 18

Wars of the Lord, Book of the, 78
Wedding Songs, 79
Westminster Confession, the, 19
Widrang, 40f.
Wisdom literature, definition of, 63; list of books, 63f.; origin and development of, 67f.; religious content of, 70; international character of, 72f.; teaching of, 73–76; permanent influence of, 76f.
Wise men, origin of, 64f.; educational aims and methods of, 65f.; relation to the prophets, 66f.
Worship, 116f., 215
Writings, the, 16f.

Xerxes I, *see* Ahasuerus

Yahweh, 23, 26f., 39f., 49f., 54–56, 66f., 101, 109, 111–115, 116f., 119f., 122f., 158–160, 215, 283
Yahwism, 21
Yedoniah, 40
Yeshibah, 66

Zadok, 291 n.
Zechariah, 25ff., 55
Zedekiah, 288
Zeno papyri, 43
Zerubbabel, 25–27, 314
Zeus, 33, 262, 325
Zion, 126f., 208ff.
Zoroaster, 344
Zoroastrianism, 344–348

INDEX OF AUTHORS

Aeschylus, 166
Ahikar, 72
Ahlemann, F., 311
Akiba, Rabbi, 179
Albright, W. F., 31, 40, 107, 109, 218, 231, 243, 275 n., 298 n., 311, 331, 351, 355
Alt, A., 362
Aristeas, 168
Athanasius, 11
Augustine, 18

Ball, J. C., 208 n.
Barton, G. A., 228, 229
Bea, A., 234 n.
Beek, M. A., 188
Begrich, J., 102
Ben Sirach, 16, 66, 139, 168, 232, 250, 269, 319, 321, 325, 326 n., 334
Bentzen, A., 107, 138 n., 162, 169, 195 n., 241, 312
Bevan, E. R., 91, 366
Bickell, G., 228
Bickermann, E., 272 n.
Blackman, A. M., 108
Bossuet, J. B., 197
Bouquet, A. C., 345 n.
Breasted, J. H., 353
Briggs, C. A., 106
Briggs, E. G., 106
Budde, K., 164, 169, 187, 208 n.
Burkitt, F. C., 239
Burnet, J., 71
Burney, C. F., 122

Castellio, S., 188
Carlyle, T., 176
Charles, R. H., 47, 58
Cheyne, T. K., 106, 208 n., 234 n., 239
Cohen, A. C., 227
Cornhill, C. H., 164, 169
Cowley, A., 41

Dante, 176
Davison, W. T., 127
Delitzsch, F., 219

Dillon, E. J., 234 n.
Driver, G. R., 108
Driver, S. R., 74, 80, 106, 164, 166, 169, 195 n., 208 n., 230, 234 n., 251
Duhm, B., 107, 109, 157
Dussaud, R., 362

Eissfeldt, O., 169, 228
Elmslie, W. A. L., 282
Engnell, I., 107
Euripedes, 176

Fairweather, W., 69 n.

Galling, K., 227, 239
Ginsberg, H. L., 218 n.
Glasson, T. F., 275 n., 358
Goethe, 203
Gordis, R., 227
Gore, C., 242
Gottwald, N. K., 205, 207 n.
Granild, E., 312
Gray, G. B., 83, 138 n., 157, 166
Gregg, J. A. F., 69 n.
Gressmann, H., 49 n., 108, 138 n., 197
Gunkel, H., 49 n., 102, 103 n., 110, 122, 123, 197
Gurney, O. R., 167 n.

Hänel, J., 297
Herder, J. G., von, 189
Herodotus, 355
Homer, 45
Hudson, W. H., 254
Humbert, P., 229 n.

Idelsohn, A. Z., 332
Isaacs, N., 366

James, M. R., 49
Jastrow, M., 234 n., 239
Jensen, P., 243
Jepsen, A., 195
Jerome, 18, 218
Johnson, A. R., 104 n.

Index of Authors

Jonge, M. de, 47
Josephus, 11, 13, 31, 32, 35, 249

Kent, C. F., 76, 233, 284
Kraeling, E, G., 41
Kramer, S. N., 167 n.
Kuenen, A., 242

Lambert, W. G., 167 n.
Langdon, S., 229
Lattey, C., 195 n.
Levita, Elias, 14
Lewy, J., 243
Lindblom, J., 66, 166
Livingstone, R. W., 355
Lods, A., 362
Löhr, M., 208 n.
Lowth, R., 187
Luther, 19, 242

Manson, T. W., 275 n.
McNeile, A. H., 228, 239
Meek, T. J., 189, 362
Milik, J. T., 258 n.
Milton, J., 176
Moffatt, J., 154, 225
Montgomery, J. A., 267
Morgenstern, J., 50 n.
Morris, A. E., 251 n.
Moulton, J. H., 345 n.
Mowinckel, S., 49 n., 104, 110, 123, 312
Mullins, T. Y., 77
Murray, G., 355

Noth, M., 66, 68, 167 n., 218, 307

Odeberg, H., 234 n.
Oesterley, W. O. E., 69 n., 297, 300, 353, 357

Paton, L. B., 242
Patton, J. H., 108
Peake, A. S., 154, 157, 166, 169, 174 n.
Pedersen, J., 169
Pfeiffer, R. H., 166, 243, 251 n., 268, 282, 296 n., 297, 311, 361
Philo, 71, 77

Philonenko, M., 47
Plato, 71, 166
Plumptre, E. H., 234 n.
Prothero, R. E., 128
Pythagoras, 71

Rad, G. von, 297
Ranston, H., 70, 228, 230
Reifenberg, A., 42
Renan, E., 187
Reuss, E., 188
Ringgren, H., 124
Robertson, A., 332
Robertson, E., 197, 199
Robinson, H. W., 234 n., 297 n.
Robinson, T. H., 85, 124, 174, 234 n., 357
Roper, H. R., 217
Rothstein, J. W., 297
Rowley, H. H., 44, 54, 58, 124, 159, 162, 174 n., 189, 196, 197, 199, 208 n., 268, 278, 297, 340, 353

Samuel, Rabbi, 241
Schoff, W. H., 189
Scott, R. B. Y., 68
Shakespeare, 176
Siegfried, C., 228
Simpson, D. C., 108, 124
Singer, C., 91, 366
Slotki, J. J., 196
Smith, G. A., 91
Smith, W. R., 217
Snaith, N. H., 104, 174, 311
Soden, W. von, 167
Staples, W. E., 197
Steinmueller, J. E., 195 n.
Steuernagel, C., 169
Stevens, D., 332
Stevenson, W. B., 163
Streeter, B. H., 77

Taylor, C., 234 n.
Theodore of Mopsuestia, 188
Theognis, 230
Thomas, D. W., 66, 68, 167 n., 218 n.
Torrey, C. C., 296 n., 298, 311
Toy, C. H., 137
Tur-Sinai, N. H., 163
Tyler, T., 234 n.

Index of Authors

Volz, P., 169
Virgil, 45, 176

Waterhouse, J. W., 348
Weidner, E. F., 243
Welch, A. C., 281, 297, 298, 311, 312
Wetzstein, J. G., 187

Whiston, W., 188
Williams, A. L., 228, 229

Xenophon, 355

Zaehner, R. C., 348
Zimmerli, W., 234 n.

For Product Safety Concerns and Information please contact our EU
representative GPSR@taylorandfrancis.com
Taylor & Francis Verlag GmbH, Kaufingerstraße 24, 80331 München, Germany

www.ingramcontent.com/pod-product-compliance
Lightning Source LLC
Chambersburg PA
CBHW071438300426
44114CB00013B/1480